MANAGEMENT SCIENCE - THEORY AND APPLICATIONS

SUSTAINABLE MANAGEMENT

MANAGEMENT SCIENCE – THEORY AND APPLICATIONS

Additional books in this series can be found on Nova's website
under the Series tab.

Additional E-books in this series can be found on Nova's website
under the E-books tab.

MATHEMATICS RESEARCH DEVELOPMENTS

Additional books in this series can be found on Nova's website
under the Series tab.

Additional E-books in this series can be found on Nova's website
under the E-books tab.

MANAGEMENT SCIENCE - THEORY AND APPLICATIONS

SUSTAINABLE MANAGEMENT

GUENNADY OUGOLNITSKY

Nova Science Publishers, Inc.
New York

Copyright © 2011 by Nova Science Publishers, Inc.

All rights reserved. No part of this book may be reproduced, stored in a retrieval system or transmitted in any form or by any means: electronic, electrostatic, magnetic, tape, mechanical photocopying, recording or otherwise without the written permission of the Publisher.

For permission to use material from this book please contact us:
Telephone 631-231-7269; Fax 631-231-8175
Web Site: http://www.novapublishers.com

NOTICE TO THE READER

The Publisher has taken reasonable care in the preparation of this book, but makes no expressed or implied warranty of any kind and assumes no responsibility for any errors or omissions. No liability is assumed for incidental or consequential damages in connection with or arising out of information contained in this book. The Publisher shall not be liable for any special, consequential, or exemplary damages resulting, in whole or in part, from the readers' use of, or reliance upon, this material. Any parts of this book based on government reports are so indicated and copyright is claimed for those parts to the extent applicable to compilations of such works.

Independent verification should be sought for any data, advice or recommendations contained in this book. In addition, no responsibility is assumed by the publisher for any injury and/or damage to persons or property arising from any methods, products, instructions, ideas or otherwise contained in this publication.

This publication is designed to provide accurate and authoritative information with regard to the subject matter covered herein. It is sold with the clear understanding that the Publisher is not engaged in rendering legal or any other professional services. If legal or any other expert assistance is required, the services of a competent person should be sought. FROM A DECLARATION OF PARTICIPANTS JOINTLY ADOPTED BY A COMMITTEE OF THE AMERICAN BAR ASSOCIATION AND A COMMITTEE OF PUBLISHERS.

Additional color graphics may be available in the e-book version of this book.

Library of Congress Cataloging-in-Publication Data

Ougolnitsky, Guennady.
  Sustainable management / Guennady Ougolnitsky.
      p. cm.
  Includes index.
  ISBN 978-1-61324-153-0 (hardcover)
  1. Management--Mathematical models. 2. Management. 3. Sustainable development. I. Title.
  HD30.25.O94 2011
  658.4'08--dc22
                              2011009081

Published by Nova Science Publishers, Inc. †New York

CONTENTS

Preface		vii
Introduction		1
Chapter 1	Rationality and Methods of Management	9
Chapter 2	Sustainable Development of Dynamic Systems	39
Chapter 3	Models of Sustainable Management	81
Chapter 4	Quality Management Principles and Sustainable Management	127
Chapter 5	Ensuring Organizational Adaptivity	155
Chapter 6	Organizational Management and Opportunistic Behavior	185
Chapter 7	Corporative Information-Modeling Systems	223
Conclusion		259
References		265
About the Author		275
Index		277

PREFACE

The most adequate tool of synthesis of the heterogeneous notions, concepts and methods is their mathematical formalization which provides a common language of the description and analysis. That is the reason why the concept of sustainable management is presented in this book on the base of mathematical modeling. Applied mathematics must use mathematical models and methods of their analysis for description of real systems and processes and connected practical problems. The results of an applied mathematical research lie beyond mathematics and belong in this case to the problems of sustainable management. The main value of the strict statements received by means of applied mathematics lies in the possibility of their interpretation and consequent usage in applied domains.

INTRODUCTION

Problems of the hierarchical management of sustainable development seem to be very actual ones. For a preliminary substantiation of this statement let's consider at least three problem domains.

First, these are environmental problems on global, regional, and local levels. A rapid growth of population, production and technologies leads to the multiple increase of the man-made impact on environment, including such unfavorable aspects as pollution of water, air, and soils, exhaustion of non-renewable natural resources, decrease of biodiversity, global warming. Environmental problems are especially acute in developing countries which have no resources to handle them. On the other side, highly developed countries solve their environmental problems at the cost of the third world states where they allocate harmful enterprises and dangerous wastes. Among sad consequences of not rational relations with Nature are deforestation, desert spreading, water and wind erosion, watersheds and animal population extinction, poaching, transformation of big territories into the zones of ecological disaster. Non-adequate impacts on local and regional levels threaten to the global ecological equilibrium and therefore to the very existence of mankind.

Second, these are problems of management of enterprises and organizations of the different economic sectors, social purposes and property forms. Productive and human resources are often used not rational, the transaction costs grow, and the raw materials, energy, time and money are wasted. Many forms of opportunistic behavior flourish and do not permit to solve organizational problems optimally from the global point of view. Interests of owners, managers, employees and consumers do not coincide, and the arising conflict situations do not always find rational trade-offs. Big corporations loose control, their departments and affiliations become a "thing in itself". Top managers and employees solve their personal problems at the cost of the organization. The externalities of production processes which have big social value are neglected.

Third, these are problems of state systems. Separatism, aggressive ambitions, and terrorism do not at all weaken as time passes. It is difficult to name a country which is free from the conflicts between different parts of territory and ethnic groups. As this takes place, both on internal and external levels the double standards which are a specific perversion of the system relativity principle are used actively. The same territory fiercely defends its sovereignty from the highly situated state and in the same time also fiercely insists on its own territorial integrity and political independence. National and territorial conflicts are very protracted and cruel and are accompanied by great financial and human losses.

All the enumerated processes: environmental impact, organizational management, territorial interaction (and many others not less important) – have definite features in common, namely:

- the dynamics of controlled systems is determined by the impact of several agents having their own objectives and interests;
- the relations of hierarchy exist in the set of agents;
- objectives and interests of the agents do not coincide as a rule; it is important that their implementation may violate the homeostatic equilibrium of the controlled system;
- there are one or more agents who are interested in the equilibrium and have some resources to preserve it; the agents may have also their private interests.

The presence of those common features permits to hope to the possibility of building a substantive theory including both descriptive and normative aspects.

It is clear that the theory must found itself on the solid base of precedent investigations, and the base really exists. But it is necessary to emphasize a principal interdisciplinary character of the considered problem which leads to the difficulties of "multilingualism" and necessity of the synthetic approach.

Let's indicate in brief the main sources of the developed theory, naming only the principal researchers (more detailed survey will be made later in the text of monograph).

1. METHODS OF HIERARCHICAL MANAGEMENT AND THEIR FORMAL MODELS

The content of this direction is formed by research in organizations theory and sociology of management. The fundamental classification of social relations (compulsory, contractual, and familistic ones) was proposed by Pitirim Sorokin. The similar approaches were used later by K. Boulding (violence, exchange, love), J. French and B. Raven (five forms of power), V. Ledyaev (kinds of power), D. Novikov (institutional, motivational, and information mechanisms of control). Terms "compulsion", "impulsion", "conviction" were used for characterization of the methods of hierarchical management in the paper (Fatkhutdinov and Sivkova 1999).

Methods of organizational management are studied by I. Adizes, Ch. Barnard, W. Edwards Deming, P. Drucker, A. Etzioni, A. Fayol, F. Herzberg, E. Mayo, D. McGregor, H. Mintzberg, M. Parker Follett, F. W. Taylor and many other specialists in management.

Formal models of hierarchical management are build in the information theory of hierarchical systems (Yu. B. Germeyer, N. N. Moiseev, V. A. Gorelik, A. F. Kononenko, I. A. Vatel et al.), theory of active systems (V. N. Burkov, D. A. Novikov, A. G. Chkhartishvily et al.), theory of contracts (P. Aghion, M. Dewatripont, G. Baker, R. Gibbons, P. Bolton, C. Bull, Y. -K. Che, Y. S. Chiu, D. Kreps, E. Fama, E. Fehr, S. Grossman, O. Hart, J. Moore, M.

Halonen, B. Holmstrom, P. Milgrom, J. J. Laffont, D. Martimort, E. Maskin, R. Myerson, B. Salanie, M. Spence, J. Stiglitz, R. Zeckhauser et al.).

2. CONTROL IN DYNAMIC SYSTEMS

We may indicate the following used directions of research:

-   notions of cybernetics and systems theory: control and controlled systems, control impact, control objective, feedback and so on (N. Wiener, W. R. Ashby, L. Bertalanfy, St. Beer et al.);
-   concepts of control in biological systems: homeostasis (C.Bernard, W.Cannon), adaptive reactions (H. Selye, L. Garkavy et al.);
-   mathematical models of optimal control (method of dynamic programming of R. Bellman, L. S. Pontryagin maximum principle) and dynamic games (antagonistic games – R. Isaaks, N. N. Krasovsky et al., non-antagonistic games – A. Haurie, F. Kidland, V. V. Mazalov, H. Moulin, L. A. Petrosyan, E. Prescott, V. V. Zakharov, G. Zaccour, D. W. K. Yeung et al.).

3. CONCEPT OF SUSTAINABLE DEVELOPMENT

The term "sustainable development" was first introduced in scientific and public usage in 1980. However, a serious attention to the problem was attracted only by the report "Our Common Future" (1987) prepared by the UNO World Commission on Environment and Development, known as "Brundtland Commission". Conclusions of the Brundtland Report formed a base for the decisions of the UNO Conference on Environment and Development (Rio de Janeiro, 1992). The complexity of the problem of sustainable development determines a necessity of its analysis on different levels and aspects (Aall 2000; Carley and Christie 1993; Coenen et al. 2000; Danilov-Danilyan and Losev 2000; Gore 1993; New Paradigm 1999; Pezzey 1989; Roseland 1992; Weizsaeker et al. 1997).

The most adequate tool of synthesis of the heterogeneous notions, concepts and methods is their mathematical formalization providing a common language of the description and analysis. That's why the concept of sustainable management if presented in the book on the base of mathematical modeling. Due to the author's conviction, applied mathematics must use mathematical models and methods of their analysis for description of real systems and processes and connected practical problems. The results of an applied mathematical research lie beyond mathematics and belong in this case to the problems of sustainable management. The main value of the strict statements received by means of applied mathematics lies in the possibility of their interpretation and consequent usage in applied domains. That's why for understanding of the most of theses of the book it is not necessary to have deep mathematical knowledge.

In the first chapter of the monograph concepts of rationality in social sciences, methods of management and their mathematical formalization are considered. The classification of rationality models is made by two foundations. From one side, "economic" and "sociological" rationality are differentiated. In the first case the agent has one criterion of optimality, in the second case several ones. From the other side, one or more agents may act in a situation. A matrix with four positions arises respectively. They are formalized by models of classic (scalar) optimization, models of multicriteria (vector) optimization, classic game theoretic models, and game theoretic models with vector payoff functions respectively. A survey of concepts of power forms and management methods analysis is made. Three principal methods of the hierarchical management (compulsion, impulsion, conviction) are characterized, real examples are driven, and known mathematical models of impulsion in different forms are described.

In the second chapter the concept of sustainable development is described. Historically it is appeared concerning the relations of society and nature. It is shown that it is possible and useful to spread the concept onto arbitrary dynamic systems which include human beings. Three principal requirements of sustainable development (homeostasis, compromise, dynamic consistency) are revealed and characterized. A concept of hierarchical control of dynamic systems is also presented. The concept is based on the classic theory of controlled dynamic systems and generalizes it for the case when the control agent (control subsystem) has a hierarchical structure. A number of optimality principles and mechanisms of hierarchical control of dynamic systems is proposed.

The central place in the book belongs to the third chapter which presents the concept of sustainable management on the base of mathematical modeling. The static and dynamic models of sustainable management formalizing methods of compulsion, impulsion, and conviction as solutions of a hierarchical game are proposed. A general model of sustainable management is specified for the case of environmental-economic systems. A number of specific models of sustainable management of forest resources, water resources, and recreational systems are analyzed.

In the fourth chapter of the monograph a connection between the concept of sustainable management and principles of quality management considering ISO 9000 standards is shown. The base of quality management is formed by process approach, and the target values of process indicators may be treated as homeostatic boundaries. The requirements of compromise and dynamic consistency are considered in development of the control processes. Monitoring is treated as a necessary part of the sustainable management which provides a feedback on the base of information of the current state of processes.

The fifth chapter is dedicated to the questions of organizational adaptivity. Basic notions of corrective and preventive actions in quality management are connected exactly with the solution of adaptation problems. Corrective actions are organizational adaptive reactions to the nonconformities as they are, meanwhile preventive actions belong to the future, direct to the "pre-adaptation" and have to rest on computer simulation modeling providing possibilities of variant forecast. Within the author's conception motivation mechanisms treated as a means for the automatic adaptation which provides employees' interest in the elimination of deviations of the current values of process indicators from the target ones.

The sixth chapter is dedicated to the organizational management and opportunistic behavior. A problem of sustainable management of a construction project is considered as an example. The possibilities of overcoming the opportunistic behavior are studied. It is necessary to emphasize that exactly opportunism, i.e. usage of different ways of satisfying personal interests at the cost of organizational interests at whole, is the most important reason for permanent monitoring and control of the sustainable development requirements. From the other side, an appropriate quality management removes a base for opportunism and in the limit permits to eliminate it completely from a corporative practice. But now the analysis of opportunism and methods of struggle with it remains an actual thing. Models of corruption in organizational management and models of consideration of private interests in resource allocation are considered.

In the seventh chapter the problems of information modeling of organizations are studied, including notion and means of the information modeling, author's concept of dynamic multidigraphs, ontological organizational models, and business process modeling including IDEF0 notation. The last chapter of the book synthesizes its results on the base of the concept of corporative information-modeling systems. Building of information models of the organizational activity and creating corporate information systems on their base have become an important branch, from one side, of computer science, from the other side, of computerization industry. The idea of addition modeling components to corporate information systems seems very fruitful. This direction is supported by many modern information technologies such as OLAP (On-Line Analytical Processing), data mining, expert systems and so on. A practical realization of the conditions of sustainable management requires an implementation of the corporative information-modeling system which provides storage and processing of the data received by process monitoring, accomplishment of forecasting and optimization calculations, assignment of expert recommendations, automation of documents flow and a number of another functions.

Basing on the fulfilled analysis it is possible to formulate the following theses which reflect the principal content of the book.

1) A correspondence between different rationality concepts and mathematical models formalizing them is established.

2) Possibility and appropriateness of generalization of the concept of sustainable development to the case of arbitrary dynamic systems including human beings are justified, and the conditions of sustainable management of a dynamic system (homeostasis, compromise, dynamic consistency) are formulated.

3) A scantiness of the classic model of controlled dynamic system is shown, a necessity of transition to the model of the hierarchically controlled dynamic system is proved.

4) A subject of the hierarchical sustainable management (subject of hierarchical rationality) is described. The subject is defined as a structured control system with a number of internal connections and relations which only conditionally could be considered as a whole unit.

5) A static game theoretic model of the sustainable management is built. The methods of the hierarchical management (compulsion, impulsion, conviction) are formalized as solutions of a hierarchical game, the necessary and sufficient conditions of their existence are found.

6) Dynamic models of sustainable management in complete and reduced form are built, their interpretation for the case of hierarchically controlled environmental-economic systems is proposed.

7) Specific models of sustainable management of the water resource, forest resource, recreational systems, and construction projects are built and investigated.

8) An approach to the consideration of corruption in the models of organizational sustainable management is realized, some models of description of private interests in resource allocation are developed.

9) A general approach to the modeling and optimization of monitoring as an integral part of the sustainable management is proposed, a technology of organizational monitoring based on mathematical models and information-modeling systems is characterized.

10) A consistency of the quality management principles and the conditions of sustainable management is shown. An interpretation of corrective and preventive actions in quality management as the adaptive behavior of organization is substantiated.

11) Dynamic multidigraphs as a means of information modeling are proposed.

12) A necessity of development of the corporative information-modeling systems as a tool of providing sustainable management is proved.

As an important result of the pursued research a technology of organizational sustainable management which includes a number of stages is received.

1. Building a system of processes in the organization including principal, supporting, and control processes.

2. Identification of process indicators and their target values, the totality of which characterizes the conditions of organizational homeostasis.

3. Monitoring of the indicators which permanently purchases information about the current state of processes basing on the indicators values to the process owners and top management.

4. Taking corrective actions in the case of nonconformity of current (actual) values of the process indicators to their target (homeostatic) values.

5. Creating a motivation system which encourages the achievement of process indicators target values and punishes the employees in the case of nonconformities. Ideally, such a system must provide automatic taking of corrective actions.

6. Taking preventive actions on the base of simulation models providing a possibility of variant calculations.

7. Implementation and maintenance of the corporative information-modeling system which plays a synthetic role in practical realization of the organizational sustainable management. The system permits: to automate the organizational document flow referring to the requirements of quality management standards; to collect, store and process monitoring data; to implement computer simulation; to find solutions of control optimization problems; to receive expert recommendations.

If the homeostasis is provided and a dynamic consistent compromise among all key organization stakeholders is achieved then the sustainable management of the organization takes place. The sustainable management provides both conditions of sustainable development and means of their realization.

The author thanks his colleagues and pupils M. I. Cherdyntseva, O. I. Gorbaneva, K. I. Denin, D. V. Dubrov, S. A. Kornienko, M. Kh. Malsagov, I. K. Nurutdinova, Ya. M.

Rusanova, E. A. Rybasov, S. V. Tikhonov, A. B. Usov for the results of joint work used in the book, and the Russian Foundation of Basic Research which has supported several stages of the work (projects 98-01-01024, 00-01-00725, 04-01-96812). The author expresses a deep respect to the activity of Professor Leon Petrosyan who is the founder of dynamic consistency concept and organizer of the remarkable conferences "Game Theory and Management" in Saint-Petersburg. The author cordially thanks Professor Dmitry Novikov, Professor Vladimir Mazalov, and Professor Alexander Tarko for their attention to the work, valuable advises and practical support. The author specially thanks Professor Irina Mostovaya who has essentially improved his understanding of the sociology of management.

Chapter 1

RATIONALITY AND METHODS OF MANAGEMENT

Two basic concepts of rationality are used in the case of individual behavior. A model of the economic person (homo economicus) originates from the definition of the only criterion of optimization such as an agent's interest is determined completely by the incentive of its maximization. A material (often financial) benefit serves as such criterion as a rule, though wider interpretations of the objective function are also possible. Economic rationality is formalized by an optimization model (more precisely – by a model of scalar optimization).

A model of the sociological person (homo sociologicus) which explains the behavior by a joint action of several incentives and norms is more appropriate but inevitably more complicate. In this case a model of vector (multicriteria) optimization is needed.

As any agent acts in a society, her possibilities of rational behavior of any type are restricted by actions of other agents. A situation of interaction is inevitably the conflict one because objectives and interests of different agents do not coincide. A trade-off which to an extent takes into consideration the interests of agents involved to the conflict serves as its resolution. Building and investigation of conflict models and their compromise solutions is the subject of game theory. It is game theoretic models of different classes that are treated as the models of compromise rationality. Models of the collective choice theory are also widely used for the description of a compromise decision making.

A hierarchical structure of big systems including human beings generates a necessity of the specific methods of hierarchical management. Analysis of the methods is based on the investigation of social relations and power forms. Three groups of the methods of hierarchical management are set off as a result of the analysis.

In the case of compulsion the agent of higher level puts the agent of lower level in such conditions that the former is obliged to use a strategy desirable for the first agent. This impact has a forcing character and an administrative or legislative base. The interests of the agent of lower level are completely ignored therefore the relations between agents have a subject-to-object nature. If the relations are described as a hierarchical game then compulsion means an impact of the Leader to the set of admissible strategies of the Follower.

In the case of impulsion the Leader creates conditions in which it is more advantageous for the Follower to use Leader's desirable strategy then not to do it. This method has a nature of economic motivation and is implemented as a feedback mechanism of penalties and bonuses. The Follower's interests are considered to an extent in this case. From the point of view of game theoretic modeling impulsion means an impact of the Leader to the Follower's payoff function.

In the case of conviction the Follower voluntarily shares the Leader's position and uses a strategy desirable for the Leader (which becomes desirable for the Follower too). This method has a social-psychological nature and gives subject-to-subject character to the relations between the agents. In the game theoretic model conviction means a transition of both players to the cooperation and joint maximization of the summary payoff function of their coalition.

1.1. ECONOMIC AND SOCIOLOGICAL RATIONALITY

An eminent sociologist Max Weber has differentiated four types of social action which interpretation is closely connected with a concept of rationality: instrumental (goal-instrumental) action, value-rational action, traditional action, affectional action (Runciman 1991). In the case of instrumental action an agent evaluates its consequences and compares the admissible ways of achieving the goal so as to choose the optimal one. In the case of value-rational behavior the principal role is played by moral and cultural values and norms which have a self-sufficing character. Traditional action delivers an agent from thinking: she just conducts such as it seems appropriate in her social community: family, nation, tribe and so on. At last, affectional behavior is conducted by spontaneous feelings and emotions which could move the agent to an economic damage and other losses.

For example, when a young man chooses his way of life he can:

- to prefer a profession which is highly wanted in present and guarantees a stable income in future (instrumental type);
- to get a fundamental education which allows to master a wide range of achievements of sciences and arts (value-rational type);
- to continue the family business (traditional type);
- to not enter a university and to joint the Army because of the quarrel with his girlfriend (affectional type).

The concept of economic rationality mostly corresponds to the instrumental Weberian type of social action. This type is the most widespread; Weber himself called it the highest type of social conduct. The base of the concept is formed by the model of "economic person" (homo economicus) which substantiates optimization theory, game theory and mathematical economics.

The following prerequisites form a base of the concept of "economic person" (Avtonomov 1998: 10-11). A subject of economic rationality disposes of a bounded quantity of resource that does not permit her to achieve her goal without difficulty. That's why the economic person has to make a choice from a set of available variants of actions. The key model prerequisite is the hypothesis due to which the choice is determined completely by the incentive to maximize a value function reflecting the subject's preference structure uniquely. The preference structure is supposed to be known and stable enough in the classic version of the model. There are also restrictions which should be considered by the subject. The classic model version also prerequisites that the agent has the information required to make an optimal decision (criterion of optimization, set of admissible variants of decision and other restrictions).

The model of economic rationality has been developing for more than two centuries. First a holistic approach to building of the model was proposed within British school of political economy by Adam Smith and David Ricardo. A known American economist George Stigler called the Smith's system "a grand palace built on the granite of personal interest" (Stigler 1971:265). Smith has accentuated egoistic interests of the individual who is searching for the most profitable application of his capital. Along with it in Smith's interpretation the objective function (criterion of optimality) of the economic person is treated widely and is not reduced only to the maximization of financial profit. Smith also takes into consideration such factors as pleasantness or unpleasantness of work, difficulty or easiness of education, social prestige of profession, probability of success (Smith 2008). Ricardo has followed the similar approach (The Works 2005).

At a later time the model of economic person has been developing in the context of two theoretical approaches: anthropological and methodological ones (Hartfiel 1968). The anthropological approach affirms with confidence that the model of homo economicus corresponds to the human nature completely and human beings in their real life conduct exactly as it is described in the model, i.e. tend to maximize a value function connected at most with financial benefit. The disciples of methodological approach consider more modestly that the model of economic person is a useful abstraction which does not embrace the whole totality of human incentives but seizes their principal characteristics and is therefore quite appropriate in descriptive and normative aspects.

A British researcher Nassau W. Senior was a founder of the anthropological approach. He has considered that a base of human conduct if formed by the wish to get much more things with the least possible losses (Senior 1827:30). In this direction the founder of utilitarianism Jeremy Bentham has affirmed that human behavior is conducted by two and only two factors: sorrow and delight (Bentham 1952:1). So an objective function of economic person in the sense of Bentham may be written as

$$ U = \sum_{i=1}^{m} a_i p_i - \sum_{j=1}^{n} b_j s_j, $$

where p_i is a value of i-th delight; a_i – its weight; s_j is a value of j-th factor of sorrow; b_j – its weight; m – number of delight factors; n – number of sorrow factors.

Another bright representative of the anthropological approach was a German scientist H.H.Gossen, the author of known Gossen laws. He has considered an aspiration to maximize delights the objective of life of all human beings without exception that is moreover corresponds to the God's will. This statement is proved by extreme force of the aspiration which overcomes any moral (Gossen 1927:3). The founders of marginalism (William Jevons, Leon Walrace) also have considered that a striving for the maximal satisfaction of needs is a fundamental property of human nature. Jevons also has used the results of psychological experiments to prove the statement (Jevons 1924:55). Such representatives of the Austrian economic school as Eugen von Boem-Bawerk and Friedrich von Wieser have also supported the anthropological approach. They have pointed at the fact that not only businessmen but the average men and women constantly calculate their profit and try to maximize it. The founder of neoclassical trend in the economic science Alan Marshall also was a convinced anthropologist. He has considered that economists deal with not an abstract economic person but with a real man from flesh and blood. Marshall acknowledged a big variety of human needs and incentives such as social activity, creative work, prestige and glory. But Marshall has substantiated money as the base for realization of any objectives, egoistic or altruistic.

The extreme expression of the anthropological approach is so-called universalism which identifies economic rationality with rationality at whole. The founder of universalism was the same scientist H.Gossen who has spread a principle of delight maximization to the whole human conduct. The leader of the new Austrian economic school Ludwig von Mises has affirmed that domains of rational and economic activity coincide, any rational action is in the same time the economic one, and any economic activity is rational (Mises 1996). A British economist William Wicksteed has insisted that the economic science investigates a real man and accentuates the aspect of optimal use of a limited resource. Because the resource scantiness is universal (at least due to the scantiness of time), the economic science is also universal and described the whole human activity (Wicksteed 1933).

A new impetus was given to the universalism in the end of the last century due to the development of so-called "economic imperialism" which tries to spread the model of economic person to the whole domain of social sciences. A leader of that current George Stigler has written that a man maximizes a value function permanently in all spheres of his activity such as scientific work, households, church and so on (Stigler 1980).

The founder of another approach to the description of economic person, a methodological one, was a British philosopher John Stuart Mill who has considered the homo economicus model only a necessary abstraction. Mill acknowledged that political economy did not describe a social conduct completely. The abstract character of the model of economic person determines its one-sidedness because other incentives are neglected (Mill 1970). The economic theory of Karl Marx has also a high level of abstraction. His main objects of analysis, a capitalist and a worker, are only personifications of capital and labor, specific social characters. The main objective of the capitalist is to maximize his surplus value.

The extreme expression of the methodological approach is a transition from a descriptive interpretation of the model of economic person to the heuristic one. This approach treats the model only as a convenient tool of analysis of the market processes irrelative to its content and prerequisites. This idea was first appeared in Wilfredo Pareto works; he used the notions of value and utility irrespective to their nature. An eminent modern British economist John Richard Hicks has used an axiomatic approach to the building of a value function. In his model the real incentives of behavior are not considered, therefore a real content of the value function is not required. Within that current Paul Samuelson has substituted a maximization of objective function by the sequential rational choice of strategies. Samuelson has proved that those two approaches are equivalent in some conditions, and the real content of the objective function is not important (Samuelson 1948).

It should be noted that an abstraction of the only one from the variety of incentives of the human conduct which substantiates the methodological approach is absolutely correct logical operation which lies in the base of any modeling. It is this abstraction that permits to build the mathematical microeconomics on the base of optimization theory. Let's consider the principal classes of optimization models and give their interpretation from the point of view of the economic rationality concept.

Models of Unconditional and Conditional Optimization

A model of unconditional optimization has the form

$$f(x) \to \max. \tag{1.1.1}$$

This is an extremely abstract, "pure" expression of the idea of economic rationality. It is required to find the set of maximum points of a function, any restrictions are absent, i.e. variable x can take arbitrary values. In the form (1.1.1) an objective function f (payoff function, utility function, criterion of optimality – these terms are used as synonyms) has a sense of utility (than more than better) therefore a maximum problem is formulated. Without loss of generality a minimum problem could be considered, in that case the objective function has a sense of losses, damage, or expenditures.

Expression (1.1.1) means that the goal of a subject of economic rationality is described completely by her striving to maximize the objective function and no other considerations exist. From the point of view of mathematical formalization a real sense of the objective function is not important. As a rule in the models of mathematical economics a quantity $f(x)$ has a sense of income or profit and may be expressed in financial units. But we have already mentioned that many classics of the political economy have given to the objective function a wider sense, and in modern heuristic models the optimization procedure may be moreover treated as "a black box".

It is really important that the objective function is unique, i.e. a subject of economic rationality has no more interests but maximization of that function. It is this hypothesis that expresses the essence of the model of homo economicus.

Evidently in reality a maximization of the objective function of a subject of economic rationality always has some restrictions. Thus the problem (1.1.1) is added by the condition

$$x \in X \tag{1.1.2}$$

which determines that the variable x can take not any but only some values from a set X. Entirely the expressions (1.1.1) and (1.1.2) form a model of conditional optimization which is an appropriate formalization of the concept of economic rationality. The model (1.1.1)-(1.1.2) means that a subject has the set of variants of actions X from which she must choose an optimal variant $x \in X$, which gives maximum to the function f (in general case several optimal variants can exist). It is such conduct that is acknowledged as economically rational.

In dependency of the type of objective function f and set of admissible solutions X different classes of optimization models exist (Handbook 1978; Reklaitis et al. 1983; Taha 1982).

Linear and Nonlinear Programming

One of the best studied class of optimizations models are models of linear programming in which the function $f(x)$ is linear and the set X is given by a system of linear equations or inequalities. In this model a set of admissible solutions is a polyhedron and the optimal decision is achieved in one of its vertices in general case. Well developed methods of solution of linear programming models exist (Dantzig 1963; Taha 1982).

Though linear programming models have favorable recommendations in practical applications, the hypothesis of linearity is too strong and does not correspond to modern paradigms of the functioning of natural and social systems. Thus in the context of modeling of the economic person different classes of nonlinear models of the type (1.1.1)-(1.1.2) are developed where an objective function and a set of admissible decisions have more complicated structure (Zangwill 1969).

Static and Dynamic Optimization Models

One of the most important "watersheds" in optimization modeling is connected with a consideration of time factor. Static models describe a momentary act of decision making. It is natural that such models are simpler in investigation and application, and in consequence they form a base of optimization theory. But real economy represents a totality of processes which have to be described by dynamic models. Specifically, the subject preferences can change in time. For example, if a subject faces to the evident impossibility of the satisfaction of her requirements, she is inclined to decrease their value. An American economist Kenneth Boulding (1979:15) called this effect "a sour grapes syndrome" by analogy with the known Lafontaine fable, and a Norwegian sociologist Jon Elster has dedicated to this phenomenon a special monograph (Elster 1983).

In this case the variable x becomes a function of time, and a criterion of optimality represents a sum or integral of the utility values during a period of time. As a rule dynamic models include discounting that allows to commensurate the utilities received at different moments of time. The theory of dynamic optimization is developed quite well (Bellman 1957; Pontryagin et al. 1962).

Discrete and Continuous Models

Another criterion of classification is connected with the nature of decision variants which form a set X. In the majority of cases the set contains a finite number of variants (alternatives, projects, strategies). Then the variable x can take a finite number of values that leads to the models of discrete optimization which are natural for description of the economic activity.

Sometimes a criterion of optimization can be considered as a continuous function of the variable x. It is this proposition that has allowed to marginalists to build a mathematical theory of the economic equilibrium. As Jevons wrote: "My theory of economy is pure mathematical. An economic theory must be mathematical because it operates with quantities" (Jevons 1924:3). But building of a mathematical theory based on the differential calculus requires additional formal conditions for the model (1.1.1)-(1.1.2). A utility function must be not only nonlinear and continuous but also differentiable and convex. These conditions are very restrictive and narrow the domain of applicability of the marginal economic theory. Indeed, a continuous objective function supposes an infinite divisibility of the evaluated goods which is possible only for a big number of subjects (Jevons 1924:15-16), but in this case the subjective preferences of consumers loose their sense. Moreover, a marginal analysis of the economic equilibrium is static.

Deterministic and Stochastic Models

At last, another principal question is concerned to the consideration of uncertainty in the models of economic rationality. If the complete information about the situation is available to the subject then deterministic models are sufficient in which all quantities are considered to be known exactly. Such models are simpler for theoretical investigation and practical applications.

But the hypothesis of complete information is not appropriate in reality. The prerequisite of incomplete information available to economic subjects forms a base of the theoretical system of John Maynard Keynes. A special monograph by Frank Knight is dedicated to the investigation of microeconomic problems of risk and uncertainty (Knight 1971). A consideration of the uncertainty factor leads to the necessity of usage of a stochastic version of the model (1.1.1)-(1.1.2). In this case the variable x is random, and the expectation of objective function is maximized as a rule. As in comparison of static and dynamic models we should acknowledge that stochastic models are more appropriate but more complicated. The necessity of a trade-off between adequacy and complexity is an immanent property of the mathematical modeling.

The concept of economic rationality was criticized repeatedly. In the second half of the nineteenth century a so-called historical school in economy was established in Germany. Its representatives have accused Adam Smith, David Ricardo and their disciples for universalism, primitive psychology based on egoism, and abuse of deductive method. The economists-historians considered the model of homo economicus not appropriate both from scientific and from ethical position. First, the German economists treated as the main object of economic studies not an individual but a nation as "ethnically and historically determined totality united by the State" (Knies 1880:157). Second, an individual is also a product of history and civilization. His needs, education and relations to the material goods and human beings are not constant, and they permanently change geographically and historically.

An eminent critic of the model of economic person was the founder of American institutionalism Thorstein Veblen. He has developed the theory of prestigious consumption which explains the economic action that seems irrational from the point of view of the homo economicus theory. Veblen has noticed that the demand for some goods can increase while their price is increasing. The subjects of prestigious consumption want to demonstrate their social status by buying very expensive goods which set their owners over the main mass of consumers. It is this striving to increase the social status that Veblen considered as the main incentive of the economic behavior (Veblen 1899). Developing Veblen's ideas, an American economist T. Skitovsky has shown that the domain of applicability of the classic model of economic person is restricted by static analysis and non-creative behavior (Skitovsky 1976).

Later on another paradoxical effects which do not agree with the classic model of economic person: effect of joining the majority (demand depends positively on the demand of other people for this commodity) and snob effect (demand depends negatively on the demand of other people for this commodity) were discovered (Leibenstein 1976). Those effects of consumer demand can be explained as means of non-verbal communication between people (Hargreaves 1989:99-100) which lie beyond the model of the model of homo economicus.

Experimental research (Kahneman, Twersky, 1979; Selten 1990) has also shown that real people not always act economically rational.

In the works by Herbert Simon (1982, 1997), Richard Heiner (1983) and Reinhardt Selten (1988, 1990) was established a base of the bounded rationality concept in which it is considered that due to lack of information, time and other resources a subject does not try to find an optimal decision but bounds herself by a rational approximation to it. Simon has defined the acceptability of a decision variant on the base of a notion of dynamic level of pretensions introduced by Kurt Lewin (1935). Developing the idea, Heiner has proposed so-called universal condition of reliability as the criterion of decision acceptability. Namely, a person changes her behavior if the ratio of probability to make choice in the right moment to the probability to change it in the wrong moment is more than a threshold value which in turn is equal to the ratio of possible loss from the decision making in the wrong moment to the benefit of the decision in the right moment. Selten has developed a three-level theory of decision making including the levels of habit, imagination, and logical reasoning. Though the levels are ordered hierarchically, in the case of contradiction the final choice will be not necessary logical; it is determined by a motivational center in the brain which is unavailable to a rational analysis (Avtonomov 1998: 176-180).

A concept of variable rationality belongs to a Harvard professor Harvey Leibenstein. In accordance to the concept, a rational behavior is determined by joint action of two groups of factors. From one side, a physiological human nature impels him to save his efforts. From the other side, social norms and rules require from him essential expenditures of physical and mental energy. In practice this contradiction is resolved as a compromise strategy of behavior which is not obliged to coincide with the economically rational strategy (Leibenstein 1976).

In the institutional theory an economic behavior is explained by striving to the maximization of transactional costs of economic interaction. In Oliver Williamson's interpretation each employee in a firm exerts an opportunistic maximization of her personal utility, therefore the firm functioning at whole can not be described by the classic model of economic rationality or even by the model of bounded rationality (Williamson 1970). Another direction of the institutional theory, an evolutionary theory of economic change, put forth a category of "routine" which substantiates a relative stability of the enterprise behavior (Nelson and Winter 1982:134).

One of the most rigid critics of the economic rationalism was a British philosopher Michael Oakeshott. By his opinion, any activity can be subdivided into two parts. The first part is technical and can be studied by books. It is this part, more simple and less important, that is explained by rationalism. The second part which is the essence of any activity can not be formalized and may be mastered by an individual only in her personal practical activity and interaction with more experienced teachers, it is impossible to understand it before the personal activity begins. Oakeshott deduced from it that it is impossible to define the goal of activity before the activity itself (Oakeshott 1949), that's why the problem (1.1.1)-(1.1.2) is senseless.

A principal way of overcoming the scantiness of the concept of economic rationality is a transition from the model of economic person to the model of sociological person (The Sociology 1992). The subject of sociological rationality is first of all oriented to the values and norms, and she behaves in accordance to the role complex acquired during her socialization. By the opinion of Ralph Dahrendorf, the behavior of a sociological person is determined not by her own intentions but by external social impact (Dahrendorf 1973).

The self-sufficient importance of social norms, standards, and rules was underlined by Jon Elster who has noticed that a social norm is not a taxi which can be left at any moment. If a person following a social norm, she must obey it even if it contradicts to her current interests. In the same time Elster acknowledges the role of economic rationality as an incentive. His final conclusion is that human actions are conditioned by both norms and interests (Elster 2007). A plural impact of different incentives to the human behavior was also noticed by Eugen von Boem-Bawerk.

So, the principal distinction of the homo sociologicus from the homo economicus is that the sociological behavior is determined by several incentives (criteria of optimality) meanwhile the economic behavior is determined by only one factor. Here it is worthwhile to remind the Weberian types of social actions. If a subject of economic rationality is conducted only by her goal then a subject of sociological rationality considers also values, norms, traditions and emotions.

From the formal point of view it means that the expression (1.1.1) has to be substituted by the following one:

$$f_i(x) \to \max, \, i = 1,..., n. \tag{1.1.3}$$

The model (1.1.2)-(1.1.3) represents a problem of vector (multicriteria) optimization (Steuer 1986). Its sense is determined by that in choosing a decision (1.1.2) the subject of optimization strives to maximize several functions (1.1.3) simultaneously.

The principal problem of multicriteria optimization is the absence of a single decision concept. If a maximum point is defined strictly and finding of the set of maximum points is connected with only technical (though quite serious sometimes) difficulties then what does mean the requirement (1.1.3)? It is evident that a simultaneous maximization of several (at least two) functions is possible only in degenerate and not interesting cases because in the majority of real situations the criteria of optimality contradict each other. Thus, the problem of multicriteria optimization is more complicated both in formulation and in solution in comparison with the problem of scalar optimization which expresses the idea of economic rationality.

The most widespread approach to the solution of multicriteria optimization problems is the idea of Pareto optimality. The solution of the problem (1.1.2) is called Pareto-optimal if does not exist other solution in which all criteria (1.1.3) take not smaller values and even one a strictly greater one. In other words, an improvement of a Pareto-optimal solution by one criterion can be achieved only at the cost of its worsening by another criterion. Therefore, the set of Pareto-optimal solutions of the problem (1.1.2)-(1.1.3) formalizes a reasonable non-improved compromise between intentions of a subject of sociological rationality.

The problem is that in the majority of cases a set of Pareto-optimal solutions contains several (and often infinite number of) variants, in consequence a final solution of the multicriteria optimization problem is not reached in fact on the base of this approach. That's why for selection of the unique solution from the set of Pareto-optimal ones it is necessary to use some additional procedures which have a subjective character.

First, one can try to ascribe specific weights a_1, ..., a_n to the criteria f_i so that $0 \le a_i \le 1$, $a_1 + ... + a_n = 1$, i.e. to define a relative significance of the criteria. If it ends successfully then instead of the multicriteria problem (1.1.2)-(1.1.3) one can consider a classic optimization problem

$$\sum_{i=1}^{n} a_i f_i \to \max, \ x \in X,$$

i.e. to search the maximum of a weighted sum of the initial objective functions (so-called linear convolution). In this case the problem is reduced to the ordering of optimality criteria on the base of a system of weights.

Second, it is possible consider one of the criteria (for example the first one) as the main one and to maximize it, and for other criteria to fix some threshold values f_i^* which give the lower bound of their admissible values. Then a classic optimization problem

$$f_1(x) \to \max, \ f_i(x) \ge f_i^*, i = 2,...,n, x \in X$$

arises again. This approach is also subjective that expresses itself both in the definition of the main criterion (what in fact reduced the sociological rationality to the economic one) and in fixation of the threshold values for consideration of another criteria. Thus a sociological decision making rests ambiguous and this ambiguity has a principal character.

Is it possible to model an irrational behavior? In our opinion, the behavior of an irrational subject is characterized by absence of optimality criteria on which she could orientate herself. As a preliminary idea we could suppose that the mathematical formalism of synergetics (Haken 1983) could be useful for the modeling. It is impossible to forecast the behavior of an irrational subject in the bifurcation point but some probabilistic evaluations on the base of the Bayes theorem are possible.

1.2. COMPROMISE RATIONALITY

As any agent acts in the society, her possibilities of the rational behavior of any type are restricted by actions of other agents. The situation of interaction inevitably becomes a conflict one because goals and interests of different agents do not coincide. A resolution of the conflict is given by a certain trade-off which considers to an extent the interests of all agents participating in the conflict. Building and investigation of the models of conflict and their compromise solutions are analyzed by game theory. It is game theoretic models of different classes that should be considered the models of compromise rationality.

The basic model of compromise rationality is a game in normal form (Moulin 1986):

$$G = \left\langle N, \{X_i\}_{i \in N}, \{u_i\}_{i \in N} \right\rangle. \tag{1.2.1}$$

Here $N = \{1,...,n\}$ is a finite set of players, i.e. agents who have their own goals and interests and certain resources for their realization; X_i is a set of strategies of i-th player, i.e.

her admissible variants of behavior; $x_i \in X_i$ is a specific strategy of i-th player from her admissible set; when each player chooses her strategy a game situation (outcome) $x = (x_1, ..., x_n)$ arises. On the set of all situations X a payoff function, i.e. a map $u_i : X \to R$ is defined for each player. A value of the function $u_i(x)$ describes the payoff of the player i in the situation x.

In accordance to the concept of economic rationality which lies in the base of the theory of games in normal form, the interests of each player are described completely by striving of maximization of her payoff function. The problem is that similarly to the model of multicriteria optimization, in general case the players can not maximize their payoff functions simultaneously. Let's denote $x = (x_i, x_{N \setminus i})$, where x_i is a strategy of i-th player, $x_{N \setminus i} = (x_1, ..., x_{i-1}, x_{i+1}, ..., x_n)$ is a vector of strategies of other players. Then by virtue of the economic rationality the problem of i-th player has the form

$$u_i(x_i, x_{N \setminus i}) \to \max_{x_i \in X_i}.$$

The possibilities of i-th player of maximization of her payoff function are thus seen to be restricted by the choice of her own strategy $x_i \in X_i$, meanwhile the result of maximization will depend on actions of all other players. As in the case of multicriteria optimization, a single notion of solution of the game in normal form (1.2.1) is absent. Some sets of situations $x \in X$ having certain compromise properties are accepted as solutions (optimality principles) for different classes of the games in normal form. An investigation of the principles forms the content of the game theory.

If the condition

$$\forall x_{N \setminus i} \in X_{N \setminus i} \forall y_i \in X_i : u_i(x_i, x_{N \setminus i}) \geq u_i(y_i, x_{N \setminus i}) \tag{1.2.2}$$

is fulfilled then x_i is called a dominant strategy of i-th player. An application of the dominant strategy gives to a player not smaller payoff than application of any other admissible strategy with any admissible strategies of other players, i.e. this strategy (or a set of the strategies if there is more than one such strategy) is her best one from the point of view of the economic rationality. If each player has even one dominant strategy then the set of situations $x = (x_1, ..., x_n)$ where each component of the vector x is a dominant strategy of the respective player is called the set of equilibria in dominant strategies in the game (1.2.1). Let's note that the definition (1.2.2) depends only on actions of the player i, therefore the players can choose their dominant strategies independently from each other. The problem is that dominant strategies exist not at all always.

If the condition

$$\forall x_{N \setminus i} \in X_{N \setminus i} : \inf_{x_{N \setminus i} \in X_{N \setminus i}} u_i(x_i, x_{N \setminus i}) = \sup_{y_i \in X_i} \inf_{x_{N \setminus i} \in X_{N \setminus i}} u_i(y_i, x_{N \setminus i}) = \alpha_i \tag{1.2.3}$$

is fulfilled then x_i is called a cautious strategy of i-th player. The quantity α_i is called a guaranteed payoff of i-th player. An application of the cautious strategy guarantees to the player a payoff not smaller than α_i for any actions of other players. As a dominant one, a player can use her cautious strategy independently from other players; it makes sense in the cases when the player expects the worst (for example hostile) actions of other players and strives to make herself secure by receiving at least her guaranteed payoff.

If the inequality

$$\forall i \in N \; \forall y_i \in X_i : u_i(x_i, x_{N\setminus i}) \geq u_i(y_i, x_{N\setminus i}) \qquad (1.2.4)$$

is fulfilled then the situation $x = (x_1, ..., x_n)$ is called the Nash equilibrium in the game (1.2.1). The set of Nash equilibria is the most widespread optimality principle for the games in normal form. The condition (1.2.4) means that if all players use strategies from the Nash equilibrium then for each of them is not profitable to choose any other admissible strategy y_i instead of the strategy x_i. In other words, the Nash equilibrium is stable against individual deviations of players. The problem is that:

- Nash equlibria not always exist;
- several Nash equilibria can exist; in this case it is not clear which one should be chosen, the more so as they could be not equivalent for different players;
- a situation could exist which is not a Nash equilibrium but all players receive greater payoffs in it. The examples and discussion see in (Case 2007; Luce and Raiffa 1957; Moulin 1986).

Another shortage of Nash equilibrium is that the situations in equilibrium are stable against individual deviations but not necessary against the group ones. In other words, if two or more players come in collusion then it could be advantageous for them to break the initial agreement and to choose strategies which do not belong to the Nash equilibrium. Thus it is natural to generalize the condition of Nash equlilibrium as follows. Let's denote $K \subset N$ an arbitrary subset of players (a coalition) and $x_K \in X_K$ let be a set of strategies of the players from K. A situation $x \in X$ is called a strong equilibrium in the game (1.2.1) if $\forall K \in N, \forall y_K \in X_K$ it is impossible to satisfy simultaneously the conditions

$$\forall i \in K : u_i(y_K, x_{N\setminus K}) \geq u_i(x_K, x_{N\setminus K})$$

$$\exists i \in K : u_i(y_K, x_{N\setminus K}) > u_i(x_K, x_{N\setminus K})$$

So, the requirement of strong equilibrium makes not advantageous not only individual but also coalitional deviations from the preliminary agreed strategies. Specifically, if K={i} then we receive the requirement of Nash equilibrium, and if K=N then we receive the requirement of Pareto optimality. In the case of two players the set of strong equilibria is a set of situations which are in the same time Nash equilibria and Pareto optima. The problem is that the requirement of strong equilibrium is really strong and one succeeds to satisfy it quite rarely.

A situation $x^\alpha \in X$ belongs to the α–core of the game (1.2.1) if $\forall K \subset N, \forall y_K \in X_K \ \exists x_{N \setminus K} \in X_{N \setminus K}$ such as it is impossible to satisfy simultaneously the conditions

$$\forall i \in K : u_i(y_K, x_{N \setminus K}) \geq u_i(x^\alpha)$$

$$\exists i \in K : u_i(y_K, x_{N \setminus K}) > u_i(x^\alpha)$$

A situation $x^\beta \in X$ belongs to the β–core of the game (1.2.1) if $\forall K \subset N \ \exists x_{N \setminus K} \in X_{N \setminus K}$ such as $\forall y_K \in X_K$ it is impossible to satisfy simultaneously the conditions

$$\forall i \in K : u_i(y_K, x_{N \setminus K}) \geq u_i(x^\beta)$$

$$\exists i \in K : u_i(y_K, x_{N \setminus K}) > u_i(x^\beta)$$

The notions of α–core and β–core for a game in normal form are connected with objections by which the players stabilize initial agreements. In the case of α–core for each specific deviation $y_K \in X_K$ of the coalition K the complementary coalition N\K selects the specific objection $x_{N \setminus K} \in X_{N \setminus K}$ which makes the deviation not advantageous. In the case of β–core a universal objection $x_{N \setminus K} \in X_{N \setminus K}$ exists which makes not advantageous for the coalition K any deviation from the preliminary agreed strategies. That's why in the case of β–core a complementary coalition has no need to know exactly which deviation was made to execute the objection.

Let's denote in the game (1.2.1) SE the set of strong equilibria, C_α the α–core, C_β the β–core. Then the consequence of inclusions $SE \subset C_\beta \subset C_\alpha$ takes place. The strong equilibrium ensures its stability automatically (it is the strongest requirement), if the β–core is not empty then the stability is provided by the universal objection, in the case of α–core for each possible deviation of the coalition K from the agreed set of strategies the complementary coalition N\K has to select a specific objection which neutralizes the danger of deviation.

A strategy x_i dominates a strategy y_i if

$$\forall x_{N \setminus i} \in X_{N \setminus i} : u_i(x_i, x_{N \setminus i}) \geq u_i(y_i, x_{N \setminus i}),$$

$$\exists x_{N \setminus i} \in X_{N \setminus i} : u_i(x_i, x_{N \setminus i}) > u_i(y_i, x_{N \setminus i})$$

Let's denote D_i the set of all non-dominated strategies of the player i. Let each player knows the payoff functions and sets of admissible strategies of other players. Then it is natural to expect that all players will exclude the dominated strategies from their decision making. The sequence $X_i^0 \supset X_i^1 \supset ... \supset X_i^t \supset ...$, where $X_i^{t+1} = D_i(X_j^t, j \in N)$ is called a procedure of sequential exclusion of dominated strategies for the player i. If such a value t of time exists that $\forall i \in N \ \forall x_i, y_i \in X_i^t$ are equivalent, i.e. $\forall x_{N\backslash i} \in X_{N\backslash i} : u_i(x_i, x_{N\backslash i}) = u_i(y_i, x_{N\backslash i})$ then the game (1.2.1) is called dominance solvable, and the set $X^t = X_1^t \times ... \times X_n^t$ is called a set of complicate equilibria in the game (1.2.1). To find the complicate equilibria it is convenient to use so-called games in extensive form (Kuhn 1953; Moulin 1986).

A specific form of conflict interaction arises when the hierarchical relations between players exist. Let's consider the case of two players when one of them (Leader denoted by index L) has a hierarchical priority in comparison with the other one (Follower denoted by index F). From the point of view of game theoretic formalization the hierarchy means that the Leader has a right of the first move: she chooses her strategy $x_L \in X_L$ and informs the Follower about it. Then it is natural to expect that the Follower will choose her strategy from the set of optimal reaction (response)

$$R_F = \left\{ x_F \in X_F : u_F(x_L, x_F) \geq u_F(x_L, y_F) \forall y_F \in X_F \right\}. \tag{1.2.5}$$

The following actions of the Leader depend on her evaluation of the Follower attitude. If the Leader expects for the benevolence of Follower then she can choose her strategy $x_L \in X_L$ from the condition

$$u_L(x_L, x_F) = \sup_{y_L \in X_L} \sup_{y_F \in R_F(x_L)} u_L(y_L, y_F) = S_L. \tag{1.2.6}$$

The set of situations (x_L, x_F) which satisfy the condition (1.2.6) is called the set of Stackelberg equilibria in the game (1.2.1). If the Leader expects for the malevolence of Follower (or just takes caution) then she chooses her strategy $x_L \in X_L$ from the condition

$$u_L(x_L, x_F) = \sup_{y_L \in X_L} \inf_{y_F \in R_F(x_L)} u_L(y_L, y_F) = \gamma_L. \tag{1.2.7}$$

This way of choice is called the principle of guaranteed result (Germeyer 1976) and the set of situations (x_L, x_F) which satisfy the condition (1.2.7) is natural to call the set of Germeyer equilibria in the game (1.2.1) (Ougolnitsky 2005). Comparing the expressions (1.2.7) and (1.2.3), it is easy to see that $S_L \geq \gamma_L \geq \alpha_L$. Indeed, the right of the first move gives to the Leader a possibility to foresee the Follower's reaction (to narrow her set of optimal response) and therefore to improve the guaranteed result.

Now let's suppose that to the moment of her choice the Leader will know the choice of Follower $x_F \in X_F$. It is evident that in this case the strategy of Leader is no more a constant parameter $x_L \in X_L$ but a function $\widetilde{x}_L = x_L(x_F)$ which maps to any value $x_F \in X_F$ a value $x_L \in X_L$, i.e. $\widetilde{x}_L : X_F \to X_L$. Thus, a set of strategies of the Leader is the set of functions (maps) $\widetilde{X}_L = \{\widetilde{x}_L = x_L(x_F): X_F \to X_L\}$ and her move is a choice of a strategy $\widetilde{x}_L \in \widetilde{X}_L$ and a transmission to the Follower of the information about it. Then the Leader's guaranteed result has the form

$$\widetilde{\gamma}_L = \sup_{\widetilde{x}_L \in \widetilde{X}_L} \inf_{x_F \in \widetilde{R}_F(\widetilde{x}_L)} u_L(\pi(\widetilde{x}_L, x_F)). \tag{1.2.8}$$

Here a set of Follower's optimal reaction $\widetilde{R}_F(\widetilde{x}_L)$ is defined similarly to (1.2.5):

$$\widetilde{R}_F(\widetilde{x}_L) = Arg \sup_{x_F \in X_F} u_F(x_L(x_F)).$$

Note that a function $u_L(x_L, x_F)$ is defined on the set $X_L \times X_F$ of initial constant strategies of the players. Because now the first argument u_L is a map $\widetilde{x}_L \in \widetilde{X}_L$ then it is necessary to introduce a special projective function $\pi: \widetilde{X}_L \times X_F \to X_L \times X_F$ which "returns" the function u_L to the initial domain (Gorelik and Kononenko 1982).

Let's consider another modification of the game. Let now Follower's strategy coincides to the Leader's strategy from the previous version and the Leader also will have information about the Follower's choice. It is evident that in this case the strategy of Follower is $\widetilde{X}_F = \{\widetilde{x}_F = x_F(x_L): X_L \to X_F\}$ and for definition of the Leader's set of admissible strategies two waves are required already: $\widetilde{\widetilde{X}}_L = \{\widetilde{\widetilde{x}}_L = x_L(\widetilde{x}_F): \widetilde{X}_F \to X_L\}$, i.e. to each map chosen by the Follower $\widetilde{x}_F \in \widetilde{X}_F$ the Leader in her turn maps a value $x_L \in X_L$ according to the rule $\widetilde{\widetilde{x}}_L = x_L(\widetilde{x}_F)$. Leader's move includes choice and transmission to the Follower a complicated map strategy $\widetilde{\widetilde{x}}_L = x_L(\widetilde{x}_F) = x_L(x_F(x_L))$ from the set $\widetilde{\widetilde{X}}_L$.

Then Leader's maximal guaranteed result is equal to

$$\widetilde{\widetilde{\gamma}}_L = \sup_{\widetilde{\widetilde{x}}_L \in \widetilde{\widetilde{X}}_L} \inf_{\widetilde{x}_F \in \widetilde{\widetilde{R}}_F(\widetilde{\widetilde{x}}_L)} u_L(\pi(\widetilde{\widetilde{x}}_L, \widetilde{x}_F)) \tag{1.2.9}$$

where Follower's set of optimal reactions has the form

$$\widetilde{\widetilde{R}}_F(\widetilde{\widetilde{x}}_L) = Arg \sup_{\widetilde{x}_F \in \widetilde{X}_F} u_F(\pi(x_L(\widetilde{x}_F)), \widetilde{x}_F),$$

$\pi : \widetilde{\widetilde{X}}_L \times \widetilde{X}_F \to \mathrm{X}_1 \times \mathrm{X}_2$ is the projective function.

Do more complicated reflexive propositions result in increasing of the number of waves to the infinity? The next statement delivers from it. Denote the considered game versions with Leader's maximal guaranteed results (1.2.7), (1.2.8), (1.2.9) as Γ_1, Γ_2, Γ_3 respectively (Germeyer 1976). Then

$$\gamma_L^{2k} = \widetilde{\gamma}_L, \gamma_L^{2k+1} = \widetilde{\widetilde{\gamma}}_L, k \geq 2, \qquad (1.2.10)$$

where $\gamma_L{}^m$ is Leader's maximal guaranteed result in the game Γ_m, $m > 3$. Besides, the following important inequalities take place:

$$\gamma_L \leq \widetilde{\widetilde{\gamma}}_L \leq \widetilde{\gamma}_L .$$

It is easy to interpret them on the base of relative information availability of Leader and Follower (Gorelik and Kononenko 1982).

Reflexive game theoretic models are studied in more details by Dmitry Novikov and Alexander Chkhartishvily (2003). The authors have proposed a generalization of the model of game in normal form (1.2.1) as follows:

$$G_I = \left\langle N, \{X_i\}_{i \in N}, \{u_i(\bullet)\}_{i \in N}, I \right\rangle. \qquad (1.2.11)$$

As earlier $N = \{1,\ldots,n\}$ is a finite set of players; X_i is a set of strategies of i-th player. It is supposed that an indefinite parameter $\theta \in \Omega$ is present in the situation (the set Ω is known for all players) thus a payoff function of i-th player is a map $u_i : X \times \Omega \to R$.

The essence of the approach is determined by an information structure I of the game which is defined as follows. An information structure of i-th player includes the following elements. First, a view of i-th player of the parameter θ which is denoted $\theta_i \in \Omega$. Second, the views of i-th player of the views of other players about the parameter θ which are denoted $\theta_{ij} \in \Omega, j \in N$. Third, the views of i-th player of the views of j-th player of the views of k-th player about the parameter θ which are denoted $\theta_{ijk} \in \Omega, j,k \in N$, and so on. In doing so along with real players so-called phantom players are taking into consideration. The phantom players exist in mind of real and other phantom players. Theoretically the level of reflection may increase as much as desired but in fact it can be restricted by considerations similar to (1.2.10) and a bad infinity in Hegel's sense does not arise.

Thus, the information structure of i-th player I_i is given by the set of parameters $\theta_{ij_1 \cdots j_p}$ where $p \in Z, j_1,\ldots, j_p \in N$, $\theta_{ij_1 \cdots j_p} \in \Omega$. The information structure I of the total game is defined similarly by the set of parameters $\theta_{i_1 \cdots i_p}$ where

$p \in Z, i_1,...,i_p \in N, \theta_{i_1 \cdots i_p} \in \Omega$. But the total structure I is not available for the players observation, each of them knows only a part of it. Therefore the information structure is a specific graph – an infinite n-tree, to each vertex of which an amount of information of the real and phantom players is prescribed (Novikov and Chkhartishvily 2003).

A known financier George Soros has developed an original theory of reflexivity for stock markets (Soros 1994). Soroc criticizes the concept of economic rationality which does not consider a number of important real factors. His idea is that the dynamics of stock market is influenced by subjective expectations of its agents. Soros treats the reflexivity as an interaction between the agents' efforts to understand the situation and the influence of their reasoning to the situation.

The model of game in normal form (1.2.1) describes an independent competitive behavior of economically rational subjects. A coalitional behavior of the subjects (cooperation) is described by the models of cooperative games (games in form of characteristic function). In this case the main agents are not individual players but their unions (coalitions), and the essence of optimality principles is in finding of a compromise not among the strategies of players but among the ways of distribution of their joint payoff (Neumann and Morgenstern 1953; Rosenmuller 1971).

The model of cooperative game has the form

$$\tilde{A}_v = \langle N, v \rangle . \qquad (1.2.12)$$

As in the model of game in normal form, here $N = \{1,...,n\}$ is a finite number of players, i.e. agents who have their own goals and interests and certain resources for their realization. But now the principal role is played by coalitions of the type $K \subset N$, i.e. subsets of the set of players. The following specific cases are of special interest:

- $K = \varnothing$ - the empty coalition which has a technical character;
- $K = \{i\}$ - a one-element coalition which consists of the only player. From this point of view the theory of games in normal form may be treated formally as a specific case of the cooperative game theory but in fact they are built absolutely differently;
- $K = N$ - the grand coalition which includes all players.

Each coalition is characterized by a numerical value the interpretation of which depends on the nature of modeled agents. For example, in economics that value is the income (profit) provided by a coalition of economic agents (firm, holding, regional or national economy). In politics that value is the political capital (a number of voices in elections, a number of places in a legislature) disposed by a coalition of political agents (party, movement).

To formalize the described notion a map

$$v : 2^N \rightarrow R \qquad (1.2.13)$$

is introduced which is called a characteristic function. This function maps to each coalition $K \subset N$ its characteristic value v(K). As a rule it is required that the characteristic function (1.2.13) satisfies two properties:

$$v(\varnothing) = 0$$

$$\forall K, L \subset N : K \cap L = \varnothing \Rightarrow v(K \cup L) \geq v(K) + v(L). \qquad (1.2.14)$$

The first property has an evident technical sense. The second property (1.2.14) is principal; it is called superadditivity. According to this property, the characteristic value of the union of nonintersecting coalitions is not smaller than the sum of the separate values. Thus, superadditivity means the advantages of coalitional unions (the grand coalition is the most advantageous).

The subject of the cooperative game theory is a just distribution of the characteristic value of grand coalition v(N) among all players. In economic applications v(N) is interpreted as the maximal (due to the superadditivity) income which may be provided to the whole community of agents by the formation of grand coalition.

Denote a distribution of the maximal income among the players as

$$x = (x_1, ..., x_n). \qquad (1.2.15)$$

To some extent it is similar to the notion of outcome in the theory of games in normal form. The optimality principles of the cooperative game theory are sets of distributions (1.2.15) which satisfy certain notions of justice.

It seems indisputable that the distributions (1.2.15) accepted as optimality principles (solutions of a cooperative game) should satisfy the following two properties:

$$\forall i \in N : x_i \geq v(i) \qquad (1.2.16)$$

$$\sum_{i \in N} x_i = v(N). \qquad (1.2.17)$$

The property (1.2.16) is called an individual rationality of the distribution (1.2.15). The violation of this property means that even one player receives in the distribution smaller than she is able to gain herself when not entering to coalitions.

The property (1.2.17) is called Pareto optimality of the distribution (1.2.15). Its violation (i.e. the inequality $\sum_{i \in N} x_i < v(N)$, because the condition $\sum_{i \in N} x_i > v(N)$ is physically impossible due to the maximality of v(N)) would mean that a part of the maximal income is hidden by someone and does not take part in the distribution.

The distributions (1.2.15) which satisfy the properties (1.2.16) and (1.2.17) are called imputations, their set in the game (1.2.12) is denoted I(v). It results from the above reasoning that all practically realizable optimality principles of the cooperative games are subsets of the set of imputations I(v). The problem is that in the majority of cooperative games this set contains more than one imputation and even can be infinite that leaves a question of the final decision open.

To narrow the set of imputations and to receive the substantive optimality principles it is necessary to learn how to compare imputations. As far as imputations are vectors, a special agreement is needed to define the comparison. An imputation x dominates an imputation y by the coalition K if the following two conditions are fulfilled:

$$\forall i \in K : x_i > y_i \tag{1.2.18}$$

$$\sum_{i \in K} x_i \le v(K). \tag{1.2.19}$$

The condition (1.2.18) expresses the sense of dominance: all participants of the coalition K receive in the imputation x strictly greater than in the imputation y, therefore they prefer x to y. The condition (1.2.19) describes a technical restriction; the participants of coalition K can not receive greater than the value v(K).

It is accepted later than if an imputation x dominates an imputation y by even one coalition K than x dominates y ($x \succ y$). This definition is not at all evident: it may appear that x dominates y by a coalition K but in the same time y dominates x by another coalition L. But the definition permits to formulate one of the most widespread optimality principles in the theory of cooperative games: the set of all non-dominated imputations of a game is called the C-core. To find all imputations from a C-core it is convenient to use the following criterion: an imputation x belongs to the C-core if and only if for any coalition K it is true that $\sum_{i \in K} x_i \ge v(K)$. The former condition has a clear interpretation which explains the essence of C-core: if the condition is violated then even one coalition K receives in the imputation smaller than v(K). It is clear that the coalition K does not approve the justice of the imputation x.

Let's call a subset B(v) of the imputations set:

-   internal stable if any two imputations from B(v) dominate each other;
-   external stable if $\forall y \in I(v) \setminus B(v) : \exists x \in B(v) : x \succ y$.

An internal and external stable set of imputations is called a Neumann-Morgenstern solution of the cooperative game (NM-solution). The interpretation of this optimality principle is also clear: the imputations from NM-solution are not comparable, and for any outside imputation there is an imputation from the NM-solution which dominates "the stranger".

It should be noted that C-core and NM-solution include more than one imputation as a rule, and in many games they contain an infinite number of imputations that leaves a question of the final solution of the game in fact open. Besides, in some games C-core and NM-solutions may be absent.

Another optimality principle – a Shapley value is free from the enumerated shortages. An imputation $\Phi(v) = (\Phi_1(v),\dots,\Phi_n(v))$ is called a Shapley value of the game Γ_v if the following axioms are fulfilled.

1) A renumbering of the players does not change their shares in the imputation.
2) $\sum_{i \in N} \Phi_i(v) = v(N)$.
3) 3. If for any coalition K it is true that $v(K) = v(K \setminus \{i\})$ then $\Phi_i(v) = 0$.
4) If for any coalition K it is true that v(K) = u(K) + w(K) then $\forall i \in N : \Phi_i(v) = \Phi_i(u) + \Phi_i(w)$.

This set of axioms for a Shapley value is categorical, i.e. permits to define its components uniquely by the formula

$$\Phi_i(v) = \sum_{i \in K} \gamma(k)[v(K) - v(K \setminus \{i\})], \qquad (1.2.20)$$

where $\gamma(k) = \dfrac{(k-1)!(n-k)!}{n!}$, k is a number of players in the coalition K, n is a total number of players. Thus, a Shapley value always exists and is unique. It is seen from the formula (1.2.20) that the share of a player in the Shapley value is determined by her potential contribution in different coalitions.

The consideration of time factor in compromise decision making is formalized by the models of multistage (in the case of discrete time) and differential (in the case of continuous time) games (Isaaks 1965; Basar and Olsder 1995; Leitmann 1974; Petrosyan and Zenkevich 1996). Here the question of dynamic stability (time consistency) of solutions of the game has a principal importance (Kidland and Prescott, 1977; Petrosjan 1977; Petrosyan and Zenkevich 1996).

The consideration of uncertainty factor in compromise decision making is formalized by the models of games with incomplete information (Vaisbord and Zhukovskiy 1988). The incompleteness of information of a player may be concerned both to the sets of admissible strategies and to the payoff functions of other players. The incompleteness of information is especially essential in game theoretic models of the hierarchical management systems where the Leader may be informed better or worse than the Follower (Fudenberg and Tirole 1991; Gorelik and Kononenko 1982). In general case it is necessary to consider not only one objective model of the game but a set of the subjective descriptions from the point of view of different players (Gorelik and Kononenko 1982; Novikov and Chkhartishvily 2003).

Similarly to the cases of economic and sociological rationality (1.1) in the models of compromise decision making it is natural to consider the case when each player has several optimality criteria. This generalization leads to the game theoretic models with vector payoff functions or vector characteristic functions, i.e. the models in which in (1.2.1) a payoff function of i-th player has the form $u_i = (u_{i1},\dots,u_{im_i})$, where m_i is a number of optimality criteria of i-th player, and the function (1.2.13) is a many-valued map $v : 2^N \to R^m$. The theory of games with vector payoff functions and all the more many-valued characteristic functions is in the very beginning of its formation. One could say that if classic game theoretic models formalize a conflict interaction of the economic persons (homo economicus) then game theoretic models with vector payoff functions formalize the interaction of sociological persons (homo sociologicus).

The correspondence of the different concepts of rationality and respective mathematical models is shown in Table 1.2.1.

Table 1.2.1. The correspondence of the different concepts of rationality and respective mathematical models

	Economic rationality (one optimality criterion)	Sociological rationality (several optimality criteria)
One agent	[Scalar] optimization models	Vector (multicriteria) optimization models
Several agents	Game theoretic models	Game theoretic models with vector payoff functions and many-valued characteristic functions

A compromise decision making is also studied by the theory of collective choice (Luce and Raiffa 1957; Moulin 1988; Roberts 1984). The theory investigates models of deducing a final opinion of the group on the base of individual preferences of the group members. The main results of the theory (Arrow theorem, Sen paradox, Gibbard-Satterthwaite theorem and others) are negative. It is explained by a paradoxical nature of the problem of collective choice.

1.3. FORMS OF POWER AND METHODS OF MANAGEMENT

A hierarchical structure of the big systems including human beings generates a necessity of special methods of the hierarchical management (control). Analysis of the methods is based on the study of social relations and power forms.

In the fundamental work by Pitirim Sorokin (1957) three types of the social relations: compulsory, contractual, and familistic ones are differentiated. For the classification Sorokin has used the following attributes of social interaction: 1) one-sided or two-sided interaction; 2) extensiveness; 3) intensiveness; 4) duration and continuity; 5) direction; 6) organization.

The relations can be symmetrical or hierarchical: in the case of one-sided interaction it is more correct to say about an impact of the subject to the object and respective one-sided dependence, meanwhile the two-sided interaction means interdependence and equality of the subjects.

Sorokin has proposed to measure an extensiveness of interaction as the share of actions and feelings connected to the interaction in the total volume of physical and mental activity of the subject. The limit case is a total extensiveness when the interaction determines the activity of subjects practically completely (for example, an infant and his mother, a loving couple).

However, in the majority of cases social interactions are restricted by their extensiveness and concern only a small part of subject's activity (for example, her professional activity).

The intensiveness of interaction is determined by the importance that the interaction has in subject's life. The relations between a teacher and his pupil may be formal but may also be all-absorbing and making the sense of life for the pupil. The unification of the attributes of extensiveness and intensiveness permits to perceive more complete characteristics of the type of relations between subjects.

The role of duration and continuity of interaction is clear. The majority of interactions are episodic and do not leave an essential trace in subject's life but some of them keep their importance during a long period which sometimes continues even after the death of one of the interaction participants.

From the point of view of direction Sorokin has differentiated solidary, antagonistic, and mixed interactions. In the case of solidarity the goals and interests of subjects coincide or at least coordinate, so they can join their efforts. In contrary, in the case of antagonism the intentions of subjects contradict each other that result in opposition and hostility. The most widespread is a mixed type in which the subjects of interaction have both coinciding and contradicting interests: in this case a trade-off is possible.

At last, an interaction is organized if it has a solid institutional base and not organized otherwise. Sorokin has underlined that the organization of interaction always results in social differentiation and stratification.

The familistic type of social relations is defined by Sorokin as total, highly intensive, solidary and protracted interaction. In this case the persons need each other, search for each other and are connected in a whole just to be together. The examples are relations between the loving members of a family, especially mother and infant, genuine friends, persons in love.

The contractual type of social relations is characterized as a strict limitation in extensiveness, intensiveness, and duration defined in a contract, solidarity within the contractual relations. In contractual relations the partner is treated as means or tool for achieving a goal, getting a pleasure, taking an advantage or profit, being served. The Latin formula of contractual relations is "do ut des". As a rule, the contracts have a written form and prepared by professional lawyers. This form of relations is the most widespread in the market economy.

The compulsory type of social relations is first of all a forced one. In this case one side of the interaction thrusts to the other side a manner of conduct, certain functions and commitments, press the other subject to do something without consideration of her desire and intentions and even despite them. The typical examples are relations between master and servant, victor and vanquished, robber and robbed.

Sorokin has noticed that in reality some mixed forms of the characterized pure types are observed. But in any social group one of the types prevails. Familistic relations prevail in families, unofficial and religious groups; contractual relations are typical for financial and trade organizations; compulsory relations flourish in military and penitentiary institutions (Sorokin 1957).

The most common analysis of power forms belongs to French and Raven (1960). They have described coercive, reward, legitimate, referent, and expert power. Coercive power forces someone to do something against their will. Its main goal is compliance: this is a power of dictators and despots. As a rule, coercive power is based on physical or other threats. Reward power exchanges money to work. More generally this power is the ability to give other people what they want, and hence ask them to do something in exchange. Legitimate power is connected with a social status: presidents, judges, and policemen possess this type of power. The legitimate power is often accompanied (implicitly or explicitly) by the coercive one. The referent power is determined by fame and charisma, it is the power of celebrities and leaders. Expert power is based on knowledge and professional skills.

Specialists in organizations theory distinguish three groups of methods of the hierarchical management:

1) compulsion when a subject thrusts an object to provide the achievement of the subject's goal despite the goals and interests of the object;
2) impulsion when a subject creates for an object such conditions in which it is more advantageous for the object to provide the achievement of the subject's goal than not to do it;
3) conviction when a subject-to-object interaction is organized in such a way that the object herself strives voluntarily for the achievement of the subject's goal which is interiorized as the object's own goal (Fatkhutdinov and Sivkova 1999).

The triad of methods of hierarchical management is ordered by: 1) decrease of rigidity of the impact of Leader on Follower; 2) decrease of necessary degree of dependence of Follower on Leader; 3) increase of progressiveness of the managerial paradigm. In the same time, the tendency of using conviction does not eliminate impulsion and even compulsion in a big number of real situations.

A correlation of the methods of compulsion, impulsion, and conviction with the traditional and modern approaches to management is shown in Figure 1.3.1.

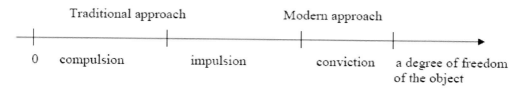

Figure 1.3.1. Correlation between the methods of management and approaches to management.

The left boundary of the range corresponds to the total absence of freedom, the right one if determined by restrictions of the solved problem. Certainly, the boundaries between methods are conditional and have rather an interval than a point character. The method of impulsion takes an intermediate place; its elements can belong both to the compulsion (especially in the negative form of punishment) and to the conviction (in relation to the needs of high levels). So, the impulsion may be used both in traditional and in modern managerial approaches. As for compulsion and conviction, they are incompatible and therefore do not intersect: the first method belongs completely to the traditional approach meanwhile the second gives tendencies of the modern management. All three methods are used in the real practice of management. The transition to the post-industrial society diminishes a share of compulsion and then impulsion, and extends the share of conviction. An ideal management should be based on the conviction completely though it is hardly possible in real life.

The method of conviction is the worst analyzed in sociological and social-psychological aspects and is the hardest to formalize. Its essence consists in the transformation of hierarchical relations to the cooperative ones, in the conversion of the Follower from a subordinate to the partner and ally of the Leader. But the cooperation should be preceded by a hierarchical impact. An eminent social psychologist Kurt Lewin thought undisputable the fact that it is impossible to teach democracy by means of authoritarian methods. But in the same time he has noticed that a democratic leader who wants to change a group atmosphere into a democratic type should possess the power and to use it for active learning (Lewin 1935).

More detailed analysis of the methods of compulsion, impulsion, and conviction can be found in (De Crespigny 1968; French and Raven 1959; Ledyaev 1998; Wrong 1988).

In this book compulsion, impulsion, and conviction are considered as principal methods of hierarchical sustainable management. Their interpretation somewhat differs from the above presented though based on it.

In the case of compulsion the agent of higher level puts the agent of lower level in such conditions that the former is obliged to use a strategy desirable for the first agent. This impact has a forcing character and an administrative or legislative base. The interests of the agent of lower level are completely neglected therefore the relations between agents have a subject-to-object nature. If the relations are described as a hierarchical game then compulsion means an impact of the Leader to the set of admissible strategies of the Follower.

In the case of impulsion the Leader creates conditions in which it is more advantageous for the Follower to use Leader's desirable strategy then not to do it. This method has a nature of economic motivation and is implemented as a feedback mechanism of penalties and bonuses. The Follower's interests are considered to an extent in this case. From the point of view of game theoretic modeling impulsion means an impact of the Leader to the Follower's payoff function.

In the case of conviction the Follower voluntarily shares the Leader's intentions and uses a strategy desirable for the Leader (which becomes desirable for the Follower too). This method has a social-psychological nature and gives subject-to-subject character to the relations between the agents. In the game theoretic model conviction means a transition of both players to cooperation and joint maximization of the summary payoff function of their coalition.

Compulsion and impulsion may be accompanied by Leader's manipulation, i.e. the deliberate misrepresentation of the information transmitted to Follower for mercenary motives. In turn the Follower can use a counter-game, i.e. the transmission to the Leader of the misrepresentative information about strategies chosen by the Follower. Control of the counter-game requires from the Leader additional costs which increase proportionally to the rigidness of Leader's demands to the Follower's strategies. In the case of conviction manipulation and counter-game are not used.

Let's borrow as a conditional but obvious case of the methods of hierarchical relations a modified situation from the famous novel "The Adventures of Tom Sawyer" by Mark Twain. Tom is the Follower, his aunt Polly is the Leader. The Leader's goal is to whitewash her fence. In the case of compulsion Aunt Polly forces Tom to whitewash the fence using her position of the older relative and head of the family. In the case of impulsion she could offer Tom some dollars or other reward for the work. In the case of conviction (that was in fact realized in the novel) Tom revaluates the situation and mentally transfers the work into the category of a pleasant amusement. Then he whitewashes the fence voluntarily and even excites envy in his friend. The manipulation could take place if Aunt Polly had promised to Tom some reward but did not keep the promise after the end of work. Tom's counter-game could consist in careless whitewashing.

Now let an environmental protection agency be the Leader, an industrial enterprise situated near a river be the Follower, the river ecosystem be the object of hierarchical control. It is natural to treat the desirable strategy for Leader as such a strategy in which the industrial sewage doesn't exceed the maximum allowable concentration of pollutants in the river. In the case of compulsion the objective is reached by establishing some sewage limits and license recall from the enterprise if the limits are forced. In the case of impulsion if the enterprise exceeds the maximum allowable concentration of pollutants in the river then a penalty is charged. At last, in the case of conviction the enterprise administration is environmentally minded and it ensures the required sewage disposal voluntarily. Manipulation may arise if a penalty rate increases antedate. Counter-game consists in that the enterprise reports to the agency understated date about the pollution. To control it the Leader is obliged to organize a water quality monitoring.

Let's consider a managerial example. Let the Leader be the chief of sales department, the Follower be a time-work sales manager, and the control object be the enterprise sales market. Leader's objective is to provide a given amount of monthly sales. In the case of compulsion if the condition is forced at least twice then the sales manager is fired. In the case of impulsion a motivation system is introduced such as if the sales plan is overdone then the sales manager gets a bonus and if it is underdone then she is charged a penalty. In the case of conviction the sales manager tries to do and overdo the sales plan voluntarily because she likes a social-psychological atmosphere in the enterprise, career prospects, and so on. Manipulation may consist in refusal to pay a promised bonus (for example, with reference to the financial crisis). The manager counter-game is to overstate the sales volume in her reports: to discover the deception a special revision is required.

Let's consider in more details the methods of compulsion, impulsion, and conviction in the domain of environmental protection and rational use of natural resources.

The method of compulsion is realized here by environmental laws and norms. The main mechanisms of environmental standardization are limiting, passport system, licensing, certification, and environmental impact assessment.

Limiting establishes the limits of a harmful environmental impact and the restrictions of natural resource use. Maximal allowable concentration and maximal allowable emission of different pollutants, limits of water resource use, boundaries of protected territories, limits and rules of cutting and hunting relate to this direction.

The passport system includes environmental passports of separate objects, resources, sources of emissions and waste disposal systems. The passports permit to optimize the usage of objects and to control an environmental impact and observance of the norms and rules. The environmental passports make an information support of the environmental management.

Licensing means a delivery of permits for certain kinds of activity, in this case connected with an environmental impact or protection. Licensing has two main functions: the preventive one (fixing some standards of resource use in the license) and the control one (monitoring of the activity of licensed agent by an official federal or state agency).

Certification means an official confirmation of the conformity of a certified object with certain environmental requirements. New devices and technologies, substances and materials can be the objects of environmental certification.

At last, an environmental impact assessment is an attempt to evaluate the consequences of a proposed action on each of the descriptors for the physical, biological, and cultural environment. The essential steps of the process are:

- prediction of the anticipated change in an environmental descriptor;
- determination of the magnitude or scale of the particular change;
- application of an importance or significance factor to the change.

In order to accomplish an environmental assessment, as well as to prepare an inventory and write an impact statement, it is necessary that the approach used be interdisciplinary, systematic, and reproducible (Canter 1977). The environmental impact assessment in the US is regulated by the National Environmental Protection Act which became effective on January 1, 1970.

The method of impulsion in the environmental protection is realized by an economic regulation (taxes, resource fees, penalties) and market mechanisms, and the method of conviction by the activity of environmentally minded enterprises.

In the second part of the last century in the USA an extensive environmental legislation was accepted which includes permanent and temporary norms, permission and control procedures, restrictions and interdictions.

The principal property of the multilevel system of federal management of the environmental protection programs is that specialized agencies (Council on Environmental Quality, Environmental Protection Agency) accomplish only regulative functions meanwhile practical actions of the environmental protection are organized by other federal and state agencies and institutions. A regional level of the environmental protection is also enhanced in the last years.

The central place in the system of environmental standardization in the USA is occupied by the state environmental expertise in the following directions:

1) control of important economic projects as well as small projects which are accompanied by an essential environmental impact;
2) licensing;
3) state control of the quality of new products.

A great role is played also by the penalty system: the most serious violations envisage fines up to 25 thousands dollars per day and even an imprisonment up to two years. But in fact those punishments are used very rarely and serve rather as a base for negotiations with the violators.

The growing expenditures on environmental protection also should be noticed: for example, means for the protection from pollution have increased from 1972 till 1994 year from 52.8 to 115.1 billions of dollars in the prices of the 1992 year (Statistical Abstract of the US 1997:333). From 1980-s an accent in the environmental quality management has shifted to the side of economic regulation.

The taxes for natural resource use are raised if the price of the usage differs from their real social value. An economic sense of the taxation consists in the transmission of producer's externalities into his direct internal production costs. One form of the taxation is direct payments for exceeding of the allowable norms of pollution. Another form is fees for the environmental services. Environmental taxes and payments are not widespread in the USA due to a serious resistance of the industrial circles.

Another side of the economic regulation is preferential duties, accelerated amortization of the waste disposal equipment, special grants, and bonds system. All the actions are examples of positive sanctions of the environmental impulsion.

Market methods of regulation are widespread in the environmental domain. A typical example is so-called "bubble" principle according to which the restrictions are fixed not for a separate source of pollution but for the whole group of enterprises which can allocate their expenditures on waste disposal arbitrarily within the group. This approach was developed by the creation of "environmental banks" which consider pollution disposal as deposits.

A serious attention paid by the state to the environmental problems resulted in creation of new branches of production in the domain of pollution prevention, environmental consulting and other services. By the middle of 1990-s more than 200 federal and 58,000 private enterprises were occupied in the environmental business (Competitive Challenges 1995:93). In the USA is prepared a list of 400 social responsible firms which provide an environmentally rational industrial activity (Environmental Finance Program 1995:7-11). A presence in the list gives serious competitive advantages both from the point of view of possible receiving of the profitable state orders and due to the favorable consumer attention.

A final characteristic of the methods of hierarchical management is given in Table 1.3.2.

Table 1.3.2. Characteristic of the methods of hierarchical management

	Compulsion	Impulsion	Conviction
General description of the method	Leader ensures choosing the desirable strategy of Follower by force	The strategy desirable for Leader is more profitable for Follower than undesirable ones	Follower chooses the strategy desirable for Leader voluntarily and consciously
Nature of impact	Administrative or legislative	Economic	Social-psychological
Type of relationships	Subject-to-object	Subject-to-object with partial consideration of Follower's interests	Subject-to-subject
Mathematical formalization	Leader's impact on the Follower's set of admissible strategies	Leader's impact on the Follower's payoff function	Transition of Leader and Follower to the cooperation and maximization of the summarized coalitional payoff function

Formal models of the hierarchical management are developed in the frame of three main directions: information theory of hierarchical systems, theory of active systems, and theory of contracts. The first direction (Germeyer 1976; Gorelik and Kononenko 1982) is characterized in the paragraph 1.2.

The theory of active systems (Burkov 1977; Burkov and Novikov 1999) investigates the properties of mechanisms of functioning of the social-economic systems determined by the activity of their elements. A model of the active system is given by enumeration of the following parameters: a content (set of elements of the active system), a structure (set of relations between the elements), regulations of functioning (the sequence of acts of information exchange and decision making), a number of periods of functioning (static or dynamic model), preferences of the elements (optimality criteria), admissible sets of strategies of the elements, an available information at the moment of decision making.

The set of enumerated parameters defines a mechanism of functioning of the active system in the broad sense as a totality of rules and procedures of interaction of the elements. In the narrow sense the mechanism of functioning is treated as a totality of rules of decision making by the elements when the content, the structure and other parameters are given.

The basic model of active system has a tree-like structure with a selected element on the higher level of control (Center) and active elements on the lower level. Denote $y = (y_1, ..., y_n) \in A$ a vector of strategies of the active elements, the components of which they can choose independently. Preferences of i-th active element are reflected by the objective function $f_i(y, \eta)$ where $\eta \in U$ is Center's control. A set of solutions of the game of active elements $P(\eta)$ is defined as the set of equilibrium strategies of the active elements when the control of Center $\eta \in U$ is given. In the one-element active system $P(\eta)$ is the set of maximum points of the objective function of the active element, and in the system with many elements it is a set of game theoretic solutions (for example, Nash equilibria).

The problem of control of an active system consists in finding of an admissible control which maximizes the Center objective function: $\eta^* \in Arg \max_{\eta \in U} \max_{y \in P(\eta)} \Phi(\eta, y)$ if the active elements are supposed benevolent or $\eta^* \in Arg \max_{\eta \in U} \min_{y \in P(\eta)} \Phi(\eta, y)$ if they are supposed malevolent. This game theoretic model is the game Γ_1 in the sense of Germeyer (1976).

Two specific cases of the control problem are distinguished: the problem of stimulation and the problem of planning. In the problem of stimulation the strategy of the Center consists in choosing of an incentive mechanism, i.e. a set of functions $\sigma(y) = \{\sigma_i(y)\}$ which map the actions of elements on their reward from the Center: $\eta = \sigma(y)$. In the problem of planning the strategy of the Center consists in choosing of a set S of admissible reports of the active elements and a mechanism of planning $\pi : S \to X$ which maps the set of reports of the elements about unknown to the Center essential parameters of the system on a vector of plans.

The main directions of research in the theory of active systems are investigation of the incentive mechanisms in deterministic active systems, in the active systems with probabilistic and fuzzy uncertainty, their application to the different domains (Burkov et al. 2008; Novikov 2007).

In the theory of contracts (theory of incentives) a basic model is the principal-agent model which describes a hierarchical interaction of the subjects with asymmetrical information (Bolton and Dewatripont 2004; Laffont and Martimort 2002; Fudenberg and Tirole 1991; Salanie 1997). Three main modifications of the model are selected: a model of adverse selection and a model of signaling as its version, a model of moral hazard, and a model of nonverifiability.

In the model of adverse selection at the moment of conclusion of the contract the principal does not know certain essential parameters of the agent (her type). The problem consists in the revealing of information and finding the optimal contract depending from the type of agent. In the model of signaling the agent can send to the principal a message about her type, naturally not free of charge, i.e. the message is a strategy of the agent. The most important is the model of moral hazard in which the agent can realize actions unknown to the principal after the conclusion of contract. The problem of principal is to impel the agent to act in a way acceptable for the principal. In the model of non-verifiability all variables are known to both players but can not be written in the contract because their values are not verified by an arbitrage. In this case renegotiation and a special mechanism design are of great importance. All the models can be generalized for the case of several players and are investigated in different formulations (discrete and continuous, deterministic and stochastic, and so on), in so doing a number of important mathematical results is received.

Thus, all three directions are close to each other, based on game theoretic models and formalize mainly the method of impulsion – an impact of the Leader (Principal, Center) to the objective function of the Follower (agent, active element).

Chapter 2

SUSTAINABLE DEVELOPMENT
OF DYNAMIC SYSTEMS

A concept of sustainable development in connection with relations between mankind and nature became very popular after the UNO Conference on Environment and Development in Rio de Janeiro in 1992. But the unity in interpretations of the concept is still absent though it is possible to enumerate a number of its essential conditions acceptable by the majority of researchers, namely: satisfaction of requirements of both economic growth and ecological equilibrium; protraction of the conditions for a long or even infinite period of time; necessity of the hierarchical management of sustainable development which provide a consistency of the not coinciding interests together with realization of the key requirements. For a formalization of the concept and a solution of the management problems it is expedient to use mathematical models.

The following general requirements of the sustainable management of a dynamic system can be formulated: homeostasis, compromise, dynamic consistency. Separately, those requirements may be considered as necessary, and in the totality as sufficient conditions of the sustainable management of a dynamic system including human beings. The condition of homeostasis contains basic requirements to all aspects of sustainable development of the system, the condition of compromise ensures appropriate impacts on the system by all associated agents with an acceptable consideration of their interests, the condition of dynamic consistency means a conformity of the short-term and long-term optimality criteria of the agents and the resulting disadvantageousness for them to break the initial agreed compromise solution in the current of time. So, the sustainable management provides both conditions of sustainable development and means of their realization.

A classic notion of the controlled dynamic system (CDS) includes an active control subject (control subsystem) and a passive control object (controlled subsystem). The subject has an effect to the object for achievement of the control goal and chooses in a sense optimal variant of control in consideration with the restrictions.

However, in a number of practical situations the model of CDS is not sufficient because the goal of control does not express the condition of homeostasis which exists objectively for the CDS, and the striving for maximization of the optimality criterion violates the homeostasis. It comes to a thought about necessity to introduce an additional (the highest) control level with the goal to provide "super-system" requirements to the state of the controlled object. In this case a new subject of hierarchical rationality arises – the structured system with its own internal connections and relations that only conditionally can be treated as a whole in relation to the control object. The control system has a hierarchical structure, and it is considered in the frame of proposed concept that the highest level of control first of all provides the goals of the whole system though it can also have its own goals. To provide the goals of the whole system which are identified with the conditions of homeostasis, the highest level of hierarchy uses three methods of management: compulsion, impulsion, and conviction. It is appropriate to describe an interaction of the elements of the hierarchical control system by game theoretic models where the methods of management are formalized as specific solutions of a hierarchical game.

2.1. SUSTAINABLE DEVELOPMENT OF THE RELATIONS BETWEEN NATURE AND SOCIETY

The term "sustainable development" was first introduced in scientific and public usage in 1980. However, a serious attention to the problem was attracted only by the report "Our Common Future" (1987) prepared by the UNO World Commission on Environment and Development, known as "Brundtland Commission". Conclusions of the Brundtland Report formed a base for the decisions of the UNO Conference on Environment and Development (Rio de Janeiro, 1992). The Brundtland Report defines sustainable development as the development which satisfies the needs of present generation and does not undermine the possibility of future generations to satisfy their needs (Our Common Future 1987:43). The Declaration on Environment and Development accepted at the Rio-92 Conference includes 27 principles, such as principle 3 "A right to the development should be realized to provide a just satisfaction of the needs of the present and future generations in the domains of development and environment" and principle 4 "To ensure the sustainable development an environmental protection should be an immanent part of the development process and can not be considered apart of it".

In spite of the active discussion of the concept of sustainable development and a number of accepted official documents, a unity in the definition and interpretation of the notion is still absent. Already in the work (Pezzey 1989) more than 60 definitions of sustainable development given by different authors are cited. Let's quote some of later definitions: "A sustainable development is the economic development which does not undermine a natural base for the future generations and increases per capita"; "a sustainable development is the economic development which ensures the stability of environment and stable permanent economic growth"; "co-evolution of man and biosphere, i.e. such an interaction between nature and society which permits their joint development"; "a way of maximization of the long-term advantages for the humanity"; "increase of the quality of people within the carrying capacity of ecosystems", and so on (Danilov-Danilyan and Losev 2000:104). An extensive synthetic definition is proposed by a Russian geographer G.Sdasyuk: "Sustainable development is the multilevel-hierarchical controlled process of co-evolutional development of nature and society (including mass and realized participation of the population), the goal of which is to ensure healthy and productive life in harmony with nature for the present and future generations on the base of protection and enrichment of the cultural and natural heritage" (Transition... 2002:18).

The complexity of the problem of sustainable development determines a necessity of its analysis on different levels and aspects (Aall 2000; Carley and Christie 1993; Coenen et al. 2000; Gore 1993; Pezzey 1989; Roseland 1992; Weizsaeker et al. 1997). Strictly speaking, the complete realization of sustainable development is possible only on the global level because the biosphere of Earth is an entity and a local violation of the requirements of sustainable development can result in global consequences. That's why a global coordination of the state efforts and a common decision making in providing the sustainable development are required obligatory.

But this does not mean that a formulation of the problem of sustainable development on a local or regional level is absolutely senseless. First, theoretically the Earth is also an open system essentially influenced by the Sun and other external sources of impact. But the solution of the problem of sustainability in the cosmic scale is hardly possible in the near future therefore the strict requirements of system dependency have to be omitted. Second, in any case the global solution of the sustainability problem is a result of the separate efforts on local, national, regional and other levels.

It is mentioned in the UNO Recommendations on Environment and Development that local authorities are the principal factor in the solution of the sustainability problem. They create, use and support an economic, social, and environmental infrastructure, determine and regulate a local environmental policy, take part in the implementation of national and regional environmental policies. Being the closest to the population administrative level, the local authorities play a vital role in drawing the population in the process of transition to the sustainable development.

The methodology and results of work of providing sustainability on the local level are generalized in (The Local Agenda 1996). Due to the recommendations, the main elements of providing of the sustainable development on the local level are partnership of all interested agents, analysis of the local conditions and problems, planning of the sustainable development, implementation and monitoring of the project, evaluation and feedback.

The following aspects of the notion of sustainable development should be noticed:

- the environmental aspect which forms a base of the notion. The most important side of the notion of sustainable development is the requirement of refusal of the man-made impact to the natural ecosystems which exceeds their carrying capacity. It is convenient to assume to this requirement the name of environmental imperative. A violation of the imperative can result in a degradation of the natural systems and environmental catastrophes;
- the economic aspect which forms the second immanent side of the notion of sustainable development. In fact, the concept of sustainable development supposes a transition from the formulation of the problem of environmental protection at the cost of economic growth to the formulation of the problem of the both economic development and environmental protection when economics supports ecological equilibrium.

It should be noted that the environmental imperative is a necessary but not sufficient condition of the sustainable development. Some authors propose to consider as sustainable "such development of the mankind which does not undermine its natural base, i.e. an acceptable environment is reproduced, a sufficient resource base is supported, a human genome is conserved" (Danilov-Danilyan and Losev 2000:253). But then an evident solution of the problem is the strategy of "zero growth" – a complete refusal of the economic development for the sake of the environmental imperative. It is obviously impossible. Thus the environmental imperative should be complemented by an economic imperative which means a certain level of satisfaction of the material needs by an economic activity (production of goods and services, support of infrastructure);

- the cultural aspect which plays an exceptionally important role in spreading of the idea of sustainable development and its practical realization. First of all it should be mentioned a variety of cultures of the people on Earth which determines essential distinctions in relation to the idea of sustainable development. A number of the Eastern cultures (Buddhism, Confucianism) well conform to the main requirements of sustainable development that simplifies their acceptance by the population of those countries. In contrary, the western Hebrew-Christian culture of the "Faust" type is antagonistic to those ideas because it is oriented to the conquest of nature, anthropocentrism, expansion and maximization of consumption;
- the social aspect which reflects the problem of sustainable development from the point of view of different social communities, structures, institutions, and political problems in this domain as well. The historical experience has shown that it is impossible to succeed the requirements of sustainable development within the limits of totalitarian states in which the ideological dominance leads to the irrational waste of human and natural resources, unreasoned big-scale projects, man-made catastrophes. But a democratic state itself is not at all a panacea in the environmental problem solving which is witnessed by the very origin of the concept of sustainable development in the wealthiest states of modern world. Environmental problems are especially serious in developing and transitory countries in which the problems have a much smaller priority in comparison with those seemingly more urgent;
- the control aspect which is the last but not at all the least. It is evident that the harmonization of conditions of economic and environmental development can not be provided automatically and requires special control efforts. An adequate functioning of the market mechanisms in all domains including the environmental protection supposes not only freedom of exchange of goods, services, resources and so on but also quite rigid centralized control efforts.

Professor Nikita Moiseev has strongly insisted on the insufficiency of particularly market mechanisms and the necessity of centralized control: "It is required a new system of demands which restricts a human activity and controls the market which is so much discussed now. The state and the civil society are obliged to intervene effectively in the industrial activity and economic process ... And the intervention should be even more rigid and total than the New Course by Roosevelt during the Great Depression of 1929-1933 years. The intervention should become really total because the environmental degradation which is inevitable in the case of insufficient activity of the state and its power bases would turn in a disaster for all nations" (Moiseev 1998:214). The necessity of the state regulation of national economies was confirmed during the last world economic recession.

An ambiguity of the interpretation of sustainable development results in the distinctions of approaches to its realization (Olson 1994). The most widespread is still the idea of so-called "environmental protection economics" according to which certain standards of environmental quality and quotas on natural resource exploitation are established and should be kept under the threat of economic and administrative sanctions. This approach means that the economic development keeps its extensive character and the costs are paid at the expense of the economic growth. This approach forms a base of the national strategies of sustainable development of almost all countries with highly developed economics which are ready to pay for the environmental protection but are not ready to the qualitative changes in economic activity and consumption standards for the sake of the sustainable development. More than 30-year experience has shown that such an economics solves successfully local problems but is not able to cope with regional and moreover global environmental problems. Because of this some modifications of the "environmental protection economics" which strengthen its environmental orientation are proposed (Danilov-Danilyan and Losev 2000:113-116).

Another approach to the solution of the problem of sustainable development is a technological transformation which means a transition to the resource and energy saving, rigid waste and pollution control. A manifesto of this direction is stated in the book "Factor Four. Doubling Wealth – Halving Resource Use" (Weizsaeker et al. 1997) prepared as a next report to the Club of Rome. The authors consider that it is possible to double the output of industrial and agricultural production and in the same time to halve the expenditures of energy and raw materials. This direction seems to be the most prospective for the present time.

There is also a third approach to the solution of the problem of sustainable development – a transition from the quantitative growth to the qualitative development that means an essential socio-cultural transformation. This is the most principal approach that permits to solve the problem of sustainable development completely but its realization in present is hardly possible due to the great economic disproportions between regions and countries, political and military tension, unilateral globalization.

Many researchers criticize the concept of sustainable development for the ambiguity and uncertainty, deny its constructive content. Some authors treat the concept as an ideological basis of the concept of the "gold billion" directed against the interests of the majority of population of the Earth for the sake of privileges of the population of highly developed Western countries.

More soft criticism treats the sustainable development as a vague idea which can be formulated in general but can not be described by precise analytical categories. We do not agree with this opinion and will try to refute it in the book. We are convinced that it is possible to precise a notion of sustainable development using the mathematical model.

A special part of the book (Danilov-Danilyan and Losev 2000:250-253) is dedicated to the role of mathematical models in the problem of sustainable development. Reluctantly we are obliged to agree with the authors' statements about a low-grade prognostic value of the majority of known models. But the authors themselves notice a number of positive consequences of the application of mathematical models in the environmental science, namely: a considerable propagandistic effect (for example, the great importance for the formation of environmental conscience of the famous book (Meadows et al. 1972) which has first informed wide circles of population about the ideas of natural resource limits and necessity to restrict the economic growth), analysis of the specific phenomena on the base of known principles, and the most important thing: "building and investigation of mathematical models help to order the conceptual tools" (Danilov-Danilyan and Losev 2000:252). It is this property of mathematical models that has a key importance.

Basing on the experience of many years of modeling of the big economic and environmental systems in the Computing Center of the Russian Academy of Sciences, Professor Alexander Petrov formulates the following principles of building of the computer information systems of evaluation of the environmental consequences of economic decisions and search for the environmental-economic compromises:

- to use information technologies for the evaluation of changes in the state of ecosystems it is necessary to build models describing environmental and economic models in their totality;
- the models should reflect structural changes in the modeled system; the relations of a macro-model should be deduced from the analysis of the interacted elements using expert data;
- due to the application needs it is necessary to build a multilevel hierarchical system of the environmental models which also reflects a hierarchy of the temporal scales of modeled processes;
- it is possible to consider in the models hardly formalized socio-cultural factors by the scenario representation of different concepts;
- a system of interconnected models of the environmental and economic processes forms the model of a control object. To model the control subject it is necessary to use game theoretic models of the different classes;
- the problem of mathematical modeling of the evaluation of social and environmental consequences of decision making has a fundamental character, therefore for its solution it is first of all necessary to develop the general principles and its appropriate mathematical expression (New Paradigm ... 1999:267-268).

Klavdia Matrosova proposes a mathematical model of the global system which modifies the famous model of world dynamics by Forrester (1978). The model includes:

- equations for the principal variables:

$$dP/dt = [Bn(t) - D(t)]P(t);$$

$$dV/dt = (1-n_L)E_r(R(t))(1-S(t)-U_z(t)-U_r(t)-U_w(t))Y(t) - V(t)/T_v - V_w(W(t))V(t);$$

$$dZ/dt = C_zZ_v(V_r(t))Z_u(U(t))P(t) - Z(t)/T_z(Z_r(t)) - Y(t)U_z(t)/C_z^u(U(t)) + C_{zw}Z_w(W_r(t));$$

$$dR/dt = -C_rR_m(M(t))R_u(U(t))P(t) + Y(t)U_r(t)/C_r^u(U(t));$$

$$dB/dt = C_{B0}(1-dZ^2(t))-kB(t);$$

$$dU/dt = \begin{cases} n_{vu}Y(t)\kappa U(t) , t<t^* , \\ \kappa U(t^*)n_{vu}Y(t^*)(U^*-U(t))/V(t^*)/(U^*-U(t^*)),t > t^*; \end{cases}$$

Sustainable Development of Dynamic Systems

- equations for the control variables:

$$T_s dS/dt + S(t) = C_s S_q(Q_m(M(t))/Q_f(F_r(t)))S_f(F_r(t));$$

$$T_{uz} dU_z/dt + U_z(t) = C_{uz}U_{uz}(Z_r(t));$$

$$T_{ur} dU_r/dt + U_r(t) = C_{ur}(Rr(t));$$

$$U_w(t) = U_{uw}(W(t));$$

- equation for the quality of life:

$$Q(t)=C_q(t)Q_m(M(t))Q_p(P_r(t))Q_z(Z_r(t))Q_B(B(t))Q_r(F_r(t))Q_w(W(t)),$$

and a number of dependences for supporting variables and initial conditions. Here P is a number of population; V - basic funds; S – the share of funds in agriculture; R – a quantity of the non-renewable natural resource; Z – volume of pollution; index r denotes a relative value of the parameter in comparison with the basic year; $M(t)$ – material level of life; $F(t)$ – food level; B – biomass of land plants; U_z – waste disposal; U_r – regeneration of the non-renewable resources; Y – gross world product; U – level of scientific-technical process (STP); n_L – salary norm; n_u – norm of STP payments in the product Y; n_v – norm of industrial accumulation; T_v – funds amortization factor; t* - a moment of initial change of the STP rate; U* - a limit technological level; n_{uv} – general norm of accumulation; κ - quality of the newest technologies; E – efficiency of the gross world product; B_n – birth rate; D – mortality rate; other quantities are constant.

The conditions of global security are:

$$0 \leq D_r(t) \leq D_r^* ; 0 \leq Z_r(t) \leq Z_r^* ; F_r(t) \geq F_r^* ;$$

$$M(t) \geq M^*; Q(t) \geq Q^*; B(t) \geq B^*; R_r \geq R_r^* , \tag{2.1.1}$$

where variables with star denote maximum allowable (critical) values of the parameters of global security for the given initial conditions (New Paradigm... 1999:345-349). Then model calculations were made for the different scenario of development. A big number of empirical dependences and problems of identification of the variables make the results quite conditional but building of the model permits to formalize the conditions of sustainable development of the global system as follows:

- for certain values of the control variables a stationary state exists;
- this solution satisfies the conditions of global security (2.1.1);
- the stationary solution is stable for the constant fluctuations bounded in mean (in the sense of Krasovsky);
- a process of global development with real initial data without consideration of fluctuations approximates to the stationary solution and satisfies the conditions of the

type (2.1.1) with more rigid maximally allowable values New Paradigm... 1999:353).

A very original concept of the sustainable development is proposed by Oleg Kuznetsov and Boris Bolshakov (2002). The mathematical model has a form

$$P(t+\tau_0) = \eta\varepsilon N(t);$$

$$N(t+\tau_0+\tau_P) = \xi P(t+\tau_0);$$

where $N(t)$ is a full power of the social system (a total consumption of the energetic resource in a certain time); $P(t)$ – a real ability of the social system to impact on the environment; η - factor of technological perfection; ε - quality of labor organization; ξ -resource return factor. Expensing power P, in the time τ_P the society receives a resource flow N. The ratio of P to N is a measure of efficiency of using the full power by the society in time τ_0 denoted $0<\eta_0<1$. The ratio of N to P is a measure of the potential ability of the system to extended reproduction denoted by $\xi_P>1$.

A simplified equation of motion of the mankind in interaction with the environment has the form

$$N(t+\tau_0+\tau_\pi) = \eta_0\xi_P\varepsilon N(t).$$

On the base of these models authors formulate the conditions of extensive growth

$$dN/dt > 0; \quad d\eta_0/dt = 0; \quad d\xi_P/dt = 0;$$

and intensive growth (development)

$$dN/dt > 0; \quad d\eta_0/dt > 0; \quad d\xi_P/dt > 0.$$

The authors propose the following definition: "A society is being sustainable developed if the following historical process takes place: a preservation of the non-decreasing rate of efficiency of using of the full power all over the time" (Kuznetsov and Bolshakov 2002: 244-247):

$$P + P_1t + P_2t^2 + P_3t^3 + \ldots \geq 0.$$

A model of the regional sustainable development is proposed by Vladimir Gurman and his colleagues. As the authors correctly notice: "It is impossible to prove mathematically that the sum of all regional programs ensures exactly the sustainability of Mankind but it is indisputable that the solution of regional problems is a necessary condition of achieving of the global objective" (Gurman et al. 1999:69). The authors build the model in the form

$$dV/dt = u \; ;$$

$$dZ/dt = w;$$

$$dR/dt = Q(R-R^*) - Cv - Du - D^{(z)}w - F^L L + Iz + r_i - r_e;$$

$$dP/dt = p;$$

$$p = (E-A)v - Bu - A^{(z)}z - B^{(z)}w;$$

$$0 \le v \le V, \ (v,u,z,w) \in \Omega(t);$$

$$0 \le z \le Z, \ 0 \le V \le V_{max}(t), \ R \in R(t),$$

where v,z,V,Z are vectors of gross outputs of products and services of the traditional and environmental protective sectors (control variables) and respective maximal outputs; p – vector of the non-industrial consumption; R, R* are vectors of present and conditionally mean state of the natural and social environmental and resources respectively; u,w are rates of the maximal outputs; r_i, r_e are immigration and emigration flows; P is an accumulated final product; λ - row vector of prices; Ω(t) – a bounded set of the admissible states of the system reflecting real views about the sustainability and respective requirements; Q – a matrix of interdependences of the natural and social state variables; $A,A^{(z)},B,B^{(z)}$ – matrices of per capita direct and funds-forming costs; $C,D,D^{(z)}$ – matrices of sensitivities of the natural and social variables to the influence of different activities; L – a number of population; E – an identity matrix. In the general case all the matrices depend on time. An application of the scenario method permit to find the scenario of regional sustainable development in which the decreasing of the pollution level is accompanied by the improvement of social parameters (Gurman et al. 1999).

The analysis of present concepts of the sustainable development and corresponding mathematical models permits to deduce a number of conclusions.

First, a sustainable development supposes a necessity of the simultaneous realization of both environmental and economic imperatives. The sustainable development requires both non-exceeding of the maximal allowable human-made environmental impact and an economic growth which provides a satisfaction of human needs on the level determining by the historically specific social and cultural conditions of life. A one-sided dominance of the economic imperative results in non-appropriate concepts of the "environmental protective economics" and a one-sided dominance of the environmental imperative leads to the non-appropriate concepts of the "zero growth". Respectively, in the mathematical modeling of sustainable development it is necessary to consider equally parameters, principles and criteria which relate to both environmental and economic subsystems.

Second, it is necessary to acknowledge the benefit of mathematical modeling for the solution of the problem of sustainable development. Though the majority of mathematical models do not permit to receive a precise forecast of the dynamics of environmental-economic systems and to give the exhaustible recommendations for decision makers, the models play an exceptionally important role in précising the notions, creating the common language, forming a conceptual thesaurus for scientists, politicians, and citizens. For separate processes of the environmental-economic interaction the models can generate quantitative estimations.

Third, the sustainable development cannot be ensured by itself and requires special managerial efforts. As a rule, the direct agents of environmental impact have for their object the goals that differ from the goals of sustainable development and even contradict them. Thus the actions of higher levels of the hierarchical management systems directed to providing the conditions of sustainable development are necessary. Though a prospective way of the environmental problems solving are environmental education and environmental conscience in the nearest future a realization of the environmental imperative demands to use serious means of impulsion and even compulsion. That's why it is appropriate to talk about the sustainable management which unites the conditions of sustainable development and the means of their realization. In mathematical models the description of mechanisms of the hierarchical control is provided by game theory.

2.2. GENERALIZATION OF THE CONCEPT OF SUSTAINABLE DEVELOPMENT

It is supposed to be appropriate to generalize the concept of sustainable development considered in the previous paragraph in the case of environmental-economic interaction for the case of arbitrary dynamic systems including human beings. The following general conditions of the sustainable development of a dynamic system can be formulated.

1. A Condition of Homeostasis

Highly organized systems of the real world should resist to the external impacts or accommodate to them ensuring a conservation of the conditions of their existence and goal-oriented development. As a French physiologist Claude Bernard has said: "The constancy of the internal milieu is a condition of the free life of organism" (1878). The term "homeostasis" was introduced in 1932 by Walter Cannon who treated it as a relative dynamic constancy of the whole organism (Cannon 1932).

There is no escape from the conclusion about a similarity between the concepts of homeostasis as a dynamic constancy of the organism and sustainable development as a combination of the economic development (dynamics) and the environmental stability (constancy) on the biosphere level. We think that the concept of homeostasis could be considered not only on the level of a separate organism but also on the levels of populations, ecosystems, environmental-economic systems, and arbitrary dynamic systems including human beings.

Let's name the homeostasis of a system the domain of values of the essential parameters of the system in which its normal existence and development are possible. Functioning of any dynamic system is characterized by a set of parameters the values of which change in the time. The condition of homeostasis means that all parameters of the system functioning during a considered period of time (long enough or even infinite) take their values from a given range, and in the specific case take given point values. For example, the point requirements to the physiological parameters of a human organism are well known: temperature 36.6 degrees centigrade, blood pressure 120 on 80 millimeters of mercury column, and so on. In the same time certain deviations from the standard values are allowable: they form the admissible ranges of functioning of a healthy organism. The point and interval requirements of homeostasis of any dynamic system including human beings can be given similarly.

In the mathematical modeling a set of the essential parameters of functioning of a dynamic system is called its vector of state (phase vector) and is denoted as $x(t) = (x_1(t), ..., x_n(t))$. Its components (state variables) $x_i(t)$ $(i=1,...,n)$ are the values of parameters which characterize the system state in the moment of time t from the point of view and with the degree of detail which are determined by the objectives and resources of the research. For example, an enterprise can be characterized by one parameter (annual profit) or, more precisely, by dozens of parameters (basic funds, working funds, number of employees, technical equipment, nomenclature of products, and so on). This relates as well to any dynamic system.

In the most widespread case the state variables take numerical values. But other variants are also possible: for example, the data of a personal file can be the symbolic ones ("Jones", "Peter", "male", and so on). The components of a state vector can also take qualitative values from an ordinal scale, for example, "very weak", "weak", "moderate", "strong", "very strong".

Then a condition of homeostasis has the form

$$\forall t \in [0, T] : x(t) \in X^*,$$

where X* is the domain of homeostasis.

2. A Condition of Compromise

Many agents are associated with any big dynamic system. From one side, their objectives and interests are determined to an extent by the state and dynamics of the system. From the other side, the agents impact the system and exert some effect on its functioning. Thus the sustainable development is possible only if a condition of the consideration and coordination of interests of the associated agents is satisfied. As the objectives and interests of agents do not coincide in the majority of cases then their interaction is conflict. But in the same time the objectives and interests are not antagonistic, therefore a compromise is possible. In the light of the requirements of sustainable development the compromise should consider the condition of homeostasis. It is this compromise between all agents associated with the system that forms another condition of its sustainable development. The main approaches of the compromise rationality are considered in the paragraph 1.2 of the book. In the mathematical formalization of a conflict interaction by game theoretic models the compromises are described by the optimality principles for different classes of games. Thus from the mathematical point of view the condition of compromise means an existence of solution of the game describing a conflict interaction of the agents associated with the system. The condition of homeostasis reflects the requirement to the state of the system meanwhile the condition of compromise formalizes the demands to the impact on it. If a compromise is not achieved then the system will be permanently threatened by not appropriate impacts violating the homeostasis.

3. A Condition of Dynamic Consistency

A key problem of the sustainable development is a possible nonconformity of the short-term and long-term criteria of optimality. The condition of homeostasis is a long-term one because it should be satisfied along the whole period of existence and functioning of the system. In the same time the agents associated with the systems are often guided by short-term criteria with much smaller character times. As a result the compromise is under the threat of violation by those participants of the initial agreement for which it could be more advantageously in the current moment of time to take another strategy corresponding to their short-term interests.

In this connection a realization of the requirements of sustainable development is possible only for those compromises which keep their optimality for all associated agents along the whole period of existence of the system. In the game theoretic formalization this principle was called a time consistency (Petrosjan 1977; Petrosjan and Zenkevich 1996; Kidland and Prescott 1977). The property of time consistency of the solution of a game means that a truncation of the solution is still optimal in all subgames arising along the optimal trajectory of the system development. This property ensures a practical realization of the compromise solution from which it is not advantageously for any agent to deviate all along the time of system functioning.

It could be stated that separately the characterized conditions of homeostasis, compromise, and dynamic consistency are necessary, and in their totality also sufficient conditions of the sustainable development of any dynamic system including human beings. The condition of homeostasis expresses basic requirements to all aspects of the system functioning, the condition of compromise provides the adequacy of impacts by all agents associated with the system with acceptable consideration of their interests, the condition of dynamic consistency means a coordination of short-term and long-term optimality criteria of the agents and the consequent non-advantageousness for them to deviate from the initially agreed compromise solution all along the time. If the homeostasis is provided and a dynamic consistent compromise between all the associated agents is achieved then a sustainable management of the system takes place. The sustainable management ensures both conditions of sustainable development and means of their realization.

The conditions of sustainable development are characterized in Table 2.2.1.

Sustainable Development of Dynamic Systems

Table 2.2.1. The conditions of sustainable development of a dynamic system including human beings

Conditions of the sustainable development	Description of content	Mathematical formalization
Homeostasis	All essential parameters of the system functioning take the values from the given ranges	$\forall t \in [0,T] : x(t) \in X^*$ where $x(t)$ is a vector of state of the system (phase vector), X^* is the domain of homeostasis, T is a period of functioning
Compromise	Consideration and coordination of the interests of all agents associated with the system	Existence of a solution of the game theoretic model of a conflict interaction of the agents
Dynamic consistency	Coordination of the short-term and long-term criteria of optimality which makes it non-advantageous for all agents any deviation from the initially agreed compromise solution all along the time of system functioning	Time consistency of the solution of the game theoretic model

Let's give a couple of examples of the conditions of sustainable development.

The Regional Sustainable Development

The condition of homeostasis in this example contains three groups of requirements: environmental, economic, and social-political ones which relate to the corresponding components of the vector of state of the regional system. The environmental requirements include: an observance of the maximal allowable concentration of pollutants in all natural environments; an observance of the maximal allowable waste from all sources of pollution on the regional territory; ensuring of the necessary level of biodiversity (species structure and critical number of populations); an observance of the limits of hunting, fishing, cutting, mining; supporting an allowable level of the radiation and noise; a conservation of natural landscapes and a number of other conditions. The economic parameters are a gross product of the regional economy, parameters of profitableness of the enterprises, a share of the highly technological production in the regional export, a share of the imported food, and so on. The social-political subsystem is characterized by such parameters as a ratio of the maximal and minimal salaries, a share of the population which lives under the poverty limit, a level of unemployment, an average duration of life of the regional population, its age structure, rates of birth and mortality, levels of crime, drugs and alcohol consumption, number of suicides and mental pathologies, a budget of culture and education, a share of students, and so on.

The agents of regional development are the regional administration (for example, state government), administrations of the territorial communities within the region, political parties, civil organizations, big enterprises of the different economic sectors and forms of property. The condition of compromise means an existence of a solution of the game theoretic model describing a conflict interaction between the named agents. In more detailed scale in the role of agents can be economic subjects: firms, businessmen, households. The solution of the game theoretic model should be time consistent.

The Sustainable Development of an Industrial Enterprise

The concept of sustainable development is proved to be fruitful not only in the solution of environmental problems but also in analysis and management of a wider class of social organizations (Ougolnitsky 2002b). A necessity of the approach is determined by the presence of two extreme strategies of organizational management. In the first strategy an accumulation is absolutely prevailing and the current needs of the staff and organizational development are ignored by the owners. In the USSR and other socialist countries it was a strategy of postponing the solution of material problems and promising "the communism for future generations". At last this strategy became one of the main causes of the disintegration of the Soviet Union and the whole socialist system.

Another extremity is an absolute orientation for the immediate enrichment independently on any spiritual, moral, environmental factors, accompanied with an extinction of non-renewable natural and cultural resources, pollution of the environment and social consciousness, wasting of time and creative capacities of the highly qualified specialists for the satisfaction of short-term utilitarian needs. This strategy is very widespread in the transitory states. In the sense of the theory proposed by Pitirim Sorokin (1957) those "Scylla and Charybdis" of the development of social organizations could be connected with "ideational" and "sensual" directions in the development of culture which repeat cyclically all along the human history throughout the world.

The concept of sustainable development in its broadened interpretation opens a prospect of "the golden mean" and more precisely "the golden section", the optimal proportion which permits to coordinate the high ideals of Eternity and the barest present necessities, to pilot a ship of the social organization between "Scylla of ideationality" and "Charybdis of sensuality". A harmonic character of the concept of sustainable development permits to make its analogy with the "idealistic" cultural type in the sense of Sorokin (1957). The main accent in the concept of sustainable development is made on ensuring the long-term conditions of stable functioning of a social organization. However on each stage of its development the current problems of satisfaction of urgent material needs should also be solved that forms a base for achieving the objectives of higher levels.

Let's consider the conditions of sustainable development of an industrial enterprise as a very important and widespread type of social organizations. The condition of homeostasis includes the following requirements: an output of qualitative production that fits the needs of a target consumer group; providing the given values of profit; ensuring an appropriate material reward of the personnel; conservation and modernization of the industrial complex, technological and economic relations; creating a favorable image of the enterprise in the eyes of population and a serious business reputation in the eyes of partners; forming a necessary professional and qualification structure; creating a favorable social-psychological atmosphere and conditions for self-realization of the employees; an observance of the requirements of environmental safety of the industrial process determined by the enterprise specifics.

A description of the conflict interaction on the level of an industrial enterprise supposes an analysis of at least following principal agents: owners (shareholders), management, and staff that results in building of a game theoretic model of the interaction.

A dynamic consistency of an industrial enterprise (and an arbitrary social organization) is treated as a coordination of the short-time objective and interests of different groups and separate individuals within the organization with the long-term strategic goals determined by the requirements of the internal organizational development and its interaction with the environment. The strategic organizational goals include social, environmental, economic, ideological, and other components meanwhile the short-term interests are mainly economic ones.

2.3. HIERARCHICAL CONTROL OF DYNAMIC SYSTEMS

A classic notion of the controlled dynamic system (CDS) includes an active subject of control (a control subsystem) and a passive object of control (a controlled subsystem). The subject has an effect to the object for achievement of a control goal and chooses in a sense optimal variant of control in consideration with the restrictions. The subject can observe changes of the state of object in time and correct (if necessary) the control impact (a feedback). The diagram of CDS is shown in Figure 2.3.1.

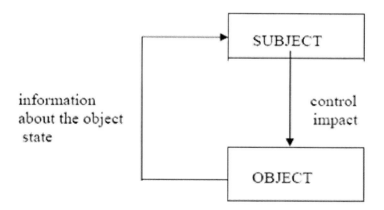

Figure 2.3.1. A controlled dynamic system.

It is convenient to write a mathematical model of the CDS in the form

$$x(t + \Delta t) = x(t) + (\Delta t)f_t(x(t), u(t), \xi(t)), \tag{2.3.1}$$

$$x(0) = x_0, \ t = 0, \Delta t, \ldots, T - \Delta t. \tag{2.3.2}$$

Here $x(t) = (x_1(t), \ldots, x_n(t))$ is a vector of state the components of which (state variables) $x_i(t)$ ($i=1,\ldots,n$) are the values of parameters characterizing the state of CDS in a moment of time t;

$u(t) = (u_1(t), \ldots, u_m(t))$ is a vector of control variables.

As the vector $u(t)$ enters in the right part of the equation (2.3.1) then the change of the state vector $x(t)$ depends on the values of its components (control variables) $u_j(t)$ ($j=1,...,m$). The values of control variables $u_j(t)$ are chosen by one or several agents associated with the CDS in accordance with an objective;

$\xi(t) = (\xi_1(t),...,\xi_p(t))$ is a vector of not objective-oriented impacts.

This vector has a nature that differs from the nature of $u(t)$ (though both vectors correspond to the external factors for the system). The variables $\xi_k(t)$ are not controlled by the subject: she can only observe their values and respective changes of the state vector. But the values $\xi_k(t)$ have an effect to the dynamics of the state vector $x(t)$ thus they say that a dynamic system develops in the conditions of uncertainty;

- $f_t(x(t),u(t),\xi(t))$ is a vector function of the same dimension as $x(t)$ which determines the dynamics of the state vector in the conditions of external impact;
- $x_0 = (x_{01},..., x_{0n})$ is a known initial value of the state vector; T is a period of modeling of the controlled system; Δt is a step of modeling (time difference between two sequential states of the system). Without lost of generality it is possible to define $\Delta t=1$ and to rewrite the model (2.3.1)-(2.3.2) in the form

$$x(t+1) = x(t) + f_t(x(t),u(t),\xi(t)), \qquad (2.3.3)$$

$$x(0) = x_0 , t = 0,1,...,T-1. \qquad (2.3.4)$$

Though the model (2.3.3)-(2.3.4) contains the principal information about a CDS it should be complemented by some explications. First, each of the vectors $x(t)$, $u(t)$, $\xi(t)$ can take their values from admissible domains denoted by $X(t)$, $U(t)$, $\Xi(t)$ respectively. The domain of admissible states $X(t)$ characterizes a range of reachable states of the system, the domain of admissible controls $U(t)$ describes control resource of the subject, and the domain $\Xi(t)$ contains possible values of the non-controlled factors (in the complete lack of information this domain coincides with the total space R^p).

Second, a presence of the goal-oriented control subject supposes an existence of the control objective (in fact, this is a tautology). It is possible to formalize the control objective in different ways. One of the most natural ways is the following: the control subject strives to keep the controlled system in a given domain $\Omega(t) \subset X(t)$, i.e.

$$x(t) \in \Omega(t) , t = 1,2,...,T. \qquad (2.3.5)$$

A widespread specific case of the condition (2.3.5) is the following:

$$x(T) = x_T , \qquad (2.3.6)$$

that means the controlled system gets in the given point in the end of considered period (for example, an arrival of the plane in an airport or providing the desirable amount of the annual dividends in a company). For consideration of the system state when $t > T$ it is necessary to add a restriction of the type

$$x(T+1) > x_{T+1}. \qquad (2.3.7)$$

Third, the control objective can be reached by different ways that generates a question of choice of the best way in a sense, i.e. the question of optimality of the control. A classic formulation of the control problem supposes that decisions are made by the only subject who is leaded by the only criterion of optimality (an economically rational agent). A criterion of optimality can be written in the form

$$J = \sum_{t=1}^{T} g(x(t),u(t),\xi(t)) \rightarrow \max, \qquad (2.3.8)$$

where g is a value of the objective function (optimality criterion) of the agent in the moment of time t. A dynamic optimization problem (2.3.3)-(2.3.5), (2.3.8) or (2.3.3)-(2.3.4), (2.3.6), (2.3.8) with a possible additional condition (2.3.7) is called a problem of optimal control, the methods of solution of which in different variants are the object of the optimal control theory (Bellman 1957; Pontryagin et al. 1962).

However, in a big number of practical situations the model of CDS is not sufficient because the goal of control does not express the condition of homeostasis which exists objectively for the CDS, and the striving for maximization of the optimality criterion violates the homeostasis.

For example, let the control subject be an industrial enterprise situated on a board of a river as the controlled object. The control objective of the enterprise is to maximize its profit, and the environmental damage from the industrial sewage is neglected. Another example is a professional activity of a manager. Her interests could be expressed as maximization of the personal income or minimization of the working efforts but hardly coincide with the total organizational interests. Due to the institutional theory, each employee of a firm exerts an opportunistic maximization of the personal utility (Williamson 1970).

Thus, in a big number of cases the actions of control object determined by her private objectives and interests according to a concept of rationality can bring the control object to a state which is not acceptable from the point of view of a subject of higher level (in the managerial example the subject is the organization, in the environmental example the subject is a regional population). In other words, the control objective (2.3.5) or (2.3.6) does not express the condition of homeostasis which exists objectively for the CDS (2.3.3)-(2.3.4), and the maximization of a criterion (2.3.8) results in violation of the homeostasis. It comes to a thought about necessity to introduce an additional (the highest) control level with the goal to ensure "super-system" requirements to the state of the controlled object. In this case a new subject of hierarchical rationality arises, the structured system with its own internal connections and relations that only conditionally can be treated as a whole in relation to the control object. The control system has a hierarchical structure, and it is assumed in the frame of proposed concept that the highest level of control first of all ensures the goals of the whole system though it can also has its own additional goals. For realization of the principal goal the new subject can have an effect on the initial control subject. For example, an environmental agency (administration) controls the water quality, establishes sewage limits and charges penalties if the enterprise violates them. A chief executive officer can develop a motivation system which impels managers to promote the goals of the whole organization.

The classic model of CDS (Figure 2.3.1) is thus generalized as a model of the hierarchically controlled dynamic system (Ougolnitsky 1999), the elementary version of which is shown in Figure 2.3.2.

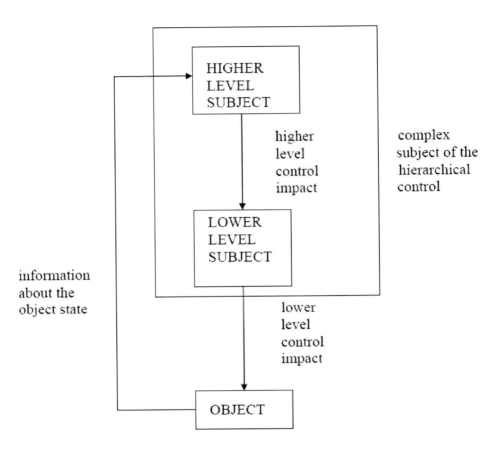

Figure 2.3.2. Hierarchically controlled dynamic system.

The elementary configuration of a hierarchically controlled dynamic system (HCDS) includes three elements:

- a control subject of higher level (Leader);
- a control subject of lower level (Follower);
- a controlled dynamic system (CDS).

It is supposed that the relations between the elements of HCDS are organized exactly as shown in Figure 2.3.2, namely: the Leader impacts on the Follower, the Follower impacts on the CDS (a direct impact of the Leader to the CDS is absent). The Leader and the Follower together can be considered as a united subject of impact on the CDS having a hierarchical structure which explains the term HCDS. In a general case more complicated configurations are possible that include tree-like, diamond-like and other structures and their combinations as a hierarchical subject of impact.

The sense of introducing a notion of HCDS is the following. In her impact to the CDS the Follower pursues certain goals which in a general case do not coincide with the objectively existing goals of keeping the CDS in a given state (a homeostatic condition). The CDS itself is a passive object and can not ensure the homeostatic conditions. That's why a Leader is required who can control the Follower to reach the homeostatic goals.

Practice gives a very big number of situations which can be described and studied in the terms of HCDS notion. Such are chains of the type "bank – enterprise – production", "International Monetary Fund – country – national economy", "superior – subordinate – work", "physician – patient – organism" and many others. Besides the main structural elements shown in the Figure 2.3.2 the following aspects form the notion of HCDS.

Dynamics of a Controlled System

Because only a Follower impacts the CDS there is no difference in comparison with the classic model of CDS. A CDS is characterized by the vector of state which components change in time by virtue of self-development, control impacts of the Follower and non-controlled external factors (random or uncertain). The initial state of CDS is supposed to be known.

An Objective Goal of Control

Here we mean the objectivity relative to the Follower who impacts the CDS in her subjective interests. The subject of the named goal is the Leader who expresses objective interests. They can be the interests of society or other system, more general than a connection "Follower-CDS". An objective goal of control (the homeostasis of CDS) may be understood and respectively formulated in different ways. It is reasonable to name two main approaches. In the first approach it is required that the CDS be in a given domain of the state space. If for each component of the state vector a range of admissible values is given in the form of segment then the admissible domain in the state space represents a parallelepiped. A similar requirement arises in presence of the "ideal state" from which the CDS should not deviate too far. In this case the admissible domain in the state space represents a ball of corresponding radius. This approach is quite widespread. For example, it is required that the vital parameters of a human organism (temperature, blood pressure, pulse, and so on) belong to a certain range, and quitting of the range means a disease. A similar approach is often used in relation to the macroeconomic parameters (budget deficit, inflation rate, exchange rate, and so on).

The second approach is connected with the notion of Lyapunov stability. The sense of this requirement is that the trajectory of a system keeps close to a given trajectory by influence of certain (as a rule small) external fluctuations (Iooss and Joseph 1980). In this connection the Le Chatelier principle can be mentioned in the strength of which external impacts that take a system out of equilibrium stimulate in it the processes that strive to weaken the results of impact (Moiseev 1998).

Actions, Interests and Resource of Follower

The interests of Follower are described by the maximization of an objective function depending in a general case on the system state and the control impacts of Leader and Follower. A set of admissible controls of the Follower characterizes her abilities in control of the dynamic system. In a general case this set and the objective function depend on the system state and actions of the Leader; the former fact determines a hierarchical nature of the relations between the Leader and the Follower. As far as a control of the dynamic system is discussed, the objective function of Follower is also a dynamic one, i.e. it represents a functional (an integral or a sum of current objective functions). This fact has a principal importance because it requires a commensurability of costs and effects in different moments of time (discounting). A period of forecasting can be finite or infinite. In the first case an additional condition of the type (2.3.7) concerning the system state beyond the period of forecasting should be introduced as a rule, otherwise an optimal solution could destroy the system in the last moment of time. In fact, this requirement relates to the objective goal of control considered above.

From the point of view of content the impact of Follower to the CDS can be very diverse. In the considered context it is the most natural to treat the impact as an "exploitation" of the CDS, usage of its resource for the maximization of the utility function of Follower. Often the utility has an economic nature (profit maximization, cost minimization) though other interpretations are also possible.

Actions, Interests and Resources of a Leader

The principal goal of Leader is to ensure certain objective requirements to the state of CDS. If this goal is unique then it is natural to call the Leader disinterested. But the Leader often has some additional interests which she tends to satisfy with the obligatory condition of achieving the principal goal. As in the considered case of Follower, the additional interests consist in maximization of a utility function. Such Leader is called interested. As far as in the accepted propositions the Leader does not impact on the CDS directly, she obtains her goals by the control of Follower. The parameters of control are determined by the Leader's set of admissible controls. If the controls can take any physically admissible values then Leader's resource is unlimited otherwise it is limited. So, the Leader can be interested or disinterested from the point of view of her goals and has limited or unlimited resource from the point of view of her control abilities.

Let's call an adaptation the activity of the conservation of homeostasis in conditions of the external impact. A modern theory of adaptation is established by Hans Selye and developed by Lyubov Garkavy with colleagues (Garkavy et al. 1979). We call a dynamic system adaptive if it is able to keep its homeostasis in a range of impacts (loads) by means of adaptation mechanisms. The adaptive systems have a hierarchical structure including the following elements: the system which is an object of impact; external impacts in a range; adaptive reactions (mechanisms of adaptation) depending on the impacts and the system state. Besides, the notion of adaptive system includes a domain of homeostasis in which a normal existence and development of the system are possible.

It is reasonable to differentiate embedded and removed adaptation mechanisms. The embedded adaptation mechanism is an integral part of the adaptive system (for example, in the human organism). The removed mechanism is relatively independent on the adaptive system but it is also directed to provide a homeostasis of the system (for example, an environmental agency which defends the interests of natural systems). So, a HCDS is the adaptive system in which the CDS is an object of impact, the Follower is a source of impact (together with non-controlled factors), and the Leader plays a role of the removed adaptation mechanism.

One of the most representative set of examples of HCDS is given by environmental-economic systems. The environmental-economic system formalizes an interaction between society and nature on different levels; its conceptual diagram is shown in Figure 2.3.3.

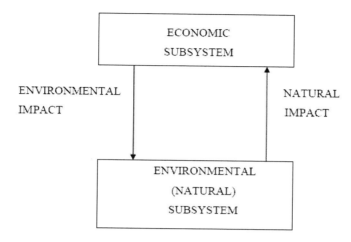

Figure 2.3.3. A diagram of the environmental-economic system.

Even on this very general level some conclusions about the structure of environmental-economic system can be made. In general it represents a loop formed by two hierarchical substructures: from one side, the economic system has an effect to the environmental one; from the other side, the natural subsystem has its effect to the economic one. But the environmental impact is more important from the point of view of its consequences both for the nature and for the mankind, and in this sense it is possible to talk about a hierarchy of the total system (the economic system as a control subsystem and the environmental subsystem as a controlled one).

Thus, the environmental-economic system includes the following aspects: the economic subsystem; the environmental (natural) subsystem; the environmental impact; the natural impact.

The economic subsystem contains among others the following elements and relations: an economic activity (industry, production of energy, agriculture, engineering, their interaction); population (settlements, demographic processes, recreation, environmental organizations, and so on); legislative and administrative regulation (environmental laws, norms, and standards, environmental quality control, environmental protection agencies). So, the name "economic" subsystem is quite limited and would better be substituted by the name "social-economic" subsystem.

The leading role in consideration of the environmental subsystem is played by the notion of ecosystem. This notion describes an interaction of animate (animals, plants, microbes) and inanimate (atmosphere, water, soil) components of the natural environment on a given territory of any scale.

The natural impact includes: a physical base (place) for the different kinds of human activity; resources of human life (air, water, food) of different quality; resources of production (raw materials, energy); protection from the cosmic emissions.

At last, the environmental impact has three main forms: pollution; natural resource use; environmental protection and natural resource renewal. A specific place is occupied by the problem of environmental impact assessment which is the central one in the total system of environmental-economic interactions (see 2.1).

In this connection it seems rational to use the concept of HCDS in the analysis of environmental-economic systems. According to the concept, the environmental (natural) subsystem is treated as CDS, and the economic subsystem consists of the Follower as a direct source of the man-made environmental impact and the Leader who controls the impact in the goal of observance of certain ecological requirements (the term "environmental imperative" is convenient here). It is natural to name the system a hierarchically controlled environmental system (HCES).

Thus, the HCES is a specific case of the HCDS and gives a comprehensive set of the examples of HCDS such as "environmental protection agency – enterprise – natural object". On regional and global level in connection with territorial-industrial and other types of interaction in the social-economic subsystem tree-like, diamond-like and more complicated hierarchical structures arise in the domain. Therefore, strictly speaking, an elementary HCES in the sense of diagram in Figure 2.3.2 is only an element of the complex environmental-economic systems but the element plays the leading role in the problem of environmental impact assessment.

Another important class of the HCDS is formed by the organizational systems. It is reasonable to consider an organization as HCDS the diagram of which is presented in Figure 2.3.2. The role of the CDS is played by a process the realization of which is the social function of the organization. An identification of the Leader and the Follower is not so simple problem and different variants of the solution are possible (Ougolnitsky 2002b).

It seems natural to give the role of Leader to the top management and the role of Follower to the personnel of an organization. As far as homeostatic requirements are identified with strategic goals of the organizational development, its top management is the best candidate to be the subject of realization of the goals, meanwhile separate employees and their groups are inclined to strive for the short-term economic objectives. But sometimes the top management also gives a priority to its private interests in comparison to the long-term strategic organizational goals. In this case the leadership has to be passed to the shareholders.

Besides, in organizations with a complex structure the diagram of the HCDS shown in Figure 2.3.2 is also complicated. The Leader and Follower loose their monolithic properties and are subdivided into a set of goal-oriented subjects having their own objectives and resources as well as criteria of optimality. Thus more complicated tree-like, diamond-like and combined hierarchical structures are substituted instead of a linear hierarchical chain.

So, a necessity of the hierarchical sustainable management of organizational systems is caused by the following factors: 1) a nonconformity of the subjective short-term goals of the staff to the objective strategic goals of the whole organization; 2) a complex organizational structure which requires a coordination of the global, group, and individual interests within the organization.

A very interesting example of the HCDS is given by a "two-storey" model of the economic theory of self-control in which on the first storey is situated a doer oriented to the short-term egoistic criteria, and on the second storey a planner who gives to the doer certain rules of behavior based upon the long-term objectives (Thaler and Shefrin 1981).

Let's discuss possible objections to the proposed concept (without pretending to be complete). The first critical argument is: isn't possible to do without introduction of the highest control level by inserting the requirements of sustainable development as additional restrictions for a traditional model of the optimal control of a dynamic system? It is really possible to an extent. However, at first, this approach is artificial because a real control subject of lower level is not interested to ensure the requirements of sustainable development. Second and principal, an introduction of the control subject of higher level permits to take into consideration her own interests and therefore to pass from an optimization model to the game theoretic model which describes more appropriately the coordination of interests in a real control system.

The second critical argument: will it be necessary to introduce one more control level to control the subject of higher level, then one more again, and so ad infinitum? A similar situation is described by Robert Sheckley in his novel "Watchbird" (1990). Such a situation could arise in fact, for example in connection with corruption. Modeling of multilevel control system considering corruption is one of the directions of development of the proposed concept. But in the majority of cases a subject interested in the sustainable development exists, and two or three levels of hierarchy are sufficient for modeling.

Thus, in analysis of the control processes in big systems including human beings (organizational, economic, environmental-economic, social) it is not sufficient to consider the only monolithic control subject leaded by the conditions of Weberian rationality even with its subsequent refinements. It is more appropriate to discuss a subject of the hierarchical rationality which is a structured system with its own internal connections and relations. This system only conditionally can be considered as a totality relative to the control object. The control system has a hierarchical structure and it is supposed within the proposed concept that the highest level of control first of all provides the goals of the whole system though it can also have its own goals. To ensure the goals of the whole system which are identified with the conditions of homeostasis, the highest level of hierarchy uses three methods of management: compulsion, impulsion, and conviction. It is appropriate to describe an interaction of the elements of the hierarchical control system by game theoretic models where the methods of management are formalized as specific solutions of a hierarchical game.

Let's write a general problem of the hierarchical control of a dynamic system in the following form (Ougolnitsky 1999):

$$x(t) \in \Omega, t = 1, 2, ..., T; \tag{2.3.9}$$

$$J_v = \sum_{t=1}^{T} g_v(t, v(t)) \to \max; \tag{2.3.10}$$

$$v(t) \in V(t), t = 1, 2, ..., T; \tag{2.3.11}$$

$$J_u = \sum_{t=1}^{T} g_u(t, x(t-1), u(t), v(t)) \to \max; \tag{2.3.12}$$

$$u(t) \in U(t,x(t-1),v(t)) \ , \ t = 1, 2, ..., T \ ; \qquad (2.3.13)$$

$$\xi(t) \in \Xi(t) \ , \ t = 1, 2, ..., T \ ; \qquad (2.3.14)$$

$$x(t+1) = x(t) + f(t,x(t),u(t),\xi(t)) \ ; \qquad (2.3.15)$$

$$x(0) = x_0 \ , \ t = 0, 1, ..., T-1 \ . \qquad (2.3.16)$$

Here $x(t) = (x_1(t), ..., x_n(t))$ is a vector of state of the CDS in a moment t;

$u(t) = (u_1(t), ..., u_m(t))$ is a vector of control impacts of the Follower on the CDS in a moment t;

$v(t) = (v_1(t), ..., v_p(t))$ is a vector of control impacts of the Leader on the Follower in a moment t;

$\xi(t) = (\xi_1(t), ..., \xi_r(t))$ is a vector of non-controlled impacts on the CDS in a moment t;

$V(t)$ is a domain of admissible controls of the Leader in a moment t;

$U(t,x(t-1),v(t))$ is a domain of admissible controls of the Follower in a moment t;

$\Xi(t)$ is a domain of possible values of external factors in a moment t;

$g_v(t,v(t))$ is an objective function of the Leader in a moment t;

J_v is an integral objective function of the Leader on a period $[0,T]$;

$g_u(t,x(t-1),u(t),v(t))$ is an objective function of the Follower in a moment t;

J_u is an integral objective function of the Follower on a period $[0,T]$;

$f(t,x(t),u(t),\xi(t))$ is an operator of transition of the CDS from its state in a moment t to the state in a moment t+1 (a given non-linear function);

$x_0 = (x_{01}, ..., x_{0n})$ a known initial state of the CDS;

T is a period of forecasting;

Ω is a domain of desirable states of the CDS (the domain of homeostasis).

The condition (2.3.9) formalizes an objective goal of control: it is required that in the each moment of time the CDS be situated in a given domain Ω of the state space R^n. Maximum in (2.3.10) is searched by all trajectories $\{v(t)\}$ which satisfy (2.3.11); so, (2.3.10)-

(2.3.11) is an optimization problem of the Leader (with an obligatory additional restriction (2.3.9)).

Respectively, the relations (2.3.12)-(2.3.13) form an optimization problem of the Follower; about the external factors $\xi(t)$ it is known in a general case only that they satisfy the condition (2.3.14).

At last, the formulas (2.3.15)-(2.3.16) describe the dynamics of CDS impacted by the Follower and external factors with the known initial conditions.

From the mathematical point of view the relations (2.3.9)-(2.3.16) define a multistage hierarchical game of two players (Leader and Follower) with consideration of the external factors $\xi(t)$. Formal requirements to the functions and sets used in the model as well as a regulation of the game are defined separately in every specific case. A specific character of the game theoretic model (2.3.9)-(2.3.16) determines an expediency of consideration of the special principles of optimality for it. Denote

$$x = (x(1),...,x(T)), \xi = (\xi(1),...,\xi(T)),$$

$$u = (u(1),...,u(T)), v = (v(1),...,v(T)),$$

X, Ξ, U, V are respective domains of the values. Then for a fixed value $\xi \in \Xi$ we have

$$J_u = J_u(x,u,v), J_v = J_v(v).$$

A solution of the game (2.3.9)-(2.3.16) is a pair of control trajectories (u,v), $u \in U(x,v)$, $v \in V$. For a fixed ξ the trajectory of CDS is determined uniquely by the choice of u: $x = x(u)$. Denote:

$$U_\Omega = \{u \in U : x(u) \in \Omega \};$$

$$U_J(v) = \underset{u \in U(x,v)}{Arg\ max}\ J_u(x,u,v);$$

$$V_J = \underset{v \in V}{Arg\ max}\ J_v(v);$$

$$V_{max} = \underset{v \in V}{Arg\ max}\ J_u(x,u,v);$$

$$V_{min} = \underset{v \in V}{Arg\ min}\ J_u(x,u,v).$$

As far as the condition (2.3.9) reflects the fundamental requirements to the state of CDS then among possible principles of optimality of the solution of game (2.3.9)-(2.3.16) should be considered only those that are given as subsets of the set

$$C_\Omega = U_\Omega \times V . \tag{2.3.17}$$

Among the subsets it is reasonable to select the following:

$$C_{\Omega J}^{u} = (U_{\Omega} \cap U_J(v)) \times V ; \qquad (2.3.18)$$

$$C_{\Omega J}^{v} = U_{\Omega} \times V_J ; \qquad (2.3.19)$$

$$C_{\Omega J}^{uv} = C_{\Omega J}^{u} \cap C_{\Omega J}^{v} ; \qquad (2.3.20)$$

$$C_{\Omega Jmax}^{u} = (U_{\Omega} \cap U_J(v)) \times V_{max} ; \qquad (2.3.21)$$

$$C_{\Omega Jmax}^{uv} = C_{\Omega J}^{uv} \cap C_{\Omega Jmax}^{u} . \qquad (2.3.22)$$

Each of the sets generates a respective optimality principle the content of which for the domain of HCES is discussed farther. It is expedient to select the following specific cases of the model (2.3.9)-(2.3.16).

1. The Case of Indifferent Leader

Here the condition (2.3.9) is omitted and $J_v \equiv$ const. In fact in this case the model (2.3.9)-(2.3.16) degenerates in a game with Nature where the Nature with its control variables $\xi(t)$ in a sense includes the Leader with her control variables $v(t)$ and without any objective. This limit case illustrates a connection with the traditional approach to the modeling of CDS and the approach based on the concept of HCDS.

2. The Case of Disinterested Leader

This case differs from the previous one in that the condition (2.3.9) is kept though again $J_v \equiv$ const. It means that the only objective of the Leader is ensuring the condition (2.3.9); she has no other "egoistic" interests. But the Leader uses her control variables (2.3.11) to ensure (2.3.9), i.e. it is no more a game with Nature. In this case a formal optimality principle is given by the condition (2.3.18) or (2.3.21) if the Leader is benevolent to the Follower.

3. An Independence of the Follower Objective Function and the Set of Admissible Controls on the State of CDS

The relations (2.3.12)-(2.3.13) give the most general form of the Follower objective function and the set of admissible controls in a HCDS. A dependence of J_u and U on $v(t)$ is principal because it determines a hierarchical nature of the relations between Leader and Follower (the Leader has an effect on the Follower but not vice versa). As for the dependence of J_u and U on the state of CDS $x(t)$ which introduces a feedback in the model, in certain cases it can be omitted. The independence of J_u on x means that the interests of Follower are not at all connected with the state of CDS impacted by her; such situations often arise in practice, especially on short periods of time.

The form of problem (2.3.9)-(2.3.16) witnesses for that in its solution analytical methods have a bounded (though very important) utility. As a rule, it is possible to find a complete analytical solution in the sense of a principle of optimality only due to the strong simplifying propositions which give to the model an illustrative character (see an example below). In a general case the investigation of the model (2.3.9)-(2.3.16) requires a combined usage of the

Sustainable Development of Dynamic Systems 65

simulative and analytical (optimization, game theoretic) methods within a simulation system ensuring the ability of realization of different heuristic algorithms in an interactive mode. Such algorithms are also considered below.

In the case of hierarchically controlled ecosystems (HCES) it is natural to interpret the model (2.3.8)-(2.3.16) as follows (Ougolnitsky 1999). The requirement (2.3.9) is treated as the "environmental imperative" (Moiseev 1998). In other words, the domain Ω is a totality of the ranges of values of the main parameters of the ecosystem state in which its normal development is ensured. It is convenient to define Ω as a parallelepiped

$$\Omega = [x^L_1, x^H_1] \times [x^L_2, x^H_2] \times \ldots \times [x^L_n, x^H_n],$$

where $[x^L_i, x^H_i]$ is a range of homeostatic values of i-th state parameter.

A Follower is treated as a source of the environmental impact. Two main kinds of the impact are natural resource use and pollution. Sources of the first kind are enterprises of the extractive industry, agriculture, hunting, fishing, cutting, and sources of the second kind are almost all industrial enterprises, agriculture, transport, energy power plants, settlements and recreational objects. Thus, the impact u(t) is either an amount of extracted natural resource in the year t (mining, harvesting, and so on), either an amount of pollution in the year t (a quantity of pollutants thrown in the environment as a result of a man-made activity).

For example, let u(t) be an amount of fish catching in the year t. Then a domain of admissible controls of the Follower is determined by three types of limitations:

1) physical limitations

$$0 \le u(t) \le x(t),$$

where x(t) is the biomass of the fish population in the beginning of year t;
2) technical and economic limitations

$$a(t)u(t) \le b(t),$$

where a(t), b(t) determine the technological capacities of an enterprise in catching and processing the fish. In a more general form of the technical and economic limitations

$$a(t,v(t))u(t) \le b(t,v(t))$$

it is supposed that the Leader can change the technological parameters of the Follower by their increase (grants) or decrease (interdictions);
3) administrative and legislative limitations

$$u(t) \le u^Q(t),$$

where $u^Q(t)$ is a catching quota established by the Leader (or established by law and controlled by the Leader).

An objective function J_u may be interpreted as the total income of an enterprise on a period [0,T], and a function g_u (t,x(t-1),u(t),v(t)) as its income in the year t. The calculation of the amount income J_u on the period [0,T] needs discounting. It means that the function g_u has the form $g_u(t,x(t-1),u(t),v(t)) = \alpha^t h_u(x(t-1),u(t),v(t))$,where α is a discount factor. As a rule it is considered that $\alpha < 1$, i.e. the utility of money in remote moments of time is smaller than in closer ones. But the case $\alpha > 1$ reflecting a hypothesis about increasing utility of the natural resource in future is also possible.

A presence of the value v(t) among arguments of the function g_u means that the Leader can change the quantity of annual income of the Follower. A positive change corresponds to a bonus (encouragement), a negative one to a penalty (punishment). So, a vector of controls of the Leader includes both variables corresponding to the economic parameters (grants, taxes, penalties) and variables corresponding to the administrative and legislative ones (quotas, limits, and so on). A role of Leader in HCES is played by an official institution of environmental control (environmental protection agency). An objective function J_v is optional but quite probably can be appropriate in practical situations. For example, the Leader can be interested in maximization in the sum of fines or in minimization of the environmental protection costs.

Let's consider an environmental-economic interpretation of the optimality principles (2.3.18)-(2.3.22).

The strategies which belong to the set $C_{\Omega J}{}^u$ (2.3.18) ensure the condition of environmental imperative (2.3.9) and maximization of the objective function of Follower J_u on the variable u. Thus, $C_{\Omega J}{}^u$ realizes the principle of optimality with a disinterested and Follower-neutral Leader. Similarly, the set $C_{\Omega J max}{}^u$ (2.3.21) realizes the principle of optimality with a disinterested and Follower-benevolent Leader (the Follower's objective function is maximized additionally by the variable v). Thus, realization of the conditions (2.3.18) or (2.3.21) means that in the same time the environmental requirements (environmental imperative) and the economic ones (maximization of the Follower's objective function) are satisfied. Based upon it the sets $C_{\Omega J}{}^u$ (2.3.18) and $C_{\Omega J max}{}^u$ (2.3.21) could be treated as the sets of homeostatic development of the environmental-economic system (or HCES) when a profitable economic activity does not contradict to the environmental requirements.

Respectively, the sets $C_{\Omega J}{}^{uv}$ (4.2.12) and $C_{\Omega J max}{}^{uv}$ (4.2.14) could be treated as the sets of hierarchically sustainable development of the environmental-economic system. In addition to the properties of $C_{\Omega J}{}^u$, $C_{\Omega J max}{}^u$ the Leader's objective function is also maximized here. In other words, in this case not only the condition of homeostasis, but also the condition of compromise is considered. The condition of dynamic consistency requires an additional checking.

As for the set $C_{\Omega J}{}^v$ (2.3.19), it could be treated as an "environmental dictatorship" in which an environmental imperative and Leader's interests are ensured for the cost of economic development. Such a strategy is practically acceptable only in some extreme cases, for example, in the regions of environmental disaster in the highly developed states.

Strategies of hierarchical management which do not belong to the set C_Ω are environmentally intolerable and contradict to the sense of the concept of HCES: their realization means that the Leader is unable to ensure the unalterable condition of environmental imperative.

Sustainable Development of Dynamic Systems 67

A very important role is played by the relation (2.3.15) which gives a man-made dynamics of the ecosystem with consideration of external factors. In fact, this relation is a system of non-linear equations each of which determines the dynamics of a respective state parameter of the ecosystem. For composition of the equations the information from ecology, geography, geochemistry, geophysics, and other environmental sciences is used.

Let's consider the following illustrative example. Let on the distance L from a river outfall a point source of pollution (an enterprise) is situated which throws industrial sewage into the river. The sewage contains a pollutant. Denote: $\pi(t,l)$ - a quantity of the pollutant in a moment t in a point l on the river ($0 \le l \le L$); $m(t)$ - a volume of the sewage in the moment t in the point $l=0$; $p(t)$ - a share of the sewage disposal in the moment t; $a(t)$ - the cost of disposal of the half of sewage in the moment t; $\kappa(l)$ - a share of dilution of the pollutant on the segment $[0,l]$; $Q(l)$ - a river outlay in the point l; v - a mean speed of the river stream; c – a maximum allowable concentration of the pollutant; λ - a factor of natural decay of the pollutant;

$\pi_0(l)$ – an initial (background) distribution of the pollutant in the water.

Assume that $\kappa(l)=kl/v$ where k is a factor of self-disposal of the river, and take a function of the sewage disposal in the form $g(p) = ap/(1-p)$.

Conserving the sense of a problem of the hierarchical control let's use a continuous time formalization on the segment $[0,T]$. Then the problem of decrease of the concentration of pollutant to the maximum allowable value with minimal costs of the disposal can be written in the form

$$J_v = \int_0^T g(p(t))dt \xrightarrow[\{p(t)\}]{} \min \tag{2.3.23}$$

$$\partial\pi(t,l)/\partial t = -\lambda\pi(t,l) + (1-kl/v)[1-p(t-l/v)]m(t-l/v) \tag{2.3.24}$$

$$\pi(0,l) = \pi_0(l) \tag{2.3.25}$$

$$\pi(T,l) \le cQ(l) \tag{2.3.26}$$

$$0 \le p(t) < 1 \tag{2.3.27}$$

$$0 \le m(t) \le M, \tag{2.3.28}$$

where M is the biggest possible quantity of sewage.

In terms of the model of hierarchical control $\pi(t,l)$ is a state of the HCES with consideration of the spatial-temporal distribution; $m(t)$ is a control impact of the Follower;

$p(t)$ is a control impact of the Leader.

The Follower is treated here as indifferent (her interests are not considered), and the adaptation mechanism is removed (waste disposal). An embedded adaptation mechanism $\kappa(l)$ is also present but its action is small in comparison with $p(t)$ especially when l is small.

From the mathematical point of view the system (2.3.24)-(2.3.28) represents a boundary-value problem for a partial differential equation with retardation the investigation of which is complicated. Let's consider as a simplified illustration the case when the running time $\tau=l/v$ from the point of sewage to the point l is small (i.e. a local dynamics of pollution). Then it is possible to write instead of the conditions (2.3.24)-(2.3.28):

$$d\pi/dt = [1-p(t)]m(t) - \lambda\pi(t) \tag{2.3.29}$$

$$\pi(0) = \pi_0 \tag{2.3.30}$$

$$\pi(T) \leq Qc \tag{2.3.31}$$

where π_0 is an initial quantity of the pollutant, Q is the river outlay (both in the point of sewage).

In the case of a constant load $m(t) \equiv m$ the problem (2.3.23), (2.3.29)-(2.3.31) is a problem of optimal control with a moving right boundary (the time may be considered as free or fixed). A substitution of the condition (2.3.31) by a stronger requirement

$$\pi(t) \leq Qc, \ 0 \leq t \leq T, \tag{2.3.32}$$

leads to an optimal control problem with a phase constraint.

Let's study a case with fixed time (that means the requirement to provide a maximum allowable concentration of the pollutant in a given time period T).

Assume $a(t) \equiv a$. A Hamilton function has the form

$$H(\psi,\pi,p)=a\psi_0(t)p(t)/[1-p(t)]+\psi_1(t)[m(1-p(t))-\lambda\pi(t)], \tag{2.3.33}$$

where $\psi(t)$ is a conjugate variable.

According to the Pontryagin principle of maximum (Pontryagin et al. 1962) $\psi(t)$ is a constant non-positive function. Denote $\psi_0(t) \equiv \psi < 0$. From the equation for the conjugate variable $d\psi_1/dt = -\partial H/\partial\pi$ we find $\psi_1(t) = C_1 e^{\lambda t}$. The necessary condition of maximum gives $0 = \partial H/\partial p = a\psi_0(t)/[1-p(t)]^2 - m\psi_1(t)$ from where the optimal control is equal to

$$p^*(t) = 1 - [a\psi_0(t)/m\psi_1(t))]^{1/2} = 1 - [aCe^{-\lambda t}/m]^{1/2} \tag{2.3.34}$$

where $C = \psi/C_1$. The condition of transversality on the right boundary gives $\theta^0\psi + \theta^1 C_1 e^{-\lambda T} = 0$ where $\theta = (\theta^0,\theta^1)$ is a tangent vector to the ray $\pi \leq Qc$. Then

$$C = \psi/C_1 = -\theta^1 e^{-\lambda T}/\theta^0 = e^{-\lambda T} > 0 \text{ from where with respect to} \tag{2.3.34}$$

$$p^*(t) = 1 - (a/m)^{1/2} e^{-0.5\lambda(T+t)}, \tag{2.3.35}$$

Sustainable Development of Dynamic Systems 69

and the optimal trajectory is

$$\pi^*(t) = \pi_0 e^{-\lambda t} + 2\lambda^{-1}(ma)^{1/2} e^{-0.5\lambda(T+t)}. \tag{2.3.36}$$

In the general case of a variable load $m(t)$ the problem (2.3.23)-(2.3.28) is a differential game with Nature where the Nature's control is $m(t)$ and the objective function $J_u = \text{const.}$ The principle of guaranteed result (Germeyer 1976) leads to the antagonistic game in which the worst for the goal-oriented player (the adaptation mechanism) situation arises when the Nature chooses the maximal value of its control variable $m(t) = M$. Therefore the antagonistic game is reduced to the studied problem of optimal control and the optimal guaranteeing strategy of adaptation has the form

$$p^*(t) = 1 - (a/M)^{1/2} e^{-0.5\lambda(T+t)},$$

that leads to the maximal guaranteed result

$$J_v^* = 2\lambda^{-1}(aM)^{1/2} e^{0.5\lambda T} - T.$$

Two main kinds of impact of the Follower to the HCES are natural resource use and environmental pollution. Let's consider quite a general model of the first kind.

Model of Natural Resource Use ("Harvesting").

$$J_u = \sum_{t=1}^{T} u(t)x(t) \rightarrow \max \tag{2.3.37}$$

$$0 \le u(t) \le 1 \tag{2.3.38}$$

$$x(t) = f([1-u(t)]x(t-1)) \tag{2.3.39}$$

$$x(0) = x_0 , \tag{2.3.40}$$

$$x(t) \ge x_{crit.} , \ t = 1,...,T. \tag{2.3.41}$$

Here $x(t)$ is a biomass of the used ecosystem in a moment t, $u(t)$ is a share of the biomass harvested in the moment t, $x_{crit.}$ is a critical value of the biomass (i.e. a condition (2.3.41) is the condition of environmental imperative).

An objective function of the Follower J_u has the sense of income from the biological resource use. From (2.3.39), (2.3.41) it is easy to get the set

$$U_\Omega = \{u(t): u(t) \le 1-(f^{-1}(x_{crit.}))/x(t) , \ t=1,...,T\}. \tag{2.3.42}$$

But the condition (2.3.41) is not obligatory for the Follower. It is known that if in the model (2.3.37)-(2.3.41) x is a scalar variable (i.e. (2.3.39) is an equation of dynamics of the used homogeneous isolated population) then an optimal harvesting strategy has the form

$$\begin{cases} 0,\ x(t) < x\,, \\ u^*(t) = \\ 1 - (f(x(t)) - x)/x(t),\ x(t) \geq x\,, \end{cases} \tag{2.3.43}$$

where x is the value of biomass which gives a maximum to the function f(x) - x . In this case the value f(x(t)) - x is harvested on each step, and the stationary value x of the biomass is supported (May 1973).

But this result does not solve the problem completely. In many cases the condition $x(t) \geq x$ becomes true only starting from a value $t^* > 1$. It means that for $t < t^*$ the Follower can prefer a harvesting strategy with positive values of u(t) and even different poaching strategies up to the immediate full extinction of the population.

In fact, in this case the Follower solves her optimal control problem (2.3.37)-(2.3.40) not for a value $T \gg 1$ but for a value $\tau \ll T$ and receives an immediate effect. If the strategy (2.3.43) definitely belongs to the set U_Ω (2.3.42) in respect to the biological sense $x \geq x_{crit.}$ then the poaching strategies do not belong to the set. More precisely,

$$\forall u \in U_\Omega\ \exists u_s \notin U_\Omega : J_u^\tau (x, u_s, 0) \gg J_u^\tau (x, u, 0);$$

it is quite possible that when $T \gg \tau$ then

$$\exists u_l \in U_\Omega : J_u^T (x, u_s, 0) < J_u^T (x, u_l, 0)$$

but the Follower does not plan her actions so far (in other words, the condition of dynamic consistency is broken).

As for a case of the vector variable x, i.e. the case of a heterogeneous population or a biological community then no general results of the type (2.3.43) are known. This is an important argument of the introduction to the model (2.3.37)-(2.3.41) a Leader who is responsible for the condition (2.3.41). The Leader should construct and realize such a mechanism of the hierarchical control v(u) that it would be advantageous for the Follower to use strategies which conform to the environmental imperative, i.e. $\forall t\ J_u^t (x, u^*, v(u^*)) > J_u^t (x, u, v(u))$, where $u^* \in U_\Omega$, $u \notin U_\Omega$.

Let's consider two heuristic algorithms called a normative and an adaptive mechanism of regulation respectively (Ougolnitsky 1999).

A Normative Mechanism of Regulation

Denote as earlier by $U_\Omega = \{u(t) : x(t, u(t)) \in \Omega,\ t = 1,...,T\}$ the set of Follower's control strategies which ensure the condition (2.3.9) with given external factors and initial conditions. In the general case the finding of the set U_Ω is a difficult problem but the HCES model is often linear on u. Besides, for each specific control strategy $u = \{u(t),\ t=1,...,T\}$ it is possible to check the condition $u \in U_\Omega$ by means of the simulation model (2.3.15)-(2.3.16). Introduce the sets of reward and punishment functions

$$v^R = \{v \in V : J_u (u, v^R) = \max_{v \in V} J_u (u, v)\}\,, \tag{2.3.44}$$

$$v^P = \{v \in V : J_u(u,v^P) = \min_{v \in V} J_u(u,v)\} \ . \tag{2.3.45}$$

Then the normative mechanism of regulation in a strict sense means that the Leader informs the Follower about the rule

$$v^*(u) = \begin{cases} v^R, u \in U_\Omega, \\ \\ v^P, u \notin U_\Omega. \end{cases} \tag{2.3.46}$$

It is supposed here that a trajectory u should be given completely for the period T and known to the Leader. A practical efficiency of the normative mechanism is determined by the following two conditions:

- importance of an objection v^P for the Follower;
- acceptability of a strategy v^R for the Leader.

The importance of an objection v^P means that the damage from its realization by the Leader for the Follower is greater that the advantage of the realization of any strategy $u \notin U_\Omega$

$$\forall u_1 \notin U_\Omega \ \exists u_2 \in U_\Omega \ J_u(u_1,v^P) < J_u(u_2,v^R) \ . \tag{2.3.47}$$

Example 2.3.1.

Assume $J_u(u,v) = u\text{-}v$, $U=V=[0,1]$, $U_\Omega = [0,1/3]$. Then $v^R = 0$, $v^P = 1$, $v^*(u) = 0$ if $0 \le u \le 1/3$ and $v^*(u) = 1$ if $1/3 < u \le 1$. It is evident that $\forall u \in U \ J_u(u,1) < J_u(u,0)$ and $J_u(1/3,0) > J_u(1,1)$. Therefore the optimal strategy of the Follower is $u^* = 1/3$; in so doing $(u^*,v^*) \in C_{\Omega J}^u$.

Another variant: assume $J_u(u,v) = uv$, $U = V = [-1,1]$, $U_\Omega = [0.1,0.5]$. It is evident that the Leader's normative mechanism

$$v^*(u) = \begin{cases} \mathrm{sgn}(u), u \in \Omega, \\ -\mathrm{sgn}(u), u \notin \Omega \end{cases} \quad \text{ensures the choice of a strategy } u \in U_\Omega \text{ by the Follower.}$$

If the condition (2.3.47) is false, i.e.

$$\exists u^0 \notin U_\Omega \ \forall u \in U_\Omega \ J_u(u^0,v^P) > J_u(u,v^R)$$

then the mechanism (2.3.46) is not efficient because the Leader can not impel the Follower to refuse from the choice of the strategy u^0 .

Example 4.2.2.

Assume $J_u(u,v) = \text{-}uv$, $U = [0,1]$, $U_\Omega = (0,1]$, $V = [0.5,1]$. Here $v^P = 1$, $v^R = 0.5$. However, for $\forall u \in U$ we have $J_u(0,v^P) > J_u(u,v^R)$ where $0 \notin U_\Omega$, i.e. the Leader's objection is not important.

The acceptability of a strategy v* for the Leader is determined by its influence on the values of the criterion J_v. If the Leader is supposed to be disinterested then this property is not essential. The ideal case for the Leader arises if

$$J_v(v^*) = \max_{v \in V} J_v(v).$$ (2.3.48)

Example 4.2.3.
Assume that $J_v(v) = v$ if $1/3 \leq v \leq 2/3$, and $J_v(v) = -v$ if $v < 1/3$ or $v > 2/3$,

$$J_u(u,v) = u - v, U = V = [0,1], U_\Omega = [1/3, 2/3].$$

Then $v^P = 1$, $v^R = 0$ and $J_v(v^*) = \max_{v \in V} J_v(v).$

In the case if $\exists v \in V : J_v(v) > J_v(v^*)$ then the Leader can use the normative mechanism (2.3.46) in a weakened form

$$v^{**}(u) = \begin{cases} v^+, u \in U_\Omega, \\ v^-, u \notin U_\Omega \end{cases}$$ (2.3.49)

where $J_v(v^{**}) > J_v(v^*)$, $\forall u \in U \; J_u(u,v^+) \geq J_u(u,v^-)$.

Thus, the normative mechanism is in fact reduced to the planning and implementation of computer simulations according to a certain algorithm which permits to the Leader and the Follower to evaluate the consequences of their control strategies for themselves and for the HCDS. The algorithm has the following form.

1. To give an arbitrary trajectory $u = (u(1),...,u(T))$.
2. To give a set of external factors $\xi = (\xi(1),...,\xi(T))$.
3. To calculate the CDS trajectory of the type $x = f(u,\xi)$ by means of the simulation model (2.3.15)-(2.3.16).
4. To check the condition (2.3.9) (or $u \in U_\Omega$ that is the same) for the found trajectory x.
5. To choose one of the values v^R или v^P as v* by the formula (2.3.46).
6. To calculate $J_u(u,v^*)$ and $J_v(v^*)$.

Computer simulation experiments on the proposed algorithm repeat for the different values of u ($u_1,..., u_R$) and ξ ($\xi_1,..., \xi_S$); in the process the properties of importance and acceptability of the strategy v* are checked and a weaker rule (2.3.49) instead of (2.3.46) is probably substituted.

Two approaches to the verification of admissibility of the Leader's strategy from the point of view of the environmental imperative are possible. First, one could require that the condition (2.3.9) be true for all values $x_{rs}(t)$ where $r=1,...,R$ are numbers of the Follower's control strategies u_r considered in computer simulations; $s=1,...,S$ are numbers of the external factors ξ_s ; $x_{rs} = f(u_r , \xi_s)$, t=1,...,T. Second, one could evaluate a probability of violation of the condition (2.3.9) by calculation of the frequency

$$P(x(t) \notin \Omega) = N^- / N \qquad (2.3.50)$$

where N is a total number of values $x_{rs}(t)$ received in all computer simulation experiences; N^- is the number of experiences in which the condition (2.3.9) is violated. After that one could require to ensure a threshold condition $P(x(t) \notin \Omega) \leq P_{crit.}$ The second approach seems more realistic.

Now let's return to the model (2.3.37)-(2.3.41) by adding it by the Leader's control (the Leader is treated as disinterested for the moment):

$$J_u = \sum_{t=1}^{T} [1-v(t)]u(t)x(t) \to \max$$

$$0 \leq u(t) \leq 1$$

$$0 \leq v(t) \leq 1$$

$$x(t) = f([1-u(t)]x(t-1))$$

$$x(0) = x_0$$

$$x(t) \geq x_{crit.} , t = 1,...,T.$$

Here v(t) is a control of the Leader (a penalty); a value 1-v(t) characterizes the share of the Follower's income withdrawn by the Leader as a penalty. Another possible interpretation of the value 1-v(t) is a price set by the Leader on the harvest gathered by the Follower.

It is evident that here $v^P(t) \equiv 1$, $v^R(t) \equiv 0$. If the penalty enters to the Follower's objective function multiplicatively (and this case is quite general) then a disinterested and having unlimited resource Leader is always able to provide the environmental imperative by the mechanism of reward and punishment in the form

$$v^*(u) = \begin{cases} 0 , u \in U_\Omega , \\ 1, u \notin U_\Omega. \end{cases}$$

An interested (for example, with the objective function

$$J_v = \sum_{t=1}^{T} v(t) \to \max$$

having the sense of maximization of penalties) or having a limited resource (when v(t) < 1) Leader should use a more general normative mechanism (2.3.49) where $0 \leq v^+ < v^- \leq 1$ which satisfies the conditions (dependence on x and u is omitted for simplicity)

$$J_u(v^P) \leq J_u(v^-) < J_u(v^+) \leq J_u(v^R),$$

$$J_v(v^R) \leq J_v(v^+) < J_v(v^-) \leq J_v(v^P).$$

Let's analyze some specific cases of the mutual disposition of the admissible domains of controls (2.3.18)-(2.3.22). Suppose at first that the Leader is disinterested.

Case 1.

$$\forall v \in V \ U_J(v) \subset U_\Omega.$$

Here a Leader is not at all needed because all strategies which are advantageous for the Follower correspond to the environmental imperative. Unfortunately, such situation is met in practice very rarely.

Case 2.

$$\exists v \in V \ U_J(v) \cap U_\Omega \neq \varnothing.$$

Using the mechanism of reward and punishment, a Leader with unlimited resource is always able to ensure a choice by the Follower of a strategy $u \in U_J(v) \cap U_\Omega$. The Leader's participation is necessary because a variant $\exists u_1 \in U_J(v) \backslash U_\Omega \ \forall u \in U_\Omega \ J_u(u_1) > J_u(u)$ is possible.

Case 3.

$$\forall v \in V \ U_J(v) \cap U_\Omega = \varnothing.$$

In this case (in a sense the most general) it is rational to distinguish two variants.

Case 3a.

$$\forall v \in V \ \forall u \in U_\Omega \ \exists u^0 \in U_J(v) : J_u(u^0,v) > J_u(u,v).$$

Here the problem of hierarchical control of the sustainable development of the dynamic system has not any solution because the Leader cannot ensure a choice by the Follower of a strategy $u \in U_\Omega$.

Case 3b.

$$\exists v \in V \ \forall u \in U_J(v) : J_u(u^*,v) > J_u(u,v).$$

For example, $J_u(u^*,v^R) > J_u(u,v^P)$, i.e.

$$\max_{v \in V} J_u(u^*,v) > \min_{v \in V} \max_{u \in U(v)} J_u(u,v).$$

In this case the Leader can impel the Follower to choose a strategy $u^* \in U_\Omega$; after that the Follower receives a payoff which is smaller than $u \in U_J(0)$, i.e. when a Leader is absent but greater than in the case when the Leader uses a punishment strategy.

A consideration of the Leader's interests requires an additional investigation of the acceptability of her control mechanism. Strictly speaking, the study made above remains valid when the Leader is interested because by the very nature of the model of HCDS the Leader should first of all ensure the environmental imperative and only after that could care for her private interests. But it is evident that from the practical point of view a disinterested Leader is a strong abstraction. Another argument against the mechanism of reward and punishment is that the Leader's control resource is probably bounded: the ability to choose $v(t) = 1$ means actually the stopping of the Follower's activity (for example, bankruptcy).

Let's characterize in more detail the results of usage of the normative mechanism by an interested Leader. Assume at first that $U_\Omega \cap U_J(v) \neq \varnothing$. Then four cases are possible.

1.$V_J \cap V_{max} \neq \varnothing$, $V_J \cap V_{min} \neq \varnothing$.

Here the normative mechanism

$$\begin{cases} V_J \cap V_{max} , u \in U_\Omega , \\ v^*(u) \in V_J \cap V_{min} , u \notin U_\Omega \end{cases}$$

ensures the choice by the Follower of a strategy $u^* \in U_\Omega$; the solution $(u^*,v^*) \in C_{\Omega Jmax}^{uv}$.

2. $V_J \cap V_{max} \neq \varnothing$, $V^J \cap V_{min} = \varnothing$.

Here the normative mechanism

$$\begin{cases} V_J \cap V_{max} , u \in U_\Omega , \\ v^*(u) \in V_{min} , u \notin U_\Omega \end{cases}$$

also ensures the choice by a rational Follower of a strategy $u^* \in U_\Omega$ and then $(u^*,v^*) \in C_{\Omega Jmax}^{uv}$.

3. $V_J \cap V_{max} = \varnothing$, $V_J \cap V_{min} \neq \varnothing$.

The normative mechanism

$$\begin{cases} V_{max} , u \in U_\Omega , \\ v^*(u) \in V_{min} \cap V_J , u \notin U_\Omega \end{cases}$$

ensures the choice by the Follower of a strategy $u^* \in U_\Omega$ after that $(u^*,v^*) \in C_{\Omega Jmax}^{u}$.

4. $V_J \cap V_{max} = \varnothing$, $V_J \cap V_{min} = \varnothing$.

The normative mechanism

$$\begin{cases} V_{max}, u \in U_\Omega, \\ v*(u) \in V_{min}, u \notin U_\Omega \end{cases}$$

ensures the choice by the Follower of a strategy $u* \in U_\Omega$; the solution $(u*,v*) \in C_{\Omega Jmax}^u$

If $\forall v\ U_\Omega \cap U_J(v) = \varnothing$ then in the respective cases 5-8 the Leader chooses the control mechanism $v*(u)$ similarly to the cases 1-4. Then the Follower should decide what is more advantageous for her:

$$\text{if } \exists u* \in U_\Omega\ J_u(u*,v^\pi(u*)) > J_u(u,v^P(u)), \forall u \in U_J\backslash U_\Omega \text{ then}$$

the Follower chooses $u* \in U_\Omega$ and in the cases 5 and 6 the solution $(u*,v*) \in C_{\Omega J}^v$; otherwise she chooses $u^0 \in U_J\backslash U_\Omega$:

$$J_u(u_0,v^P(u^0)) = \max_{u \in U_J\backslash U_\Omega} J_u(u,v^P(u))$$

and $(u^0,v*) \notin C_\Omega$, i.e. the problem of hierarchical control of the sustainable development of the dynamic system has no solution.

By virtue of economic rationality of the Follower in the cases 1-4 she always chooses the strategy $u* \in U_\Omega$ that delivers the Leader from using her punishment strategy (which can be not advantageous). In the cases 3-4, 7-8 the Leader can try to find a strategy

$$v^+(u) \in V_J : \exists u* \in U_\Omega\ J_u(u*,v^+(u*)) > J_u(u,v^P(u)), \forall u \in U_\Omega.$$

If the strategy exists then the Leader's payoff increases in comparison with the mechanism of reward and punishment and the solution of the game $(u*,v^+(u*)) \in C_{\Omega J}^{uv}$ (in the cases 7-8 if the choice of $u*$ is advantageous for the Follower). It is not necessary to substitute v^P by v^- because the strategy all the same is not realized when the Follower is economically rational.

An Adaptive Mechanism of Regulation

The algorithm of adaptive regulation may be presented in the following form. In the loop on $t = 1, 2,..., T$:

- a value $\xi(t)$ is generated;
- the Follower finds a strategy which is optimal on the step t:

$$u*(t) \in \text{Arg} \max_{u(t) \in U(t,v(t-1))} g_u(t,x(t-1),u(t)) \qquad (2.3.51)$$

Sustainable Development of Dynamic Systems   77

-    the Leader calculates $x(t) = x(t-1) + f(t,x(t-1),u^*(t),\xi(t))$;
-    the Leader chooses a corrective impact

$$\begin{cases} 0, x(t) \in \Omega, \\ v^*(t) = \\ v^C(t), x(t) \notin \Omega. \end{cases} \tag{2.3.52}$$

The rule (2.3.52) has the following sense: if the Follower's optimal strategy on the step t violates the condition (2.3.9) then the Leader impacts to the domain of Follower's admissible strategies $U = U(v)$ so that a new optimal strategy on the step t+1 transfers the CDS to the domain Ω or at least moves it closer to the domain.

Consider as an example the model of biological resource use in the form

$$J_v = v(t) \to max \tag{2.3.53}$$

$$v(t) \in V(t) \tag{2.3.54}$$

$$J_u = \sum_{i=1}^{n} c_i(t)u_i(t) \to max \tag{2.3.55}$$

$$\sum_{i=1}^{n} a_{ij} u_i(t) \le b_j(t) + v_j(t), j=1,\dots,m \tag{2.3.56}$$

$$u_i(t) \ge 0, i=1,\dots,n \tag{2.3.57}$$

$$x_i(t) = f(x_i(t)) - u_i(t) \tag{2.3.58}$$

$$x_i(0) = x_i^0 \tag{2.3.59}$$

$$x_i(t) \ge x_i^{crit.}, i=1,\dots,n, t=0,1,\dots,T-1. \tag{2.3.60}$$

Here $x(t) = (x_1(t),\dots,x_n(t))$ is a vector state variable (for example, the biomass of a biological community); $u(t) = (u_1(t),\dots, u_n(t))$ – a vector of "harvesting" (Follower's control on the step t); $b_j(t)$ – technological restrictions of j-th type for the Follower on the step t; $v_j(t)$ – Leader's grants which permit to weaken the restrictions (Leader's control in the moment t); a_{ij} – an efficiency of j-th technological method for i-th type of biological resource; $c_i(t)$ – a price of the unit of i-th type of biological resource on the step t; $x_i^{crit.}$ – a critical value of the biomass of i-th type.

The Leader should ensure the condition of environmental imperative (2.3.60) on each step t; after that she can also solve an optimization problem (2.3.53)-(2.3.54). The Follower on each step solves the problem of linear programming (2.3.55)-(2.3.57) which is a parametric one on the Leader's control variable $v_j(t)$. From (2.3.58) and (2.3.60) results

$$U_\Omega = \{u(t): u_i(t) \le f(x_i(t)) - x_i^{crit.}, i=1,\dots,n\}. \tag{2.3.61}$$

Bring the problem (2.3.55)-(2.3.57) to a canonical form by introducing the additional variables and write it in a vector form with evident denotations (Ougolnitsky et al. 2000):

$$(c^t, u^t) \rightarrow \max \tag{2.3.62}$$

$$A_t u^t = b^t + v^t \tag{2.3.63}$$

$$u^t \geq 0 . \tag{2.3.64}$$

Assume $u^t(v^t)$ is a basis solution of (2.3.63)-(2.3.64) so that $u^t(0)$ is an optimal solution of (2.3.52)-(2.3.64). Denote $A_t = (B_t, D_t)$ where B_t is the basis of solution $u^t(0)$; I_B is an index set of the basis variables; $Z_t = B_t^{-1} D_t$; $z_0^t = B_t^{-1} b^t$; $\Delta t = B_t^{-1} v^t$.

Then $u_B^t(0) + Z_t u_D^t(0) = z_0^t$; $u_B^t(v^t) + Z_t u_D^t(v^t) = z_0^t + \Delta^t$, hence in view of $u_D^t(v^t) = 0$ it is true that $u_B^t(v^t) = u_B^t(0) + \Delta^t$. As far as the estimates for non-basis variables do not depend on v^t then $u^t(v^t)$ leaves an optimal solution for all $v^t \in V^t$. If $i \notin I_B$ then $u_i^t(v^t) = 0$ otherwise $u_i^t(v^t) = u_i^t(0) + \Delta_i^t$. Then the condition $u^t \in U_\Omega$ takes the form $\Delta_i^t \leq f(x_i(t)) - x_i^{crit.} - u_i^t(0)$, from where the restrictions for v^t can be found:

$$B_t^{-1} v^t \leq f(x_i(t)) - x_i^{crit.} - u_i^t(0). \tag{2.3.65}$$

Thus, for the solution of the problem of hierarchical control of a dynamic system the Leader should solve the problem of mathematical programming (2.3.62)-2.3.65).

A more general model of the HCDS has the form

$$H = < N, A, \wp, \Sigma, \{U_i\}_{i \in N}, \{J_i\}_{i \in N} >, \tag{2.3.66}$$

where N is a set of agents; A is a binary relation on N; $\wp$ is a set of partitions (coalitional structures) on N; Σ is a controlled dynamic system; U_i is a set of strategies of i-th agent;

J_i is a payoff function of i-th agent defined on the set of situations $U_1 \times U_2 \times \ldots \times U_N$.

The following properties (axioms) supposed to be true:

A1 - hierarchy: the binary relation A is a strict order relation;

A2 - stratification: each partition $S \in \wp$ is ordered;

A3 – economic rationality: each agent $i \in N$ strives to maximize her payoff function Ji.

On the set of all subsets (coalitions) of N a characteristic function of the Neumann-Morgenstern type can be defined as

$$v(K) = \max_{u_K \in U_K} \min_{u_{N\backslash K} \in U_{N\backslash K}} \sum_{i \in K} J_i(u_K, u_{N\backslash K}), \quad K \in N, \tag{2.3.67}$$

where u_K is a set of strategies of the members of coalition K, $u_{N\backslash K}$ is a set of members of the complementary coalition $N\backslash K$.

The model (2.3.66) with the axioms A1-A3 and the characteristic function (2.3.67) which is superadditive permits to join three known constructs:

1) a directed graph without loops $D = (N,A)$ with a given set of ordered partitions of its vertices $\wp$ which characterizes an organizational structure of control of a dynamic system;

2) a game of N players in the normal form $G = <N, \{U_i\}_{i \in N}, \{J_i\}_{i \in N}>$ which models the dynamic system as a totality of independent economically rational individuals;

3) a game in the form of characteristic function $\Gamma_v = <N,v>$ which permits to describe the forming of coalition and cooperative principles of resource allocation.

Chapter 3

MODELS OF SUSTAINABLE MANAGEMENT

Basing on the given analysis of the methods of hierarchical management, the concept of sustainable development, the problem of hierarchical control of dynamic systems it is possible to formulate a synthetic concept of sustainable management. A complete reflection of the concept is appropriate only within a dynamic model which describes the process of development of a hierarchically controlled system and permits to consider the condition of dynamic consistency. Namely, the methods of hierarchical management (compulsion, impulsion, conviction) are formalized as specific versions of the Stackelberg equilibrium which ensures the condition of homeostasis by different ways. A study of the model requires a usage of the methods of applied system analysis on the base of simulation modeling. An illustrative static model of the hierarchical management of sustainable development is also proposed.

A general dynamic model of hierarchical management of sustainable development of the environmental-economic system is built, and the results of computer simulation experiments based on a scenario method are given. The results of investigation of the specific models of hierarchical management of sustainable development of the forest resource systems and recreational systems are adduced to illustrate the general concept and its practical abilities.

3.1. STATIC AND DYNAMIC MODELS OF THE HIERARCHICAL MANAGEMENT OF SUSTAINABLE DEVELOPMENT

Basing on the given analysis of the methods of hierarchical management, the concept of sustainable development, the problem of hierarchical control of dynamic systems it is possible to formulate a synthetic concept of sustainable management. A complete reflection of the concept is appropriate only within a dynamic model which describes the process of development of a hierarchically controlled system and permits to consider the condition of dynamic consistency. But for methodical purposes it is more convenient to begin the study from a static model which permits a more obvious representation of the concept and the optimality principles.

Let's consider a game theoretic model of the hierarchical management of sustainable development in the elementary static form which includes two players: a Leader (the control agent of higher level denoted by L) and a Follower (the control agent of lower level denoted by F). The model has the following form:

$$J_L(p,q,u) = g_L(p,q,u) - M\rho(u,U_L) \to \max \qquad (3.1.1)$$

$$p \in P, q \in Q; \qquad (3.1.2)$$

$$J_F(p,q,u) \to \max \qquad (3.1.3)$$

$$u \in U(q). \qquad (3.1.4)$$

The vector of Leader's controls is subdivided into two subvectors: p is a vector of impulsion controls, q is a vector of compulsion controls; P, Q are respective sets of admissible controls. Thus, the Leader strategy is a pair (p,q). Denote by u the Follower's strategy (impact on the controlled object), and by U(q) a set of admissible strategies of the Follower. According to the concept of sustainable management the Leader impacts on the Follower's payoff function J_F by her impulsion controls p and to the Follower's set of admissible strategies U(q) by her compulsion controls q. The condition $u \in U_L$ expresses the requirement of homeostasis because the general requirement $\forall t \in [0,T] : x(t) \in X_L$ for a controlled dynamic system $dx/dt = f(x(t), u(t))$ in natural conditions is equivalent to the condition $\forall t \in [0,T] : u(t) \in U_L$. To ensure the condition an indicator function $\rho(u,U_L) \begin{cases} = 0, u \in U_L, \\ > 0, u \notin U_L \end{cases}$ and an arbitrary big penalty constant M are introduced. Therefore, a maximization of the Leader's payoff function J_L is possible only if the condition of homeostasis $u \in U_L$ is satisfied. A specific Leader's payoff function without consideration of the condition of homeostasis is denoted by g_L. Two hypotheses are used in the model:

A1. $U_L \neq \varnothing$.

A2. $\exists p \in P, q \in Q : Arg \sup_{u \in U(q)} J_F(p,q,u) \setminus U_L \neq \varnothing$.

The first hypothesis means that the condition of homeostasis is reachable. According to the second hypothesis, by certain values of the Leader's controls (for example, p=q=0) the interests of Follower contradict to the condition of homeostasis, therefore the sustainable management is necessary.

Three types of equilibrium serve as solutions of the hierarchical game (3.1.1)-(3.1.4) (Ougolnitsky 2005).

Definition 3.1.1. An outcome (p,q,u) such as

$$J_L(p,q,u) \geq \gamma_L{}^{comp}(p), \qquad\qquad (3.1.5)$$

$$\gamma_L{}^{comp}(p) = \sup_{s \in Q} \inf_{z \in R(p,s)} J_L(p,s,z), p \in P;$$

$$R(p,q) = Arg \sup_{u \in U(q)} J_F(p,q,u)$$

is called a compulsion equilibrium in the game (3.1.1)-(3.1.4). Denote the set of compulsion equilibria by $Comp_L(p)$.

Statement 3.1.1. Let Q is compact, $g_L(p,q,u)$ is continuous on q. Then

$$\forall p \in P : Comp_L(p) \neq \varnothing \Leftrightarrow \exists q^* \in Arg \sup_{q \in Q} g_L(p,q,u) : U(q^*) \subset U_L.$$

Prove. Due to the compactness of Q and continuousness of $g_L(p,q,u)$ on q it is true that $Arg \sup_{q \in Q} g_L(p,q,u) \neq \varnothing$. Assume $\exists q^* \in Arg \sup_{q \in Q} g_L(p,q,u) : U(q^*) \subset U_L$. Then

$$\forall p \in P : R(p,q^*) \subset U(q^*) \subset U_L \Rightarrow \forall u \in R(p,q^*) \rho(u,U_L) = 0,$$

whence

$$\forall p \in P : J_L(p,q^*,u) = g_L(p,q^*,u) = \sup_{q \in Q} g_L(p,q,u) \geq \gamma_L{}^{comp}(p) \Rightarrow (p,q^*,u) \in Comp_L(p).$$

Now assume that $\forall q \in Arg \sup_{q \in Q} g_L(p,q,u)$ it is true that $U(q) \setminus U_L \neq \varnothing$. According to the model hypothesis A2 it is true that $\exists p \in P, q \in Q : R(p,q) \setminus U_L \neq \varnothing$. Therefore

$$\inf_{u \in R(p,q)} J_L(p,q,u) = -M < \gamma_L{}^{comp}(p) \Rightarrow \exists p \in P : Comp_L(p) = \varnothing.$$

Definition 3.1.2. An outcome (p,q,u) such as

$$J_L(p,q,u) \geq \gamma_L{}^{imp}(q), \qquad\qquad (3.1.6)$$

$$\gamma_L{}^{imp}(q) = \sup_{r \in P} \inf_{u \in R(r,q)} J_L(r,q,u)$$

is called an impulsion equilibrium in the game (3.1.1)-(3.1.4). Denote the set of impulsion equilibria by $Imp_L(q)$.

Statement 3.1.2. Let P is compact, $g_L(p,q,u)$ is continuous on p. Then $\forall q \in Q$ $Imp_L(q) \neq \varnothing$

$$\Leftrightarrow \exists p \in Arg \sup_{p \in P} g_L(p,q,u) : \forall z \in U(q) \setminus U_L \exists u \in U_L : J_F(p,q,u) > J_F(p,q,z).$$

Prove. Due to the compactness of P and continuousness of $g_L(p,q,u)$ on p it is true that $Arg \sup_{p \in P} g_L(p,q,u) \neq \varnothing$. Assume

$$\exists p \in Arg \sup_{p \in P} g_L(p,q,u) : \forall z \in U(q) \setminus U_L \exists u \in U_L : J_F(p,q,u) > J_F(p,q,z).$$

Then

$$\forall q \in Q \ R(p,q) \subset U_L \Rightarrow \forall u \in R(p,q) \ \rho(u,U_L) = 0 \Rightarrow \forall q \in Q \ \forall u \in R(p,q) \ J_L(p,q,u) = g_L(p,q,u) =$$

$$= \sup_{r \in P} g_L(r,q,u) \geq \gamma_L^{imp}(q) \Rightarrow (p,q,u) \in \mathrm{Imp_L(q)}.$$

Now assume

$$\forall q \in Q \ \forall p \in Arg \sup_{p \in P} g_L(p,q,u) \ \exists z \in U(q) \setminus U_L : J_F(p,q,u) \leq J_F(p,q,z).$$

Then

$$R(p,q) \setminus U_L \neq \varnothing \Rightarrow \inf_{u \in R(p,q)} J_L(p,q,u) = -M < \gamma_L^{imp}(q) \Rightarrow \mathrm{Imp_L(q)} = \varnothing.$$

Definition 3.1.3. An outcome (p,q,u) such as

$$(J_L + J_F)(p,q,u) = \sup_{r \in P} \sup_{s \in Q} \sup_{z \in U(s)} (J_L + J_F)(r,s,z) \tag{3.1.7}$$

is called a conviction equilibrium in the game (3.1.1)-(3.1.4). Denote the set of conviction equilibria by Conv.

Statement 3.1.3. Let P, Q, U are compact, $g_L(p,q,u)$, $g_F(p,q,u)$ are continuous. Then Conv $\neq \varnothing$.

The prove is evident.

A combined usage of the methods of compulsion and impulsion by the Leader is also possible. In this case the equilibria of compulsion/impulsion arise for which

$$J_L(p,q,u) \geq \sup_{q \in Q} \gamma_L^{imp}(q), \tag{3.1.8}$$

and the equilibria of impulsion/compulsion for which

$$J_L(p,q,u) \geq \sup_{p \in P} \gamma_L^{comp}(p).$$

(3.1.9)

Thus, the methods of hierarchical management are formalized as solutions of a hierarchical game (equilibria of compulsion, impulsion, and conviction). If the Leader is benevolent to the Follower then infimum in the formulas (3.1.5) and (3.1.6) can be substituted by supremum and the inequality by the strict equality.

In the case of environmental-economic problem domain the model (3.1.1)-(3.1.4) can be interpreted as follows: u is the Follower's environmental impact (natural resource use, pollution); U_L is a domain of the Follower's strategies which satisfy an environmental imperative; q are administrative and legislative controls of the Leader of the type of compulsion (maximum allowable concentration of pollutants, fish catching quotas, forest resource cutting rules, and so on); p are economic controls of the Leader of the type of impulsion (fines, taxes, credits, grants, and so on). Additionally to the model hypotheses A1 and A2 the following ones are accepted.

$$A3: \frac{\partial J_F}{\partial u_j} \geq 0; \frac{\partial J_F}{\partial p_j} \leq 0; \forall p \in P, q \in Q: J_F(p,q,0) = 0, i = 1,...,m; j = 1,...,n.$$

According to the hypothesis A3, it is advantageous for the Follower to increase her environmental impact and it is not advantageous for her when the Leader increases her taxes or fines (it is an appropriate interpretation of the impulsion without loss of generality). In the absence of environmental impact the income of Follower is equal to zero.

$$A4: g_L(p,q,u) = g_1(p,u) - g_2(p,q);$$

$$\frac{\partial g_1}{\partial p_i} \geq 0; \frac{\partial g_1}{\partial u_j} \geq 0; \frac{\partial g_2}{\partial p_i} \geq 0; \frac{\partial g_2}{\partial q_j} \geq 0; g_2(0,0) = 0; \lim_{q_j \to 1} g_2(p,q) = \lim_{p_i \to 1} g_2(p,q) = \infty, i = 1,...,m; j = 1,...,n.$$

Here the functions g_1 and g_2 are non-negative, continuous and differentiable on both arguments. The function g_1 describes the Follower's income and increases both when p ("tax rate") increases and when u ("tax base") increases. The function g_2 describes the Leader's cost of monitoring of her controls (overcoming of the Follower's counter-game) which increase when either p or q increase. The values p=q=1 are treated as punishment functions, and in this case the limit costs of the Leader are infinite (i.e. the practical realization of the strict punishment functions is economically impossible).

Let's consider a simplified version of the model (3.1.1)-(3.1.4) for the case of environmental-economic system when the model hypotheses A1-A4 are satisfied.

$$J_L = c_L p(u)\sqrt{u} - \frac{q + p(u)}{(1-q)(1-p(u))} - M\rho(u, U_L) \to \max$$

$$0 \leq q \leq 1; 0 \leq p(u) \leq 1;$$

$$J_F = c_F(1 - p(u))\sqrt{u} \rightarrow \max$$

$$0 \leq u \leq 1 - q; U_L = [0, a]; 0 \leq a \leq 1.$$

In the case of compulsion

$$\gamma_L^{comp}(p) = \sup_{0 \leq s \leq 1} \inf_{z \in R(p,s)} [c_L p(z)\sqrt{z} - \frac{s + p(z)}{(1-s)(1-p(z))} - M\rho(z, U_L)] =$$

$$= \sup_{0 \leq s \leq 1} [c_L p(1-s)\sqrt{1-s} - \frac{s + p(1-s)}{(1-s)(1-p(1-s))} - M\rho(1-s, U_L)] =$$

$$= \sup_{1-a \leq s \leq 1} [c_L p(1-s)\sqrt{1-s} - \frac{s + p(1-s)}{(1-s)(1-p(1-s))}] = c_L p(a)\sqrt{a} - \frac{1 - a + p(a)}{a(1-p(a))},$$

i.e. the compulsion equilibrium is (p,1-a,a). When p=0 we get $\gamma_L^{comp}(p) = -\dfrac{1-a}{a} < 0$, i.e. a

disinterested Leader ensures the condition of sustainable development with constant cost of overcoming the Follower's counter-game.

In the case of impulsion

$$\gamma_L^{imp}(p) = \sup_{p \in P^U(q)} \inf_{z \in R(p,q)} [c_L p(z)\sqrt{z} - \frac{q + p(z)}{(1-q)(1-p(z))} - M\rho(z, U_L)] =$$

$$= c_L \sqrt{a}[1 - \frac{1 - \sqrt{1+q}}{\sqrt{c_L(1-q)\sqrt{a}}} - \frac{\sqrt{c_L(1-q^2)\sqrt{a}}}{\sqrt{1-q}}],$$

i.e. the impulsion equilibrium is $(1 - \dfrac{\sqrt{1-q}}{\sqrt{c_L(1-q)\sqrt{a}}}, q, a)$. When q=0 we get

$\gamma_L^{imp}(0) = \sqrt{c_L\sqrt{a}}(\sqrt{c_L\sqrt{a}} - 2)$. This expression is non-negative when $c_L \geq 4a^{-1/2}$, i.e. the Leader's income depends on the rigidity of environmental requirements.

In the modeling of conviction two approaches are possible. In the first simpler case one could consider that the Follower's counter-game is impossible by definition and the monitoring costs are absent. Then the coalition of Leader and Follower maximizes jointly by all three variables p, q, u the payoff function $J_{LF} = c_L p\sqrt{u} + c_F(1-p)\sqrt{u} - M\rho(u, U_L)$. It is evident that u*=a, and $0 \leq q^* \leq 1 - a$. Therefore it is sufficient to solve the problem

$$\tilde{J}_{LF}(p) = \sqrt{a}(c_L - c_F)p \to \max, 0 \le p \le 1, \text{ whence } p^* = \begin{cases} 1, c_L > c_F, \\ 0, otherwise \end{cases}.$$

Thus, when $c_L > c_F$ then the conviction equilibrium is (1, q*, a), and the coalitional payoff is equal to $c_L \sqrt{a}$; when $c_L \le c_F$ then the conviction equilibrium is (0, q*, a), and the coalitional payoff is equal to $c_F \sqrt{a}, 0 \le q^* \le 1 - a$.

In the second approach it is supposed that a monitoring mechanism takes place even during the transition to conviction. Then the coalition of Leader and Follower should maximize the function $J_{LF} = c_L p \sqrt{u} + c_F (1-p)\sqrt{u} - \dfrac{p+q}{(1-p)(1-q)} - M\rho(u, U_L)$. It is evident again that u*=a, q*=0, therefore it is sufficient to solve the problem

$$\tilde{J}_{LF}(p) = \sqrt{a}(c_L - c_F)p - \frac{p}{1-p} \to \max, 0 \le p \le 1, \text{ whence a suspicious for extremum}$$

point is $p^* = 1 - (\sqrt{a}(c_L - c_F))^{-1/2}$. As far as $\tilde{J}_{LF}(0) = 0, \tilde{J}(p^*) = 1 - (\sqrt{a}(c_L - c_F))^{1/2}$ then when $\sqrt{a}(c_L - c_F) < 1$ the maximum of $\tilde{J}_{LF}(p)$ is reached by p=p* and is equal to $1 - (\sqrt{a}(c_L - c_F))^{1/2}$, and the conviction equilibrium is (p*,0,a), and when $\sqrt{a}(c_L - c_F) \ge 1$ then the maximum of $\tilde{J}_{LF}(p)$ is reached by p=0 and is equal to 0, and the conviction equilibrium is (0,0,a).

The methods of compulsion and impulsion (pure or combined) can be added by the Leader's manipulation. They say about manipulation when B does not realize the intension of A to exert an influence on him, and A is able to compel B to act in accordance with his desires (Easton 1958:179). Thus, in the case of the manipulation the ability of control subject to ensure a subordination of the control object is connected with the subject's ability to conceal some information (Ledyaev 1998).

In the model (3.1.1)-(3.1.4) the mechanism of manipulation consists in a deliberate misrepresentation by the Leader of the information about impact p on the Follower's payoff function J_F or about impact q on the Follower's set of admissible strategies U(q). The manipulation has the following reason: to compel or impel the Follower to choose homeostatic strategies the Leader often should offer her interests. For example, a punishment strategy in the impulsion mechanism could result in zero payoff of the Leader, and an introduction of quotas in the compulsion mechanism is connected with the monitoring costs, and so on. And if the Leader chooses an advantageous strategy then the Follower's optimal reaction quite probably could violate the conditions of homeostasis.

Therefore the Leader informs the Follower about a fictitious control mechanism such as the optimal reaction satisfies the condition of homeostasis and after that chooses in fact a more advantageous control.

In turn, the Follower's counter-game consists in forcing of the administrative or economic limitations established by the Leader. More precisely, the Follower can inform the Leader about the choice of a strategy and to choose in fact a more advantageous one. The overcoming of counter-game requires from the Leader additional costs for the monitoring of limitations. It is evident that an amount of the costs is proportional to the rigidity of limitations. Note that the method of conviction due to its cooperative nature eliminates both a manipulation of the Leader and a counter-game of the Follower.

A more general classification of models of sustainable management which considers two criteria of the classification, namely the methods of management and the types of Germeyer games (see 1.2) is given in Table 3.1.1. Models 1 and 5 are considered as the principal ones for the methods of compulsion and impulsion respectively because they reflect its character more appropriate but other variants are also possible.

Table 3.1.1 Methods of solution of the problem of sustainable management

	Without a feedback (Γ_1)	With a feedback (Γ_2)	With a counter feedback (Γ_3)
Compulsion	Model 1 (the principal variant)	Model 2	Model 3
Impulsion	Model 4	Model 5 (the principal variant)	Model 6
Conviction	Model 7		

Model 1. (compulsion without a feedback)

$$p = const, q \in Q, u \in U(q)$$

$$q^* : U(q^*) \subset U_L, J_L(q^*) = \sup_{q \in Q} \inf_{u \in U(q)} J_L(q, u)$$

Model 2. (compulsion with a feedback)

$$p = const, q \in Q^U, u \in U(q)$$

$$q^* : U(q^*) \subset U_L, J_L(q^*) = \sup_{q \in Q^U} \inf_{u \in U(q)} J_L(q, u)$$

Model 3. (compulsion with a counter feedback)

$$p = const, q \in Q^{U^Q}, u \in U(q)$$

$$q^* : U(q^*) \subset U_L, J_L(q^*) = \sup_{q \in Q^{U^Q}} \inf_{u \in U(q)} J_L(q, u)$$

Model 4. (impulsion without a feedback)

$$q = const, p \in P, u \in R(p)$$

$$R(p) = \{u \in U : J_F(p,u) \geq J_F(p,y), \forall y \in U\}$$

$$p^* : R(p^*) \subset U_L, J_L(p^*) = \sup_{p \in P} \inf_{u \in R(p)} J_L(p,u)$$

Model 5. (impulsion with a feedback)

$$q = const, p \in P^U, u \in R(p)$$

$$R(p) = \{u \in U : J_F(p(u),u) \geq J_F(p(y),y), \forall y \in U\}$$

$$p^* : R(p^*) \subset U_L, J_L(p^*) = \sup_{p \in P^U} \inf_{u \in R(p)} J_L(p,u)$$

Model 6. (impulsion with a counter feedback)

$$q = const, p \in P^{U^P}, u \in R(p)$$

$$R(p) = \{u \in U^P : J_F(\pi(p,u(p))) \geq J_F(\pi(p,y(p))), \forall y \in U^P\}$$

$$p^* : \pi(R(p^*)) \subset U_L, J_L(p^*) = \sup_{p \in P^{U^P}} \inf_{u \in R(p)} J_L(p,u)$$

Model 7. (conviction)

$$q \in Q, p \in P, u \in U(q)$$

$$(p^*, q^*.u^*) : U(q^*) \subset U_L,$$
$$(J_L + J_F)(p^*, q^*, u^*) = \sup_{q \in Q, p \in P} \sup_{u \in U(q)} (J_L + J_F)(p,q,u)$$

A general model of the sustainable management has the form

$$J_L = \sum_{t=1}^{T} [g_L^t(p^t,q^t,u^t,x^t) - M_L \rho(x^t,X_L^t)] \rightarrow \max, p^t \in P^t, q^t \in Q^t; \qquad (3.1.10)$$

$$J_F = \sum_{t=1}^{T} [g_F^t(p^t,u^t,x^t) - M_F \rho(x^t,X_F^t)] \rightarrow \max, u^t \in U^t(q^t); \qquad (3.1.11)$$

$$x^t = f(x^{t-1},u^t), x^0 = x_0, t = 1,2,\ldots,T. \qquad (3.1.12)$$

The explanations to the model (3.1.10)-(3.1.12) are given in Table 3.1.2. It is supposed here and everywhere that the maximums of J_L, J_F are reachable.

Table 3.1.2. Denotations in the general model of sustainable management

Denotation	Mathematical definition	Interpretation
x^t	$(x_1^t,...,x_k^t) \in R_+^k$	Set of the state parameters of a hierarchically controlled dynamic system on a step t
u^t	$(u_1^t,...,u_n^t) \in R_+^n$	Set of the Follower controls on the step t
p^t	$(p_1^t,...,p_m^t) \in R_+^m$	Set of control impacts of the Leader to the payoff function of the Follower on the step t
q^t	$(q_1^t,...,q_n^t) \in R_+^n$	Set of control impacts of the Leader to the set of admissible strategies of the Follower on the step t
f	$f: R_+^k \times R_+^n \to R_+^k$	Rule of change of the dynamic system state with consideration of the Follower's impact
x_0	$(x_{01},...,x_{0k}) \in R_+^k$	A known initial state of the dynamic system
T	$0 < T \le \infty$	A period of hierarchical impact on the dynamic system
P^t, Q^t	$P^t \subset R_+^m$; $Q^t \subset R_+^n$; compact sets for t=1,...,T	Sets of admissible controls of the Leader
$U^t(q^t)$	$U^t(q^t) \subset R_+^n$ is a compact set for t=1,...,T	A set of admissible controls of the Follower depending on Leader's impact
g_v^t	$g_v^t: R_+^m \times R_+^n \times R_+^n \times R_+^k \to R$ – a continuous number function	An amount of income of the Leader on the step t
g_u^t	$g_u^t: R_+^n \times R_+^m \times R_+^k \to R$ – a continuous number function	An amount of income of the Follower on the step t
ρ	$\rho(x^t, X) \begin{cases} = 0, x \in X, \\ > 0, x \notin X \end{cases}$	An indicator function which is equal to zero if on the step t the state of dynamic system belongs to a given set X and positive otherwise
M_v	$M_v > \max\limits_{p^t,q^t,u^t} g_v$	The Leader penalty constant
M_u	$M_u > \max\limits_{p^t,u^t} g_u$	The Follower penalty constant
J_v, J_u	$J_v \in R$; $J_u \in R$	Amounts of income of the Leader and Follower for the period T respectively
X_v^t, X_u^t	$X_v^t \subseteq R_+^k$, $X_u^t \subseteq R_+^k$ t=1,...,T	The target domains of the phase space of Leader and Follower respectively

The main objective of the Leader in the model (3.1.10)-(3.1.12) is to ensure a condition

$$x^t \in X_L^t, \ t=1,...,T \tag{3.1.13}$$

which is treated as the condition of homeostasis for a dynamic system with the state vector x.

A representation of the condition of homeostasis by means of a penalty function $M_L \rho(x^t, X_L^t)$ in (3.1.10) permits to state accurately that the condition (3.1.13) is an inalterable goal of the Leader. It is evident that if the condition is violated even on one step then a maximization of the Leader's payoff function is absolutely impossible. In the same time after the inalterable ensuring of (3.1.13) the Leader can additionally maximize her income described by a function g_L^t. Thus, the function g_L^t gives the Leader's criterion of optimality on the step t, and the integral value of her payoff function J_L permits to compare different ways of ensuring the sustainable management and to choose the best one in the sense of maximal total income of the Leader on the period T. In the general case the Follower also has a goal (the condition $x^t \in X_F^t$, t=1,...,T) which is formalized by a penalty function $M_F\rho(x^t, X_F^t)$ in the relation (3.1.11). However, in practice this goal is absent as a rule ($X_F^t \equiv R_+^k$) and will not be mentioned later. It is the reason of sustainable management that the Follower often strives only for the maximization of her current payoff meanwhile the objective of Leader is to ensure the homeostasis on a long (perhaps infinite) period of time.

A complexity of the model (3.1.10)-(3.1.12) determines a necessity of usage for its analysis a simulation modeling (computer simulation) based on the scenario method. Robert Shannon has defined the simulation modeling as a process of construction of the model of a real system and organization of experiments with the model which has a goal either to understand the system's behavior or to evaluate different strategies controlling the system functioning. Thus, the process of simulation modeling includes both the construction of a model and its application to the analysis of a problem (Shannon 1975).

The definition permits to treat the simulation modeling in a broad sense as a process of applied systems analysis, i.e. the combined usage of mathematical modeling, computer simulation, and expert procedures for the solution of complex practical problems of control of the dynamic systems (Gorstko and Ougolnitsky 1996; Ougolnitsky 1999). The process of applied systems analysis is represented by the diagram in Figure 3.1.1.

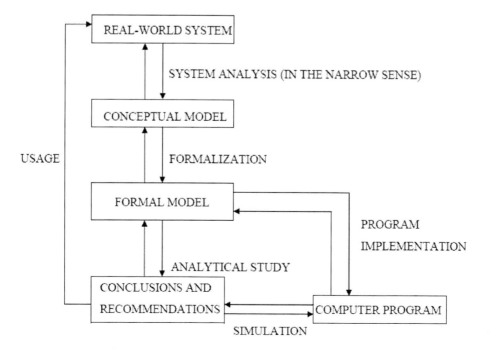

Figure 3.1.1. Principal phases and results of the applied systems analysis.

Three phases are selected in the process of applied system analysis:

- a conceptualization: a system analysis of the object in the narrow sense of the notion, formulation of goals and objectives of the study, determination of boundaries of the object, its structure and functions, construction of the final conceptual model;
- a formalization: a representation of the obtained conceptual model in the form of a system of the mathematical or other formal relations, a solution of the identification problems, a program realization of the formal model;
- a work with the formal model: an analytical research, computer simulation experiments, an interpretation and usage of the results (Gorstko and Ougolnitsky 1996; Ougolnitsky 1999).

The applied system analysis based on the simulation modeling is perhaps the only method of investigation of the model (3.1.10)-(3.1.10) in its initial complete form. For the analytical research the model (3.1.10)-(3.1.12) should be simplified.

The condition of homeostasis $\forall t \in [0,T] : x(t) \in X_L$ for a controlled dynamic system $dx/dt = f(x(t),u(t))$ in natural conditions is equivalent to the requirement $\forall t \in [0,T] : u(t) \in U_L$. This fact permits to eliminate from the model of sustainable management an explicit description of the dynamics of HCDS and therefore to simplify the model essentially. In this case the model of sustainable management takes the form

$$J_L(p,q,u) = \sum_{k=1}^{T} \delta_L^{\,k} \, [g_L(p^k,q^k,u^k) - M\rho(u^k,U_L)] \to \max \qquad (3.1.14)$$

$$\delta_L \in (0,1), p^k \in P, q^k \in Q; \qquad (3.1.15)$$

$$J_F(p,q,u) = \sum_{k=1}^{T} \delta_F^{\,k} \, g_F(p^k,q^k,u^k) \to \max \qquad (3.1.16)$$

$$\delta_F \in (0,1), u^k \in U(q^k), k = 1,...,T. \qquad (3.1.17)$$

Here δ_L, δ_F are discount factors; $p = (p^1,...,p^T); q = (q^1,...,q^T); u = (u^1,...,u^T).$

Denote

$$P^T = P \times ... \times P(T \ times), Q^T = Q \times ... \times Q(T \ times), U^T(q) = U(q^1) \times ... \times U(q^T),$$

$$R^T(p,q) = R(p^1,q^1) \times ... \times R(p^T,q^T), R(p^k,q^k) = Arg \sup_{z^k \in U(q^k)} g_F(p^k,q^k,u^k).$$

Then the set of compulsion equilibria in the dynamic game (3.1.14)-(3.1.17) has the form

$$Comp_L(p) = \{(p,q,u) : q \in Q^T, u \in U^T(q) : J_L(p,q,u) \geq \gamma_L^{comp}(p)\},$$

$$\gamma_L^{comp}(p) = \sup_{s \in Q^T} \inf_{z \in R^T(p,s)} J_L(p,s,z);$$

the set of impulsion equilibria has the form

$$\mathrm{Imp_L}(q) = \{(p,q,u) : p \in P^T, u \in U^T(q) : J_L(p,q,u) \geq \gamma_L^{imp}(q)\},$$

$$\gamma_L^{imp}(q) = \sup_{r \in P^T} \inf_{z \in R^T(r,q)} J_L(r,q,z);$$

the set of conviction equilibria has the form

$$Conv = \{(p,q,u) : p \in P^T, q \in Q^T, u \in U^T(q) : (J_L + J_F)(p,q,u) = \sup_{r \in P^T} \sup_{s \in Q^T} \sup_{z \in U^T(q)} (J_L + J_F)(r,s,z)\}.$$

It is evident that if the propositions made in Statements 3.1.1-3.1.3 for a static case remain valid then the equilibria of compulsion, impulsion, and conviction exist in the dynamic case too, and the model of sustainable management can be written both in the form of a multistage game (3.1.14)-(3.1.17) and in the form of a differential game.

3.2. A GENERAL MODEL OF THE SUSTAINABLE MANAGEMENT OF ENVIRONMENTAL-ECONOMIC SYSTEMS

A general model of the sustainable management of an environmental-economic system has the following form (Ougolnitsky 2004):

$$J_v = \sum_{t=1}^{T} [g_v^t(p^t,q^t,u^t,x^t) - M_v\rho(x^t,X_v^t)] \rightarrow \max, \ p^t \in P^t, \ q^t \in Q^t; \tag{3.2.1}$$

$$J_u = \sum_{t=1}^{T} [g_u^t(p^t,u^t,x^t) - M_u\rho(x^t,X_u^t)] \rightarrow \max, \ u^t \in U^t(q^t); \tag{3.2.2}$$

$$x^t = f(x^{t-1},u^t), \ x^0 = x_0, \ t=1,2,...,T. \tag{3.2.3}$$

The explanations to the model (3.2.1)-(3.2.3) are given in Table 3.2.1. It is supposed here and everywhere that the maximums of J_L, J_F are reachable.

Table 3.2.1. Denotations in the general model of the sustainable management of an environmental-economic system

Denotation	Mathematical definition	Environmental-economic interpretation
x^t	$(x_1^t,...,x_k^t) \in R_+^k$	Set of the state parameters of a hierarchically controlled environmental-economic system in a year t
u^t	$(u_1^t,...,u_n^t) \in R_+^n$	Set of the Follower (natural resource user) controls in the year t: natural resource use, production of goods, pollution
p^t	$(p_1^t,...,p_m^t) \in R_+^m$	Set of control impacts of the Leader (control agency) to the payoff function of the Follower on the year t: taxes, penalties, grants
q^t	$(q_1^t,...,q_n^t) \in R_+^n$	Set of control impacts of the Leader to the set of admissible strategies of the Follower in the year t: quotas, limits, norms, standards
f	$f: R_+^k \times R_+^n \rightarrow R_+^k$	Rule of change of the environmental-economic system state with consideration of the Follower's impact
x_0	$(x_{01},...,x_{0k}) \in R_+^k$	A known initial state of the environmental-economic system
T	$0 < T \leq \infty$	A period of hierarchical impact on the system
P^t, Q^t	$P^t \subset R_+^m; Q^t \subset R_+^n;$ compact sets when t=1,...,T	Sets of admissible controls of the Leader
$U^t(q^t)$	$U^t(q^t) \subset R_+^n$ – a compact set when t=1,...,T	A set of admissible controls of the Follower depending on Leader's impact
g_v^t	$g_v^t: R_+^m \times R_+^n \times R_+^n \times R_+^k \rightarrow R$ – a continuous number function	An amount of income of the Leader in the year t
g_u^t	$g_u^t: R_+^n \times R_+^m \times R_+^k \rightarrow R$ – a continuous number function	An amount of income of the Follower in the year t
ρ	$\rho(x^t, X)\begin{cases} = 0, x \in X, \\ > 0, x \notin X \end{cases}$	An indicator function which is equal to zero if in the year t the state of dynamic system belongs to a given set X and positive otherwise
M_v	$M_v > \max\limits_{p^t,q^t,u^t} g_v$	The Leader penalty constant
M_u	$M_u > \max\limits_{p^t,u^t} g_u$	The Follower penalty constant
J_v, J_u	$J_v \in R; J_u \in R$	Amounts of income of the Leader and Follower for the period T respectively
X_v^t, X_u^t	$X_v^t \subseteq R_+^k, X_u^t \subseteq R_+^k$ t=1,...,T	The target domains of the phase space of Leader and Follower respectively

The main goal of Leader in the model (3.2.1)-(3.1.3) is to ensure a condition

$$x^t \in X_v^t, \ t=1,...,T \tag{3.2.4}$$

which is treated as the condition of homeostasis for an environmental-economic system with the state vector x. As a rule, the domain X_v^t is given by inequalities of the type $x_i^t \geq a_i^t$ for those components of the state vector which correspond to the produced goods and used resources and by inequalities of the type $x_j^t \leq b_j^t$ for those components which correspond to the pollutants. Then to an extent the ensuring of condition (3.2.4) permits to satisfy the requirements of both economic development and environmental equilibrium. A necessity of consideration of the interests of future generations means that a quantity T should be big enough or even infinite.

A representation of the condition of homeostasis (3.2.4) by means of a penalty function $M_v\rho(x^t,X_L^t)$ in (3.2.1) permits to state accurately that the condition (3.2.4) is an inalterable goal of the Leader. It is evident that if the condition is violated even on one step then a maximization of the Leader payoff function is absolutely impossible. In the same time after the inalterable ensuring of (3.2.4) the Leader can additionally maximize her income described by a function g_v^t. Thus, the function g_v^t gives the Leader criterion of optimality on the step t, and the integral value of her payoff function J_v permits to compare different ways of ensuring the sustainable management and to choose the best one in the sense of maximal total income of the Leader on the period T.

In the general case the Follower also has a goal (the condition $x^t \in X_u^t$, t=1,...,T) which is formalized by a penalty function $M_u\rho(x^t, X_F^t)$ in the relation (3.2.2). However, in practice this goal is absent as a rule ($X_u^t \equiv R_+^k$) and will not be mentioned later. It is the reason of sustainable management that the Follower (natural resource user) often strives only to maximize her current payoff meanwhile the objective of Leader (control agency) is to ensure the homeostasis on a long (perhaps infinite) period of time.

A difference form of the model (3.2.1)-(3.2.3) is determined both by the character of environmental-economic data (collected in regular periods of time) and by the fact that in a general case the model can be studied only by means of the simulation modeling. Consider a general form of the simulation model of an environmental-economic system in the context of sustainable management (Ougolnitsky and Cherdyntseva 2004):

$$\Omega^{t+1} = \Omega^t + \Psi^t(\Omega^t, v^{t+1}, u^{t+1}), \Omega^0 = \Omega_0 ;$$

$$G_L^{t+1} = G_L^t + g_L(\Omega^{t+1}, v^{t+1}, u^{t+1}), G_L^0 = G_{L0} ;$$

$$G_F^{t+1} = G_F^t + g_F(\Omega^{t+1}, v^{t+1}, u^{t+1}), G_F^0 = G_{F0} , t=0,...,T-1.$$

Here $\Omega^t = (\{x_i^t\}_{i=1}^I , \{y_j\}_{j=1}^J , \{z_k\}_{k=1}^K)$ is the vector of state of an environmental-economic system on the step t where x_i^t is the quantity of i-th natural resource; y_j^t – the quantity of j-th product; z_k^t – the quantity of k-th pollutant in the end of t-th modeling step; I – the number of natural resources; J – the number of products; K – the number of pollutants;

$\Psi^t = (\{f_i^t\}_{i=1}^I , \{\varphi_j^t\}_{j=1}^J , \{h_k^t\}_{k=1}^K , \{\pi_k^t\}_{k=1}^K)$ – a generalized operator of transform of the system state on the step t where f_i^t is a function of the natural dynamics of i-th resource; φ_j^t – a production function of j-th product; h_k^t – a transformation function of k-th pollutant in consideration with the ecosystem self-refinement ability; π_k^t – an amount of disposal of k-th pollution in the production process;

- $v^t = (\{p1_i^t\}_{i=1}^I, \{p2_j^t\}_{j=1}^J, \{p3_k^t\}_{k=1}^K, \{q_i^t\}_{i=1}^I, \{d_k^t\}_{k=1}^K)$ – is a vector of the Follower's controls on the step t where $p1_i^t$ is a tax rate (rental fee) for the use of i-th resource; $p2_j^t$ – a tax rate for the production of j-th product; $p3_k^t$ – a penalty rate for k-th pollutant disposal; q_i^t – a quota on i-th resource use; d_k^t – a quota of pollution of k-th pollutant on the step t;

- $u^t = (\{\mu_i^t\}_{i=1}^I, \{\tau_j^t\}_{j=1}^J, \{v_k^t\}_{k=1}^K)$ – a vector of the Follower's controls on the step t where μ_i^t – a part of extraction of i-th resource; τ_j^t – a technology of production of j-th product; $\{\tau_{j1}, ..., \tau_{js}\}$ – a set of admissible technologies; v_k^t – a degree of removal for k-th pollutant.

In more details the given relations have the form

$$x_i^{t+1} = x_i^t + f_i^t(x_1^t, ..., x_I^t) - \mu_i^{t+1} x_i^t, \quad i=1,...,I;$$

$$y_j^{t+1} = \varphi_j^t(r_1^{t+1}, ..., r_I^{t+1}, \tau_j^{t+1}), \quad r_i^{t+1} = \mu_i^{t+1} x_i^t, \quad j=1,...,J;$$

$$z_k^{t+1} = z_k^t + h_k^t(z_1^t, ..., z_K^t) + \pi_k^t(y_1^{t+1}, ..., y_J^{t+1}, \tau_1^{t+1}, ..., \tau_J^{t+1}) - v_k^{t+1} z_k^t, \quad k=1,...,K.$$

The relations of financial balance (dynamics of payoffs of Leader and Follower) are

$$G_L^{t+1} = G_L^t + \sum_{i=1}^I a_i^{t+1}(\mu_i^{t+1}) p1_i^{t+1} \mu_i^{t+1} x_i^{t+1} + \sum_{j=1}^J b_j^{t+1}(\tau_j^{t+1}) p2_j^{t+1} y_j^{t+1} +$$

$$+ \sum_{k=1}^K c_k^{t+1} \sigma^{t+1} p3_k^{t+1} z_k^{t+1} - M\rho(\Omega^{t+1}, \Omega^*);$$

$$G_F^{t+1} = G_F^t + \sum_{i=1}^I a_i^{t+1}(\mu_i^{t+1})(1-p1_i^{t+1})\mu_i^{t+1} x_i^{t+1} + \sum_{j=1}^J b_j^{t+1}(\tau_j^{t+1})(1-p2_j^{t+1})y_j^{t+1} +$$

$$+ \sum_{k=1}^K c_k^{t+1} \sigma^{t+1} p3_k^{t+1} z_k^{t+1} - \sum_{k=1}^K w_k^{t+1}(v_k^{t+1})$$

where G_L^t, G_F^t are payoffs of the Leader and Follower respectively on the step t;

$a_i^{t+1}(\mu_i^{t+1}) = [a1_i^{t+1} - a2_i(\mu_i^{t+1})]\sigma^{t+1}$;

$b_j^{t+1}(\tau_j^{t+1}) = [b1_j^{t+1} - b2_j(\tau_j^{t+1})]\sigma^{t+1}$;

$a1_i^{t+1}$ – a price of the unit of i-th resource on the step t;

$a2_i(\mu_i^{t+1})$ – a cost price of extraction of the unit of the i-th resource on the step t+1;

$b1_j^{t+1}$ – a price of the unit of the j-th product on the step t+1;

$b2_j(\tau_j^{t+1})$ – a cost price of production of the unit of the j-th product which depends on the technology used on the step t;

c_k^{t+1} – a "price" of disposal of the unit of the k-th pollutant on the step t+1;

σ^{t+1} – a discount factor on the step t+1;

$w_k^{t+1}(v_k^{t+1})$ – expenditures for the removal of the unit of the k-th pollutant on the step t+1. For the described simulation model initial conditions should be given

$x_i^0 = x_{i0}$, i=1,...,I; $z_k^0 = z_{k0}$, k=1,...,K;

$G_L^0 = G_L^0$; $G_F^0 = G_{F0}$,

and the following restrictions should be satisfied

$$0 \le \mu_i^{t+1} \le q_i^{t+1} , \text{ i=1,...,I; } \tau_j^{t+1} \in \{\tau_{j1} ,..., \tau_{js}\}, \text{ j=1,...,J; } d_k^{t+1} \le v_k^{t+1} \le 1, \text{ k=1,...,K; } 0 \le$$
$$p1_i^{t+1} \le 1, 0 \le q_i^{t+1} \le 1, \text{ i=1,...,I; } 0 \le p2_j^{t+1} \le 1, \text{ j=1,...,J; } 0 \le p3_k^{t+1} \le 1,$$
$$0 \le d_k^{t+1} \le 1, \text{ k=1,...,K.}$$

At last, the requirement of homeostasis in the described simulation model is determined by the condition $\Omega \in \Omega^*$ where $\Omega^* = X^* \times Y^* \times Z^*$ is the domain of homeostasis of the environmental-economic system;

$$X^* = \prod_{i=1}^{I} [x_i^* ,\infty) , x_i^* \text{ - a critical quantity of the i-th resource;}$$

$$Y^* = \prod_{j=1}^{J} [y_j^* ,\infty) , y_j^* \text{ - a critical quantity of the j-th product;}$$

$$Z^* = \prod_{k=1}^{K} [0, z_k^*] , z_k^* \text{ - a maximum allowed quantity of the k-th pollutant.}$$

Taking into consideration an interaction of pollutants results in the additional restrictions

$(z_{k1} , z_{k2}) \in Z^*_{k1 , k2} ,$ k1, k2 = 1,...,K;

$(z_{k1} , z_{k2} , z_{k3}) \in Z^*_{k1 , k2 , k3} ,$ k1,k2,k3 = 1,...,K;

$\dots$

$(z_1 ,..., z_K) \in Z^*_{1,...,K} .$

To an extent ensuring of the conditions enumerated above ensures conservation of the biological and geological diversity, environmental safety, and satisfaction of the basic economic needs (i.e. the sustainable development of the environmental-economic system).

On the t-th step of modeling a transition from the value Ω^t to the value Ω^{t+1} and from the values G_L^t , G_F^t to the values G_L^{t+1} , G_F^{t+1} , t = 0,1,...,T-1 is realized.

Let's consider as an example the results of computer simulation experiments with a simplified model of the sustainable management of an environmental-economic system (Ougolnitsky and Cherdyntseva 2004). The simulation experiments based on the following propositions:

- there is only one production (one Follower) and only one technology;
- only one natural resource is used in the production process;
- a pollution in the production process has not any effect on the dynamics of the used natural resource and the pollution fine is included to the rental fee for the resource;
- the simulation experiments model the dynamics of natural resource and Follower's profit, and the Leader's profit is not modeled;
- the simulation experiments are realized for a fixed number of steps (20 steps);
- strategies, tax rates, fines, and other parameters are determined before the experiments for the whole period of modeling.

The dynamics of natural resource is described by the Verhulst-Pearl or Ricker models. In the Verhulst-Pearl model parameters are chosen so as the maximum of logistic curve be equal to 1.

The production model is based on the proposition that a quantity of the product varies in the range from 0 to1, and on each step the product increases in comparison to the previous step on K percents but does not exceed 1. The parameter K can take arbitrary values, if K=0 then the product is constant, and if K<0 then it decreases.

Two strategies were modeled:

1) without limitations on the resource extraction: if the quantity of resource becomes smaller than a normative value than a penalty for the total extracted volume of resource is charged;
2) with limitations on the resource extraction: the quantity of resource which permits to avoid a penalty is extracted, or the production is stopped for a while. Three functions of dependence of the Follower income on the production volume are considered: a linear one, an exponential one with a factor greater than 1, and an exponential one with a factor smaller than 1.

Consider the results for the linear model of income. The graphs of dependence of the final quantity of natural resource, the total incomes of the Follower for the first and second strategies on the production volume chosen by the Follower are shown in Figure 3.2.1.

The model parameters take the following values:

- a production increase rate is equal to 2%;
- a limitation on the resource quantity is equal to 0,5;
- a factor in the linear income model is equal to 0,5;
- a penalty for a violation of the limitation is equal to 30% (i.e. the rental fee for the total extracted resource increases on 30%).

Models of Sustainable Management

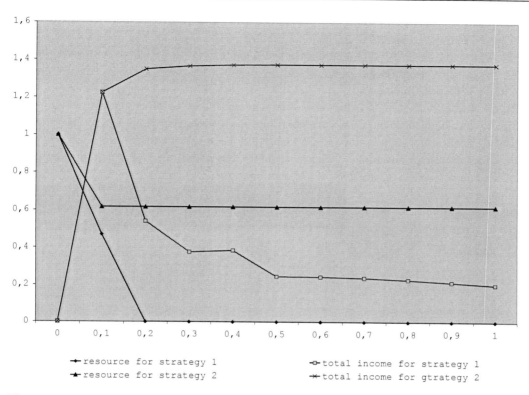

Figure 3.2.1

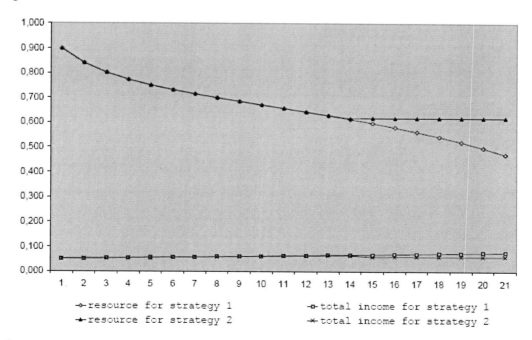

Figure 3.2.2.

It is seen from the graphs that only the choice of a value of the initial production volume equal to 0.1 permits to ensure a greater total income for the first strategy than for the second one. However, the final resource quantity is always smaller for usage of the first strategy.

Let's consider the graphs of quantities of the resource and income for the fixed values of the initial production volume equal to 0.1 and 0.3 (Figure 3.2.2 and 3.2.3 respectively).

If the initial value of production volume is equal to 0.1 then both strategies give practically similar results, only on the several last steps strategy 1 leads to greater values of the payoff function but in the same time the quantity of resource decreases quickly. And if the initial value of production volume is greater than 0.1 on several first steps than the strategy 1 leads to greater values of the payoff function but then the production stops due to the complete extraction of resource. Thus, the velocity of resource extraction and therefore the production stopping is proportional to the initial value of production volume.

To analyze the effect of restrictions on resource extraction and a penalty to the final result of production a dependence of the total payoff on the restrictions for resource extraction and the penalty was studied. The restrictions in the range from 0.1 to 0.9 were considered. The value of penalty changed from 0% to 100% by the step 10%. The analysis shows that if the initial value of production volume is equal to 0.1 then when the Leader chooses the restrictions in the range from 0 to 0.3 then both strategies give the same total income. If the restriction value is equal to 0.4 then the first strategy always gives a greater value of the total income independently on the penalty value. If the restrictive boundaries vary from 0.5 to 0.9 then to provide an advantage of the second strategy the Leader should establish the penalty not smaller than 25-35%. If the Follower chooses the initial value of production volume from 0.2 and greater then the second strategy always results in a greater total income independently on the restrictions and penalty. In this case the Leader's control is not essential because the natural resource dynamics does not permit to receive better results by the first strategy.

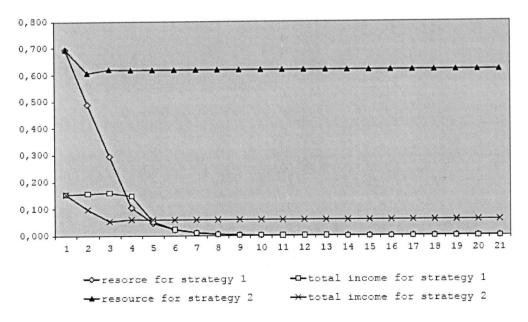

Figure 3.2.3.

Models of Sustainable Management 101

If the modeling period decreases to 10 steps then the results become the following. The second strategy is better again if the initial value of production volume is not smaller than 0.2 independently on the restrictions and penalty. If the production starts from the value 0.1 then both strategies give the same results when the restrictive boundary is not greater than 0.5. The restriction value equal to 0.6 gives advantage to the first strategy for any penalty. If the restriction range is 0.7-0.9 then to provide an advantage to the second strategy one should establish the penalty equal to 25-35%.

If a number of the modeling steps decreases to five then the second strategy could have an advantage only if the initial value of production volume is not smaller than 0.5. For smaller values (see the first column) the model results are the following:

0.1	- in restrictions range 0.1 - 0.6 both strategies give the same total income; - if the boundary value is equal to 0.7 then the first strategy is more advantageous; - in restrictions range 0.8-0.9 the second strategy gives a greater total income if the penalty is not smaller than 25-35%.
0.2	- if the boundary value is equal to 0.1 then both strategies give the same total income; - the value 0.2 gives an advantage to the first strategy; - in restrictions range 0.3-0.9 the second strategy gives a greater total income if the penalty is not smaller than 25-35%.
0.3 0.4	The second strategy is more advantageous with any restrictions if the penalty is not smaller than 25-35%.

At last, in the case of short-term resource use (three modeling steps) the second strategy has no absolute advantage for any initial values of production volume. The results are shown below:

0.1	- in restrictions range 0.1 – 0.7 both strategies give the same total income; - the value 0.8 gives an advantage to the first strategy; - in restrictions range 0.9 the second strategy gives a greater total income if the penalty is not smaller than 25-35%.
0.2	- in restrictions range 0.1 – 0.4 both strategies give the same total income; - the value 0.5 gives an advantage to the first strategy; - in restrictions range 0.6 - 0.9 the second strategy gives a greater total income if the penalty is not smaller than 25-35%.
0.3	- when the boundary value is equal to 0.1 then both strategies give the same total income; - the value 0.2 gives an advantage to the first strategy; - in restrictions range 0.3 - 0.9 the second strategy gives a greater total income if the penalty is not smaller than 25-35%.
0.4	- the value 0.1 gives an advantage to the first strategy; - in restrictions range 0.2 - 0.9 the second strategy gives a greater total income if the penalty is not smaller than 25-35%.
0.5- 0.8	- in any restrictions the second strategy gives a greater total income if the penalty is not smaller than 25-35%.
0.9	- in restrictions range 0.1-0.2 to make the second strategy more advantageous it is sufficient to establish the penalty equal to 10%; - when the boundary value is equal to 0.3 to make the second strategy more advantageous it is sufficient to establish the penalty equal to 20%; - in restrictions range 0.4-0.6 the penalty should be not smaller than 30%; - in restrictions range 0.7-0.8 the penalty should be not smaller than 40%; - in restrictions range 0.9 the penalty should be not smaller than 50%.

The most convenient and informative way of representation of the spatially determined data are geographic maps. Therefore a proposed method of the dynamic cartography could be useful in processing data with a spatial determination to which belong the environmental-economic systems (Gorstko and Ougolnitsky 1996).

The system state in every moment of time t is described by a vector

$$x(t) = (x_1(t), \dots ,x_n(t)) \tag{3.2.5}$$

where $x_i(t)$ is a value of i-th parameter in the moment t.

A spatial heterogeneity of the system is represented by a partitioning of the territory occupied by the system into cells so as within each cell the state parameters values do not vary. Then the system state in every moment of time t can be represented by a matrix

$$X(t) = \|x_{ri}(t)\| \begin{matrix} R & N \\ \\ r=1 & i=1 \end{matrix} \tag{3.2.6}$$

where $x_{ri}(t)$ is a value of i-th state parameter in r-th cell in the moment t; R is a number of cells in the partitioning; N is a number of state parameters. The vector

$$X_i(t) = (x_{1i}(t), \dots ,x_{Ri}(t)) \tag{3.2.7}$$

represents a thematic map, i.e. a distribution of the values of i-th state among the cells in the moment t.

$$A \text{ matrix } X(0) = \|x_{ri}(0)\| \begin{matrix} R & N \\ \\ r=1 & i=1 \end{matrix}$$

is an initial modeling database; matrices X(t) when $t=-T_1,\dots,-2,-1$ are spatial-temporal series of the available data; matrices X(t) when $t=1,2,\dots,T$ can be used for storing of the forecasting data on the period T. This approach permits to establish a one-to-one correspondence between a dynamic relational database and a dynamic set of thematic maps (Figure 3.2.4).

For computer building of the thematic maps the following scaling procedure is convenient: a range of admissible values $[x_i^{min} , x_i^{max}]$ for each parameter $i=1,\dots,N$ (Figure 3.2.4a) is subdivided on the segments of equal length Δ_i to which a certain intensiveness of the map coloring corresponds:

$$[x_i^{min} , x_i^{min} + \Delta_i] \rightarrow \text{intensiveness 1}$$
$$[x_i^{min} + \Delta_i , x_i^{min} + 2\Delta_i] \rightarrow \text{intensiveness 2}$$
$$\dots$$
$$[x_i^{max} -\Delta_i , x_i^{max}] \rightarrow \text{intensiveness } (x_i^{max}-x_i^{min})/\Delta_i.$$

From three to five grades of intensiveness are sufficient for research objectives and permit to build monochrome thematic maps (Figure 3.2.4b).

	Parameter 1	Parameter 2	...	Parameter N
1	x_{11}	x_{12}	...	x_{1N}
2	x_{21}	x_{22}	...	x_{2N}
...	...	...	...	...
R	x_{R1}	x_{R2}	...	x_{RN}

a

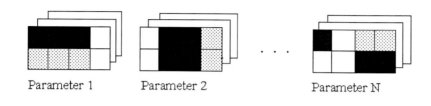

b

Figure 3.2.4. Correspondence between a dynamic relational database (a) and a dynamic set of thematic maps (b) of the system; static snapshots for a moment t=t* are shown.

3.3. SPECIFIC MODELS OF THE SUSTAINABLE MANAGEMENT OF ENVIRONMENTAL-ECONOMIC SYSTEMS

Based on the general methodology of sustainable management of environmental-economic systems a number of specific models of the forest resource use and recreation was built, implemented, and analyzed.

Let's consider a model of the forest resource use which corresponds to the general model described in Paragraph 3.2. Two variants of the solution are proposed: a static one which permits to find an analytical form of solution, and a dynamic one in which the model is analyzed by the computer simulation (Ougolnitsky et al. 2000; Dubrov and Ougolnitsky 2001).

One of the principal features of forest ecosystems which complicate their modeling is a very long time of forest reproduction (50-120 years). This peculiarity witnesses for the usage of methodology of sustainable management of environmental-economic systems.

A forest land is considered as a set of the environmental-economic sections which contain elementary forest valuation cells homogeneous both in biological and in economic aspect. The biological homogeneity is ensured by including to each section the cells of forest land with one main species and one type of natural conditions. The economic homogeneity is ensured by using the same rules of forest resource use within the section. Age of the forest and methods of cutting and transportation are used as the criteria of classification. Thus, each section is a totality of the cells of forest land which are characterized by the same natural conditions, one main species, the same age and methods of cutting and transportation.

A state vector of the forest resource use system has the form

$$\Omega^t = (\{x_i^t\}_{i=1..I}, \{y_j^t\}_{j=1..J}, \{z_i^t\}_{i=1..I}) \qquad (3.3.1)$$

where $\{x_i^t\}_{i=1..I}$ is a distribution of the forest resource by species and by age groups for each species on the modeling step t; y_j^t – a quantity of wood of the certain species, age, and quality (denoted by an index j) in the end of the step t; z_i^t – a degree of damage by cutting and transportation of i-th species of forest resource in the end of the step t; I – a number of sections; J – a number of products (wood sorts).

A discrete model with the step t=10 years is considered. Its main blocks are the following.

Dynamics of the forest resource:

$$x_i^{t+1} = x_i^t + f_i(x_1^t, \ldots, x_I^t) - \mu_i^{t+1} x_i^t, \qquad i=1..I; \tag{3.3.2}$$

$$f_i(x_1^t, \ldots, x_I^t) = \frac{\sum_{gv=1}^{I} k_{gv,i} * x_{gv}^t}{},$$

where $k_{gv,i}$ are coefficients of transition from the age group g_v to i-th age group for $g_v < i$ and from i-th group to g_v-th one for $g_v > i$; μ_i^{t+1} – a part of i-th forest resource (of the same main species, age, and natural conditions) used on the step t.

Wood production:

$$y_j^{t+1} = y_j^t + \varphi_j(r_1^{t+1}, \ldots, r_I^{t+1}, z_j^{t+1}), \quad r_i^{t+1} = \mu_i^{t+1} x_i^{t+1}, \quad j=1..J. \tag{3.3.3}$$

Dynamics of the degree of wood damage:

$$z_i^{t+1} = z_i^t + \pi_i(z_1^{t+1}, \ldots, z_I^{t+1}, \tau_1^{t+1}, \ldots, \tau_I^{t+1}) - h_i(z_i^t) \tag{3.3.4}$$

where τ_i is a technology of extraction of i-th resource (cutting) on the step t.

Operators of transform:

$$F = (\{f_i\}_{i=1..I}, \{\varphi_j\}_{j=1..J}, \{\pi_i\}_{i=1..I}); \tag{3.3.5}$$

where f_i is a model of the natural dynamics of i-th forest resource;

φ_j is a production function for j-th product (wood);

π_i is a model of the forest resource damage as a result of used technologies of cutting and transportation;

h_i is a model of the natural reproduction of the forest resource after the damage.

A diagram of the hierarchically controlled forest resource use system is shown in Figure 3.3.1.

The Leader's (forest land owner) goal is to ensure the sustainable development of the forest ecosystem on the whole long-term period of its usage. The Follower's (forest land leaseholder) goal is to maximize her income from sale of wood cut in the leased forest land.

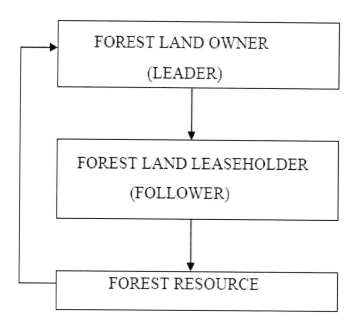

Figure 3.3.1. A diagram of the hierarchically controlled forest resource use system.

Financial balance:

$$G_L^{t+1} = G_L^t + \sum_{i=1}^{I} a_i^{t+1}(\mu_i^{t+1}) p1_i^{t+1} \mu_i^{t+1} x_i^{t+1} + \sum_{j=1}^{J} b_j^{t+1}(z_j^{t+1}) p2_j^{t+1} y_j^{t+1} + \sum_{i=1}^{I} c_i^{t+1} \chi^{t+1} p3_i^{t+1} z_i^{t+1} - M\rho(\Omega^{t+1}, \Omega^*)$$

(3.3.6)

$$G_F^{t+1} = G_F^t + \sum_{i=1}^{I} a_i^{t+1}(\mu_i^{t+1})(1-p1_i^{t+1})\mu_i^{t+1} x_i^{t+1} + \sum_{j=1}^{J} b_j^{t+1}(z_j^{t+1})(1-p2_j^{t+1}) y_j^{t+1} - \sum_{i=1}^{I} c_i^{t+1} \chi^{t+1} p3_i^{t+1} z_i^{t+1} -$$

$$- \sum_{i=1}^{I} w_i^{t+1}(v_i^{t+1})$$

(3.3.7)

Here G_L^t, G_F^t are quantities of income of the Leader and the Follower on the step t respectively;

$$a_i^{t+1}(\mu_i^{t+1}) = [a1_i^{t+1} - a2_i^{t+1}(\mu_i^{t+1})]\chi^{t+1};$$

(3.3.8)

$$b_j^{t+1}(\tau_j^{t+1}) = [b1_j^{t+1}(z_j^{t+1}) - b2_j^{t+1}]\chi^{t+1};$$

(3.3.9)

$a1_i^{t+1}$ is a price of the unit of i-th resource (wood) on the step t+1;

$a2_i^{t+1}(\mu_i^{t+1})$ – a cost price of cutting and transportation of the unit of i-th resource (wood) in consideration of the volume of cutting on the step t+1;

$b1_j^{t+1}(z_j^{t+1})$ – a price of the unit of j-th product (wood) in consideration of its damage on the step t+1;

$b2_j^{t+1}$ – a cost price of production of the unit of j-th product (wood) on the step t+1;

c_i^{t+1} – a "price" for the damage of the unit of wood of i-th section on the step t+1;

χ^{t+1} – a discount factor on the step t+1;

w_i^{t+1} – expenditures for the care cutting in i-th section on the step t+1.

Leader's vector of controls:

$$v^t = (\{p1_i^t\}_{i=1..I}, \{p2_j^t\}_{j=1..J}, \{p3_i^t\}_{i=1..I}, \{q_i^t\}_{i=1..I}, \{d_i^t\}_{i=1..I}); \qquad (3.3.10)$$

$$0 \leq p1_i^{t+1} \leq 1, \qquad 0 \leq q_i^{t+1} \leq 1, \qquad 0 \leq p2_j^{t+1} \leq 1,$$
$$0 \leq p3_i^{t+1} \leq 1, \qquad 0 \leq q_i^{t+1} \leq 1, \qquad 0 \leq d_i^{t+1} \leq 1, i=1..I, j=1..J, \qquad (3.3.11)$$

where $p1_i^t$ is a tax rate (rental fee) for cutting of i-th resource on the step t;

$\qquad p2_j^t$ – a cost price of production of j-th product (wood) on the step t;

$\qquad p3_i^t$ – a penalty rate for the damage of forest resource in i-th section on the step t;

$\qquad q_i^t$ – a quota of cutting of i-th resource on the step t;

$\qquad d_i^t$ – a quota of damage in i-th section on the step t.

Follower's vector of controls:

$$u^t = (\{\mu_i^t\}_{i=1..I}, \{\tau_i\}_{i=1..I}, \{v_i^t\}_{i=1..I}); \qquad (3.3.12)$$

$$0 \leq \mu_i^{t+1} \leq q_i^{t+1}, \tau_i^{t+1} \in \{\tau_{i1},...,\tau_{is}\}, \qquad 0 \leq v_i^{t+1} \leq 1, i=1..I; \qquad (3.3.13)$$

where μ_i^t is a part of i-th resource cut on the step t;

$\qquad \tau_i^t$ – a cutting technology for i-th resource on the step t;

$\qquad \{\tau_{i1},...,\tau_{is}\}$ – a set of admissible technologies;

$\qquad v_i^t$ – a part of care cuttings in i-th section on the step t.

Conditions of homeostasis:

$$\Omega^* = X^* \times Y^* \times Z^* \qquad (3.3.14)$$

- a domain of homeostasis of the forest ecosystem;

$$X^* = \prod_{i=1}^{I} [x_i^*, \infty], \qquad (3.3.15)$$

where x_i^* is a critical value of i-th resource (necessary to provide the biological diversity);

$$Y^* = \prod_{j=1}^{J} [y_j^*, \infty], \qquad (3.3.16)$$

where y_j^* is a critical value of j-th product (necessary to provide the basic economic needs);

$$Z^* = \prod_{i=1}^{I} \left[0, z_i^*\right],$$ (3.3.17)

where z_i^* is a maximum allowable amount of damage of the forest resource (necessary to provide the environmental safety).

Let's consider the methods of sustainable management in the model.

Compulsion (Administrative Mechanism)

For compulsion the Leader establishes quotas on cutting and damage of the forest resource. The control variables of compulsion are

$$0 \le q_i^{t+1} \le 1, 0 \le d_i^{t+1} \le 1, i=1,\dots,I.$$

Impulsion (Economic Mechanism)

For compulsion the Leader establishes tax rates (rental fees) and penalty rates for damage. The control variables of impulsion are

$$0 \le p1_i^{t+1} \le 1, 0 \le p2_j^{t+1} \le 1, 0 \le p3_i^{t+1} \le 1, i=1..I, j=1,\dots,J.$$

Compulsion-Impulsion (Administrative and Economic Mechanism)
Impulsion-Compulsion (Economic and Administrative Mechanism)

These two methods of hierarchical management are combined ones. Their distinction is that one of the methods is the principal one, the other is the auxiliary one. In the method of compulsion-impulsion the principal method of management is an administrative one and an economic method is the auxiliary one, in the method of impulsion-compulsion – vice versa.

Conviction (Cooperative Mechanism)

This method means the voluntary cooperation of a forest land owner and an environmentally minded leaseholder which is oriented to the rational forest resource use with an obligatory ensuring of the homeostatic conditions.

All methods of hierarchical management besides the conviction could be added by the Leader's manipulation and/or the Follower's counter-game.

It is supposed in the model that the Follower leases a set of the forest land cells for a long-time period and solves a problem of maximization of her income for the period. The Leader strives for the minimization of the deviations of a present state of the forest resource from the domain of homeostasis.

Let's consider the solutions of the problem (3.3.6)-(3.3.17) received by computer simulation experiments with the model implemented by means of the DELPHI visual shell. A period of modeling is equal to 100 steps, and the initial age and quantity of the forest resource are the same for all cells. The scenario method was used. The scenario is optimal for the Leader if she can ensure the conditions of homeostatic development of the forest ecosystem for the whole period of modeling.

Let's consider in more details the mechanism of impulsion-compulsion (at first the Leader uses rental fees, then quotas, and if the quotas are exceeded than a penalty is charged). The greatest fee is used for the youngest forest, and then it decreases.

The First Variant of The Leader Penalty Function

For scenarios 1-7 the Leader penalty function has two grades: a complete absence of the forest resource and a deviation from the homeostatic state. The penalty is proportional to the deviation.

Scenario 1: on each step the Follower realizes a cutting in one cell. After 25 steps the forest reproduces and the cutting repeats in the same sequence of cells. After number of steps equal to the number of cells the forest ecosystem gets into the homeostatic domain but the total income of the Follower is not the biggest among the scenarios 1-7.

Scenario 2: on each step the Follower realizes a cutting in two cells. After 12 steps the forest is not reproduced, the age is small and the wood has no economic value. Thus, the Follower continues a cutting only after several steps of waiting. The cutting repeats in the same sequence of cells. The financial estimate of the wood value and the incomes of Leader and Follower in this scenario are higher but a violation of the homeostatic condition is possible.

Scenario 3: on each step the Follower realizes a cutting in three cells. After 9 steps the forest is not reproduced, the age is small and the wood has no economic value. Thus, the Follower continues a cutting only after several steps of waiting as in the previous scenario. The cutting repeats in the same sequence of cells. The financial estimate of the wood value and the income of Leader are greater than in scenarios 1-2, and the income of Follower is greater than in scenario 1 but smaller than in scenario 2. A violation of the homeostatic condition is also possible.

Scenario 4: at first the Follower waits until the wood reaches an economic condition. Then on each step the Follower realizes a cutting in one cell. After 25 steps the forest reproduces and the cutting repeats in the same sequence of cells. After number of steps equal to the number of cells the forest ecosystem gets into the homeostatic domain. The Follower's income and the financial estimate of the wood are low.

Scenario 5: at first the Follower waits until the wood reaches an economic condition. Then on each step the Follower realizes a cutting in three cells. After 9 steps the forest is not reproduced, the age is small and the wood has no economic value. Thus, the Follower continues a cutting only after several steps of waiting as in the previous scenario. The cutting repeats in the same sequence of cells. The Follower's income is high but the financial estimate of the wood is low and a violation of the homeostatic condition is possible again.

Scenario 6: at first the Follower waits until the wood reaches an economic condition. Then on each step the Follower realizes a cutting in two cells. After 13 steps the forest is not reproduced, the age is small and the wood has no economic value. Thus, the Follower continues a cutting only after several steps of waiting as in the previous scenario. The cutting repeats in the same sequence of cells. The Follower's income is high but the financial estimate of the wood is very low and a violation of the homeostatic condition is observed more often than in the previous scenarios.

Scenario 7: at first the Follower waits until the wood reaches an economic condition. The cutting is realized periodically in a half of the cells. Between two cuttings the Follower is waiting. Then the cutting repeats in the same sequence of cells. The Follower's income is

Models of Sustainable Management 109

mean on the set of scenarios. The financial estimate of the wood is low and violations of the homeostatic condition are observed often.

The resulting data are shown in Table 3.3.1 (financial estimates are conditional).

Table 3.3.1. Results of the computer simulation experiments

Scenarios	The financial estimate of the wood ($)	The Leader's income ($)	The Follower's income ($)	Violation of the condition of homeostasis
1	178701.8	970454.6	69745.9	no
2	198305.8	1470547.4	717917.6	yes
3	296252.6	1395426.8	792173.3	yes
4	178701.8	861573.4	10304.9	no
5	530752.9	1415037.9	648927.2	yes
6	25029.4	1394384.2	711777.5	yes
7	121385.8	1012038.4	734014.1	yes

The Second Variant of the Leader Penalty Function

Now the penalty function has four grades: a complete absence of the forest resource and three values of deviation from the homeostatic state. The penalty is proportional to the deviation. The Follower uses the same strategies as in the previous scenarios 1-7. Two new scenarios are also considered.

Scenario 8: on each step the Follower realizes a cutting in one cell. After 25 steps the forest reproduces and the cutting repeats in the same sequence of cells. After number of steps equal to the number of cells the forest ecosystem gets into the homeostatic domain, and the system dynamics is similar to the scenario 1.

Scenario 9: on each step the Follower realizes a cutting in two cells. After 12 steps the forest is not reproduced, the age is small and the wood has no economic value. Thus, the Follower continues a cutting only after several steps of waiting. The cutting repeats in the same sequence of cells. The financial estimate of the wood value and the income of Leader are greater than in scenario 8 but smaller than in scenario 2. The income of Follower is greater than in scenario 2, violations of the condition of homeostasis are possible.

The comparative results are shown in Tables 3.3.2 and 3.3.3 (financial estimates are conditional).

Table 3.3.2. Comparative results for scenarios 8 and 9

Scenarios	The financial estimate of the wood ($)	The Leader's income ($)	The Follower's income ($)	Violation of the condition of homeostasis
8	178701.8	969454.6	10767.7	no
9	198305.8	1267295.1	792889.2	yes

Table 3.3.3. Comparative results for scenarios 2 and 9

Scenarios	The financial estimate of the wood ($)	The Leader's income ($)	The Follower's income ($)	Violation of the condition of homeostasis
2	198305.8	1470547.4	717917.6	yes
9	198305.8	1267295.1	792889.2	yes

In the case of disinterested Leader the scenarios 2 and 9 are equivalent. If the Leader maximizes her income then the scenario 9 is preferable for her. If the Follower is interested then the second variant of the penalty function is preferable for her. But in both variants a violation of the condition of homeostasis is possible therefore the problem of sustainable management could have no solution.

The Third Variant of the Leader Penalty Function

Now the penalty function has three grades: a complete absence of the forest resource and two values of deviation from the homeostatic state. The penalties are increased for big deviations and canceled for small ones.

Scenario 10: on each step the Follower realizes a cutting in one or two cells. In the full modeling cycle the forest reproduces completely. The cutting repeats in the same sequence of cells. The forest ecosystem quite quickly gets to the domain of homeostasis and practically does not quit it. The Follower's income is positive on each step, and the incomes of both players are the highest for the considered scenarios (Table 3.3.4).

Table 3.3.4. Comparative analysis of the Follower's optimal strategies

Scenarios	Minimal value of the forest resource ($)	Maximal value of the forest resource ($)	The Leader's income ($)	The Follower's income ($)	Violation of the condition of homeostasis
2	0	198305.8	1470547.4	717917.6	yes
9	0	198305.8	1267295.1	792889.2	yes
10	100000	200000.0	1629344.3	475226.6	no

Thus, the mechanisms of compulsion-impulsion and impulsion-compulsion permit to solve the problem of sustainable management of a forest resource use system.

Now let's consider another variant of formulation and solution of the problem of sustainable management of a forest resource use system (Ougolnitsky et al. 2000).

A combined static and dynamic formulation of the problem of sustainable management of a forest resource use system is considered. The relations between agents are shown in Figure 3.3.1. The Leader's (forest land owner) goal is to ensure the sustainable development of the forest ecosystem on the whole long-term period of its usage, i.e. she solves a dynamic control problem. The Follower's (forest land leaseholder) goal is to maximize her income from sale of wood cut in the leased forest land with restrictions on forest resource use on one step (a static model).

Assume $\forall t \in [0, T-1]$ the following optimization problem is solved:

$$\sum_{i=1}^{n} c_i(t) u_i(t) \to \max \tag{3.3.18}$$

$$\sum_{i=1}^{N} a_{ij}(t) u_i(t) \le b_j(t) + v_j(t) \quad \forall j \in [1; m] \tag{3.3.19}$$

$$u_i(t) \ge 0 \quad \forall i \in [1; n] \tag{3.3.20}$$

where $c_i(t)$ is a price of wood in the cell i in the year t;

$u_i(t)$ is a quantity of the used wood in the cell i in the year t;

$b_j(t)$ is a resource limitation in the year t;

$v_j(t)$ is an additional quantity of the resource j apportioned by the Leader in the year t;

i is a number of cell; j is a number of resource.

Dynamics of the resource is described by the following controlled dynamic system:

$$x_i(t+1) = x_i(t)\big(1 + \alpha_i(t)\big) - u_i(t)$$

$$x_i(0) = x_{i0} \ge x_i \quad \forall i \in [1; n] \quad \forall t \in [0; T-1] \tag{3.3.21}$$

The homeostatic condition has the form

$$\sum_{i=1}^{n} x_i(t) \ge x_i \quad \forall i \in [1; n] \quad \forall t \in [1; T] \tag{3.3.22}$$

Denote

$$v = \{v_j(t) \quad \forall j \in [1; m] \quad \forall t \in [0; T-1]\}$$

and define the following problem of optimization by v :

$$\begin{cases} J_v\big(v(t),t\big) \to \max \\ v(t) \in V(t) \end{cases}$$

(3.3.23)

Then the problem of hierarchical optimization if formulated as follows. On each step t supposing the optimal basis solution of the problem ((3.3.18)-(3.3.20)) when v = 0 is known it is required to find v(t) which satisfies the following objectives:

Objective I (the main one): the optimal basis solution of the problem ((3.3.18)-(3.3.20)) should satisfy the conditions ((3.3.21), (3.3.22));

Objective II (the auxiliary one): v(t) should be optimal in the sense (3.3.23).

For the solution an adaptive algorithm is used, i.e. the Follower proposes her strategy on each step then the Leader corrects her plan. Suppose that the following conditions are satisfied:

1) The Follower solves a linear optimization problem on the set of her admissible impacts to the CDS.
2) The Leader has an effect to the right part of the linear restrictions of the Follower.
3) The Leader can be either disinterested or she can solve an optimization problem on the set of her admissible impacts to the Follower on a present step.
4) The state of CDS on a next step depends linearly on the Follower's control.
5) The state of admissible states of the CDS is a linear polyhedron.

In this case to ensure the main objective of the Leader on each next step her control impact to the Follower on the previous step should satisfy linear restrictions which can be found in an explicit form.

Reduce the problem ((3.3.18)-(3.3.20)) to the canonical form. Assume

$$u(t) = \left\{ u_i(t) \quad \forall i \in [1;n] \quad u'_j(t) \quad \forall j \in [1;m] \right\}$$

Here $u'_j(t)$ are variables introduced for transforming (3.3.19) into the equalities;

$$c(t) = \left\{ c_i\big(t,\tau(t)\big) \quad \forall i \in [1;n]; 0; 0; \ldots 0 \right\}$$

$$b(t) = \left\{ b_j(t) \quad \forall j \in [1;m] \right\}$$

$$a^{(j)}(t) = \left\{ a_{ij}(t) \quad \forall i \in [1;n]; e^{(j)} \right\} \quad \forall j \in [1;m]$$

$$A(t) = \begin{pmatrix} a^{(1)}(t) \\ a^{(2)}(t) \\ \dots \\ a^{(m)}(t) \end{pmatrix}$$

Then the problem ((3.3.18)-(3.3.20)) can be written as:

$$\begin{cases} \left(c^t; u^t\right) \to \max & (3.3.24) \\ A^t u^t = b^t + v^t & (3.3.25) \\ u^t \geq 0 & (3.3.26) \end{cases}$$

Thus, the following actions are realized on each step t:

1) The Follower's problem (3.3.24)-(3.3.26) without consideration of the Leader's impact (v^t=0) is solved. The values u^t(0), G^t, and I^t_B are found.

2) Based on the known value x^t the values $\bar{u}^t$ and S^t are found.

3) Taking into consideration the Leader's optimization problem her control impact v^t is chosen.

4) The solution of the Follower's problem is found $(u^t)v^t$ where v^t is known.

5) Based on the known solution $(u^t)v^t$ the value of state of the CDS x^{t+1} on the next step is calculated.

Thus, the problem of sustainable management of a forest resource use system can be solved by means of the adaptive algorithm which combines the abilities of analytical optimization methods (linear optimization) and simulation modeling.

Now let's consider the possibilities of application of the methodology of computer simulation modeling of the hierarchically controlled environmental-economic systems on the example of a marine resort (Ougolnitsky 1999). A conceptual model of a resort as the HCES, its mathematical formalization based on the queuing theory, and the mechanisms of hierarchical management are described.

A recreational activity is the human activity in the leisure time aimed to the recovery of her physical and mental power, rest, and personal development. A complex totality of phenomena connected with the recreational activity should be considered as a system. The diagram of a recreational system is shown in Figure 3.3.2.

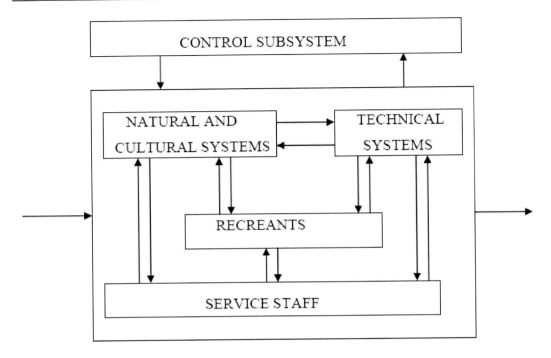

Figure 3.3.2. The diagram of a recreational system.

The recreational activity has a number of functions:

- medical (medical treatment, sanitation, recovery of health);
- social and cultural (traveling, sightseeing);
- economic (business, employment, labor resource reproduction).

The recreational activity is characterized by such properties as diversity, combination, and cyclic recurrence. It is possible to select the following recreational cycles:

- medical (climatic, balneological ones);
- sanitary (swimming, jogging ones);
- sporting (tourist, alpinist ones);
- cognitive (natural, cultural and historical ones).

Recreational cycles form a base for the organization of recreational systems.

An increase of the input recreant flow results in excessive loads on the natural and cultural systems and to the respective loss of their recreational properties. The environmental protection in a recreational system is not an optional action but one of the principal ways of conservation of the recreational functions.

Recreants take the central place in any recreational system. In this connection it is logical to consider a recreational system as the queuing system. A role of service channels is played by the objects of recreational specialization and infrastructure (medical rooms, playgrounds, shops, cafes and restaurants, hotels, and so on) and natural and cultural-historical objects (beaches, valleys, caves, museums, galleries, and others). The channels provide a possibility of the organization of different recreational cycles. The arrival of recreants is treated as an input claim flow in the queuing system.

It is natural to subdivide an annual cycle of the recreational activity for a marine resort on two seasons: summer (from July to September, 12 weeks), and non-summer (other months, 40 weeks) with evident distinctions. Besides, for consideration a heterogeneity of the recreational systems and recreant flows a subdivision on service categories is introduced. Namely, all objects of recreational specialization and infrastructure, as well as natural and cultural-historical objects are prescribed to a service category which differs from others by the quality, time, and price of the service. The examples are price categories of restaurants and cafes, categories ("stars") of hotels, importance of memorial places (global, regional, local) and so on. The recreants are subdivided respectively, i.e. it is supposed that during the season each recreant is served only by the channels of a certain category.

Inside each category the service channels are grouped in service blocks which correspond to the branches of recreational specialization and infrastructure and to the types of natural and cultural-historical objects. The channels inside each block are assumed to be homogeneous.

From the point of view of the queuing theory the principal characteristic of a service channel is a random variable – the service time for one claim in the channel. The type and parameters of distribution of the random variable are assumed to be the same for all channels of a block (with fixed season and service category). The principal characteristic of the recreant flow from the point of view of the queuing theory is also a random variable, namely an interval of time between two consequent service claims. The type and parameters of distribution of the random variable are assumed to be the same for each service block.

The conceptual diagram of a queuing system for the described propositions is shown in Figure 3.3.3.

A recreational system needs investments which are compensated after a period of exploitation. For evaluation of the compensation period and other characteristics of functioning of the resort it is necessary to get a forecast of the quantity of recreants who will visit the resort in a considered period in future. The following hypotheses are used for the evaluation. The number of recreants depends on certain parameters of attractiveness of the resort. Assume that there are two factors of the resort attractiveness: service time and environmental quality. It is exactly a hypothesis that is typical for the applied system analysis and needs validation within the research. Another hypotheses which take into consideration another factors of attractiveness or neglect the factors proposed above are also possible but the very fact of dependence of the potential number of recreants on some factors of resort attractiveness is inalterable.

An environmental quality (the quality of marine ecosystem and the shore in this case) is undoubtedly one of the principal factors of attractiveness. From the other side, recreation has an important effect to the ecosystem and can result in the recreational digression. A conceptual model of the recreational environmental impact is shown in Figure 3.3.5.

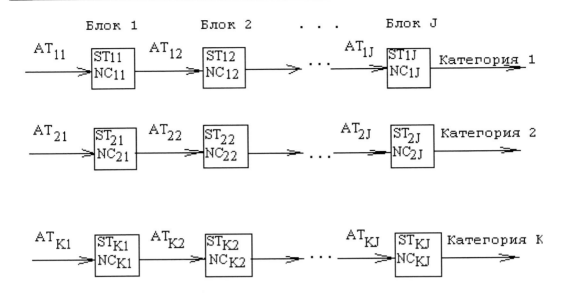

Figure 3.3.3. The conceptual diagram of a marine resort as a queuing system: K is a number of service categories; J is a number of service blocks; AT_{kj} – an expectation of the period of time between two sequential service claims in j-th block of k-th category; ST_{kj} - an expectation of the service time for one claim in j-th block of k-th category; NC_{kj} – a number of service channels in j-th block of k-th category. The quantities AT_{kj}, ST_{kj}, NC_{kj} can differ from each other for different recreational seasons; k=1,...,K; j=1,...,J.

The concept of queuing system forms a base for building of the general model of a marine resort the diagram of which is represented in Figure 3.3.4.

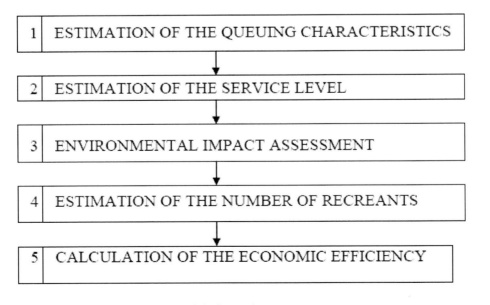

Figure 3.3.4. The diagram of the general model of a marine resort.

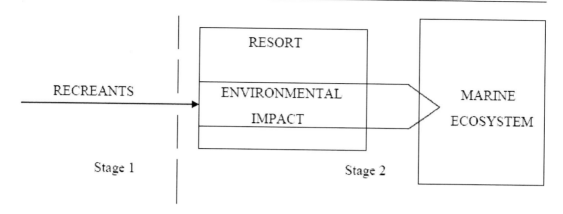

Figure 3.3.5. Two-stage conceptual model of the recreational environmental impact.

The stage 1 corresponds to the arrival of recreants to the resort, or to the input claim flow for the queuing system model. The stage 2 describes the environmental impact of the recreants together with the resort technical systems on the marine ecosystem.

The principal factors of the recreational environmental impact on the marine ecosystem are quantitative and qualitative change of the water flow from the territory of resort. Assume that the quality of marine ecosystem is determined by the concentrations of pollutants in the marine water. The concentrations are determined by the output of pollutants from the recreants and technical systems with consideration of the transformation of pollutants in marine water and its ability to self-refinement. Therefore the model represented in Fig 3.3.5 can be specified as shown in Figure 3.3.6.

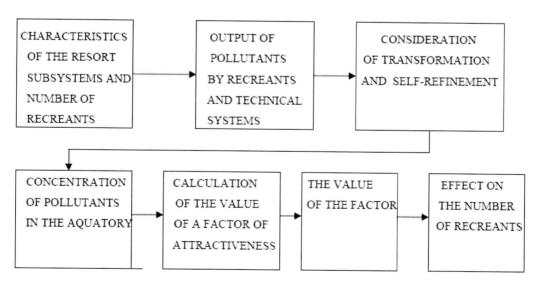

Figure 3.3.6. An algorithm of determination of the environmental quality as a factor of attractiveness of a resort.

The considerations made above determine a structure of the general model of a marine resort represented by the diagram in Figure 3.3.4. The blocks 1-3 are dedicated to the calculation of the factors of attractiveness using the queuing theory methods and the conceptual model of recreational environmental impact. Values of the factors of attractiveness permit to evaluate a number of the recreant flow according to the accepted hypothesis (block 4). At last, the found characteristics permit to calculate a balance of the recreational activity and an economic efficiency of the resort (block 5).

From the point of view of the concept of sustainable management the role of HCES is played by a marine ecosystem, the role of Follower by a recreation system (its owner and top management), and the role of Leader by an environmental protection agency. The Follower control variables are parameters of the recreational system (volumes of building of the new recreational objects) and costs of pollution control. The Leader control variables are penalties for pollution and costs of centralized pollution removal. The condition of environmental imperative is described in terms of maximal allowable concentration of the pollutants.

Go on to the mathematical formalization of the conceptual model. The input data for the block 1 "Estimation of the queuing characteristics" is a set of the values of time intervals between sequential service claims (i.e. arrivals of recreants) and the values of service time in j-th block of k-th category (for all blocks j=1,...,J and categories k=1,...,K).

Accordingly to the accepted conceptual hypothesis the times are assumed to be random variables with known characteristics of distribution. An assumption about the law of distribution is the hypothesis of the next level (a hypothesis of formalization), and the calculation of numerical values of the distribution parameters is an object of the identification problem. Let's assume as an example of the hypothesis of formalization that both a random variable describing the interval between sequential service claims and a random variable describing service time are distributed by an exponential law. Then the complete characteristics of distribution for both quantities are their expectations AT_{kj} and ST_{kj} respectively (Figure 3.3.3).

It should be noticed that the assumption about the exponential type of distribution is a hypothesis and not an obligatory requirement. It is possible to build a simulation model of the queuing system in assumption of the presence of more complicated laws of distribution of the considered random variables. A new hypothesis could be more adequate but in the same time it would require more complete data about several distribution parameters. This reasoning remains valid for any accepted hypothesis.

Any service block consists of a set of objects of the same type which can be treated as a multi-channel one-phase queuing system. Thus, a food block includes restaurants and cafes in which waiters are service channels; a rental block includes rental points in which managers are channels, and so on. That's why it is sufficient to consider a model of a separate service object (Figure 3.3.7).

A claim arriving to the system can be served by any free channel after that it leaves the system. If there are no free channels then the claim stays in queue and waits for the service. From the other side, if a channel becomes free before a claim arrives to the system then a down time arises when the service staff and equipment are idle and wait for a claim.

For calculation of the expectation AT_j of the time interval between sequential service claims the following assumptions are used. At the moment of beginning of the calculations by the queuing system model a number of recreants NN (they should visit all blocks) and a number VR_j of visits by one recreant for the objects of block j during a period of 10 days are known.

Models of Sustainable Management

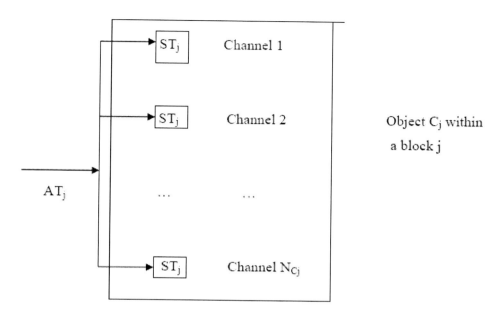

Figure 3.3.7. Representation of the service object as a multi-channel system.

Therefore a total number of visits (claims) for the block j for 10 days is equal to NN∗VR$_j$, and a number of visits for one object is equal to NN∗VR$_j$/CC$_j$ where CC$_j$ is a number of working objects in the block (it is also known). Thus the mathematical expectation AT$_j$ (in minutes) can be calculated by the formula

$$AT_j = \frac{TC \times CC_j}{NN \times VR_j} \qquad (3.3.27)$$

where TC is the number of minutes in 10 days. The formula (3.3.27) should be used with consideration of the season and service category. The values of expectations of service time ST$_j$ are assumed to be the same for all objects in a block and are estimated by experts.

Output variables in the model are mean for a block waiting time of a claim WT$_{kj}$ and mean idle time of a channel IDT$_{kj}$ (the times are supposed to be random) which are calculated by averaging by objects for all blocks j=1,...,J and categories k=1,...,K (block 2). A flow chart of the algorithm of calculation WT$_{kj}$ and IDT$_{kj}$ when AT$_{kj}$ and ST$_{kj}$ are known is proposed in the book (Naylor 1971).

Block 3 "Environmental impact assessment" realizes a conceptual diagram shown in Figure 3.3.6. Denote i=1,...,P – an index of the pollutant; IMP$_{ijk}$(τ) – a total output of i-th pollutant by j-th service block of k-th category in the moment of time τ; POL$_i$(θ) – a concentration of i-th pollutant in the aquatory in the moment θ; PDK$_i$ – a maximum allowable concentration of i-th pollutant in water; SL$_i$ – a minimal concentration of i-th pollutant which is still harmful for the ecosystem.

Then a value of the environmental quality as a factor of attractiveness ENV is calculated by the general formula

$$
\begin{cases}
0, & FACT \le FACT_1, \\[2mm]
FF = \dfrac{FACT\text{-}FACT_1}{FACT_2\text{-}FACT_1}, & FACT_1 < FACT < FACT_2, \\[2mm]
1, & FACT \ge FACT_2,
\end{cases}
\tag{3.3.28}
$$

where $ENV = 10(1\text{-}FF)$, $FACT = POL_i$, $FACT_1 = SL_i$, $FACT_2 = PDK_i$. The general formula (3.3.28) is also used for modeling of impact of different factors in the resort model.

For transition from the values of output $IMP_{ijk}(\tau)$ to the values of concentrations $POL_i(\theta)$ the following model is used (Loucks et al. 1981):

$$
c(t+\Delta t) = c(t) + F1/V - (Q/V + F2)c(t)
\tag{3.3.29}
$$

where $c(t)$ – a concentration of the pollutant in the aquatory in the moment t; V – a volume of the aquatory; Q – a constant water flow; $F1$ – a quantity of output of the pollutant; $F2$ – a part of its degradation and sedimentation.

The model (3.3.29) is used separately for all considered pollutants POL_i in assumption of the absence of their interaction. As $F1$ the total output

$$
\sum_{\tau=t}^{t+1} \sum_{j=1}^{J} \sum_{k=1}^{K} IMP_{ijk}(\tau),
$$

is taken, and as Q a sewage from all technical systems of the resort.

For estimation of the number of recreants (block 4) is used the same approach as in the blocks 2 and 3. Namely, a number of recreants in s-the season of the year t is predicted by the formula

$$
N_s(t) = N_s^{min} + k_{ENV} * f_{ENV}(t) + k_{SERV} * f_{SERV}(t)
\tag{3.3.30}
$$

where N_s^{min} is an expert estimation of the lower value of the number of recreants in season s;

$f_{ENV}(t)$, $f_{SERV}(t)$ are functions of impact of the environmental quality and service time respectively in the year t; k_{ENV}, k_{SERV} are relative weight coefficients of these factors of attractiveness;

$$
k_{ENV} + k_{SERV} = N_s^{max} - N_s^{min}
$$

where N_s^{max} is an expert estimation of the upper value of the number of recreants in season s.

The values of functions f_{ENV}, f_{SERV} monotonically increase from 0 (the worst value of the factor) to 1 (the best value). Thus, if all factors of attractiveness take their ideal values then the number of recreants reaches its maximal value N_s^{max}, and if all factors take their worst values then the number is equal to the minimal value N_s^{min}. The formula (3.3.30) is used separately for all K service categories.

An economic efficiency of functioning of the recreational system during a considered period (block 5) is calculated by the formula

$$E_0 = (1\text{-TAX}) \sum_{t=1}^{T} E(t) = (1\text{-TAX}) \sum_{t=1}^{T} [INC(t)\text{-}EXP(t)] \qquad (3.3.31)$$

where E_0 is a net profit for the period T; $E(t)$ – a total profit in the year t; TAX – a tax rate; $INC(t)$, $EXP(t)$ – total incomes and costs in the year t respectively. In turn

$$INC(t) = \sum_{k=1}^{K} \sum_{j=1}^{J} \sum_{s=1}^{S} PR_{jks} * V_{jks} * N_{ks}(t) * C_{jks}(t), \qquad (3.3.32)$$

where $N_{ks}(t)$ – a number of recreants of k-th category visiting the resort in s-th season of the year t; $C_{jks}(t)$ a number of working objects of j-th block of the k-th category in the year t; PR_{jks} a price of one visit of j-th block of k-th category in s-th season; V_{jks} a number of visits by one recreant of j-th block of k-th category in s-th season.

The costs are calculated by the formula

$$EXP(t) = \sum_{k=1}^{K} \sum_{j=1}^{J} [NB_{jk}*D_{jk}(t)+(SAL_{jk}+MNT_{jk})]C_{jk}(t)+OTH(t) \qquad (3.3.33)$$

where NB_{jk} is a total cost of the construction of one object of j-th block of k-th category; $D_{jk}(t)$ – a number of introduced objects of j-th block of k-th category in the year t; SAL_{jk} – a total salary of the personnel of one object of j-th block of k-th category; MNT_{jk} – a cost of the annual maintenance of one object of the j-th block of k-th category; $C_{jk}(t)$ – a number of working objects of j-th block of k-th category in the year t; $OTH(t)$ – an amount of other expenditures in the year t which is equal to

$$OTH(t) = INF(t) + ADV(t) + CEN(t) + MIS(t) \qquad (3.3.34)$$

where $INF(t)$ are infrastructure costs; $ADV(t)$ are advertising costs;

$CEN(t)$ are expenditures of the centralized departments of the resort management;

$MIS(t)$ are reserved expenditures in the year t. All cost parameters are calculated in the prices of a base year.

The block of calculation of the economic efficiency can be used in two ways. First, it can be considered as a part of the general resort model (Figure 3.3.4); in this case an input quantity $N(t)$ of the number of recreants is evaluated in the general model by the formula (3.3.30).

Second, the model (3.3.31)-(3.3.34) can work in an autonomous mode; in this case the number of recreants is given by a scenario. Then the model (3.3.31)-(3.3.34) is considered as a simplification of the general resort model. In this case the diagram represented in Figure 3.3.4 is specified in Figure 3.3.5.

Let's describe a data structure for the model. The data can be subdivided into two groups: constants and variables. It is convenient to classify as constants the data elements which do not change for all or at least for many scenarios of simulation.

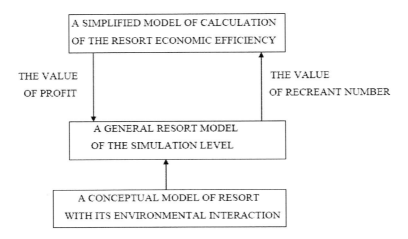

Figure 3.3.5. A concept of simplified models in the research of a resort.

A period of prediction T, a number of service categories K, a number of service blocks J, a number of seasons S etc. are related to this category. Another data are described in the variable section of the program as simple variables or arrays. The values of variables and arrays components can vary from one scenario to another. Specifically, computer simulation experiments aimed to the identification of the empirical parameters are possible.

The most numerous group is formed by the data described as arrays. A dimension of the arrays is different: for example, infrastructural, advertising and other costs depend only on the index of year and can be represented respectively by one-dimensional arrays INF[1..T], ADV[1..T], MIS[1..T]; many data vary in blocks and categories, for example, the salaries, maintenance and construction costs, and are represented by two-dimensional arrays SAL[1..J,1..K], MNT[1..J,1..K], NB[1..J,1..K]; three-dimensional arrays are also possible, such as the array of working objects of j-th block of k-th category in the year t CC[1..T,1..J,1..K], and so on.

How to determine the values of data for input and modeling purposes? The majority of variables in the resort model are the controlled ones, i.e. their values are given by the researcher's discretion. In fact, the data are chosen from an admissible range the initial boundaries of which are determined by physical restrictions: for example, all environmental-economic variables are nonnegative; any specific expenses can not be greater than the whole budget, and so on. In the majority of cases the evident estimates can be essentially specified by means of expert knowledge and common sense. Thus, the prices for recreational facilities are determined by known world standards with small deviations. Possible exceptions can be connected with investigation of an extreme variant, for example, the evaluation of an admissible period of some free services for publicity objectives.

The values of many data can be received on the base of known facts. Thus, the construction costs for all recreational objects are known quite well though some difficulties could remain: the information can be hardly available or be in the form which is not convenient for modeling; but those difficulties are technical.

Some data are not controlled but normative ones, for example, the values of maximal allowable concentration of pollutants. Such values can be found in the respective references. It should be noticed that computer simulation experiments permit to study the values of

Models of Sustainable Management

standards which differ from the actual ones; in this case the results could be used as a base for the change of standards. There are also "pure" control variables the values of which really determine a variant of the system development. For the resort model an example is given by the quantities $DD_{jk}(t)$ of introduction of the new recreational objects in time. A change of the data results in a qualitatively new scenario which corresponds to a specific concept of the resort development.

Let's formulate more specific hypotheses which are necessary for the resort model identification. Assume that the number of categories K=3 (three, four, or five "stars"); the number of seasons S=2 (s=1 - summer; s=2 – the rest of the year); the number of service blocks J=6 (hotels, restaurants, shops, entertainment, sport, medical services); the number of pollutants P=2 (biochemical consumption of oxygen, suspended substances). Some data are given in Tables 3.3.5 - 3.3.8.

Table 3.3.5. Mathematical expectation of service time by blocks and categories (minutes)

	j=1	j=2	j=3	j=4	j=5	j=6
k=3	30	15	5	60	90	30
k=4	15	10	3	60	90	30
k=5	5	5	1	60	90	30

Table 3.3.6. Number of personnel (persons)

	j=1	j=2	j=3	j=4	j=5	j=6
k=3	1	33	2	2	10	2
k=4	100	21	2	7	10	2
k=5	50	15	2	8	10	2

Table 3.3.7. Number of visits of an object by one recreant in 10 days

	j=1	j=2	j=3	j=4	j=5	j=6
k=3	10	40	2	2	20	5
k=4	20	50	3	2	10	10
k=5	30	50	4	3	10	10

Table 3.3.8. Pollution data

	F2	SL (kg/m3)	MAC(kg/m3)	POL[0]
BCO	0.2	0.0003	0.003	0.0003
SS	0.8	0.00015	0.00075	0.00015

According to the accepted concept, a resort is considered as the hierarchically controlled dynamic system which consists of the Leader (an environmental agency), the Follower (a resort management), and the environment (a marine ecosystem). The Follower's control variables are amounts $DD_{jk}(t)$ of introduction of the new recreational objects of j-th block of k-th category in time and a part of sewage removal u(t). In turn, the Leader can charge penalties if the Follower exceeds the normative pollution, and to fix a lower boundary of the pollution removal v(t).

Consider in more details the following mechanism of hierarchical management. The Follower's payoff function has the form

$$J_u(t) = G(C(t) + D(t)) - a_u u(t)/(1-u(t)) \rightarrow \max \qquad (3.3.35)$$

where C(t) is a number of working objects in the year t; D(t) – a number of objects introducing in the year t; $G(C(t)+D(t))$ – an income function (see (3.3.32)); $a_u u(t)/(1-u(t))$ – a function of removal costs. The Follower chooses the part of pollution removal from the range

$$0 \leq v(t) \leq u(t) \leq u_{max} < 1$$

where the lower boundary v(t) is fixed by the Leader using the rule

$$v(t) = \begin{cases} 0 \, , c(t) \leq MAC, \\ (c(t)-MAC)/c(t) \, , c(t) > MAC. \end{cases} \qquad (3.3.36)$$

In this case a quantity

$$J_v(t) = a_v u(t)/(1-u(t)) \qquad (3.3.37)$$

can be treated as "income" of the Leader received by penalties and used for the centralized pollution removal.

Computer simulation experiments based on the proposed control mechanism have followed the algorithm below.

1. To give a matrix D of the objects introduced in the year t (the development scenario in the narrow sense).
2. To calculate concentration of the pollutants without consideration of the removal c(t, C+D).
3. To calculate a part of removal v(t) by the formula (3.3.36).
4. To calculate the concentration with consideration of the removal c(t, D, v(t)).
5. To calculate the incomes of Leader and Follower by the formulas (3.3.35), (3.3.37).
6. If the value of income satisfies the Leader then go to the next year else change the scenario on the step 1.

Consider some scenarios which permit an obvious interpretation. In the scenarios it was allowed to change the variables $DD_{kj}(t)$ during the first five years after that it was fixed for the next five years ("a project capacity").

1. "Minimal construction" – the construction stops after the introduction of one object of each block of each category in the first year.

2. "Development of the first category" – a number of objects of the first category increases annually by one.
3. "Development of the second category" – a number of objects of the second category increases annually by one.
4. "Development of the third category" – a number of objects of the third category increases annually by one.
5. "Expansion of the hotels" – a number of hotels of all categories increases annually by one.
6. "Resort development" – a number of all objects increases annually by one.
7. "Intensive resort development" – a number of all objects increases annually by five.
8. "Intensive expansion of the hotels" – in the first year five objects of all categories are built then a number of hotels of all categories increases annually by five.
9. "Choice" - in the first year five objects of all categories are built then a number of hotels of a category is introduced.
10. "Long-term exploitation" – in the first a big number of objects is introduced after that the building stops.
11. "Short-term exploitation" – in the first year one object of each type is built after that the building stops up to the fifth year when a big number of objects are built again.

An example of calculations by the scenario 7 is shown in Table 3.3.9. The absolute values of data are conditional but their comparison for different scenarios permit to give a relative evaluation.

Table 3.3.9. Calculations by the scenario 7

	$t=1$	$t=2$	$t=3$	$t=4$	$t=5$
Environmental quality	3.91	2.83	1.45	0.23	0.00
A part of removal of BCO	0.00	0.00	0.00	0.00	0.16
A part of removal of SS	0.02	0.36	0.54	0.61	0.67
Follower's income	249941	217265	450202	- 48377	-349757
Leader's income	248	5691	11794	15625	22323

The following interpretation of the results is proposed.

Scenario 1. The environmental quality in the whole period is close to the maximal value, the removal is not required. From the second year the Follower's income is positive but not very big.

Scenario 2. The environmental quality slightly decreases but remains attractive for all categories of recreants therefore the resort is full. The pollution removal is not required. The income increases with introduction of the new objects after that it remains constant.

Scenario 3. The environmental quality decreases more essentially but the pollution removal is still not required. The hotels of second category have more rooms that permits to increase the Follower's income.

Scenario 4. The best scenario which combines the maximal income and the minimal environmental impact. High prices permit to receive a big profit with smaller number of the recreants.

Scenario 5. This scenario demonstrates the advantages of expansion of the hotels. The resort becomes profitable from the third year. The environmental impact is acceptable.

Scenario 6. The environmental impact reduces the resort attractiveness and the number of recreants decreases but the pollution removal is still not required.

Scenario 7. This scenario shows that an unlimited growth of the resort capacity is not allowable. The environmental quality decreases to zero which results in the lost of attractiveness and big removal costs. An initially big income quickly transforms into big losses.

Scenario 8. It is similar to the previous scenario. Smaller losses are determined by the smaller number of introduced objects.

Scenario 9. It is preferable to build hotels oriented to the middle class of recreants with the same environmental impact.

Scenario 10. A sharp reduction of the environmental quality leads to the same sharp reduction of the number of recreants and big removal costs.

Scenario 11. The critical reduction of the environmental quality lies beyond the considered period of modeling.

The problems of sustainable management of the river water resource systems are considered in (Ougolnitsky and Usov 2008, 2009a,b).

Chapter 4

QUALITY MANAGEMENT PRINCIPLES AND SUSTAINABLE MANAGEMENT

Quality management has a leading position in theory and practice of the organizational management since the 1950-s. The basic principles of the quality management are marketing philosophy, consideration of interests of different stakeholders of the organization, orientation to the persuasion and cooperation, continual quality improvement, cybernetic approach, use of statistical methods and information technologies. The principles of quality management are formalized by the International Organization for Standardization which develops official standards ISO 9000. A certification of the enterprises for the conformity of their management systems to the standard ISO 9001 is in fact a necessary condition of the competence of an enterprise as a business agent. The "core" of quality management is the process approach which considers an organizational functioning as a set of activities using resources, and managed in order to enable the transformation of inputs into outputs. To characterize processes the indices of their functioning are developed and the target values of indices are fixed. A correspondence between the actual and target values of the indices means that the conditions of homeostatic organizational development are satisfied. For the successful functioning of an organization it is necessary to ensure a compromise of the interests of all stakeholders associated with the organization. An essential requirement to the compromise is its dynamic consistency (stability). This property means that in the whole period of realization of the compromise it is not advantageous to any one of its participants to deviate from the initial agreement. The realization of the conditions of homeostasis and dynamically consistent compromise is treated as a sustainable development of the organization.

4.1. QUALITY MANAGEMENT AND ISO 9000 STANDARDS

The twentieth century was characterized by an active development of theory and practice of the organizational management determined by the swift growth of the industrial production, trade and services, state sector. A necessity of rationalization and standardization of the processes of production and management has become evident. The patriarchal methods of enterprise management have left in the past and have been substituted by the scientific methods of labor organization.

In the first half of the XX century the dominating place in the organizations theory was occupied by the classic direction connected with names of Frederick Winslow Taylor, Henry Ford, Henri Fayol, and Harold Emerson (Mescon et al. 1988). Within this direction a notion of an industrial mechanism including workers and employees as "small screws" was developed. The principal results of the classic theory of organizational management are:

- structuring and description of the main functions of management (planning, organization, leadership, and control);
- detailed development of the linear and linear-functional organizational structures;
- a notion of industrial process as a totality of operations which are to be analyzed and optimized;
- development of the systems of economic motivation;
- attention to the problem of quality control.

The classic theory was essentially added by the school of human relations (Elton Mayo, Frederick Rotlisberger, Mary Parker Follett) which had given a principal attention to the study of interests of employees, their motivation, origin and interaction of different groups within an organization.

After the World War II the theory and practice of organizational management have reached a new level based on the notion of industrial organism. A number of new concepts has appeared: the Peter Drucker management theory (Drucker 1996), an effective management (Malik 2006), an evidence-based management (Pfeffer and Sutton 2006), a lean production (Womack and Jones 2003), corporate lifecycles (Adizes 2004), business processes reengineering (Hammer and Champy 1993), a balanced scorecard (Kaplan and Norton 1996) among others. The system approach, mathematical methods and information technologies were widely introduced in management.

But the central place in the management research of this period is occupied by the management quality concept which combines many ideas of the enumerated theories. The main contribution to the development of the concept was made by William Edwards Deming (1986) as well as by other researchers often called "the gurus of quality management": W. Shewhart, J. Juran, A. Feigenbaum, F. Crosby, K. Ishikava, H. Taguchi (Neave 1990). The most widespread practical application of the quality management approach was reached in Japan but in the Northern America and Western Europe they are also highly estimated. The essence of the concept of quality management is expressed by its principles, namely: customer focus; top management responsibility; personnel participation; process approach; system approach; continual improvement; decision making on the base of facts; consideration of interests of the suppliers.

The principles of quality management are officially formalized by the International Organization of Standardization (ISO). Since 1987 the ISO 9000 standards dedicated to the quality management systems were spread (there are also other ISO standards). The quality management is interpreted as a coordinated activity of organizational management from the point of view of quality. Now three ISO 9000 standards on quality management systems are actual (ISO 9000:2008, ISO 9001:2008, ISO 9004:2008): basic principles and glossary, requirements, recommendations on improvement.

The ISO 9000 standards try to formulate a quintessence of the quality management concept which fits the organizations of any sector, size, kind of activity and form of property.

Quality Management Principles and Sustainable Management 129

In comparison with the theoretical works on quality management the standards are written in more precise and unambiguous manner but in the same time their generality and laconism does not permit to say about some specific and univalent recommendations and allows a broad and free interpretation. That's why it is impossible to find two identical management systems built in accordance to the standard ISO 9001:2008.

The following basic theses of the modern theory of organizational management having their reflection in the quality management principles and ISO 9000 standards can be formulated:

1) marketing philosophy;
2) consideration of interests of the organization stakeholders;
3) focus on persuasion and cooperation;
4) principle of the continual quality improvement;
5) system-cybernetic approach;
6) use of the mathematical (especially statistical) methods and information technologies. Consider the theses in more details.

Marketing Philosophy

The first and the most important principle of the quality management is customer focus. It is here where the principal watershed between the modern and the antiquated business philosophy, between the consumer market and the producer market, between the industrial and the post-industrial social structures is situated. A center of gravity is shifted irrevocably from the production problems to the study and to a great extent creation of customers' needs, i.e. marketing. The situation is caused by the increase of wealth of the major part of population of the leading economic powers, the growth of competition, the origin of the big transnational corporations, the total globalization, and the creation of a "consumer society". An eminent management theorist Peter Drucker affirms that the only true definition of the objective of a business enterprise is to form its customer (Drucker 1996). Drucker opposes the thesis to a widespread but false idea that the objective of a business enterprise is to provide a profit. Certainly, the profit is an important quantitative estimate of the enterprise efficiency and thus the profit maximization can form the base of a formal model of the business activity but the profit is only a consequence of the adequate marketing policy.

In fact, the first of Deming's "fourteen theses", a constancy of objective, also determines the marketing philosophy. In his personal manner Deming treats his principles very broadly that results in an intersection with the ideas of sustainable management. Thus, Deming proposes to evaluate the effectiveness of management not by the amount of quarterly dividends but by its ability to ensure the stability of business and safety of investments, to guarantee the future dividends, to keep working places (Deming 1986). Deming interprets the constancy of objective as a continual improvement of products and services but not as an end in itself, rather as a means of satisfaction of the public needs. It is important to underline here a public character of the marketing philosophy of Deming's teaching which requires both working places, and stable profit, and satisfaction of needs in commodities and services. This principle is opposed by a "mortal disease" of short-term orientation, a lack of the constancy of objective when the strategic interests are sacrificed for the sake of immediate profit, a maximization of the quarterly dividends. Certainly, the short-term objectives can not be ignored completely therefore the constancy of objective means a trade-off between the short-term and long-term interests with a priority of the former ones.

The idea of customer focus according to the standard ISO 9001:2008 is that the top management of an organization shall ensure that customer requirements are determined and are met with the aim of enhancing customer satisfaction (p.5.2). For that the organization shall determine a) requirements specified by the customer, including the requirements of delivery and post-delivery activities, b) requirements not stated by the customer but necessary for specified or intended use, where known, c) statutory and regulatory requirements related to the product, and d) any additional requirements considered necessary by the organization (p.7.2.1).

Two moments are to be accentuated here. First, in the quality management internal and external customers are distinguished. The external customers are clients of the organization who consume its products or services in the final form. The internal customers are employees of the organization who use in their work the working results of other employees of the same organization. From this point of view two main situations can be selected: a) a consequent product processing of a conveyor type when an output of the previous stage of production process is an input of the next stage, b) a functioning of the supporting departments (personnel, accounting, legal, security and others). The ideas of quality management reflected in the ISO 9000 standards requires to determine, analyze, and consider the needs of both customer categories.

Second, actual and potential needs exist. The actual needs are evident to deal with, namely they should be determined and considered by the fact of their existence. The anticipation of potential needs is an "acrobatic flying" of marketing which means not only study but also creation of the consumer audience. This circumstance was meant by Drucker when he had told about customer forming as a principal objective of a business enterprise and had selected in its activity two main functions, a marketing one and an innovative one. If and only if an enterprise is an innovator who can propose to the market principally new products and services then it can become a leader in the post-industrial economy. The bright examples are given by the modern software, Internet resources, cellular phones and personal computers, smart houses, nanotechnologies, e-learning and so on.

Consideration of Interests of the Organization Stakeholders

The groups of interested agents (stakeholders) are associated with each organization. The principles of quality management explicitly demand to consider the interests of four groups of stakeholders: customers (customer focus), top management (its responsibility), personnel (participation of personnel), and suppliers (consideration of interests of the suppliers). In more wide and detailed approach the organization owners (shareholders), its different partners, and the whole society are also included in the set of stakeholders.

The principle of customer focus occupies the first place in the list of quality management principles therefore customers are the principal group of stakeholders. According to the marketing philosophy the main objective of an organization is determination, analysis, consideration, anticipation, and creation of the interests of its customers.

The next principle of quality management is responsibility of the top management. According to that principle, it is the top manager of an organization (president, CEO) who shall personally head the work of development and maintenance of the management system, formulate the mission of organization, its quality objectives and policy, and mobilize all employees to the realization of the policy. Deming formulates the idea very categorically when he calls "a sincere fool" the president of a company who entrusted his managers with the quality management (Neave 1990).

Unfortunately, in real life the top manager (especially in big organizations) very rarely heads the works of quality management personally and directly. As a rule, one of the vice-presidents or even a chief of department is appointed to the position of management representative. The first variant could be acceptable if the president shares the ideas of quality management, considers that its development in the organization is necessary, supports the management representative and heads the management system strategically (participation in the preparation of the principal documents of the system, regular meetings on quality, management reviews).

The third principle of the quality management is a participation of personnel. It is clear that the top manager and his management representative themselves can not ensure the satisfaction of all management quality principles and requirements of the standard ISO 9001 with the best will in the world. The participation of all staff from the deputy directors to the ordinary employees is necessary for it. According to Deming, one of the management tasks is to regulate the required changes and to involve everybody in it (Neave 1990). Here the principle of consideration and coordination of interests is spread to the internal level of organization where certain groups of interests, supporters and opponents of the quality management as well as neutral observers also exist. A management system can be successfully introduced only if it is supported by the majority of the staff including the key figures on all organizational levels which permit to win an inevitable resistance.

The last but not least principle of the quality management is a consideration of the interests of suppliers which as though closes the loop "supplier – organization – customer". Deming paid a great attention to that principle: he criticized a formal approach to the choice of supplier based on prices only and insisted on establishment of the long-term partner relationships with suppliers which in the limit should lead to the presence of the only exclusive supplier for each type of the necessary input resources. Deming notices that an organization of tenders for the choice of a supplier contributes to the corruption and, moreover, increases variability and therefore deteriorates the statistical characteristics of the quality of input resources. Deming determines the principal demand to a supplier as his hunger and ability of the long-term partnership. Such long-term and even lifelong partner relationships are widespread in Japan, the country of triumphant quality management, where a supplier considers the satisfaction of his customer as the matter of honor.

In the standard ISO 9001:2008 the section 5 "Management responsibility" is dedicated mainly to those principles. The standard determines management commitment (5.1), quality policy (5.3), planning (5.4), responsibility, authority and communication (5.5.), management review (5.6). Requirements to the suppliers are determined in the point 7.4 "Purchasing". According to the point 7.4.1, the organization shall ensure that purchased product conforms to specified purchase requirements. The type and extent of control applied to the supplier and the purchased product shall be dependent upon the effect of the purchased product on subsequent product realization or the final product. The organization shall evaluate and select suppliers based on their ability to supply product in accordance with the organization's requirements. Criteria for selection, evaluation and re-evaluation shall be established. Records of the results of evaluations and any necessary actions arising from the evaluation shall be maintained.

It should be noticed that those formulations, as all theses of the standard ISO 9001:2008, give to the organization an alternative to bound itself by some formal criteria (for example, to organize a tender for suppliers) or to use a creative approach by Deming and his followers. From the point of view of official certification, both approaches are acceptable, and the first one is even more simple and convictive but its long-term efficiency is much smaller.

Focus on Persuasion and Cooperation

This principle is represented in the standard ISO 9001:2008 only indirectly. In the same time Deming's philosophy pays a great attention to the ideas of cooperation: eleven from the fourteen of his theses (1-2, 6-14) are dedicated partly or completely to the creation of the new type of relationships in organizations.

The matter is that a traditional management which is still deeply implanted in organizations in spite of the efforts made by Deming and his pupils and followers, is based on the exactly opposite ideas qualified by Deming as "mortal diseases". They are:

- striving for an immediate profit which is inconsistent with the long-time strategic interests of an enterprise;
- formal systems of personnel certification and ranging which undermine a genuine labor motivation and encourage competition, denunciations, and intrigues;
- fluctuation of labor which deprives the employees of specific information and of the base of strategic decision making;
- primary orientation to the quantitative criteria which do not permit to consider important hardly formalized.

Those "mortal diseases" are inherited from the Taylorian model of an organization as an industrial mechanism managed primarily by formalization and compulsion. In its time the concept was progressive and effective but now it is out of date and shall be substituted by the organic concept based on impulsion and transition to the conviction (see Paragraph 2.3).

The first Deming's thesis "Constancy of objective" forms a base for supporting of motivation and striving for cooperation for the staff on all organizational levels. The second thesis "New philosophy" definitely affirms that a new economic era has begun (primarily in Japan) in which the competitiveness of an enterprise is determined by the new management principles. The sixth thesis accentuates the necessity of continual personnel learning which is connected to the incentives of social recognition, self-perfection and self-realization situated on the highest levels of the Maslow pyramid. The seventh thesis "Establish a leadership" underlines an important role of the top organizational management in the creation of the atmosphere of trust and cooperation. The eighth thesis "Ban the fears" encourages the relations of partnership and trust between leaders and subordinates, excludes the fear of punishment which inevitably results in formalism and opportunism. The ninth thesis "Remove the barriers" appeals to the effective cooperation between the organizational departments. The tenth thesis proposes to refuse from idle slogans and appeals and therefore delivers from the demoralization the employees who are trying in vain to satisfy the impracticable demands. The eleventh thesis requires to remove arbitrary quantitative norms and tasks and to substitute them by the leaders support. The twelfth thesis "Give to the employees an opportunity to be proud of their work" is very important and its moral sense does not require any comments. The thirteenth thesis "Encourage the education" supports the idea of the sixth one and permits to the personnel to fit modern demands of the "knowledge society". At last, the fourteenth thesis "Involvement and activity of the top management" again draws an attention to the key role of the leaders of an organization in the practical development, introduction and maintenance of the quality management system.

Principle of the Continual Quality Improvement

This basic principle is formulated literally both in the standard ISO 9000 and in the Deming's theses. Deming steadfastly insisted on the interpretation of quality as a striving for the ideal which can be reached only in the limit of the process of continual improvement. This idea is principal and is discussed in more details in the next paragraph.

Deming selects two aspects of the process of continual improvement. First, it is the search of problems and of the ways to overcome them. Second, it is innovations which are considered as the only method of real quality improvement. All items of the Deming program are closely interconnected. Thus, the continual improvement of the production includes a work with suppliers targeted in the limit to the choice of the only supplier and the only delivering point for each article (thesis 4). The improvement of the production is concerned with the optimization of efforts of the workers that is connected to their learning (theses 6 and 13) and to the removal of barriers between functional departments (thesis 12).

In the standard ISO 9001:2008 the paragraph 8.5 is dedicated directly to the continual improvement. According to the standard, the organization shall continually improve the effectiveness of the quality management system through the use of the quality policy, quality objectives, audit results, analysis of data, corrective and preventive actions and management review (8.5.1). The requirement underlines a dynamic character of the enumerated actions, a necessity of their continual revision and updating.

The processes of quality management shall perform according to the so-called Plan-Do-Check-Act (PDCA) methodology or Shewhart-Deming cycle. This methodology is described as follows (0.2):

Plan: establish the objectives and processes necessary to deliver results in accordance with customer requirements and the organization's policies.

Do: implement the processes.

Check: monitor and measure processes and products against policies, objectives and requirements for the product and report the results.

Act: take actions to continually improve process performance.

A spiral containing at each coil the next Shewhart-Deming cycle is a model of the process of continual improvement.

System-Cybernetic Approach

Cybernetics as the science of general laws of control is a fundamental theoretical source of the quality management. A known specialist in this domain Stafford Beer has defined the principal problem of cybernetics as a transformation of a fuzzy notion to the precise and clear one so that to know exactly how to use it (Beer 1959). The following basic theses of cybernetics find their reflection in the quality management:

- an isomorphism, i.e. one-to-one correspondence between structures and functions of different organizations and therefore between their management systems. As it is said in the paragraph 1.2 of the standard ISO 9001:2008: "All requirements of this international Standard are generic and are intended to be applicable to all organizations, regardless of type, size and product provided";
- a feedback which pass to the control system the information about state of the control object, specifically about the conformity of the present values of state indices to their target values. In the standard ISO 9001:2008 the notion of feedback is used in definition of the monitoring, improvement, corrective and preventive actions (see paragraph 4.3 and chapter 5 of the book for more details);
- a principle of system relativity according to which each system, from the one side, is a part of a system of higher level (a super-system), and from the other side, it consists itself of the systems of lower level (subsystems). For example, a section of human resources is a part of the department of corporative relations and includes several human resource managers. From the functional point of view an organization is represented as a totality of interacting processes consisting of smaller processes and elementary operations;
- a hierarchy of control which corresponds to the hierarchical organizational structure and to the methods of hierarchical management;
- a William R. Ashby principle of necessary diversity according to which a complexity of a control system shall be not smaller than a complexity of the controlled object. It means that a top management shall be competent and able to solve the problems of organizational development basing on the control theory and modern methods of implementation of its principles.

The system-cybernetic approach is reflected by the process and system approach as principles of the quality management. Deming has defined a system as a sequence of functions or activities (subprocesses) within an organization which works in common for the organizational objective (Neave 1990). Deming did not use the terms "system" or "process" in the titles of his theses but he often pointed that the theses should be considered as a total system and it would be dangerous to pull out one or two theses from the general context. Specifically, he underlines an unalterable requirement to consider all examples only on the base of a theory of the system nature.

Use of the Mathematical (Especially Statistical) Methods and Information Technologies

As the majority of other "gurus", Deming was an eminent statistician, and the use of statistical methods is one of pivotal ideas of the quality management. By his own words, the essence of management consists in the decreasing of variations (Neave 1990). In the Deming's understanding the statistical process control is not a technical method but a new management paradigm. One should understand clearly that the statistical approach is not at all obligatory connected to a mass character of the quality controlled objects: a large-series production or unique services are also influenced by the whole number of random factors that results in variations (variability). According to the statistical paradigm, it is the decreasing of variations that is a main way of the quality improvement.

The bases of the statistical approach to the quality management were established in the works by Walter Shewhart who had selected two groups of causes resulting in process variations: general and specific ones. In the first case a process is situated in a statistically controlled state, i.e. the variations could be controlled; in the second case the process is not statistically controlled and the variations are not controllable.

If a process is not statistically controlled then all efforts on the quality improvement are useless and even harmful. Fortunately, a number of the not statistically controlled processes is small: according to the estimates made by Joseph Juran and William Edwards Deming in different times, it varies from 15% to 2%. Once specific causes of variations have been eliminated and the process is in a controlled state, the managers (but not the ordinary employees!) can improve the system and decrease the variations. As a working tool for the distinction of the named above principally different types of situations W. Shewhart has proposed the control charts which have been perfected later by K. Ishikawa.

Though statistical techniques form the main array of mathematical methods used in the quality management and in the management in general, they can not pretend for exclusiveness. The modern theory and practice of organizational management use a wide range of the mathematical techniques and information technologies. The founder of cybernetics Norbert Wiener has proclaimed categorically that cybernetics is nothing if it is not based on mathematics. A Russian researcher Alexander Shadrin has modified the idea so as the quality management is nothing if it is not based on mathematics. Together with statistical techniques based on the probability theory it seems reasonable to use the following mathematical methods and models in the quality management:

- graph theory for the description of an organizational structure;
- differential equations for the description of process dynamics and stability analysis;
- optimization and game theoretic models for the finding of the best in a sense decisions, including the cases of several criteria and different agents;
- simulation modeling for the variant evaluation of the long-term consequences of control strategies and implementation of preventive actions.

Besides, an integral part of the modern management is information technologies which permit to process and analyze big volumes of data in the real time. A key role is played here by the corporative information systems which solve actual problems of the document flow automation and decision support. In the final chapter of the book their important modification, so-called information-modeling systems is considered as a tool of ensuring of the sustainable management.

Table 4.1.1.The principles of quality management and the sustainable organizational management

Principles of quality management	Homeostasis	Compromise	Dynamic consistency
Customer focus	Determination of the indices of customer satisfaction	Consideration of interests of the customers	Coordination of the long-term and short term interests of the customers
Top management responsibility	A general guidance of the construction of system of the management system processes indices, their monitoring and improvement	Consideration of interests of the top manager	Coordination of the long-term and short term interests of the top manager
Personnel participation	Participation of the employees in the construction of system of the management system processes indices, their monitoring and corrective and preventive actions	Consideration of interests of the employees, their motivation	Coordination of the long-term and short term interests of the employees
Process approach	Forming of the system of the processes indices, their target values and monitoring of their achievement (homeostasis)	Procedures of resolution of the conflict situations in control processes	Providing the coordination of the long-term and short term interests of the associated agents in the control processes
System approach	Interpretation of the system of the processes indices, their monitoring and corrective and preventive actions as a system	Complex consideration of the interests of all agents associated with the system	Complex coordination of the long-term and short term interests of the associated agents
Continual improvement	Continual improvement of the built management system	More detailed consideration of the interests of all agents associated with the system, their needs and incentives	More detailed consideration of the conditions of the coordination of the long-term and short term interests of the associated agents in the control processes
Decision making on the base of facts	Implementation of corrective and preventive actions in the presence of actual or potential nonconformities to the homeostasis	Collecting data about the agents' interests and decision making on the base	Collecting data about the conditions of the coordination of the long-term and short term interests and the decision making on the base
Consideration of interests of the suppliers	Determination of the suppliers satisfaction parameters	Consideration of interests of the suppliers	Coordination of the long-term and short term interests of the suppliers

There are two aspects of advantages received by an organization from the use of a quality management system. First, it is a formal image value. The quality management is more and more widely spreading around the world. More than half a million of enterprises are certified by the standard ISO 9001 – the main quality management standard.

Second, a presence of the acting management system gives to the organization real possibilities for the improvement of its corporative management and therefore the whole business. Deming has proposed the following logical chain in this connection: improve the quality – owing to a smaller amount of mistakes, alterations and delays as well as better use of machine time and materials the costs will decrease - the productivity will increase – you will occupy the market by proposing better quality for lower cost – you will stay in business – you will keep and augment the working places (Deming 1986).

A rationalization of management permits to reach greater effectiveness and efficiency in the achievement of both operative and strategic objectives. Therefore it is reasonable to treat the quality management as a technology aimed to the sustainable organizational management. We think that the principles of quality management are compatible with the proposed conditions of the sustainable management formulated in the Paragraph 2.2 (see Table 4.1.1).

4.2. PROCESS APPROACH AND ORGANIZATIONAL HOMEOSTASIS

The "core" of quality management is the process approach. The standard ISO 9001:2008 refers the approach as the application of a system of processes within an organization, together with the identification and interactions of these processes, and their management to produce the desired outcome, where a process is considered as an activity or set of activities using resources, and managed in order to enable the transformation of inputs into outputs. The main task of a process is to receive the output which satisfies the customer (to achieve the process' objective).

It is conventional to select three groups of processes: main processes connected to the product realization, supporting processes and control processes. The main processes are specific in dependence on the products or services realized by the organization. So, the real estate development organizations realize the following main processes: development of the project concept; preparation of the draft and working project documentation; providing of the necessary permissions and agreements; realization of the construction works; financing; selling or rental of the real estate development objects; their maintenance. The supporting processes are the same for the overwhelming majority of organizations and include human resource, accounting, legal, informational, analytical, security support of the main organizational activity. The control processes are also universal by their functions of planning, coordination, control and motivation within organization. A more detailed characteristic of the organizational processes is given in Table 4.2.1.

Table 4.2.1. (Eliferov 2005:102)

Types of process	Character features	Clients
Main processes	The destination is a product realization. The result is a final product or a half-finished product for its realization. The processes are on the way of product realization. The processes add to the product a value for the customer	1. External clients 2. Final customers 3. Internal clients – other processes within the organization
Supporting processes	The destination is a support of the activity of the main processes. The result is resources for the main processes. The processes are not connected to the product realization. The processes add to the product a value	Internal clients – other processes within the organization
Control processes	The destination is a management of the whole organization. The result is the organizational activity	Interested persons: owners (investors); customers (clients); personnel (employees); suppliers and subcontractors; society

The key role in a process is played by its owner, i.e. an employee who is responsible for the achievement of the process result and is provided with necessary resources (human, financial, technological). In the quality management system of any organization all processes shall be described by regulations or other obligatory documents. The responsibility for a process description and its conformity to the regulations also bears for the process owner.

For the convenient description of processes special language and program means are used. The most widespread language of process description is a methodology of functional modeling IDEF0. Methodologies ARIS and UML are also widely used.

In the ideal case a functional structure determined by the identified processes should coincide with the organizational structure, and then the heads of structural departments become naturally the respective process owners. It is possible to realize several processes in one department or, in contrary, to realize one process in several departments. In these situations it is necessary to regulate very strictly a distribution of the responsibility and authorities. In any case the following rule is true: he who has realized a product is responsible for its transmission.

Two notions are used for the characteristic of a process result (its objective): effectiveness and efficiency. The effectiveness answers to a qualitative question whether the objective is reached or not reached. The efficiency gives a quantitative characteristic of the objective achievement by comparison of the result with the costs. So, the effectiveness can be ensured with different efficiencies. Formally, the standard ISO 9001:2008 requires from organizations only to be effective though it is evident that any reasonable management can not do without an evaluation of the efficiency.

The very important role in the process management is played by indices of their realization. The system of indices should satisfy the following requirements: a simple connection to the strategic organizational indices; "transparency" for the top management; convenience for the process owners using the indices for control; plainness for the personnel participating in the process; numerical measurability (expert estimates are allowable). In the general case the indices shall cover the following aspects of the organizational functioning: 1) indices of the product realization. This group of indices characterizes the result of a process and answers the question "What has produced the process?" 2) indices of the process efficiency. This group of indices characterizes the costs of resources for the production and answers the question "What are the production costs?" 3) indices of the satisfaction of process's customers. This group of indices characterizes the satisfaction of customers of the process results and answers the question "How content is the client with the process results?" (Eliferov 2005:123-124). If an organization finds it difficult or unreasonable to use the three groups of indices it can bound itself by one or two indices for each process which characterize its effectiveness – the main process property.

For the practical usage of a system of indices it is necessary to fix their target (plan) values the achievement of which witnesses about the normal functioning of the process. It is the achievement of the target values that we interpret as the satisfied condition of homeostasis – the key condition of the sustainable organizational development.

The notion of homeostasis was initially introduced in physiology by Claude Bernard in 1878 and means a dynamic stability of the internal milieu of an organism (Cannon 1932). It seems natural to generalize the notion for an industrial enterprise considered as an "industrial organism" as well as for organizations of other types also treated as "social organisms". But development of the methods of measuring the homeostasis which permits to deduce valid conclusions about the fact and moreover the degree of its presence in an organization is not at all simple and has driven a great attention by William Edwards Deming.

How to measure a degree of correspondence of the actual values of process indices to their target values and therefore to evaluate the effectiveness or "homeostatic level" of the organization? It is natural to calculate a general number of points of the plan or all plans that are to be realized in a present period and a number of the realized points. The ratio of the second number to the first one may be considered as a degree of realization of the planned activity or as the effectiveness. But an application of this approach causes a number of questions. Suppose that from the ten points of plan eight ones are realized: it is sufficient for the effectiveness or not? And 95 points from 100? Moreover, each point in its turn can be realized in a degree. For example, a house is to be built on February 23. If the act of putting into operation is really signed not later than February 23 then the effectiveness has no doubt. And if the act is signed on February 24? And on March 7?

There are two ways of answering these questions. The traditional way is based on so-called admittances. Suppose that the length of a detail shall be equal to 25 millimeters. Then the effectiveness is considered to be achieved (and the detail is qualitative) if the real length belongs to the range, for example, from 24.8 to 25.2 millimeters. Similarly, a house is considered to be put into operation in time if the delay does not exceed, for example, two weeks or one month from the date written in the contract (and in this case a penalty is not charged). The effectiveness is considered to be achieved (and the process is qualitative) if not less than nine points from the ten points of plan are realized.

The approach based on admittances is simple, clear and really used in practice in the overwhelming majority of cases. Moreover, it is theoretically grounded because any complex process is influenced by a number of random factors and therefore its result will be received with an inevitable deviation from the target value (we even do not speak here about an error of the measurements themselves). Thus, it is possible to say only about a rigidity of the requirements to the admittances: to demand 0.2 mm, or 0.02 mm, or 0.0002 mm, or so on.

In spite of this Deming has severely criticized the approach based on admittances and has proposed an alternative approach. Of course, an eminent statistician Deming does not deny the objective character of errors which arise in the realization of any process. Moreover, he insisted that an operational definition of any "true" value is impossible because an observed numerical value of everything depends on the used definitions and operations which will differ from one expert in the problem domain to another (Deming 1986). Deming and his commentator Henry Neave bring long discussions talking about subjectivity and therefore, by their opinion, senselessness of the numerical values of admittances.

Thus, the true value is unavailable, and the attempts to fix a range for its evaluation are not correct. Deming sees the exit from the vicious circle in the consistent application of the principle of continual improvement. If the required value of the length of a detail is equal to 25 millimeters then is it possible to ensure the value for each of the made ten thousand or hundred thousand details? Probably not, but Deming appeals to strive for it instead of bounding himself by the requirement that the length shall belong to a range 25 plus-minus 0.2 mm, plus-minus 0.02 mm or some other arbitrary given range from the very beginning. In this approach the target (plan) value of a parameter (an index) is treated as an ideal which can be reached in the limit, and the striving for the limit permits to mobilize physical and intellectual abilities of the workers and to realize the principle of continual improvement completely. By Deming's opinion, the approach based on admittances damps the workers' ardor.

In fact, the alternative approach proposed by Deming reinforces the requirements of the approach based on admittances. Deming himself said: "usage of admittances is not a mistake, it is just not sufficient", "we surely do not want to break the admittances but we shall do better". The admittances become an initial point of reading but not the final objective (Neave 1990).

The reasoning by Deming permits to precise the definition of the organizational homeostasis given in Table 2.2.1. We have defined the homeostasis as the realization of condition

$$\forall t \in [0, T] : x(t) \in X^* \tag{4.2.1}$$

where x(t) is a vector of state of an organizational system, X^* is the domain of homeostasis, T is a period of functioning of the system. Suppose that for each state variable x_i its target (plan) value x_i^* is determined, and the domain of homeostasis represents a parallelepiped

$$\prod_{i=1}^{n} [x_i * - \varepsilon, x_i * + \varepsilon] \tag{4.2.2}$$

where n is a total number of the considered state parameters. Then the segments [x_i^*- ε, $x_i^*+\varepsilon$] are exactly the admittances for the parameter x_i, and the condition (4.2.1) when $t \to \infty$

Quality Management Principles and Sustainable Management 141

means the condition of neutral stability of the stationary point x* for the controlled dynamic system

$$\frac{dx}{dt} = f(x(t), u(t)) \tag{4.2.3}$$

which describes the development of an organizational system with the state vector x(t) with a certain set of control impacts u(t).

The requirement of continual improvement by Deming is described by the additional condition

$$\lim_{t \to \infty} x(t) = x* \tag{4.2.4}$$

which together with the condition (4.2.1) and taking account of (4.2.2) means the asymptotic Lyapunov stability of the stationary point x*.

Thus, if the development of an organizational system is modeled by the equation (4.2.3), and the set of target values for its state parameters by the stationary point x* then the traditional approach is formalized as a requirement of the neutral stability of the stationary point, and the Deming approach of continual improvement as a requirement of the asymptotic Lyapunov stability of the equilibrium point. The requirement of neutral stability can be considered as a weak form of the condition of organizational homeostasis, and the requirement of asymptotic stability as its strong form. The asymptotic stability (the strong condition of homeostasis) includes the neutral stability (the weak condition). In other words, if the strong condition is fulfilled then the weak one is also fulfilled but the inverse statement is not always true. Thus, the Deming approach reinforces the approach based on admittances (Table 4.2.2).

Table 4.2.2. Conditions of homeostasis and their interpretation

Conditions of homeostasis	Interpretation	Mathematical formalization
Weak form	An approach to the quality problem based on admittances	$x(t) \in [x*-\varepsilon, x*+\varepsilon]$ when $t \to \infty$ (neutral stability)
Strong form	Deming's principle of continual improvement	Additionally $\lim_{t \to \infty} x(t) = x*$ (asymptotic stability)

Homeostasis as one of the conditions of sustainable management means that the indices of quality management system processes take their values from the target range. Therefore the realization of the conditions of homeostasis satisfies the quality requirements.

A formalization of the conditions of homeostasis in the terms of the stability theory has the following advantages. First, operational definitions of both approaches to the achievement of quality on the base of the formal model of a controlled dynamic system are given. Second, in the context of these definitions it is stated definitely that the approach based on admittances is a first stage of the Deming approach of continual improvement (because the neutral stability is a necessary condition of the asymptotic one). Deming himself has used even more categorical statements: "to follow the requirements of admittances is a sure way to the decline" (Neave 1990) but a subsequent approach seems to be more balanced. Third, if an organization is described by the model of a controlled dynamic system (4.2.3) then it is possible to solve the questions of stability basing on formal criteria developed by the stability theory (Iooss and Joseph 1980).

It is evident that the approach based on the stability theory caused certain technical complexities both in the construction of a model of the controlled dynamic organizational system and in the investigation of stability of its equilibrium point which requires a calculation of the eigenvalues of the matrix of the linearized dynamic system. That's why in the quality management practice for a formalization of the Deming principle of continual improvement another approach based on so-called Taguchi function of losses is more widespread (Neave 1990).

Taguchi function of losses is a parabola in the form

$$L(x) = c(x - x^*)^2 \qquad (4.2.5)$$

where x is a measured value of a quality index; x* - its target (nominal, plan) value; c − a scaling coefficient chosen in accordance with a money unit used in the losses measurement.

The Taguchi approach according to Deming's ideas supposes that the best (nominal, plan, target) value of the quality index exists and any deviation from it results in losses which increase when the deviation increases. The main form of Taguchi function (4.2.5) may be modified. For example, if the value of a quality index shall be not greater than a fixed one (as for a project put into operation) then the first part of the function of losses will be horizontal with zero value, and after the critical value the second part will be parabolic.

The Taguchi function has the following advantages: 1) it has a logical ground as opposed to the arbitrary admittances; 2) it supports a necessity of continual improvements. Any deviations from the ideal value result in losses which cause the need in improvements and variations decrease. It differs from the hope that a complete satisfaction of the admittances is sufficient for providing quality; 3) the evaluations based on the function of losses give a reference point for the process of improvement, permit to range the problems in accordance with a cybernetic principle of the main chain; 4) it permits to evaluate quantitatively an efficiency of the quality improvement (Neave 1990).

An application of the process approach entails a number of consequences:

- a necessity of monitoring of the actual values of the quality indices (the state of process) for their comparison with the plan values (Paragraph 4.3);
- a necessity of corrective actions in the case of nonconformity of the actual values to the plan ones (Chapter 5);

Quality Management Principles and Sustainable Management 143

- a necessity of preventive actions which stave off potential nonconformities in the future basing on the methodology of simulation modeling (Chapter 5).

So, conditions of the homeostatic development of an organization are formulated as the neutral (a weak form) or the asymptotic (a strong form) stability of its target state defined in terms of the indices of the organizational functioning processes. These conditions express the essence of the organizational sustainable development and are necessary for its achievement but they can not be called sufficient.

The matter is that in general case the requirements of homeostasis can not be realized by themselves. A question of the subject of their realization arises: who will ensure the homeostasis and why is she interested in it? The experience shows that it is the absence of an interested and solid subject that causes fails of the most beautiful plans and programs on all levels of management. In the absence of the real subject any program is only a declaration. That's why the requirements of homeostasis of an organization formulated in terms of the state of a controlled system shall be complemented by the requirements to the control impacts aimed for the achievement of the desirable state. These impacts shall correspond to the subject's interests and be provided by the necessary resources.

As it was shown above, a whole set of subjects (stakeholders) having their own interests and resources is associated with each organization. These interests are neither antagonistic nor coincident, they contain certain contradictions. Therefore the process of organizational management is inevitably conflict, and the successful management is possible only on the base of a compromise between the interests of the stakeholders. Building and investigation of the models of conflict is the subject of the game theory. It is game theoretic models of different classes that are to be considered as models of compromise rationality which are adequate for the description of organizational management.

The activity of an organization is a conflict controlled dynamic process which can be adequately described by the models of multistage (in the case of discrete time) and differential (in the case of continuous time) games (Isaaks 1965; Basar and Olsder 1995; Leitmann 1974; Petrosyan and Zenkevich 1996). Here the question of dynamic stability (time consistency) of solutions of the game has a principal importance (Kidland and Prescott, 1977; Petrosjan 1977; Petrosyan and Zenkevich 1996).

The property of dynamic stability of the optimal control was first formulated by Richard Bellman (1957). Independently of the initial states and solutions, the consequent solutions (which are components of the optimal solution) must be the optimal control relative to the state received as a result of the first solution. The majority of problems of the classic theory of optimal control possess this property.

A transition to the mulicriteria problems of optimal control, multistage and differential games complicates the situation. First, a unique principle of optimality is absent, and the property of time consistency has to be checked separately for each class of solutions. Second, the majority of used optimality principles which have good static properties do not possess the property of time consistency. Thus, at a moment of time one or more players can find it advantageous to deviate from the trajectory which corresponds to the initially agreed principle of optimality. Thereby the initial agreement is violated that results in unfavorable practical consequences (the abatement from the accepted agreements). That's why only time consistent optimality principles may be considered as practical recommendations in dynamic compromise decision making.

Another aspect of ensuring the stability of an agreement is a strategic stability, or Nash equilibrium. This requirement means that if all players use the strategies which form the Nash equilibrium then it is not advantageous for anyone to choose other admissible strategy instead of the Nash one. That's why the Nash equilibrium is stable against individual deviations of the players (a strategic stability).

As a whole the conditions of applicability of a compromise in the organizational management are given in Table 4.2.3.

Table 4.2.3. Conditions of applicability of a compromise and their interpretation

Conditions of compromise	Interpretation	Mathematical formalization
Strategic stability	For each stakeholder it is not advantageous to deviate from the strategy agreed in the compromise solution	Nash equilibrium: if it is true $\forall i \in N \; \forall y_i \in X_i : u_i(x_i, x_{N\backslash i}) \geq u_i(y_i, x_{N\backslash i})$, then the situation $x = (x_1, ..., x_n)$ is called a Nash equilibrium
Dynamic stability	The initially agreed compromise keeps optimal in any subsequent moment of the conflict controlled process development	Dynamic stability (time consistency) (Petrosjan and Zenkevich 1996)

In their totality the conditions of homeostasis and compromise give the conditions of sustainable management of an organization. A general characteristic of the conditions in the weak and strong form taking into consideration the consequences of their possible violation is given in Table 4.2.4.

4.3. CONCEPT OF MONITORING IN QUALITY MANAGEMENT

In the Paragraph 2.3 an organization is characterized as the hierarchically controlled dynamic system (HCDS) with a Leader and a Follower as the control agents in the elementary case. To ensure the objectives of sustainable management the Leader needs information about the system state and its changes in the process of organizational activity. Based upon the information the Leader and the Follower evaluate and forecast the state of HCDS. In organizations the monitoring of Leader is realized by the top management and the monitoring of Follower by the heads of departments and employees. Thus, in general case the Leader's monitoring system includes observation, evaluation and forecast of the HCDS state, the impact of Follower on the HCDS and the state of Follower.

Table 4.2.4. Conditions of sustainable management of an organization

	Homeostasis		Compromise	
	Realized	Not realized	Realized	Not realized
Weak form	$x(t) \in [x*-\varepsilon, x*+\varepsilon]$ when $t \to \infty$ (neutral stability) Observance of admittances which provides minimal quality requirements	The admittance are not observed that causes to evident defects	A situation $x = (x_1,...,x_n)$ is a Nash equilibrium, i.e. it is true $$\forall i \in N \, \forall y_i \in X_i :$$ $$u_i(x_i, x_{N\backslash i}) \geq u_i(y_i, x_{N\backslash i})$$ Strategic stability of a compromise: for each stakeholder it is not advantageous to deviate from the strategy agreed in the compromise solution	A mutually acceptable compromise is absent, and destructive conflicts among the stakeholders are inevitable
Strong form	Additionally $$\lim x(t) = x*$$ $$t \to \infty$$ (asymptotic stability) A continual improvement on the base of striving for the achievement of an ideal quality	A step by step lag from the competitors who use more rigid quality requirements	Dynamic stability (time consistency) (Petrosjan and Zenkevich 1996) A long-term cooperation among the stakeholders is guaranteed	An opportunistic behavior is inevitable because a part of the stakeholders acquires more advantageous strategies in time

The Leader's monitoring is the main kind of monitoring because it ensures a solution of the control problems of the whole organization. In turn, the Follower observes, evaluates and forecasts the state of HCDS from the point of view of her aims and objectives (Figure 4.3.1). Here x_{SL} – a Leader's information about the state of HCDS; x_{FSL} – a Leader's information about the impact of the Follower on the HCDS; x_{FL} – a Leader's information about the state of the Follower; x_{SF} – a Follower's information about the state of HCDS.

According to the monitoring diagram shown in Figure 4.3.1 the model of the hierarchical management of a dynamic system (3.1.1)-(3.1.4) can be specified as follows:

$$J_L = g_L(q, p, u, x_{SL}, x_{FSL}, x_{FL}) - M\rho(u, U_L(x_{SF})) \to \max; \tag{4.3.1}$$

$$q \in Q(x_{SL}, x_{FSL}, x_{FL}); \quad p \in P(x_{SL}, x_{FSL}, x_{FL}); \tag{4.3.2}$$

$$J_F = g_F(q, p, u, x_{SF}) \to \max; \tag{4.3.3}$$

$$u \in U(x_{SF}). \tag{4.3.4}$$

As it results from the model (4.3.1) – (4.3.4), the decision making in HCDS depends essentially on the information available for the Leader and the Follower. From the mathematical point of view the model (4.3.1) – (4.3.4) is a game with incomplete information. The better is a monitoring quality the more accurate can be evaluated the parameters x_{SL}, x_{FSL}, x_{FL}, x_{SF} that in turn ameliorates the quality of the decision making.

In organizations the presence of information about employees has an essential effect to the management quality. It should be noticed that in the organizational applications monitoring parameters are often used as an object of manipulation because a misrepresentation could be advantageous for some employees (Kurbatov and Ougolnitsky 1998).

An extensive system description of the monitoring includes the following functions: 1) an observation of the impact on HCDS; 2) an observation of the state of HCDS; 3) a forecast of the HCDS state; 4) an estimation of the present state of HCDS; 5) an evaluation of the future state of HCDS; 6) a standardization of the HCDS state; 7) a standardization of the impact on HCDS; 8) a regulation of the impact on HCDS; 9) a regulation of the state of HCDS.

The key moment of realization of the two first points of the program are methods of observation including a number of the required actions. First, it is necessary to prepare a list of the observed parameters which forms the state vector of HCDS. If the organization has a quality management system then the observed parameters are the indices of QMS processes. A monitoring of the values of the indices permits to judge about a degree of conformity to the requirements of the organizational homeostasis.

Second, methods of measurement of the observed parameters and a necessity of using of the special equipment shall be determined. The standard ISO 9001:2008 contains serious demands to the measurement. According to the point 7.6 of the standard, the organization shall determine the monitoring and measurement to be undertaken and the monitoring and measurement equipment needed to provide evidence of conformity of product to determined requirements.

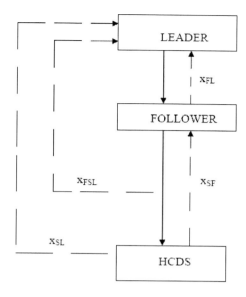

Figure 4.3.1. The diagram of monitoring in a hierarchically controlled dynamic system (HCDS).

Where necessary to ensure valid results, measuring equipment shall a) be calibrated or verified, or both, at specified intervals, or prior to use, against measurement standards traceable to international or national measurement standards, where no such standards exist, the basis used for the calibration or verification shall be recorded, b) be adjusted or re-adjusted as necessary, c) have identification in order to determine its calibration status, d) be safeguarded from adjustments that would invalidate the measurement result, e) be protected from damage and deterioration during handling, maintenance and storage.

When used in the monitoring and management of specified requirements, the ability of computer software to satisfy the intended application shall be confirmed. This shall be undertaken prior to initial use and reconfirmed as necessary (it is self-evident that the software shall be open or licensed).

Third, the methods shall establish spatial-temporal characteristics of the observation. The spatial characteristics are geographic coordinates of the points (domains) of observation; for example, in the organizational monitoring they are affiliations of an enterprise moved away from the main office. The temporal characteristics are the frequency of observation (every day, every week, every month and so on).

Fourth, it is necessary to determine the methods of processing and analysis of the collected observation data. Here the principal role is played by statistical techniques as one of the main directions of the quality management. The standard ISO 9001:2008 connects an application of statistical techniques to the demonstration of conformity to product realization, of the quality management system, and the continual improvement of its effectiveness (8.1). The statistics permits to order big volumes of collected observation data, to confirm their representativeness, to prove some statistical hypotheses. A forecasting of the state of an organization as HCDS requires building and usage of its dynamic model.

An evaluation of the present and future state of the HCDS requires fixing of the respective evaluative parameters. The most adequate representation of the system state is given by the set of all observed characteristics. However, a work with such multidimensional arrays of data is often complicated if at all possible. Therefore some aggregated parameters are used which are scalar functions of a vector argument – the total set or a subset of the observed characteristics (the quality indices). There is no doubt that it is appropriate to use the indices in the organizational monitoring. For an evaluation of the future state of HCDS the indices should be used together with dynamic forecasting models within a two-stage procedure: 1) calculation of the future characteristics of HCDS; 2) calculation of the values of quality indices.

The problem of standardization of the HCDS state may be formulated as a problem of determination of the admissible range for the values of observed variables (the values of quality indices in the aggregated case). This problem depends on the specific domain and should be solved by the experts in the domain. In the organizational monitoring the admissible ranges (or admissible points) are the plan values of the indices of organizational functioning (QMS processes if it is developed) which determine the homeostatic requirements.

The problem of standardization of the impact is an inverse problem of the HCDS theory: to find the values of the control variables which ensure a hit of the HCDS trajectory to the given (on the stage of the state standardization) domain. The domain could be determined in the form of phase limitations of the model which formalize the condition of homeostasis for the HCDS: for any t it is required $x(t) \in X(t)$. In the strong form of the homeostatic condition it is required that in the limit the actual value be equal to the plan value.

At last, the problems of regulation of the impact on a HCDS and of its state are formalized as problems of hierarchical management of a dynamic system (see Paragraph 2.3).

From the above-stated a principal conclusion about a close connection of the monitoring with mathematical modeling is deduced. Mathematical models together with conceptual models, expert estimates and information technologies form an integral part of the solution of problems of forecasting and evaluation of the HCDS state, standardization of impacts on the HCDS, regulation of the impacts and its state. Specifically, a struggle against an opportunistic behavior demands building of game theoretic models of the hierarchical management of monitoring.

Thus, a very important part of the organizational control is a feedback which permits to the top management:

- to get information about the state of the organization and the realized processes taking consideration of external impact to the organization;
- to compare the parameters of an actual state with the target values;
- if the actual values deviate from the plan ones then to use control impacts aimed to the elimination of the deviation and return to the plan trajectory;
- to control the effectiveness and efficiency of the control impacts, to form some additional impacts if necessary.

It is the monitoring that realizes a feedback in organizational control because:

- it provides the top management by a regular information about the organizational dynamics taking into consideration the environment;
- it permits to control the effectiveness and efficiency of the control impacts;

Quality Management Principles and Sustainable Management 149

- in the presence of respective models it gives a possibility to forecast the organizational state for different scenarios of the dynamics of its internal and external milieu.

Thus, the monitoring is a necessary integral part of the procedures of organizational control for organizations of any type, size and product provided.

Development of the quality management system (QMS) of an organization based on the standard ISO 9001:2008 seems to be a prospective platform for the description and realization of the organizational monitoring. The idea of QMS is that the quality of products or services of an organization depends on the quality of its management. As it was mentioned above, QMS is based on the following principles: customer focus, top management responsibility; personnel participation; process approach; system approach; continual improvement; decision making on the base of facts; consideration of interests of the suppliers. From the point of view of organizational monitoring the principles can be interpreted as follows.

Customer focus is the most important principle of the quality management which expresses the essence of the marketing philosophy of modern organizations – its client orientation. Any business or non-commercial activity is not an end in itself but should satisfy as completely as possible actual and even potential customer needs. This idea results in the necessity to collect information about the customer preferences and the degree of their satisfaction – it is a problem of the monitoring of customer satisfaction. One should remember that besides external customers there are also internal ones – the departments and employees of the same organization who use the results of other departments in their work.

The principle of top management responsibility fixes the key role of the chief executive officer in the introduction of all innovations including QMS. For the realization of her leader functions the CEO should have the complete, accurate and actual information about the organizational functioning which is provided by the monitoring procedures. The volume of information should be sufficient but not redundant.

A necessity of the personnel participation is explained by the fact that the success of development, introduction and maintenance of QMS depends not only on the top management but on all employees of the organization. The employees are taking part in the monitoring in two ways: from one side, they provide information for their chiefs and top managers, and from the other side they need some information for the realization of their official duties. The most rational form of support of the information needs of the employees is a corporative information system which provides possibilities for collection, storage and processing of the required information.

The process approach has the central place in the ideology of QMS. According to this approach, the functioning of organization is represented as a set of activities using resources and managed in order to enable the transformation of inputs into outputs. As a rule the main processes of product realization, the supporting and control processes are selected. A process system is the hierarchical one: the processes of higher level include the processes of lower level. A rational process system should correspond to the organizational structure though exceptions are possible (for example, several processes can be realized in the same department). According to the standard ISO 9001:2008 (0.2), the process approach emphasizes the importance of a) understanding and meeting requirements, b) the need to consider processes in terms of added value, obtaining results of process performance and effectiveness, and d) continual improvement of processes based on objective measurement. The item d) is directly connected to the monitoring as a tool of measurement.

For example, a real estate development company can determine the following process system.

- A1: to realize the strategic and operative management.
- A11: to realize the strategic analysis and planning.
- A12: to realize the current analysis and planning.
- A13: to maintain internal audits.
- A2: to manage resources and work environment.
- A21: to manage the finances.
- A22: to manage the personnel.
- A23: to provide accounting.
- A24: to provide legal support and security.
- A25: to provide information support.
- A26: to provide technical support.
- A3: to manage the project realization.
- A31: to manage the project preparation.
- A32: to manage the project documentation.
- A33: to manage the advertisement.
- A34: to manage the construction works.
- A35: to manage the sells.

It is natural that a process management needs a process monitoring which in turn is based on the determination of a system of the process indices, regular control of their current values and their comparison with the plan values (see Paragraph 4.2).

The system approach forms a base for the idea of a cybernetic control pattern with a feedback which requires a continual monitoring. Certainly the organizational monitoring shall be based on the system principles and envelop the organizational activity as a whole, in all aspects and on a required level of accuracy (the term "monitoring system" is not accidental).

The principle of continual improvement means an analysis of the present organizational state and a search of the variants of its changes which permit to optimize the solution of problems fixed in the Mission and Vision of the organization, its Quality objectives and policy. Respectively, a comprehensive analysis shall be provided by the required information ensured by the monitoring procedures. The procedures also realize a control of the efficiency of improvements.

The principle of decision making on the base of facts in the most explicit form fixes a necessity of the monitoring which provides the facts about the present state of the organization for the top management. Statistical techniques and methods of the aggregation of data play an important role in this aspect.

At last, the principle of consideration of interests of the suppliers determines a necessity of collection the respective information which concerns the contracts with suppliers, their satisfaction of the relationships with the organization, and in a broader sense the information about the organizational environment.

Thus, all principles of the quality management imply the necessity and expediency of the organizational monitoring. The third stage of the Shewhart-Deming cycle is also dedicated to the problems of organizational monitoring.

According to the standard ISO 9001:2008 (4.1) the organization shall establish, document, implement and maintain a quality management system and continually improve its effectiveness. The assets of monitoring are considered in more details in the paragraph 8.2 "Monitoring and measurement" which includes the following sections: customer satisfaction, internal audit, monitoring and measurement of processes, monitoring and measurement of products.

In the process of monitoring of the customer satisfaction the organization shall collect and analyze the information about the customer perception of the conformity of its activity to their requirements. It is not simple to measure a subjective perception therefore the development of special methods of collection and usage of the information is required. The most widespread methods are interrogatories (especially by the Internet site of the organization), questionnaires, and regular meetings with the customers.

The standards ISO 9000 and ISO 14000 consider audits as a management method which ensures monitoring and verification of the effectiveness of the quality policy introduction and/or environmental management1. The following types of audit are selected: the first side audit (internal) is implemented by the organization itself; the second side audit is taken by the agents interested in the organizational activity (for example, its customers); the third side audit is taken by external independent organizations (for example, the organizations which are authorized to certify another organizations to the conformity of its QMS to the requirements of ISO 9001:2008). The second and third side audits are external in relation to the organization.

The auditors shall follow a number of principles: ethic behavior as a base of professionalism; impartiality as a commitment to report truthfully and accurately; professional diligence and common sense; independency as a base of the objectiveness and impartiality; approach on the base of facts – a rational method of achievement of the reliable and reproducible conclusions in the systematic audit process.

There are different audit programs. The internal audits are taken at least once a year and are directed to the verification of conformity of the QMS to the ISO 9000 requirements. During an internal audit all organizational departments are examined in accordance to the audit plan. The certification audits are taken once in three years and officially confirm the conformity of the QMS to the ISO 9000 requirements. Between the certification audits the annual supervising audits are organized which check and analyze the present state of a QMS.

It should be noticed that the audits themselves are also monitored in the process of "meta-monitoring", or second level monitoring. After it an analysis of the audit program is realized which permits to take into consideration: results and trends received by the monitoring; conformity to the procedures; growing needs and expectations of the interested parts; records of the audit program; alternative methods of audit; cooperation of actions of the different groups of auditors in similar situations, and so on.

The process monitoring has the central place among monitoring processes because the processes form a base of the QMS. The aim of process monitoring is the confirmation of their effectiveness. If the planned results are not achieved then corrections and corrective actions

---

[1] Standard ISO 19011-2002.

are made in the end of monitoring. For checking the effectiveness (and probably the efficiency) of the QMS processes a system of indices characterizing the processes is used (see Paragraph 4.2).

For example, for the process A34 "To manage the construction works" of a real estate development organization the following indices in the proposed above groups may be chosen:

1.1. An exceeding of the deadlines of construction works fixed in the contract.

2.1. An exceeding of the construction works budget.

2.2. A number of deviations made in the construction works from the parameters determined in the project working documentation.

3.1. Customer criticism of the quality of the bought or rented lodging.

For the practical use of the system of indices it is necessary to fix their plan values the achievement of which witnesses about the normal process realization. For the indices proposed above the following plan values (for every month) are possible respectively: three days; not more than 5%; no one; no one.

On each stage of the product realization the organization shall monitor and measure the product characteristics for checking the product requirements. For a real estate development organization the product monitoring represents a control of the contracts with organizations-contractors (project bureaus, construction work firms, advertisement agencies and so on).

The market monitoring is not mentioned explicitly in the standard ISO 9001:2008 but is important without any doubt for all organizations. A study of the market is necessary for marketing decisions. For example, for a real estate development organization the market monitoring permits to determine the most appropriate target customer audience for each land cell and therefore to establish the basic parameters of the concept of an investment project: a real estate type (residential, commercial, office, warehouse); a real estate class (social, economy, business, premium); an expected profile of the future owners and/or tenants; recommendations on the size, design and style decisions, and so on. An information about the activity of the competitors permits to determine adequate prices.

Thus, the organizational monitoring includes: the monitoring of customer satisfaction; the process monitoring; the product monitoring; the market monitoring; internal and external audits.

The monitoring is an integral part of the quality management technology which includes the following stages:

- selection and description of the business processes;
- determination of the parameters of functioning for each process (a vector of state);
- determination of the plan (target) values of the parameters (conditions of homeostasis);
- regular measurement of the present values of the internal parameters and the parameters of the organizational environment;
- analysis of the results of measurement;
- evaluation of the state;
- development and realization of the corrective actions (adaptation) as necessary;
- development and maintenance of the motivation mechanism;
- forecast of the state of internal and external milieu of the organization (modeling);

- development and realization of the preventive actions (pre-adaptation);
- automation of the documents flow and decision making on the base of a corporative information-modeling system.

This technology ensures the organizational adaptivity on the base of monitoring, system analysis and forecast of the organizational dynamics (see the next chapter).

Chapter 5

ENSURING ORGANIZATIONAL ADAPTIVITY

Organizational systems should accommodate themselves to the internal and external changes keeping their competitiveness and integrity. Such accommodative mechanisms are called adaptive reactions. The theory of adaptive reactions is developed quite well for the case of an organism and allows a comprehensive generalization on the organizations level. The notions of adaptive (A.Toffler) and creative (V.Inosemzev) corporation are known in the management theory; they are formulated as a result of the analysis of adaptation of the modern organizations to the impetuous changes in their conditions of functioning.

In the quality management the ideas of adaptation are realized by the notions of correction (elimination of nonconformities), corrective and preventive actions. According to the standard ISO 9001:2008, the organization shall take action to eliminate the causes of nonconformities in order to prevent recurrence. An important role is played here by the organizational monitoring which permits to determine the nonconformities and to classify them. An elimination of the special causes of nonconformities requires special actions, and an elimination of the system causes demands a general improvement of the management system. An appropriate motivation system permits to create the conditions for an automatic ensuring of the adaptation.

The standard ISO 9001:2008 also says that the organization shall determine action to eliminate the causes of potential nonconformities in order to prevent their occurrence. Thus, the preventive actions have a function of the pre-adaptation. By virtue of the prognostic nature of preventive actions the necessary tool of their realization is simulation modeling (computer simulation). The scenario method permits to predict possible consequences of the different variants of management strategies with taking into consideration the external impacts.

5.1. CONCEPT OF ADAPTIVITY AND ITS ORGANIZATIONAL SPECIFICITY

An activity aimed for keeping the homeostasis with taking into consideration the external impacts is called an adaptation. The modern theory of adaptation is founded by Hans Selye and developed in the works by L.Garkavy et al. (1979). In these studies a concept of the adaptive reactions as the ways of accommodation of an organism to external impacts is created. It is found that as a response to the action of irritants of arbitrary nature different by their power the qualitatively different reactions arise in the organism, namely: the training reaction as a response to the weak irritants, the activation reaction as a response to the middle irritants, and the stress reaction as a response to the strong ones. In turn, the training reaction includes the phases of orientation, restructuring and trainedness, the activation reaction includes the stages of primary and steady activation, and the stress can be subdivided into eustress, distress and the final exhaustion. In the same time, a general model of the reaction of an organism to the external impacts is more complicated: as a power (quantity) of the impact increases from a negligibly small to the lethal one, a multiple change of the triads of adaptive reactions (training, activation, stress) divided by an non-reactivity domain is observed.

The adaptive reactions are closely connected to the resistance (stability) of an organism. In the case of training the resistance increases gradually, in the case of activation it increases quickly, meanwhile the stress decreases the resistance because the organism is obliged to offer its essential resource for the adaptation to the strong damaging impacts. However, there are special methods which permit to transform a stress even on the stage of exhaustion into the reactions of training and activation using the functional resource of the organism and saving it from the death. The specialists notice that a development of mathematical and cybernetic models of the adaptive reactions should promote the solution of the problem of resistance control (Garkavy et al. 1979:108).

It seems appropriate and prospective to generalize the ideas, notions and methods of the physiological theory of adaptive reactions on a broader class of arbitrary dynamic systems. We call a dynamic system the adaptive one if it is able to keep its homeostasis in a range of the impacts (loads) by means of the adaptive mechanisms. The adaptive systems have a hierarchical structure which includes the following elements: a system − object of impact; external impacts in a range; adaptive reactions (mechanisms of adaptation) depending on the impact and the system state. Besides, the notion of adaptive system includes a homeostatic domain inside which a normal functioning and development of the system are possible.

It is reasonable to differentiate embedded and removed adaptation mechanisms. The embedded adaptation mechanism is an integral part of the adaptive system (for example, in the human organism). The removed mechanism is relatively independent upon the adaptive system but it is also directed to ensure a homeostasis of the system (for example, an environmental agency which defends the interests of natural systems). So, a HCDS is the adaptive system in which the CDS is an object of impact, the Follower is a source of impact (together with non-controlled factors), and the Leader plays a role of the removed adaptation mechanism (Ougolnitsky 1999).

A very important role is played by the adaptation in the case of an organization as a social organism which should react to the changes in its external and internal milieu and to accommodate to them being threatened to loose its competitiveness and to perish. The problem of organizational adaptivity has become especially urgent in the second half of the past century when the conditions of organizational functioning have become much more dynamic in comparison with the precedent historical periods.

In the 1970-s a notion of the mechanisms of control adjustment (administrative, information, structural ones) ensuring the organizational adaptivity was determined by the group headed by Ivan Syroegin in the USSR. An arising problem situation is met by the information mechanism which ensures its identification and resolution. This mechanism works well in the case of typical problem situations for which the ways of resolution are already known and installed in the organizational structure. If a problem situation is new and the present distribution of responsibility and authorities does not ensure its resolution then the administrative mechanism begins to act. It helps to find a structural element which possesses the resource and competence required for the solution of the new problem. If the attempt is successful then the adjustment is considered to be finished otherwise the structural mechanism is taken into action. This mechanism changes the present resource allocation and control regulations. If the structural mechanism does not work too then the organization shall receive additional resource from outside or decline (Methods of Structural Adjustment 1976:21-22).

A broader interpretation of the organizational adaptivity is given in the works of researchers of the post-industrial society. The founder of the post-industrialism Daniel Bell characterizes the transformation of corporations in the second half of the last century as a motion from "economization" to "sociologization". The main features of the corporations in the beginning of the XX century were a rational concept of production and management, a strict hierarchical structure, bureaucratic regulations, a usage of quantitative methods. One of the most eminent American management theoreticians and practical workers, a chief of the General Motors Corporation in that period Alfred Sloan has written that in the automobile industry one cannot act without programming and planning, it is necessary to base on numbers in predicting the future (Sloan 1964:136).

Daniel Bell has defined the "economization" as a science of the best allocation of a bounded resource between competitive parties (Bell 1976). In the process the competitive interactions corresponding to the concept of economic rationality are spread both on the relations between different corporations and on the internal corporative relations. In this case the principal value is a satisfaction of the interests of an individual that results in a number of contradictions between the individual and the society. Taking down of the contradictions is ensured by the transition to the "sociologized" model of a corporation. If in the "economized" model the growth of production and profit maximization are regarded as of paramount importance then now the satisfaction of the employees becomes the main direction of resource expense. As Bell notes, a corporation cannot more stay an organization with a narrow destination, in the case of an industrial company only an instrument of the production of goods and services, but shall become an acceptable style of life for its members. It shall not only satisfy its customers but also be pleasant for itself (Bell 1976). Later this concept finds its reflection in the quality management which requires the satisfaction of not only external customers but also the internal ones, i.e. the employees of the organization.

The consideration by D. Bell of a corporation as a social institution requires an extension of the set of its state parameters and therefore the set of conditions of its homeostasis. If in the "economized" model the conditions of homeostasis concern only industrial and economic parameters of the organizational functioning then in the "sociologized" one they envelop also the characteristics of the employees' self-appraisal, self-realization and self-actualization. Bell enumerates a number of aspects which should be considered in building and implementing of the "sociologized" model: a satisfaction of the work, a hire of national minorities, a ratio of the salaries of managers and employees, a responsibility against the local community and an environmental responsibility, moral problems. A consideration of these aspects is necessary for providing the complex adaptivity of a modern corporation, at least as a trend.

To a big extent one speaks here about an often used notion of the social responsibility of business. As it is known, an extreme point of view belongs here to Milton Friedman who thought that the social responsibility of the corporative top managers consisted exclusively in the defense of financial interests of the owners, of course with necessary legal and ethic restrictions. But his critics note that this concept is acceptable only from the point of view of short-term interests meanwhile a long-term strategy should include the solution of social problems. Any profit is useless in the conditions of growth of the social tension and conflicts which can acquire a very undesirable and dangerous form. Besides, it is not correct to consider a corporation only as an artificial tool made for the satisfaction of needs of its shareholders. The corporation is a self-sufficient social organism which possesses its complex internal structure and its own conflict objective-making. The corporation itself determines a ratio between current interests of its owners and long-term social needs, including its employees as a part of the society.

Thus, the adaptivity is connected with problems of the sustainable management which demands balancing of the short-term and long-term interests during which a role of the former ones continually increase. The organizations which strive only for the maximization of current profit inevitably loose their competitiveness and let the place to more farsighted colleagues.

The term "adaptive corporation" belongs to an American sociologist and publicist Alvin Toffler (1985). Toffler considers that a key to the adaptivity is a qualified management and an attention to the external customers of the corporation. He points out to the following problems which should be solved to ensure the adaptivity:

- an addition of the material incentives by the possibilities of a creative self-realization of the employees;
- an attention to the information which plays a more important role than the traditional production factors;
- a transition from the production of standardized uniform articles to the making of the individualized goods and services taking into consideration specific requirements of customer groups and even separate clients;
- a transformation of organizational structures from the rigid bureaucratic hierarchy to the flexible structures which are able to react more efficiently to unexpected changes of the internal and external milieu, to provide a quick feedback, to motivate an initiative of the employees;
- a creation of the modular structural units organized by the team principles and having a fixed period of existence – from several years to several days.

Toffler underlines that the changes of the corporative functioning accelerate qualitatively what makes impossible the traditional management and requires a serious decentralization and a resolute delegation of authority. By his opinion, effective decisions should be made on lower and lower levels of the organization. The requirements of participation of the employees in management are dictated not by a political ideology but by the practical inability of the actual structural configuration of organizational systems to react efficiently to the quick changes in its environment (Toffler 1985).

The ideas of changing of the nature of a modern corporation are developed by a Russian researcher of the post-industrial society Vladislav Inosemzev (1997). By his opinion, an essential feature of a modern corporation is its functioning as a social organism which unites workers having a labor ability and means of production. A formation of the bases of the post-industrial society is connected with a gradual overcoming of the economic motivation of workers that leads to a change of the nature of corporations.

By the opinion of a known specialist in management Mike Hammer, a present corporation represents something more than a set of products and services and even more than an association of the working people: it is also a human community (Hammer 1996:153). Therefore the main incentive characteristics of the organizational dynamics are determined not so much by external as by internal factors, namely by the interests of the employees.

V. Inosemzev selects the following groups of factors of the transition of corporations from the industrial type to the post-industrial one which form the necessary conditions of their adaptivity. First, it is an augmentation of the proportional share and therefore the role of intellectual workers. In the knowledge-based society a proletariat is added and to a great extent excluded by a "cognitariat". Its representatives are neither farmers nor workers nor businessmen but only the employees of their organizations, they do not belong to the proletariat and cannot be exploited as a class. Changing their work they do not change their economic and social positions (Drucker 1996:22-23). As far those people have completely satisfied their material needs and strive primarily for the self-realization, they cannot be managed by traditional methods. As Peter Drucker writes, the intellectual workers should be managed as if they were volunteers (Drucker 1997:148), i.e. on the base of conviction. Second, an industrial activity is transformed, the accent shifts from separate operations to the whole product realization. Therefore the process approach which is the key quality management principle is regarded as of paramount importance. As already cited Mike Hammer notices the process time comes. The processes are not more the business step-children, they should take the central place in the organization (Hammer 1996:13). Respectively, a role of the individuality of an employee increases, primarily of the process owners but also of other participants whose creative efforts are obligatory in the achievement of the common aim. Third, management changes after the production. The principal role is played here by modular structures and team-building. The teams most naturally and efficiently provide the conditions for the self-realization of creative personalities and promote the augmentation of adaptivity.

All this permits to speak about an origin of the next, even more advanced in comparison with the adaptive corporations level of the organizational development, namely the creative corporations (Inosemzev 1997). A creative corporation is directed not so much to the solution of traditional economic problems as to the satisfaction of post-economic needs of its founders. The creative corporations are engendered inside the traditional ones and follow the way from a gradual individualization of produced goods and services to the socialization of their founders as the owners of the company which becomes the reason of their activity. Respectively, the key role in creative corporations is played by the creative personality of their owner who personifies the company and in fact becomes the main factor of its market value. The persons like Bill Gates, Steve Jobs, Roger Branson and others are inseparable from the corporations they head. The key point is not that they are the principal shareholders but that they personify the community created by them, rear a volunteer responsibility for it and relate to the business as their creation. The creative corporations realize the concept of constructive marketing which refuses from a passive following to the customers' requests and forms the principally new needs. The creative corporations continually engender new companies that form a new environment of the post-industrial society. They do not exclude the previous types of corporative structures but determine the trends of development of the new society and become the main source of economic and social progress.

Another eminent researcher of the post-industrial society Manuel Castels sees the main trend of the organizational dynamics in arising of the network type of enterprises which includes an organization of interactions among firms, strategic corporative alliances, and global business networks. Two moments should be noticed here. First, small and middle enterprises occupy the more and more important place. But Castels resumes dialectically that from one side small and middle enterprises are the organizational forms that are well adapted to the flexible system of the new informational economy, and from the other side they are still controlled by big corporations which stay in the center of the economic structure of a new global dynamics (Castels 1996). Second, the leading role in the functioning of enterprises of the new economics is played by information technologies. American specialists J. Boyett and H. Cohn notice that the ability of big American companies to restructure themselves so as to look and to act as small enterprises is at least partly explained by the development of a new technology which makes useless the whole layers of managers (Boyett and Cohn 1991:23).

Thus, the problem of adaptivity of modern organizations includes the following aspects:

- the adaptivity should envelop not only the relations of an organization with its environment but in the resolute degree the challenges arising inside the organization. An adaptive management is based on the consideration of interests of the employees, their incentives which lie beyond the traditional economic needs;
- it is necessary to ensure a balance between short-term interests of the shareholders and long-term interests of the employees and the whole society that underlines the nature of the corporative adaptive reactions as a mechanism of the sustainable management;
- the adaptivity is closely concerned with new features of the springing up post-industrial society: a creative character of the industrial activity, a post-economic motivation of the intellectual workers, flexible organizational structures;
- an active use of information technologies is a necessary condition of the successful adaptation;
- the problems of organizational adaptation are reflected in such principles of the quality management as customer (external and internal) focus, process approach, continual improvement.

5.2. CORRECTION AND CORRECTIVE ACTIONS

A theoretical base for the actions named in the title of the paragraph is formed by cybernetic principles. Let's consider a respective mathematical model (Moiseev 1981).

Suppose a controlled dynamic system exists

$$\frac{dx}{dt} = f(t, x(t), u(t), \xi(t)) \tag{5.2.1}$$

where x(t) is a vector of state (phase vector), u(t) – a vector of control impacts, $\xi(t)$ – a vector of external impacts in the moment of time t. Assume that the control objective is a transfer of the system from an initial state $x(0)=x_0$ to a final state $x(T)=x_T$. As the system (5.2.1) if influenced by the external factors $\xi(t)$ then for any control the phase vector x(t) is a random function of time. Therefore the control objective $x(T)=x_T$ should be substituted by a stochastic condition like

$$J_1 = E((x(T)-x_T)^2) \to \min \tag{5.2.2}$$

where E is a mathematical expectation, or

$$J_2 = P\{\| x(T)-x_T \| < \varepsilon\} \to \max \tag{5.2.3}$$

where P{y<a} is a probability of the fact that a random quantity y does not exceed a deterministic quantity a. It is also better to write a control quality functional in a stochastic form of the type

$$J_0 = \int_0^T E(F(x(t),u(t)))dt. \tag{5.2.4}$$

In the first approximation the external fluctuations can be considered as small ones ($\xi=0$). Then the function x(t) is no more a random process and the control quality functionals become the finite expressions. For example, the functional (5.2.2) takes the form

$$J_1 = (x(T)-x_T)^2$$

and reaches the maximal value if

$$x(T) = x_T. \tag{5.2.5}$$

Thus, a standard problem of optimal control arises: to find the control u(t) which satisfies certain deterministic restrictions and transfers the system

$$\frac{dx}{dt} = f(x(t),u(t),t,0)$$

from the state $x(0)=x_0$ to the state $x(T)=x_T$ so as to maximize a quality functional

$$J_0 = \int_0^T F(x(t),u(t))dt. \tag{5.2.6}$$

The trajectory x(t) which solves the problem is called a program trajectory (an optimal program) and the control u(t) which realizes the trajectory is called a program (optimal) control.

However, there is a problem that in the strength of disturbing factors the system is unable to move along the optimal trajectory without additional efforts. As specialists say, a real rocket never flies along the program trajectory. It is necessary to build special control mechanisms which ensure a correction of the trajectory influenced by disturbing random factors. It is this activity that is an adaptation to the external impacts. In techniques such mechanisms are called "automatic pilot". In the quality management the role of autopilot is played by corrections and corrective action.

It is possible to show mathematically that a corrective control is a function of the disturbing factors $\xi(t)$. But it is difficult to choose the control as a function of ξ because it requires a measurement of the disturbing factors. Therefore the dependency is considered indirectly by the measurement of values of the phase variables or their deviations from the program motion, i.e. the corrective control is searched in a form

$$v = v(t, x(t)).\tag{5.2.7}$$

This problem is called a control problem with a feedback or a synthesis problem (Moiseev 1981). The form of function (5.2.7) underlines the necessity of measurement of the values of the state variables, i.e. a connection between the control problem and the problem of monitoring.

The standard ISO 9001:2008 also underlines that the methods of monitoring and measurement of the quality management processes shall check an achievement of the planned results for the processes. If the planned values of process indices are not achieved then corrections and corrective action shall be taken (point 8.2.3 of the standard).

In the quality management a correction is understood as the elimination of nonconformities themselves, and corrective action as the elimination of their causes. Therefore, the corrective actions are deeper and more essential in comparison with the correction. In a number of cases the correction could be complicated because the nonconformity has already appeared (for example, a house is not put into operation in time). Certainly, all the same it should be put later but the main thing is to escape the deviations from planned data in the future by the elimination of their causes.

In accordance to the standard ISO 9001:2008, the organization shall take action to eliminate causes of nonconformities in order to prevent recurrence. A documented procedure shall be established to define requirements for a) reviewing nonconformities (including customer complaints), b) determining the causes of nonconformities, c) evaluating the need for action to ensure that nonconformities do not recur, d) determining and implementing action needed, e) records of the results of action taken, and f) reviewing the effectiveness of the corrective action taken.

Thus, the procedure of implementation of corrective action includes primarily the methods of reviewing of arising nonconformities. The principal role is played here by the monitoring system described in the precedent chapter which ensures a possibility of comparison of the present values of process indices with the plan ones. The more detailed is the system of indices and the higher is the precision of measurement the more accurate and well-founded could be the conclusions about nonconformities.

After revealing of the nonconformities their causes shall be determined. It is a creative activity implemented by process owners and their subordinates. This work is essentially supported by statistical techniques which are accustomed to the quality management by Walter Shewhart, William Edwards Deming and their colleagues and followers. Here it should recall again the problem of differentiation of special and system causes of deviations (variations). The special causes should be eliminated by the special actions, and the system ones by the general improvement of a management system. A practical tool of the differentiation is control charts and other statistical instruments (Deming 1986; Neave 1990).

It is this differentiation that is primarily meant by the evaluating the need for action to ensure that nonconformities do not recur required by the standard. There are two aspects here. If the nonconformity is generated by a special cause and has a unique character then the correction could be sufficient. If the cause is system then corrective actions are obligatory but a serious caution is required. The matter is that according to Deming's principles an attempt to eliminate the nonconformities generated by system causes by the impact to separate employees and separate elements of the production process is a big mistake. Such actions only deteriorate the situation because they continue to unbalance the system. The system causes of nonconformities (which form the overwhelming majority of them) require the system actions for their elimination. These actions can affect not only considered process but other processes too and demand the intervention of managers on higher levels.

After the revealing of a nature of the nonconformity the respective corrective action can be determined and implemented. These actions shall be documented as records for the consequent analysis and usage including the evaluation of effectiveness. The most convenient and efficient means of the documenting is a corporative information system containing the respective blocks.

We think that the effectiveness and efficiency of corrections and corrective action are closely connected to the system of motivation used in an organization. In the ideal case the system should ensure an automatic realization of the corrections and corrective actions. In other words, the employees should be motivated to eliminate nonconformities and their causes independently without some special control efforts from the top management.

Let's consider a mathematical model of stimulation (incentive model) in an organizational system (Nurutdinova and Ougolnitsky 2010). The simplest game theoretic incentive model is the model of interaction of two players – principal and agent. The principal is an organization having a labor contract with the agent, and the agent is respectively an employee. The agents can choose their actions (strategies) from an admissible set. The incentive system is completely determined by an incentive function which defines the dependence of the agent reward on her strategies.

The strategy of i-th agent is a choice of the action $y_i \in A_i$ where A_i is a set of admissible actions. The action can be a number of working hours, a production volume, a value of a key working parameter of the agent, the vector of parameters or a combination of them. Assume that n agents exist and $y=(y_1,...,y_n)$ is the set of their strategies. The principal's strategy is a choice of the incentive function $\sigma(y)=(\sigma_1(y),..., \sigma_n(y))$, $\sigma(y) \in M$ where M is the admissible set, $\forall i=1,...,n$ $\sigma_i(y) \geq 0$. The choice of an action requires from the agent i a quantity of costs

$c_i(y_1,\ldots,y_n)$ and returns to the principal the revenue $H(y_1,\ldots,y_n)$. It is assumed that c_i does not decrease and $c_i(0)=0$.

The interests of principal and agent are reflected by their payoff functions. The principal's payoff $F(y,\sigma)$ is a difference between her revenue and stimulation cost, and the agent's payoff $f_i(y,\sigma_i)$ is a difference between her stimulation and cost:

$$F(y,\sigma) = H(y) - \sum_{i=1}^{n} \sigma_i(y); \qquad (5.2.8)$$

$$f_i(y,\sigma_i) = \sigma_i(y) - c_i(y), \quad i = 1,\ldots,n. \qquad (5.2.9)$$

Denote $P(\sigma)$ – the set of solutions of the game. Then the quantity $K(\sigma)$ is called the efficiency of the incentive system σ:

$$K(\sigma) = \max_{y \in P(\sigma)} F(y,\sigma). \qquad (5.2.10)$$

A problem of finding of the most efficient incentive system has the form (Novikov 2007):

$$K(\sigma) \underset{\sigma \in M}{\to} \max. \qquad (5.2.11)$$

The solution (perhaps not unique) is an incentive system $\sigma^*(y) = (\sigma_1^*(y),\ldots, \sigma_n^*(y))$:

$$\sigma_i^*(y) = \begin{cases} c_i(y) + \delta_i, & y_i = y_i^* \\ g_i(y), & y_i \neq y_i^* \end{cases}, \quad i = 1,\ldots,n. \qquad (5.2.12)$$

where $g(y)=(g_1(y),\ldots, g_n(y))$, $g_i(y) \leq c_i(y)$ $\forall y \in P(\sigma)$, y^* is an optimal action of the principal, $\delta=(\delta_1,\ldots, \delta_n)$ is a vector with arbitrarily small components. If the hypothesis of benevolence is true then one can assume $\delta=0$.

The value y^* (optimal plan) is found from the problem of optimal planning:

$$H(y) - \sum_{i=1}^{n} c_i(y) \underset{y \in A}{\to} \max. \qquad (5.2.13)$$

The set of admissible actions A is defined by the restrictions on the wage fund and the actions of agents:

$$\begin{cases} \sum_{i=1}^{n} c_i(y) \le R \\ a_i \le y_i \le b_i, \quad i = 1,\ldots,n \end{cases} \tag{5.2.14}$$

The standard problem of conditional optimization (5.2.13)-(5.2.14) arises the solution of which is the maximal payoff of the principal $\Phi(R)$:

$$\Phi(R) = \max_{y \in A} \left(H(y) - \sum_{i=1}^{n} c_i(y) \right). \tag{5.2.15}$$

If the wage fund is a variable quantity then its optimal value R^* can be found as a solution of the problem

$$R^* = \arg \max_{R \ge 0} [\Phi(R)]. \tag{5.2.16}$$

An introduction of the optimal incentive system generates a number of questions and difficulties:

1) Which minimal value of δ has the incentive effect?
2) A small value of δ does not provide a sufficient stability of the cost function c(y) the identification of which generates the most principal problems.
3) If an incentive system (not optimal) already exists in the organization then its change can result in discontent and opposition.

Let's try to solve the problems. Assume that an incentive system (not optimal) $w(y)$ already exists in the organization and realizes a vector of actions y'. It means specifically that each agent receives a non-negative reward. Assume for simplicity that $\forall i=1,\ldots,n$ $\sigma_i(y)=\sigma_i(y_i)$ and $c_i(y)=c_i(y_i)$.

Suppose that y^* is the optimal action of the principal. Formulate a problem of increasing her profit by reapportionment of the constant wage fund so that each agent receives the same payoff (5.2.9) as in the previous incentive system. It solves the problems 1) and 3). Let's build an incentive function $\sigma(y)$ in the form:

$$\sigma_i(y_i) = \begin{cases} c_i(y_i) + w_i(y_i') - c_i(y_i') + \delta_i, & y_i = y_i^*, y_i \ne 0 \\ g_i(y_i), & y_i \ne y_i^*, y_i \ne 0, \\ 0, & y_i = 0 \end{cases} \tag{5.2.17}$$

$i=1,\ldots,n$, where $\forall y_i \in A_i$ $g_i(y_i) \le c_i(y_i)$, $i=1,\ldots,n$ $\delta=(\delta_1,\ldots,\delta_n)$ is a vector with arbitrarily small components, perhaps even equal to zero if the agent's payoff in the previous incentive system was positive. For the calculation of y^* denote

$$s_i(y_i) = \begin{cases} c_i(y_i) + w_i(y_i') - c_i(y_i'), & y_i > 0 \\ 0, & y_i = 0 \end{cases}, \qquad (5.2.18)$$

$$R' = \sum_{i=1}^{n} w_i(y_i') \qquad (5.2.19)$$

is a wage fund in the old incentive system. The problem takes the form:

$$\begin{cases} H(y) - \sum_{i=1}^{n} s_i(y_i) \xrightarrow[y]{} \max \\ \sum_{i=1}^{n} s_i(y_i) \leq R' \\ a_i \leq y_i \leq b_i, \quad i = 1,...,n \end{cases} \qquad (5.2.20)$$

An admissible solution of the problem y' exists (we assume that the vector y' is admissible) therefore an optimal solution y^* also exists.

If $\forall i\ 0 \notin A_i$ then go to the problem (5.2.21):

$$\begin{cases} H(y) - \sum_{i=1}^{n} c_i(y_i) \xrightarrow[y]{} \max \\ \sum_{i=1}^{n} c_i(y_i) \leq \sum_{i=1}^{n} c_i(y_i') \\ a_i \leq y_i \leq b_i, \quad i = 1,...,n \end{cases} \qquad (5.2.21)$$

In this case the principal's payoff $\widetilde{F}$ is calculated by the formula (5.2.22):

$$\widetilde{F} = H(y) - \sum_{i=1}^{n} c_i(y) - \sum_{i=1}^{n} (w_i(y_i') - c_i(y_i')). \qquad (5.2.22)$$

It is seen from the problem formulation that the solution of the problem (5.2.21) y^* is a vector of actions which provides to each agent not greater total expenditures and not less income.

Now let's consider the case when the wage fund reapportionment should concern not more than m employees, $1 \leq m \leq n$. Denote:

$$z_1 = y_{i_1}, z_2 = y_{i_2}, ..., z_m = y_{i_m}; \qquad (5.2.23)$$

$$y = (y_1', y_2', ..., z_1, ..., z_m, ..., y_n')$$

(5.2.24)

is a vector where $n - m$ coordinates are fixed but i_1, i_2, ..., i_m, which are the optimization variables. Then the optimization problem takes the form:

$$\begin{cases} H(y) - \displaystyle\sum_{i \in \{1,...n\}/\{i_1,...i_m\}} w_i(y_i') - \sum_{i \in \{i_1,...i_m\}} s_i(z_i) \underset{\substack{z_1,...z_m \\ \{i_1,...i_m\} \subset \{1,...n\}}}{\longrightarrow} \max \\ \displaystyle\sum_{i \in \{1,...n\}/\{i_1,...i_m\}} w_i(y_i') + \sum_{i \in \{i_1,...i_m\}} s_i(z_i) \leq R' \\ a_{i_k} \leq z_k \leq b_{i_k}, \quad k = 1,...,n \end{cases}$$

(5.2.25)

Here the set of indices of agents $\{i_1,...,i_m\}$ and their actions (5.2.23) are the variables of optimization.

If $\forall i \; 0 \notin A_i$ then go to the problem (5.2.26):

$$\begin{cases} H(y) - \displaystyle\sum_{i \in \{i_1,...i_m\}} (c_i(z_i) - c_i(y_i')) \underset{\substack{\{i_1,...i_m\} \subset \{1,...n\} \\ y_1',...y_m'}}{\longrightarrow} \max \\ \displaystyle\sum_{i \in \{i_1,...i_m\}} c_i(z_i) \leq \sum_{i \in \{i_1,...i_m\}} c_i(y_i') \\ a_{i_k} \leq z_k \leq b_{i_k}, \quad k = 1,...,n \end{cases}$$

(5.2.26)

where the principal's payoff $\widetilde{F}$ is calculated by the formula (5.2.27):

$$\widetilde{F} = H(y) - \sum_{i \in \{i_1,...i_m\}} (c_i(z_i) - c_i(y_i')) - \sum_{i=1}^{n} \sigma_i(y_i)$$

(5.2.27)

where $\widetilde{F}$ is the payoff function of the problem (5.2.25). This problem is reduced to the C_m^n problems of the type (5.2.8). In the same model by fixing a number of variables it is possible to consider the case when it is not desirable to change the reward system for specific agents.

Now let's consider the algorithm of solution. In the general case the problem (5.2.25) and its specific case (5.2.20) are problems of non-linear optimization, moreover the functions $s_i(y)$ are not continuous. Suppose that $y_i \in A_i$ where A_i is a finite set.

The problem could be solved by the exhaustive search but this variant is not the best. As it is assumed that the stimulation depends only on the agent's actions and the agent costs are separable, i.e.

$$\sigma_i(y) = \sigma_i(y_i), \quad c_i(y) = c_i(y_i), \quad \forall i = 1,...,n \quad \forall y \in A$$

(5.2.28)

Then a more efficient algorithm can be considered in which the vectors of actions such as their first k components do not satisfy the restrictions for any values of other components are cut off from the very beginning.

Assume also that the principal's payoff function is additive:

$$H(y) = \sum_{i=1}^{n} h_i(y_i).$$

(5.2.29)

Then the vectors which are Pareto-dominated on the plane "payoff – wage fund after the reward" are also cut off from the very beginning.

Let's consider the case when the payoff function is additive relative to the several groups of indices inside of which the payoff is not additive. For example, $H(y)=y_1+y_2 \cdot y_3$, the first group is {1}, the second is {2,3}. Then for each group of components the Pareto-dominated vectors can be cut off, and inside the group the proposed algorithm can be used if the respective conditions for the cost functions inside the group are satisfied. Otherwise the problem can be solved by the exhaustive search inside the group if all costs inside it depend only on the actions of members of the group. In general case the agents should be partitioned into the groups of indices so that the payoff function is additive relative to them and the costs inside the group are separable from the costs of other groups.

It is also possible to consider the iterative process of successive change of the salary for a pair of employees instead all of them. The process converges because the received sequence of payoffs do not decrease and bounded above by the payoff corresponding to the solution of the problem for m=n.

Let's consider a simplified version of the model (5.2.21) which includes one principal and two agents of different types. The principal's payoff function is linear:

$$H(y) = h_1 y_1 + h_2 y_2.$$

(5.2.30)

Expenditures of i-th agent c_i have the form:

$$c_i(y_i) = a_i y_i^2, i=1, 2.$$

(5.2.31)

Suppose that an incentive system given by the function $w(y)=(w_1(y_1), w_2(y_2))$ already exists in the organization:

$$w_i(y) = b_i y_i, i=1, 2.$$

(5.2.32)

Assuming that no additional restrictions are introduced one can find the maximum point y_i' of i-th agent's payoff function $f_i(y_i, w_i)$:

$$f_i(y_i, w_i) = w_i(y_i) - c_i(y_i) = b_i y_i - a_i y_i^2, i=1, 2.$$

(5.2.33)

$$y'_i = \frac{b_i}{2a_i}, \; i=1, 2. \tag{5.2.34}$$

The agent's payoff in this case is equal to

$$f_i(y'_i, w_i) = \frac{b_i^2}{4a_i}, \; i=1, 2. \tag{5.2.35}$$

Respectively, the principal's payoff is equal to

$$F(y', w) = \frac{(h_1 - b_1)b_1}{2a_1} + \frac{(h_2 - b_2)b_2}{2a_2} \tag{5.2.36}$$

with the wage fund

$$R' = \frac{b_1^2}{2a_1} + \frac{b_2^2}{2a_2}. \tag{5.2.37}$$

Let's build a new incentive function in the form

$$\sigma_i(y_i) = \begin{cases} c_i(z_i) + \dfrac{b_i^2}{4a_i}, & y_i = z_i, \\ 0, & y_i \neq z_i \end{cases} \; , \; i=1, 2. \tag{5.2.38}$$

Here $z = (z_1, z_2)$ is the action for which the agent is stimulated by the principal. It is natural that exactly this action will be chosen in the presented incentive system. The optimal (for the principal) value z^* of action z is received as a solution of the problem

$$\begin{cases} H(z) - c_1(z_1) - c_2(z_2) \xrightarrow[z]{} \max \\ c_1(z_1) + c_2(z_2) \leq R' \\ z_i \geq 0, \; i = 1, 2. \end{cases} \tag{5.2.39}$$

If the wage fund constraint is not considered then the optimal action for the principal is the point z^0 such as

$$z^0 = (\frac{h_1}{2a_1}, \frac{h_2}{2a_2}). \tag{5.2.40}$$

If the constraint named above is satisfied in the point then $z^* = z^0$. It could be noticed that on the plane Oz_1z_2 the part of the plane bounded by the coordinate axes and the following ellipse corresponds to the restrictions of the problem (5.2.39):

$$a_1 z_1^2 + a_2 z_2^2 \leq R'. \tag{5.2.41}$$

The set of points z which supply to the principal the same payoff F is also determined by an ellipse (with its center in the point z^0):

$$F = h_1 z_1 + h_2 z_2 - a_1 z_1^2 - a_2 z_2^2 - \frac{b_1^2}{4a_1} - \frac{b_2^2}{4a_2}. \tag{5.2.42}$$

$$a_1(z_1 - z_1^0)^2 + a_2(z_2 - z_2^0)^2 = \frac{h_1^2}{4a_1^2} + \frac{h_2^2}{4a_2^2} - \frac{b_1^2}{4a_1} - \frac{b_2^2}{4a_2} - F. \tag{5.2.43}$$

The greater is payoff, the less is the radius of the ellipse. In the case when the point z^0 is not admissible the point of tangency of the two ellipses z^* corresponds to the maximal value of F if the wage fund restriction is satisfied (Figure 5.2.1). This point can be found by the solution of the respective system of equations.

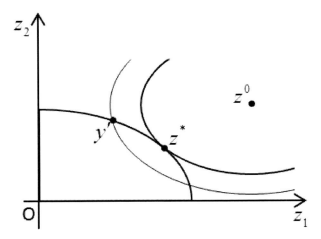

Figure 5.2.1. Graphical representation of the problem (5.2.39).

Let's notice that if the principal chooses as z the point y'(it is admissible) then her payoff with the old incentive system is equal to the payoff for the new incentive system which does not exceed the payoff for the value z= z*:

$$F(y', w) = \frac{(h_1 - b_1)b_1}{2a_1} + \frac{(h_2 - b_2)b_2}{2a_2} = F(y', \sigma) \leq F(z^*, \sigma) \tag{5.2.44}$$

Thus, the payoff of the principal for the new incentive system (5.2.38) is not less than for the old system (5.2.32), and the agents' payoff and the wage fund are the same.

Now let's consider an example of the problem of the type (5.2.25). The results of the text example are received by means of a computer program developed for the realization of the proposed algorithm. Let an organization system contains ten members (Table 5.2.1).

Table 5.2.1. Data about the present incentive system

i	A_i	$\sigma_i(x)$	$c_i(x)$	y_i	$\sigma_i(y)$
1	0, 10,..., 100	5% of the income	$x^2/80$	10	11.65
2	0, 1,..., 8	3x	$x^2/2$	3	9
3	0, 1,..., 20	2x, x≤10 3(x-10)+20, x>10	$x^2/6$	6	12
4	0, 1,..., 20	2x, x≤10 3(x-10)+20, x>10	$x^2/6$	6	12
5	0, 1,..., 20	2x, x≤10 3(x-10)+20, x>10	$x^2/6$	6	12
6	0, 0, 5;...; 2	0, x=0 2+x, x>0	$1,5x^2$	0.5	2
7	0, 0, 5;...; 2	0, x=0 2+x, x>0	$1,7x^2$	0.5	2
8	0, 1,..., 15	0, x=0 3+2x, x>0	$x^2/6$	6	15
9	0, 1,..., 8	0, x=0 3+3x, 0<x≤5 19+4(x-5), x>5	4x	1	6
10	0, 1,..., 8	0, x=0 4+3x, 0<x≤5 18+4(x-5), x>5	4x	1	7
Profit				84.35	
Wage fund				88.65	

The denotations are: i is the index of an agent, A_i – the set of admissible actions, $\sigma_i(x)$ – a present incentive function, $c_i(x)$ – a cost function, y_i – a realized action. The payoff function is a linear one:

$$H(y) = y_1 + 8y_2 + 5(y_3 + y_4 + y_5) +$$
$$+ 3(y_6 + y_7) + 4y_8 + 11(y_9 + y_{10}). \qquad (5.2.45)$$

The employees with indices 3, 4, 5 have the same position (the same incentive system) and the same cost functions, the employees 6 and 7 have the same position but different cost functions, and the employees 9 and 10 have different positions but the same cost function. The employee 1 receives 5% of the organizational income.

Now let's solve the problem (5.2.25) for the values of parameter m= 1, 2,..., 10. The results of the solution are shown in the Table 5.2.2. Here F is the profit of the principal, R –

the wage fund, d – an increase of the profit in percents relative to the old incentive system. All values are rounded to the second digit after the decimal point.

Table 5.2.2. Results of solution of the problem (5.2.25)

m	F	R	d
1	86	77	2
2	100	85	18.55
3	119	86	41.08
4	126.5	88	49.97
5	127.33	87.67	50.95
6	130	88.5	54.12
7	132.5	88	57.08
8	133.83	88.17	58.66
9	136.83	88.17	62.22
10	136.83	88.17	62.22

The incentive system (5.2.17) permits to increase the profit up to 62.22%. To increase the profit on 50% it is sufficient to change a realized action for four persons. For m=1 the profit increases on 2% only. For m=2 and m=3 a sharp jump of the profit increase is observed then it decelerates. It is shown in Figure 5.2.2 that m=3 is a point of inflection.

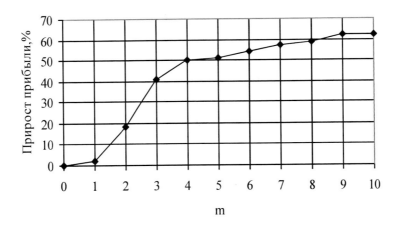

Figure 5.2.2. Graph of the dependence of the profit increase on m.

Let's consider the ratio d/m, denote it as p(m) (Table 5.2.3).

Table 5.2.3. Dependence p(m)

m	1	2	3	4	5
p	2	9.28	13.69	12.49	10.19
m	6	7	8	9	10
p	9.02	8.15	7.33	6.91	6.22

All values are rounded to the second digit after the decimal point. The respective graph is shown in Figure 5.2.3. It is seen that the maximal relative profit increase is observed when m=3.

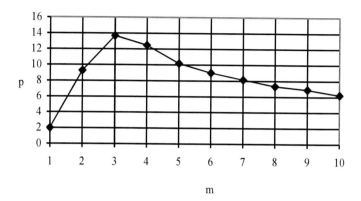

Figure 5.2.3. Graph of the dependence p(m).

5.3. PREVENTIVE ACTIONS

The difference between corrective and preventive actions in the quality management is that the corrective actions are aimed to the elimination of the causes of real present nonconformities meanwhile the preventive actions aim to eliminate the causes of potential nonconformities which could arise in the future. This notion is connected with a frequently used in the quality management term "anticipation of expectations" which means that not only real but even potential requirements of the internal and external customers are satisfied and no nonconformities arise even in the future.

The standard ISO 9001:2008 establishes (Paragraph 8.5.3) that the organization shall determine action to eliminate the causes of potential nonconformities in order to prevent their occurrence. Preventive actions shall be appropriate to the effects of the potential problems. A documented procedure shall be established to define requirements for a) determining potential nonconformities and their causes, b) evaluating the need for action to prevent occurrence of nonconformities, c) determining and implementing action needed, d) records of results of action taken, and e) reviewing the effectiveness of the preventive action taken.

As preventive actions relate to the future they should be based on certain forecasts. Therefore, by our opinion, a necessary tool of their realization is simulation modeling (computer simulation) which ensures a possibility of the forecast.

In a general form the simulation model can be written as follows (see Paragraph 2.3):

$$x(t + \Delta t) = x(t) + (\Delta t) f_t(x(t), u(t), \xi(t)), \qquad (5.3.1)$$

$$x(0) = x_0, \, t = 0, \, \Delta t, \, ..., \, T - \Delta t. \qquad (5.3.2)$$

The essence of the method of simulation modeling (computer simulation) is in the following. The model (5.3.1)-(5.3.2) and a computer are used for answering the question

"What will happen with the CDS if ...?" Instead of dots in this question should be substituted that a) control variables take certain values for t=1,2,...,T; non-controlled variables take certain values for t=1,2,...,T. Though formally these sentences are similar they have absolutely different meaning. The control impacts u(t) can be chosen by a control subject from an admissible domain U(t) arbitrarily. The non-controlled values $\xi(t)$ can not be chosen by the subject, it is only known that they belong to the domain $\Xi(t)$. However, after that the values u(t) and $\xi(t)$ for t=1,2,...,T are determined by a way, the relations (5.3.1) give the algorithm of transfer of the CDS from the initial state x_0 to the final state x(T). It is not necessary to give the function f explicitly, instead of it a rule of transfer from x(t) to x(t+Δt) could be determined.

The main reason of using the model (5.3.1)-(5.3.2) in computer simulation experiments is a complexity of CDS which bounds the possibilities of traditional analytical methods of study of the mathematical models. However, the simulation modeling is not at all an alternative to the mathematical modeling: the computer simulation develops the possibilities of the mathematical modeling and reinforces them by the computer and a human expert in the dialogue with computer.

The following stages of the simulation modeling are selected.

1. Determination of simulation objectives, problems and resource.
2. Analysis of the CDS and building its conceptual model.
3. Formulation and structuring of the simulation model.
4. Program implementation of the simulation model.
5. Analysis and correction of the simulation model.
6. Design and realization of the simulation experiments.
7. Processing and analysis of the simulation results.
8. Introduction and maintenance of the simulation results.

Let's give a brief characteristic of the enumerated stages (Ougolnitsky 1999).

1. Determination of Simulation Objectives, Problems and Resource

One of the most important theses of system analysis states that it is impossible to study a complex system as a whole, in the totality of its elements and connections between them. A study is always directed to the specific problem concerned with the whole system. In the case of preventive action the main objective of simulation modeling is a determination of the conditions which could result in the violation of the requirements of an organizational homeostasis (Table 4.2.2).

For computer calculations with the model (5.3.1)-(5.3.2) the initial conditions x_0, the vector of control impacts u(t) and the vector of non-controlled factors $\xi(t)$ for t=1,2,...,T-Δt (it is supposed that the identification problem is solved, i.e. the form of function a and its numerical parameters are known) should be given. The set of enumerated quantities is called a scenario of simulation. Its own trajectory of the CDS calculated by the algorithm (5.3.1)-(5.3.2) corresponds to each scenario. Therefore the main question of simulation modeling could be reformulated as follows: "Which will be the CDS trajectory in the given scenario?"

The essence of our approach is the following: if for a scenario the simulation shows that the conditions of homeostasis are forced then it means a potential nonconformity caused by the scenario.

Another factor which determines a selection of the considered problem of the whole variety of aspect concerned with the system is research resource. Theoretical, financial, temporal and other resources can be selected. The subject of research is a process owner, an authorized employee or a quality manager.

Theoretical resource determines the data and methods which the researcher is able to use for the problem solving based on her professional knowledge and experience. If they are not sufficient then the researcher should receive a consultation from an expert or a special team is to be formed by the top management decision. Financial resource limits the usage of equipment, the volume of experiments and observations, the number of specialists and supporting personnel. It is clear that straitened circumstances do not promote the enthusiasm of workers and the success of research though sometimes could result in unexpected economic decisions. Any research should be maintained in certain period which influences essentially to the scale of problem formulation and the depth of its investigation.

The research objectives can be subdivided as follows:

- description of the system functioning;
- forecasting of the functioning for different impacts;
- searching for the optimal variant of functioning.

A description of the system functioning is a basic objective of any research and a necessary element of the achievement of higher level objectives (forecast, optimization). It is meant here not a complete description of the whole CDS (which is principally impossible for big systems) but the description within a problem already formulated, i.e. the description of an aspect of the system functioning. The description permits to represent a present state of the system (perhaps with consideration to the past states) and its change in time. The description can be formal (for example, statistical) or can explain a mechanism of the system functioning (for example, the striving for self-conservation or expansion).

The objective of the forecasting of the functioning is the prediction of the system state in the future for different variants of internal and external impacts to the system. The decisions of system management relate to the internal impacts and the influence of the environment to the external ones. For example, in the case of enterprise the internal impacts are management decisions about the profit distribution, personnel hiring and firing, purchasing of raw materials, advertisement and so on; the external impacts are official documents, actions of the suppliers and competitors, political situation and so on. The internal impacts always have on objective because they are concerned with a control meanwhile the external impacts can be either objective-oriented (actions of suppliers and competitors) or not (natural phenomena). Thus, the objective of a forecast can be once more briefly formulated as an answer to the question "What will be with the system if the set of internal and external impacts takes certain values?" It is this objective that is the principal one in preventive action.

The searching for the optimal variant of functioning first of all supposes the choice of an optimality criterion. For big systems the criterion is rarely unique. Thus, for an industrial enterprise the income (or profit), the quality of product (and therefore the reputation), the working conditions, good relations with the local population and administration and many other criteria could be determined. Sometimes one of the criteria could be considered as the principal one (for example, profit) and others as the restrictions. In the majority of cases the organization is not a monolithic one and contains many subjects with their own interests and preferences expressed by different criteria of optimality. Thus, in the case of an enterprise instead of a global view of optimality (personified by the individual or collective owner) there are also multiple views of the departments, separate workers and their groups. Therefore the objective of choice of the optimal variant of the system functioning should include a consideration and coordination of interests of the associated subjects.

It should be mentioned that in the formulation of a forecasting objective the estimative parameters of the system functioning quality are also formulated and their values are calculated for each scenario. In this case a partial solution of the problem of searching for the optimal variant of functioning is realized for a subset of variants determined by the considered scenarios. Therefore the objective of searching of the best variant could be considered as an element of preventive action.

2. Analysis of the CDS and Building its Conceptual Model

A formulation of the research problem permits to outline the borders of an object and therefore to select it from the environment. It should be noticed that the selection is possible exactly within the limits of the studied problem; for another problem a division between the considered system and its environment will also be different. For example, a whole enterprise (a factory) could be considered as an object; then the borders are determined by the territory of the factory (may be also by other objects like affiliations) and the environment is formed by the suppliers, the competitors, the customers, the local administration and so on. However, it is simple to imagine a research objective which requires the consideration of not the whole factory but one of its subsystems (for example, the assembling department). Then the department becomes the analyzed system and other departments form its environment. According to the principle of system relativity any element of a complex system could be considered as a system which includes the subsystems on lower levels and is a subsystem of the system on higher level. For each selected level determined by the research objective and resource the respective intra-system relations treated as stronger than the relations between the system and its environment. A role of the interaction with the environment also varies in dependence on the situation. Sometimes a system could be considered as practically closed and it is possible to ignore its connections with the other world meanwhile in other cases the connections are essential. Certainly the assumption about closure is stronger and leads to a simpler model. A further analysis of the system in its determined borders should result in the formulation of a list of the elements which form the system including their composition and interconnections as well as processes in which the elements and their connections change. The sets of elements and relations characterize the structure of the system and the change of the system parameters within the structure – its functions.

The result of a system approach to the problem is so-called conceptual model. The model reflects a research concept and is determined by the research objectives and resources. The conceptual model includes:

- the description of the borders of the considered system;
- the set of system elements;
- the set of state parameters for each;
- the set of connections between the system elements (containing the values of flows of energy and matter if necessary);
- the list of processes realized in the system;
- the list of internal and external impacts to the system.

It should be noticed again that each item of the conceptual model includes those and only those elements which correspond to the research objectives and resource. A conceptual model could be described by different means: there are no strict rules and limitations here, only the maximal clarity is required. Verbal descriptions are the most widespread, different visual means such as charts, diagrams, graphs, tables which permit to represent the required information in the obvious and compressed form are also broadly used. A conceptual model could include formalized elements (algorithms written in a programming language, flow models, mathematical relations) what facilitates the consequent stage of formalization. For the very complex objects the conceptual model could be built as a multilevel system the higher level of which gives a general representation of the object and the subsequent levels specify the representation in different aspects.

3. Formulation and Structuring of the Simulation Model

The next stage of the simulation modeling is a formalization of the received conceptual model that results in building of the formal model. We call "formal" such model the elements of which can be transformed by certain formal rules. The general form of a simulation model is given by the formulas (5.3.1)-(5.3.2). The initial point of formalization is a determination of the state vector the components of which are characteristics of the CDS selected in the conceptual models as the basic ones bearing the necessary and sufficient information for the solution of the formulated problem.

In dependence on the research objective so-called system time is introduced which models the course of time in a real CDS. Uniform and event-driven scales of the model (system) time are differentiated. For the first type a constant step Δt of the time change is introduced. In this case the model state vector is considered in the moments of time $t + k\Delta t$ where k is a natural number. The model (5.3.1)-(5.3.2) is built just so. In this case each moment of the real time t_i^r maps to the moment of model time t_i^m, and $t_1^m - t_2^m = A(t_1^r - t_2^r)$ where A is a scaling coefficient. If a modeling object varies only if an event occurs and does not vary in other moments then it is not convenient to use the uniform scale because the state vector remains constant on time segments between the events. In this case an event-driven time reading is better, i.e. the every next moment of time comes in the model only when an event is modeled. There are typical cases for which the appropriate way of real time modeling is clear. For example, for queuing systems the event-driven approach is traditional meanwhile in the ecological systems the time changing is considered as uniform. The length of the time step is determined as usual by the research objectives and resource.

After and sometimes in the same time with determination of the state vector and time step a decomposition of the model and revealing of its block construction are made. For this purpose the set of model variables is divided into nonintersecting subsets each of which contains a group of homogeneous variables. As a rule, a block contains the variables describing a separate process, a subsystem or an element of the object, or a group of factors of the same nature (for example, the marketing factors). In the result of decomposition the model is represented as a complex of the interconnected blocks which interact by certain rules and permit finally to realize the simulative research of the CDS.

The block principle of the model building has a number of advantages which are especially important for the complex simulation models. First of all, if a model requires a big amount of computer memory and time then it is quite difficult to use the model in computer simulation experiments. A good solution in this case is a decomposition of the model so that the programs implementing separate blocks could work in a parallel way and change information in accordance to certain rules. However, the block structure of simulation models is determined not only by the possibilities of computers. The model development requires regular contacts between the researcher and the experts in a specific problem domain. The block structure permits to use the expert knowledge of owners and participants of different processes more efficient without troubling the mutual understanding by specific problems which do not relate to the given block. Besides, it is the block principle that permits to establish the best ratio between the accuracy of modeling and the providing of information. The matter is that in the research of CDS separate aspects are studied less than others as a rule: a smaller amount and worse quality of data correspond to them. In this case there no reason to develop the "well-being" block (provided by complete and accurate data) in details because in a whole the accuracy of results of this block will be neutralized by the roughness of calculations in "bad" blocks. Thus, a principle of equal accuracy of the blocks of a simulation model is important.

As the blocks describe different subsystems, processes and factors then a system time for them could also differ. The time is determined by the internal needs of a block. If the block describes "quick" changes then the time is calculated by seconds, hours, days (for example, technological processes); if a CDS changes in time quite slowly (realization of investment projects) then the time is calculated by months, years and even decades. However, it is necessary to ensure the consequence of times used in the model by their reduction to the united system time.

After the decomposition of the model its blocks are developed separately. For each of them:

- the hypotheses which relate directly to the processes, aspects and elements forming the block are specified and made more exact;
- the respective subset of input and output data is determined; the data could belong either to the sets of "inputs" and "outputs" of the whole model or to the sets of local input and output data of other blocks;
- the set of parameters if formed;
- the principal laws of interaction of the block elements are formalized.

In the process a transition from the qualitative dependences of the conceptual model to the precise quantitative dependences and logical charts of interaction of the elements within each block is realized. It should be noticed that in the practice of simulation it is not at all always possible to represent all the connections of a conceptual models as analytical functions. Often the researcher is obliged to introduce empirical dependences based on the data of natural observations, of the generalization of experience of the modeling of similar objects and so on. An invaluable role on the stage of formalization is played by the expert estimates of the received empirical dependences and parameters.

4. Program Implementation of the Simulation Model

A realization of the computer simulation experiments with a model requires that the formal model be implemented as a computer program. The program realizes a respective research algorithm: a numerical solution of the system of algebraic or differential equations or the optimization problem, a transfer of the system from an initial state to the final one and so on. A program implementation of the model means a solution of the following problems:

- a choice of the hardware;
- a choice of the software;
- a choice of the programming technology.

The choice of hardware is restricted practically only by the financial resource of the research organization or an individual researcher. There are problems that can be solved only by using powerful supercomputers but a very big number of problems concerned with complex objects are solvable by means of minicomputers and even personal computers (especially workstations). It is obviously more pleasant to have a powerful computer that permits to solve broader classes of problems but sometimes the hardware limitations could have a wholesome effect because they impel to investigate the problem deeper and to find a shrewder algorithm. In this sense the hardware limitations could be treated as an additional restriction of the problem.

The software consists of operational systems, programming languages, database management systems, application packages and other software tools. The choice of a specific tool is determined primarily by the researcher preferences and resources because the same objective could be achieved by the usage of different software. From the point of view of systems modeling the programming languages could be subdivided on two big groups: universal and specialized ones. The universal programming languages (ADA, C, Pascal, Fort and others) are destined for the implementation of arbitrary algorithms meanwhile the specialized languages (GPSS, SIMULA, SLAM and others) are intended to the research of the specific classes of systems (queuing systems, process control, dynamic systems and so on). Thus, advantages and shortages of the two groups of languages are complementary: universal languages permit to write any program but for some classes of problems the specialized language is more efficient. The choice of a specialized programming language is connected with technical difficulties (a translator for the language is needed, the programmers should master the language and so on) and could be recommended in the cases when only one well-defined class of problems should be investigated and there are strict requirements to the efficiency; in other cases a universal language is more appropriate.

The application packages which propose finished solutions for the widespread classes of problems (methods of the numerical solution of different classes of systems of algebraic and differential equations and optimization problems, graphical output of data, input data processing and so on) could be very useful. The situations in which it is simpler to write the program independently than to use a package also happen but for the complex systems they are rather an exception.

In the past century the most widespread and approbated was the structured programming technology in different modifications. The main principles of the technology are top-down development, stepwise refinement and structured walk-through. One of the features of the structured technology is modular (block) program composition which was discussed above.

In the last decades the technology of object-oriented programming is first and foremost. Special object-oriented programming languages are developed (C++, Object Pascal, CLOS and others). The object-oriented technology also supports the modular principle of program composition. The mastering of a programming technology and its subsequent use permits to simplify essentially and "automate" the solution of many technical programming problems (testing, debugging, modification, maintenance and so on).

5. Analysis and Correction of the Simulation Model

Before using the built simulation model the following problems should be solved:

- a choice of the values of structural and numerical parameters of the model (identification);
- an examination of the adequate correspondence of the model parameters to the modeled CDS (verification).

For calculation of the specific numerical values of the CDS state variables by a simulation model the form of all functions used in the model and the numerical values of their parameters should be known. A problem of determination of the values of the model parameters is called the problem of identification; it is expedient to distinguish the identification in the narrow and broad sense (numerical and structural identification respectively). In the problem of identification in the broad sense it is necessary to determine the form of functions used in the model. Practically a class of functions is chosen from the set of known classes approbated in the description of the respective classes of real systems. The functions contain parameters the values of which are determined by the solution of the identification problem in the narrow sense.

One of the most widespread methods of solution of this problem is the method of least squares the essence of which is the following. Suppose that on the stage of structural identification a function $y = f(x,a)$ depending on a set of parameters a is chosen as a connection between the variables y and x. It is assumed that the system is observable, i.e. values of the input variable $x(t)$ could be given and the respective values of the output variable $y(t)$ could be measured in the moments of time $t = t_1, ..., t_N$ where the number of observations N is big. Let's divide the segment $[t_1, t_N]$ in two parts: $[t_1, t_m]$ – the learning part и $[t_{m+1}, t_N]$ – the examining part. Compose the expression

$$S(a) = \sum_{t=t_1}^{t_m} [y(t) - f(x(t),a)]^2 \tag{5.3.3}$$

in which the first summand in the square parentheses is the real value of the variable y in t-th observation and the second summand is the value calculated by the model with the set of parameters a. Then it is clear that the set of parameters a* minimizing the expression (5.3.3) solves the identification problem in the narrow sense because for this set the sum of squares of deviations of the model values of y from the real ones is minimal.

The identification problem in the narrow sense is widespread and better known therefore when they say "the identification problem" it is exactly this problem that is meant and it is supposed tacitly that the model structure is already determined. However, for the simulation modeling the identification in the broad sense (structural identification) is just more important. Often in the investigation process it becomes clear that between several variables there is a dependence of a form $y = f(x_1, ..., x_n)$ and a "direction" of the dependence is known (for example, if x_1 increases then the value of y also increases and if x_2 increases then y diminishes); sometimes some quantitative estimates are also known (for example, if x_5 increases in 100 times then y increases in 3 times). Such estimates arise on the stage of analysis and building conceptual model of the CDS: for the formalization the received qualitative dependences should be parameterized, i.e. the problem of structural identification should be solved. As differentiated from the problem of numerical identification formal methods like the least squares method are absent here and the researcher is obliged to be content with a qualitative approach based on experience and expert estimates.

Return to the problem of numerical identification. Using the found optimal set of parameters a* one could receive the output characteristic in the form $y^*(t) = f(x(t),a^*)$, $t=t_1,...,t_m$. The problem of verification is first of all aimed to check that on the examining segment of time $[t_{m+1}, t_N]$ the model trajectory $y^*(t)$ is close to the actual one. A comparison of these two trajectories permits to judge whether the model is appropriate. There are special methods of evaluation of the proximity of trajectories, for example, a calculation of the Tail coefficient

$$U = \frac{\sqrt{\dfrac{1}{T}\sum_{t=1}^{T}(y(t)-y^*(t))^2}}{\sqrt{\dfrac{1}{T}\sum_{t=1}^{T}(y(t))^2} + \sqrt{\dfrac{1}{T}\sum_{t=1}^{T}(y^*(t))^2}} \quad (0 \leq U \leq 1).$$

The closer is U to zero the closer is a model trajectory to the actual one. In the case of U=1 the model is wittingly inadequate and requires restructuring, substituting of data or the new identification with more valid data. However, a closeness of the model and actual trajectories still does not guarantee that the model is adequate to the real object. It is natural to demand the satisfaction of the following additional conditions:

- the computer implementation corresponds to the formal model;
- the model dynamics corresponds to the real object dynamics;
- the modeling results are interpreted correctly.

The correspondence between computer and formal models means that 1) their algorithmic structures are identical (a program implementation keeps the logic of model building) and 2) the coincidence of the domains of variation of the state vector components of the formal and computer models. The second requirement means that the numerical methods used for the program implementation do not generate the error which leads a component out of the domain of admissible values. For example, if a step of integration for a system of differential equations with positive variables is chosen too big then it is possible to get negative values of the variables which contradict to the common sense.

A correspondence of the simulated and real dynamics is partly checked already on the stage of the model verification. It is known that practically any simulation model could be reduced to the required degree of coincidence of the model and actual trajectories by the special selection of parameters but this model is not obliged to be adequate. Therefore for the evaluation of the model adequateness it is necessary to investigate its dynamic properties qualitatively by a series of test calculations. Two main types of tests could be selected. The first type contains tests in which plausible values of external impacts (controlled and non-controlled) are given. If in this case model calculations do not contradict the known laws of a real object behavior then it witnesses about the model adequacy. The second type of tests is based on usage of the critical (extreme, urgent) situations, i.e. the values of data which are not typical for the modeled CDS but could happen. These tests are extremely important for complex models intended for a long-term prediction because the better the model describes the object behavior in critical circumstances the more reliable will be the results of calculations in normal conditions.

The model adequacy is also characterized by its sensitivity to the variations of parameters and initial values of the state vector. If the results of model investigation change essentially for small variations of the parameters and initial data, i.e. the model is unstable then the model is not adequate because real systems are stable. The less accurate the model parameters could be determined the more important is the requirement of stability.

The analysis of model adequacy recalls again about the research objective. The same model could correspond quite well to one research objective and be absolutely useless for the solution of other problems. Therefore a question of the domain of applicability of the model is important: a model is suitable if and only if it permits to achieve the research objective.

The main methods of evaluation of the model adequacy and suitability are not formal (expert estimates, common sense and so on). However, sometimes the procedure could be formalized. Specifically, statistical techniques are quite useful here.

It should be noticed that the process of simulation modeling is iterative. A situation in which the built simulation model satisfies all requirements from the first time and permits to solve the formulated problems at once is exceptional and practically does not occur. As a rule multiple modifications and corrections of the model are required which lead to the success only in the limit.

6. Design and Realization of the Simulation Experiments

In fact, in the simulation modeling a computer is playing a role of the experimental plant which outputs the trajectory of CDS as a response to the given values of control variables, non-controlled factors and initial conditions. As a number of admissible combinations of the external impacts is huge even for finite sets U and Ξ and often not observable at all then a role of design of the simulation experiments becomes clear. The planning is based on the general theory of design of experiments with taking into consideration the specifics of computer simulation (Ougolnitsky 1999).

7. Processing and Analysis of the Simulation Results

As a rule, the direct results of simulation are still not suitable for the solution of formulated problems. The results should be systemized, transformed to a more convenient form, shown to the top management and analyzed together. On this stage negative from the point of view of the model adequacy results are quite probable that requires a model correction and return to the previous stages. The statistical techniques used for the processing of modeling results include fixation and storage of the statistical data, determination of the confidence intervals for the output variables, finding of a functional dependence between variables by means of the regression analysis, identification of the distribution law by a histogram.

The analysis of the modeling results includes an evaluation of the accuracy of simulation experiments, a diminution of the number of model parameters, a determination of admissible ranges of the variables, a determination of the sources of mistakes, a choice of the coordinate system for the results representation, an analysis of the response function and so on (Law and Kelton 1991).

8. Introduction and Maintenance of the Simulation Results

Returning to the requirements of the standard ISO 9001:2008 let's recall that we consider the simulation modeling as a tool of preventive action. Therefore the problems of introduction and maintenance of the modeling results should be regulated by the respective documented procedure (p.8.5.3). This procedure determines a place and a role of simulation models in the corporative information-modeling system (see Chapter 7 of the book).

Chapter 6

ORGANIZATIONAL MANAGEMENT AND OPPORTUNISTIC BEHAVIOR

As an example of the models of organizational management a problem of the sustainable development in a construction project management system is considered. A tree-like management system which consists of an Administration on the higher level and real estate development companies (Developers) on the lower level, $i = 1,\ldots,n$, is investigated. Each Developer maximizes its profit (restrictions on solvent demand are possible). The Administration has a double problem. First, it is interested in the construction works development, i.e. in maximization of the total profit of the developers taking consideration with management costs. Second, it should ensure the conditions of sustainable development which are interpreted here as construction of a given amount of the social class lodging.

In the modern economic science opportunism is treated as the striving of agents for satisfaction of their own personal interests for the sake of public ones. The main mathematical models of opportunism are studied by the theory of contracts. An important and dangerous modification of the opportunistic behavior is corruption the mathematical models of which are also actively investigated in the last decades. A principal direction of the struggle with an opportunistic behavior which is able in the limit to eliminate the opportunism at all is a transfer to the cooperation based on conviction strongly recommended by Deming's philosophy. In this case all participants of the interaction win and a ground for manipulation and opportunism disappears. But this is an ideal result achieved gradually by usage of the palliative actions based on compulsion and impulsion. In the book the author's models of corruption based on the main model of the hierarchical control of sustainable development are considered. The principal innovations consist here in the differentiation between three kinds and two types of corruption. In the case of q-corruption the object of a bribe is the set of admissible values of the bribe-giver, in the case of p-corruption the payoff function, in the case of a-corruption the conditions of homeostasis. In the case of connivance the bribe-taker apportions to the bribe-giver normative values of a resource free and more profitable values for a bribe. In the case of extortion the bribe-taker requires money already for the normative resource and puts a dependent subject in less profitable conditions than provided by the law if the former refuses to give a bribe.

The problem of coordination of private and public interests plays an important role in the context of opportunism. A bright example of the mathematical formalization of the problem is the known Germeyer-Vatel model which describes a situation of the type "travelers in the same boat". It seems rational to consider as a generalization of the Germeyer-Vatel model a so-called game with partly coincident interests the examples of which in static and dynamic formulation are considered in the book.

6.1. SUSTAINABLE MANAGEMENT OF CONSTRUCTION PROJECTS

A real estate development (RED) project ensures implementation of the whole cycle of investments in capital building. The subject of the activity is a real estate development company, or developer.

Real estate development objects are subdivided into types and classes. The main types are urban and suburban residential real estate, commercial real estate, trade and entertainment centers, stores, industrial buildings. The principal classes are premium class (A), business class (B), economy class (C), social class (of the residential real estate as a rule). Intermediate classes as B^+, B^- and so on are also possible. There are professional classifiers which can define the class of an object. The class of an object determines the production costs and possible prices. Each RED-object may be characterized by an index which combines its type and class.

It is evident that there are many developers on each territory. Their "horizontal" interaction may be considered either from the point of view of competition (supply of the same product, tenders), either from the point of view of cooperation (common resources, mergers and acquisitions of development companies). Besides, there are "vertical" hierarchical relations which have a big importance. Those are relations between developers and banks, administrative agencies, different suppliers (consulting, project, construction work and other companies). A problem of control of the sustainable development of the RED-activity has a special interest.

It is rational to use mathematical models for the investigation and control of the RED-activity. There are many publications on project management including mathematical models and methods. Consider a system of optimization and game theoretic models of the RED-activity (Ougolnitsky 2009); its structure is shown in Figure 6.1.1.

The basic role in the proposed system is played by aggregated models of a RED-company. First, these are static optimization models which are aimed to the determination of optimal prices of the real estate development considering constraints on solvent demand and credit return. Second, these are dynamic models of search of the optimal ratio between sales and rentals of a RED-object.

There are two natural directions of generalization of the basic models: "horizontal" and "vertical". First, it is possible to consider interaction between developers as equal economic agents. In turn, two modeling variants are possible in this case. If we consider competitive relations of RED-companies without formation of coalitions then non-cooperative games of n players in normal form arise. If cooperation is possible (common resource, mergers and acquisitions of RED-companies) then the cooperative games are formulated. Second, RED-companies have economic relations with organizations of other types. These relations are hierarchical as a rule, and a RED-company can be both a Leader (in relations with its suppliers) and a Follower (in relations with its investors, credit institutions, administrative agencies). Respectively, hierarchical game theoretic models arise.

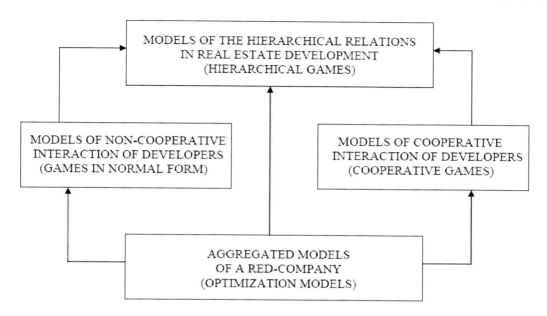

Figure 6.1.1. Hierarchical system of mathematical models of the RED-activity.

A static optimization model of finding optimal sales price with constraints on non-satisfied solvent demand has the form

$$u = \sum_{j=1}^{N} [\alpha_j(p_j)p_j - c_j] S_j - C \to \max \qquad (6.1.1)$$

$$\sum_{j=1}^{N} \alpha_j(p_j) S_j = S^{max}, \ 0 \leq p_j \leq p_j^{max}, \ j=1,\ldots,N, \qquad (6.1.2)$$

where j is a RED-project index (combination of the RED type and class); N is a quantity of RED-projects realizing by the developer in the current year; u is an annual profit of the developer ($); S_j is an annual building volume on j-th RED-project (m^2); c_j is a cost price in j-th RED-project ($/m^2); p_j is a sales price in j-th RED-project ($/m^2); $\alpha_j(p_j)$ is a share of the sold m^2 of the total amount S_j; C are constant expenditures ($); S^{max} is a maximal solvent demand of the developer target consumer group (m^2); p_j^{max} is a maximal possible sales price in j-th RED-project ($/m^2). Let's accept the following considerations:

- variables which don't depend on p may be excepted from the payoff function;
- it is convenient to describe a solvent demand by the parameter $\beta = S^{max} / S_j$, $0 \leq \beta \leq 1$;
- index j may be omitted without lost of generality. Then we get

$$u = \alpha(p)p \to \max \qquad (6.1.3)$$

$$\alpha(p) \leq \beta, \ 0 \leq \beta \leq 1, \ 0 \leq p \leq p^{max}, \qquad (6.1.4)$$

where all variables relate to a separate RED-project.

Models (6.1.1)-(6.1.2) or (6.1.3)-(6.1.4) are static ones, i.e. they describe an activity of a RED-company during a year. The key role in the model (6.1.3)-(6.1.4) is played by the function $\alpha(p)$ which describes the dependence of sales share on sales price. A parameterization of the function $\alpha(p)$ is based on the following proposals which don't constraint a generality:

- $\alpha(p)$ is a decreasing function of sales price, $0 \le \alpha(p) \le 1$;
- $\alpha(0) = 1$, $\alpha(p^{max}) = 0$.

The simplest function which satisfies the constraints is a linear function

$$\alpha(p) = 1 - p / p^{max} ; \qquad\qquad (6.1.5)$$

The solution of the problem (6.1.3)-(6.1.4) with (6.1.5) gets

$$p* = \begin{cases} p^{max}(1-\beta), 0 \le \beta < 1/2; \\ p^{max}/2, 1/2 \le \beta \le 1; \end{cases} \qquad\qquad (6.1.6)$$

and

$$u(p*) = \begin{cases} \beta(1-\beta)p^{max}, 0 \le \beta < 1/2; \\ p^{max}/4, 1/2 \le \beta \le 1. \end{cases}$$

So, if β decreases from ½ to 0 then the optimal sales price $p*$ increases from $p^{max}/2$ to p^{max} but the profit $u(p*)$ nevertheless decreases from $p^{max}/4$ to 0.

The dynamic model of search of the optimal ratio between sales and rentals in commercial RED-projects has the form

$$U = K_1(s,c) \sum_{t=1}^{T} \alpha_t \beta_t + K_2(r,z) \sum_{t=1}^{T} (T-t+1)(1-\alpha_t) \beta_t \to max$$

$$\sum_{t=1}^{T} \beta_t \le 1 , \beta_t \ge 0, 0 \le \alpha_t \le 1.$$

Here U is a total developer's profit ($/m^2); T is an implementation period (months); s is sales price ($/m^2); c is cost price ($/m^2); r is rentals rate for a month ($/m^2); z is maintenance cost for a month ($/m^2); $K_1(s,c)$ is profit from sales considering taxes ($/m^2); $K_2(r,z)$ is profit from rentals considering taxes ($/m^2); β_t is the total share of m^2 sold and rented in the month t; α_t is the share of sold m^2 in the month t.

Considering that the payoff function is linear on the controlled variable α_t we get the optimal solution in the form

$$
\begin{cases}
1, \ K_1(s,c) \sum_{t=1}^{T} \beta_t > K_2(r,z) \sum_{t=1}^{T} (T-t+1)\,\beta_t, \\
0, \ \text{otherwise.}
\end{cases}
$$

For example, if the whole RED-object is sold or rented in the first month then rentals are more profitable than sales if $K_1(s,c) < TK_2(r,z)$, and if the object is sold and rented uniformly during the whole period T then the condition becomes $K_1(s,c) < 0.5(T+1)\,K_2(r,z)$.

Now let's consider several RED-companies acting on a territory. Let's designate them by an index $i=1,\ldots,n$. Then a competitive interaction of the RED-companies is described by n-person game in normal form

$$
G = <\{1,\ldots,n\}\,,\,\{X_1,\ldots,X_n\}\,,\,\{u_1,\ldots,u_n\}> \tag{6.1.7}
$$

where payoff functions u_i are given by the formula (6.1.1) and sets of admissible strategies X_i defined by the constraints of the type (6.1.2). The following hypotheses about the game theoretic model (6.1.7) were investigated:

1) $\alpha_i = \alpha_i(p_i)\,,\,0 \le p_i \le p_i^{\ max}\,,\,i=1,\ldots,n,$

where $p_i^{\ max}$ is the maximal admissible sales price, i.e. $\alpha_i(p_i^{\ max})=0$;

2) $\alpha_i = \alpha_i(p_i^{\ rel})\,,\,p_i^{\ rel} = p_i\,/\,p_{max}\,,\,p_{max} = \max\,\{p_1\,,\ldots,\,p_n\};$
3) X_i is determined by constraints $\alpha_i S_i = S_i^{\ max}$ for each RED-company $i=1,\ldots,n$ independently;
4) X_i is determined by common constraints $\sum \alpha_i S_i = S^{max}$ for the total solvent demand of the population of the territory.

In all four cases of possible combinations α_i and X_i the character of solution (6.1.6) is qualitatively the same.

As far as the solution (6.1.6) is a dominant strategy of the player i then the vector

$$
p^* = (p^*_1\,,\ldots,\,p^*_n) \tag{6.1.8}
$$

could be considered as an equilibrium in dominant strategies in the game (6.1.7). But it is important that the players' behavior is absolutely independent only in the case $\alpha_i = \alpha_i(p_i)$, $\alpha_i S_i \le S_i^{\ max}$. In other three cases the calculation of dominant strategy requires from a player the knowledge of other players' parameters hence the solution (6.1.8) should be more correctly treated as Nash equilibrium which allows some informational exchange between players.

Let's consider again several RED-companies acting on a territory and designate them by an index $i=1,\ldots,n$. Let's suppose that the companies can exchange information, join the resources and realize common projects. Let A_i be the amount of actives of i-th RDE-company.

Then cooperative interaction of the companies may be formalized as a voting game $(A^{min}\,;\,A_1\,,\ldots,\,A_n)$, i.e. the characteristic function has the form

$$
v(S) = \begin{cases} 1, \sum_{i \in S} A_i \geq A^{min}, \\ \\ 0, \text{ otherwise.} \end{cases} \tag{6.1.9}
$$

So a coalition is winning if and only if for this coalition $\sum A_i \geq A^{min}$. The threshold value A^{min} may be treated for example as a deposit necessary for participation in a tender or for providing a bank credit.

It is possible to mark the following specific cases of the game (6.1.9):

1) dictator game $\exists \, i \in \{1,\dots,n\}: A_i \geq A^{min}, \forall j \neq i \, A_j < A^{min}$. In this case the game is non-essential, $v(S)=1 \Leftrightarrow i \in S$, and the only imputation $(0,\dots,0,1,0,\dots,0)$ ($x_i = 1$) exists which forms C-core, is the only Neumann-Morgenstern solution and the Shapley value;

2) symmetrical game of k-th order

$$
v(S) = \begin{cases} 1, s \geq k, \\ \\ 0, \text{ otherwise, } s=|S|, \, 1 \leq k \leq n. \end{cases}
$$

In this case C-core of the game is empty, the Shapley value has the form $(1/n,\dots,1/n)$, an example of the Neumann-Morgenstern solution is the set

$$
\{(x_{i1},\dots, x_{ik},0,\dots,0) : x_{i1} \geq 0,\dots, x_{ik} \geq 0; \, x_{i1} + \dots + x_{ik} =1\}.
$$

It is possible to consider cooperative games in general form where a coalition formation $S \cup T$ means merger (acquisition) of RED-companies S and T or simply joining of their resources.

Let's consider as an example of the hierarchical relations the interaction between RED-companies and a bank (supposing for simplicity that the only bank credits developers on the territory). The game is based on the following rules.

Stage 1: Preparation of Credit Application by RED-Companies

This stage includes for each RED-company $i=1,\dots,n$: formation of concepts of the RED projects $j=1,\dots,n_i$; working out schedules of projecting, construction, and financing for each project; estimating of the actives and cost prices; investigating the needs in credits and applying the bank for credit

$$
K_i^0 = \sum_{j=1}^{n_i} K_{ij}^0 .
$$

Organizational Management and Opportunistic Behavior

Stage 2: Decision Making by the Bank

In this stage the bank analyzes credit applications $K_1^0, ..., K_n^0$; estimates credit risks r_i for each application; determines credit rates $s_i = s_i(r_i)$; makes a decision on credit payments $K_1, ..., K_n$ and corresponding credit rates $s_1, ..., s_n$; informs RED-companies about the decision.

Stage 3: Decision Making by Developers

In this stage each RED-company $i=1,...,n$: corrects real volumes of construction works and corresponding schedules based on credit amount K_i and credit rate s_i; determines the optimal sales price by solving an optimization problem (6.1.3)-(6.1.4).

The model of bank decision making is based on the following simplifying hypotheses:

- credit risks are estimated as

$$r_i = K_i /A_i , \; i=1,...,n ,$$

(6.1.10)

where A_i are actives of i-th developer, K_i are credit amounts. Then the condition of crediting is given by inequality $r_i \leq r^{max}$, where r^{max} is a normative of acceptable risk for the bank;

- credit rate is an increasing linear function of the risk:

$$s_i = ar_i + b = aK_i /A_i + b = a_i K_i + b , \; i =1,...,n.$$

Let's consider that

$$0 < s_{min} \leq s_i \leq s_{max} < 1, \; r_{min} \leq r_i \leq r_{max} , \; s(r_{min}) = s_{min}, \; s(r_{max}) = s_{max} .$$

Then we get

$$a_i = (s_{max} - s_{min})/[A_i (r_{max} - r_{min})], \; b = (s_{min} r_{max} - s_{max} r_{min})/(r_{max} - r_{min}), \; i=1,...,n.$$

Considering the accepted propositions the model of bank decision making in stage 2 is an optimization problem

$$u_0 = \sum_{i=1}^{n} s_i K_i = \sum_{i=1}^{n} (a_i K_i + b) K_i \rightarrow max$$

(6.1.11)

$$\sum_{i=1}^{n} K_i = K , \; 0 \leq K_i \leq L_i , \; i=1,...,n,$$

(6.1.12)

where K is a total capital of the bank in the current year, $L_i = min \{ K_i^0, A_i r^{max} \}$. Solving the problem (6.1.11)-(6.1.12) by the Lagrange method we find optimal values

$$K_i^* = min \{L_i, M_i \} , \; M_i = K / (a_i \sum a_i^{-1}) ;$$

(6.1.13)

$$s_i^* = [(s_{max} - s_{min}) K_i^* + A_i (s_{min} r_{max} - s_{max} r_{min})] / [A_i (r_{max} - r_{min})], \quad i = 1,\ldots,n. \qquad (6.1.14)$$

The model of developer decision making in stage 3 has the form (6.1.3)-(6.1.4) with additional constraint

$$c_i S_i \leq A_i - C_i + (1 - s_i^*) K_i^*,$$

from where we get optimal values of construction works volume

$$S_i^* = [A_i - C_i + (1 - s_i^*) K_i^*] / c_i, \qquad (6.1.15)$$

and the corresponding value $\beta_i^* = S_i^{max} / S_i^*$, which has to be substituted in the formula (6.1.6) to calculate the optimal sales price.

Let's consider the case of interaction of the only RED-company with the bank. Then we get a hierarchical game "Bank-Developer" in the following form:

$$u_0(K_1) = a_1 K_1^2 + b K_1 \to max \qquad (6.1.16)$$

$$0 \leq K_1 \leq min \{K, K_1^0, A_1 r^{max}\} \qquad (6.1.17)$$

$$u_1(K_1, p_1) = [\alpha_1(p_1)p_1 - c_1] [A_1 - C_1 + (1 - s_1) K_1] / c_1 \to max \qquad (6.1.18)$$

$$0 \leq \alpha_1(p_1)[A_1 - C_1 + (1 - s_1) K_1] / c_1 \leq S_1^{max}, \quad 0 \leq p_1 \leq p_1^{max}. \qquad (6.1.19)$$

The outcome (K_1^*, p_1^*) where K_1^* is calculated by formula (6.1.13), and p_1^* by the formula (6.1.6) after substituting the values s_i^* and S_i^* by formulas (6.1.14) and (6.1.15) respectively, is the Stackelberg equilibrium in the game (6.1.16) − (6.1.19).

The problem of sustainable management in the case of RED may be formulated as follows. A tree-like control system is considered where the upper level is presented by an Administration, and the lower level by Developers designated by index $i = 1,\ldots,n$. Each Developer maximizes its profit (probably with constraints on the solvent demand). Administration solves two problems. First, it tends to develop the regional construction works complex, or in model terms to maximize the summary profit of Developers with consideration of control expenditures. Second, it has to ensure sustainable development conditions which mean in model terms some necessary constraints on social class residential RED volumes.

In general model of the sustainable management the Principal can use methods of compulsion (administrative impact), impulsion (economic impact), and conviction (psychological impact). In the described model of hierarchical sustainable management of the regional construction works complex Administration can't use compulsion because it has no legal possibilities to compel Developers to build social class houses. In return, it has many economic possibilities of impulsion: warranties of buying of social class apartments on the previously stated price, state warranties for bank credits, direct grants and so on. Theoretical possibility of conviction (voluntary cooperation of Developers with Administration) also exists. The model of the sustainable management of the regional construction works complex may be presented in the following form:

Organizational Management and Opportunistic Behavior 193

$$u_0(p,S) = \sum_{i=1}^{n} u_i(p_i, S_i) - f_0(p) \to \max, \tag{6.1.20}$$

$$p_i \in P_i, \ i = 1,\dots,n; \tag{6.1.21}$$

$$\sum_{i=1}^{n} S_{i1} \geq S_1^{min}; \tag{6.1.22}$$

$$u_i(p_i, S_i) \to \max, \tag{6.1.23}$$

$$S_i \in \Omega_i, \ i = 1,\dots,n. \tag{6.1.24}$$

By the index $j=1$ are designated social class RED projects; S_{ij} are volumes of construction works for j–th project for i–th Developer; S_1^{min} is the necessary volume of social class construction works, i.e. inequality (6.1.22) reflects social requirements to the sustainable development of the regional construction works complex; $S_i = (S_{i1},\dots, S_{ini})$, where n_i – is total quantity of projects implemented by i–th Developer; $S = (S_1 ,\dots, S_n)$; $p = (p_1 ,\dots, p_n)$ is a vector of impulsion controls used by Administration; $f_0(p)$ is control expenditures function of Administration; u_i is payoff function of i-th Developer; Ω_i – set of constraints for i-th Developer. In this model Developer's strategies are not sales prices but construction works amounts; sales prices are determined by the combination of type and class of the RED project.

An outcome

$$(p_1^*,\dots, p_n^*,\dots, S_1^*,\dots, S_n^*) \in P_1 \times \dots \times P_n \times \Omega_1 \times \dots \times \Omega_n$$

is named the solution of the hierarchical game (6.1.20)-(6.1.24) if

$$u_0(p_1^*,\dots, p_n^*,\dots, S_1^*,\dots, S_n^*) = \max_{p_i \in P_i} \min_{S_i \in R_i(p_i)} u_0(p_1,\dots, p_n,\dots, S_1,\dots, S_n), \ i = 1,\dots,n$$

where $R_i(p_i) = \{S_i \in \Omega_i : u_i(p_i, S_i) = \max_{z_i \in \Omega_i} u_i(p_i, z_i)\}$, $i = 1,\dots,n,$

with the obligatory condition (6.1.22).

Now let's consider a pricing model of the sustainable management of the regional construction works complex. It has the form

$$u_L(\overline{p}, p_0, p) = \delta p \alpha(p) - M \rho(p, p_0) \to \max \tag{6.1.25}$$

$$0 < p_0 \leq \overline{p} \leq p_{max} \tag{6.1.26}$$

$$u_F(\overline{p}, p_0, p) = p\alpha(p) + p\xi(p)(1 - \alpha(p)) \to \max \tag{6.1.27}$$

$$0 \le p \le p_{max} \qquad (6.1.28)$$

Here p is sales price; p_0 — normative price of social class residential real estate development; $\overline{p}$ - limit price of social class residential real estate development; M $>>1$—

penalty constant; $\rho(p, p_0) = \begin{cases} 0, p \le p_0 \\ 1, p > p_0 \end{cases}$; δ - Administration bonus parameter for social

class residential real estate development sales; p_{max} — «overlimit» price of social class residential real estate development (there are no sales if $p > p_{max}$); $\alpha(p)$ is share of residential real estate development bought by Administration with warranty; $\xi(p)$ - share of another residential real estate development successfully sold by Developer without help.

Variable p is Developer's strategy and variables p_0 and $\overline{p}$ are strategies of Administration which tries to satisfy the condition of homeostasis

$$p \le p_0. \qquad (6.1.29)$$

Functions $\alpha(p)$ and $\xi(p)$ decrease on the segment $[0,1]$ and satisfy the assumptions

$\alpha(p) = \begin{cases} 1, 0 \le p \le p_0 \\ 0, p \ge p_0 \end{cases}$, $\xi(0) = 1, \xi(p) = 0, p \ge p_{max}$. Let's consider as illustration

linear functions $\alpha(p)$, $\xi(p)$, then we get

$$\alpha(p) = \begin{cases} 1, 0 \le p \le p_0, \\ \dfrac{\overline{p} - p}{\overline{p} - p_0}, p_0 < p < \overline{p}, \\ 0, p \ge \overline{p}; \end{cases} \quad \xi(p) = \begin{cases} 1 - p/p_{max}, 0 \le p \le p_{max}, \\ 0, p > p_{max}; \end{cases}$$

$$u_F = \begin{cases} p, 0 \le p \le p_0, \\ \dfrac{p_{max}(\overline{p} - p_0)p + p_0 p^2 - p^3}{p_{max}(\overline{p} - p_0)}, p_0 < p < \overline{p}, \\ p - \dfrac{p^2}{p_{max}}, \overline{p} \le p \le p_{max}, \\ 0, p > p_{max}. \end{cases}$$

Hence we have:

- when $0 \le p \le p_0$ then the maximal value u_F achieved by $p=p_0$ and is equal to p_0;

- when $p_0 < p < \bar{p}$ $\dfrac{\partial u_F}{\partial p} = 0$ if $p = \dfrac{p_0 \pm \sqrt{p_0^2 + 4 p_{max}(\bar{p} - p_0)}}{2}$; one of the roots is negative but the positive root is more than $\bar{p}$, hence the maximal value u_F achieved by $p = \bar{p}$ and is equal to $\bar{p} - \dfrac{\bar{p}^2}{p_{max}}$;

- when $\bar{p} \le p \le p_{max}$ the condition $\dfrac{\partial u_F}{\partial p} = 0$ gives $p* = \dfrac{p_{max}}{2}$. If $\bar{p} < \dfrac{p_{max}}{2}$, then the maximal value u_F achieved by $p=p*$ and is equal to $\dfrac{p_{max}}{4}$, otherwise $(p > \dfrac{p_{max}}{2})$ it achieved by $p = \bar{p}$ and is equal to $\bar{p} - \dfrac{\bar{p}^2}{p_{max}}$; let's gather the found values in a table.

Values of p	$[0,p_0]$	$[p_0, \bar{p}]$	$[\bar{p}, p_{max}]$	
			$\bar{p} \le \dfrac{p_{max}}{2}$	$\bar{p} \ge \dfrac{p_{max}}{2}$
p*	p_0	$\bar{p}$	$\dfrac{p_{max}}{2}$	$\bar{p}$
u_F^*	p_0	$\bar{p} - \dfrac{\bar{p}^2}{p_{max}}$;	$\dfrac{p_{max}}{4}$	$\bar{p} - \dfrac{\bar{p}^2}{p_{max}}$;

Note the following:

- closed ranges (segments) of p values may be used because values of u_F on the ends are equal on each side;

- for each $\bar{p}$ is true that $\bar{p} - \dfrac{\bar{p}^2}{p_{max}} \le \dfrac{p_{max}}{4}$;

- if limit price of social class residential real estate development is high ($\bar{p} > \dfrac{p_{max}}{2}$) then the optimal price is bigger than if it is low ($\bar{p} < \dfrac{p_{max}}{2}$), and the Developer payoff is less in this case. But it is dangerous for Administration to establish lower limit price because in this case to achieve the maximal payoff $u_F^* = \dfrac{p_{max}}{4}$ Developer

uses the strategy p*= $\dfrac{p_{max}}{2}$, which may force the condition of homeostasis (6.1.29).

Administration can ensure the sustainable development by the control mechanism $p_0 > \dfrac{p_{max}}{4}$, $\overline{p} > \dfrac{p_{max}}{2}$. Then the strategy p= $\overline{p}$ is not profitable for Developer because $u(\overline{p}) < \dfrac{p_{max}}{4}$, and the strategy p= $\dfrac{p_{max}}{2}$ is not admissible. That's why Developer has the only optimal response p=p$_0$ which satisfies (6.1.29), and $u_F = \dfrac{p_{max}}{4}, u_L = \dfrac{\delta p_{max}}{4}$. The outcome ($\dfrac{p_{max}}{2} + \varepsilon$, $\dfrac{p_{max}}{4}$, $\dfrac{p_{max}}{4}$) is a conviction equilibrium.

Thus, the problem domain of real estate development is conceptualized in terms of optimization and game theoretic models. A system of such models is proposed. The system is based on optimization models of separate RED-companies which are generalized as games in normal form, cooperative games, and hierarchical games. The problem of sustainable management is also adapted for the RED problem domain. Some examples are driven.

6.2. MODELS OF CORRUPTION IN ORGANIZATIONAL MANAGEMENT

In the modern economic science opportunism is treated as pursuing the personal interests, perhaps fraudulently including such forms of deception as lie, stealing, and swindle among others. But more often opportunism means more sophisticated forms of fraud which could have active or passive form, appear ex ante and ex post (Williamson 1970).

The mathematical formalization of the opportunistic behavior is a subject of the theory of contracts (Bolton and Dewatripont 2004; Laffont and Martimort 2002; Salanie 1997). The principal model of the theory is a system "principal-agent" in which the agent realizes different forms of opportunistic behavior.

The institutional economic theory interprets opportunism as a natural phenomenon including the domain of organizational management. Along it a correct management satisfying Deming's principles to a great extent eliminates the causes of opportunistic behavior and in the limit is able to exclude it from the corporative practice. It is not accidental that one of the chapters of Deming's commentator Henry Neave's book (1990) is called "New Climate". In this new climate based on cooperation and conviction there is no place for deception and manipulation, and managers and employees form a united team which realizes friendly and efficiently the common collective objectives and aims.

The key ideas of Deming in this context are "joy of work" and "cooperation". He was sure that the principal management objective has been to create conditions in which everybody could get joy and satisfaction from the work. Unfortunately, the evaluation of a number of workers who get the joy from their work made by Deming in the 1980's does not exceed 2% of managers and 10% of ordinary employees and it seems too much optimistic.

Cooperation is a backbone of the Deming's management philosophy because in this case all the participants of an interaction win. Deming himself has determined the objective of his book "Out of crisis" (1986) as a qualitative comprehensive transformation of management in the direction from competition to cooperation. In this case the process system within an organization functions in the most efficient way because the internal suppliers voluntarily ensure the best conditions for the work of their internal customers along the whole process chain that results in the optimal product realization.

Deming's philosophy means spreading of the relationships of cooperation to the organizational environment, i.e. its relations to the partners including suppliers and clients.

It is traditionally assumed that competition makes a positive contribution to the stimulation of the activity of organization's employees and to the defense of customers' interests for the sake of overcoming of a monopoly. But Deming proves that cooperation is able to solve the same problems on the essentially higher level avoiding a number of unnecessary material and psychical losses. The results of cooperation are not equal for everybody but everybody's payoff is greater than the one in the conditions of competition where by definition it is possible to win only for the sake of others. The "win-win" principle is one of the main ideas of the quality management.

Thus, opportunism is an inevitable consequence of a bad management. If an organization is managed by conviction, i.e. there is a voluntary agreement of all stakeholders about the objectives and means of their activity and an acceptable compromise is achieved then opportunism is substituted by cooperation. However, the complete realization of the ideas of cooperation based on conviction is possible only in the limit as well as the complete satisfaction of the conditions of homeostasis. Therefore a striving for the ideal does not cancel the investigation of an existing opportunism and the search of means of its elimination by less efficient but yet necessary methods of compulsion and impulsion.

One of the most important and dangerous modifications of opportunism is corruption (Rose-Ackerman 1975; Bac 1996; Bardhan 1996). A basic model of the sustainable management with consideration of corruption proposed by us has the form (Rybasov and Ougolnitsky 2004):

$$J_v = \sum_{t=1}^{T} \left[g_v^t\left(p^t, q^t, u^t, \beta^t\right) - M\rho\left(u^t, U_v^t\right) \right] \to \max \ p^t \in P^t, q^t \in Q^t;$$

$$J_u = \sum_{t=1}^{T} \left[g_u^t\left(p^t, u^t, \beta^t\right) - M\rho\left(u^t, U_u^t\right) \right] \to \max$$

$$u^t \in U^t(q^t), \quad \beta^t \in B^t.$$

Here $\beta^t = (\beta_1^t, \ldots, \beta_n^t) \in R_+^n$ is a set of additional control variables of the Follower which are interpreted as a bribe proposed by the Follower to the Leader for getting some privileges;

$B^t \subset R_+^n$, t=1,...,T are the respective sets of admissible controls. Other denotations are given in Table 3.1.2 (see Paragraph 3.1).

Let's classify the kinds of corruption in dependence on the kind of privilege provided to the Follower by the Leader for a bribe. Three kinds of corruption are selected.

1. *p-corruption.* In this case the Leader for a bribe gives to the Follower economic (for example, tax) privileges, i.e.

$$p^t = p^t(\beta_p^t)$$

In the simplest case the dependence could be represented as a linear function $p^t = p_0 - \gamma\beta_p^t$, $\gamma > 0$.

2. q-corruption. In this case the quota fixed by the Leader depends on the bribe, i.e.

$$q^t = q^t(\beta_q^t).$$

Similarly to p-corruption the simplest form of the $q^t(\beta_q^t)$ is a linear dependence $q^t = q_0 - \delta\beta_q^t$, $\delta > 0$.

3. a-corruption. In this case for a bribe the Leader extends a set of strategies corresponding to the condition of homeostasis, i.e.

$$U_v^t = U_v^t(\beta_q^t).$$

In fact, in the case of a-corruption the Leader ignores the condition of homeostasis artificially extending the set U_v and respectively the freedom of action of the Follower. This kind of corruption is the most dangerous because it could result in critical consequences for the sustainable development of the environmental-economic system.

Consider the proposed kinds of corruption in more details.

The bribe has an effect to the tax rate (*p-corruption*):

$$J_v = \sum_{t=1}^{T} \left[c^t p_\beta^t \left(1 - \beta_p^t\right) u^t + c^t \beta_p^t u^t - g_2(p^t, q^t) - M\rho(u^t, U_v^t) \right] \to \max$$

$$J_u = \sum_{t=1}^{T} \left[c^t \left(1 - p_\beta^t\right)\left(1 - \beta_p^t\right) u^t \right] \to \max;$$

where

$$p_\beta^t = p^t - \gamma\beta_p^t + d^t, \gamma > 0$$

$$0 \le p_\beta^t \le 1; \quad 0 \le q^t \le 1;$$

$$0 \le \beta_p^t \le 1$$

$$0 \le u^t \le 1 - q^t \, ;$$

$$U_v^t = \left[0, a^t\right], \qquad 0 \le a^t \le 1 \, , t = 1, \dots, T \, .$$

Thus, a bribe part β_p^t permits to the Follower to get tax privileges. The parameter d^t characterizes so-called degree of "roughness" of the corruption. Assume for definiteness that the value $d^t = 0$ corresponds to the "soft" corruption (connivance) and the value $d^t = \gamma$ - to the "rough" corruption (extortion). In the case of connivance the bribe-taker apportions to the bribe-giver normative values of a resource free and more profitable values for a bribe. In the case of extortion the bribe-taker requires money already for the normative resource and puts a dependent subject in less profitable conditions than ensured by the law if the former refuses to give a bribe. Connivance and extortion are defined similarly for other kinds of corruption too.

The bribe has an effect to the quota (*q-corruption*):

$$J_v = \sum_{t=1}^{T} \left[c^t p^t \left(1 - \beta_q^t\right) u^t + c^t \beta_q^t u^t - g_2(p^t, q^t) - M\rho(u^t, U_v^t) \right] \to \max$$

$$J_u = \sum_{t=1}^{T} \left[c^t \left(1 - p^t\right)\left(1 - \beta_q^t\right) u^t \right] \to \max;$$

$$0 \le p^t \le 1; \qquad 0 \le q_\beta^t \le 1;$$

where

$$q_\beta^t = q^t - \delta \beta_q^t + d^t, \delta > 0$$

$$0 \le \beta_q^t \le 1$$

$$0 \le u^t \le 1 - q_\beta^t \, ;$$

$$U_v^t = \left[0, a^t\right], \qquad 0 \le a^t \le 1 \, , t = 1, \dots, T \, .$$

Here a bribe permits to the Follower to receive a greater amount of resource because the quota increases. Similarly to p-corruption the value $d^t = 0$ corresponds to the "soft" corruption and the value $d^t = \delta$ to the "rough" one.

The bribe weakens the condition of homeostasis (*a-corruption*):

$$J_v = \sum_{t=1}^{T}\left[c^t p^t \left(1 - \beta_\alpha^t\right)u^t + c^t \beta_\alpha^t u^t - g_2(p^t,q^t) - M\rho(u^t,U_v^t(\alpha^t))\right] \to \max$$

$$J_u = \sum_{t=1}^{T}\left[c^t\left(1 - p^t\right)\left(1 - \beta_\alpha^t\right)u^t\right] \to \max;$$

$$0 \le p^t \le 1; \quad 0 \le q^t \le 1;$$

where

$$\alpha^t = \lambda\beta_\alpha^t + d^t, \; \lambda > 0$$

$$0 \le \beta_\alpha^t \le 1$$

$$0 \le u^t \le 1 - q^t;$$

$$U_v^t = \left[0, a^t + \alpha^t\right], \; 0 \le a^t + \alpha^t \le 1, \; t = 1,...,T.$$

In this case the Follower is able to increase the used amount of resource for the sake of extension of the domain of strategies satisfying the weakened requirements of homeostasis. Similarly to p- and q-corruption the value $d^t = 0$ corresponds to the "soft" corruption and the value $d^t = a^t$ to the "rough" one.

A comparative analysis of the model for different kinds of corruption with the usage of the methods of compulsion, impulsion and conviction is made in the paper by Rybasov and Ougolnitsky (2004). It is clear that the presence of corruption is advantageous for the Leader in all cases. Besides, the "rough" corruption is always more advantageous for the Leader than the "soft" one and, in contrary, is less advantageous to the Follower. In the case of compulsion the "rough" a-corruption is more advantageous to the Leader than the "rough" q-corruption if $p > 2a - 1$. This condition is identically true if $a < \frac{1}{2}$. Thus, for the rigid conditions of homeostasis the a-corruption is more advantageous for the Leader. Very often it is more advantageous for the Follower too that makes it especially dangerous. For example, in the case of compulsion the "soft" corruption is more advantageous for the Follower than a "pure" situation without corruption. Even "rough" corruption in the case $a < \frac{1}{2}$ is more advantageous for the Follower than a "pure" case. In the case of impulsion the "rough" a-corruption is more advantageous for the Leader than the "rough" p-corruption if $a < 1 - \dfrac{\varepsilon}{2}$ that is true almost always.

The next model by Denin and Ougolnitsky (2010) develops the basic model of the hierarchical management of an environmental-economic system considering corruption. The new elements are a possibility of the bribe-giver to give several bribes at once and a generalization of the notion of benevolence of the Leader in the case of corruption. A static two-level game theoretic model of the multiple corruption (two types of bribes) using the methods of hierarchical management and the conditions of homeostasis is considered. The model can be used in different problem domains such as environmental-economic or social-economic ones. The terminology of environmental-economic systems is the most convenient for interpretative purposes.

The agents of game theoretic interaction are a functionary who delivers quotas for a renewable biological resource and gathers taxes for the usage, referred further by name Leader (the agent of higher level), and a person or organization who uses and processes the resource, referred further by name Follower (the agent of lower level).

As a basis game theoretic model of the hierarchical interaction is used a Germeyer (1976) game of the class Γ_2 with an additional assumption about knowledge of both agents of the values of all exogenous parameters. For the quantitative evaluation of the level of benevolence of the Leader special parameters named quantities of the corruption roughness are introduced. In accordance to the concept of sustainable management it is the Leader that is the only person who shall ensure the condition of homeostasis. A violation of the homeostatic condition leads to the serious fining of the Leader if the Follower uses more resource than it is allowed by the quota taking bribes into consideration. The penalty function is realized by an infinitely big constant M (6.2.12) entering in the last summand of the criterion (6.2.1). A tax rate is fixed exogenously (by the law) but the Leader can change it for a bribe or being influenced by the factor of benevolence.

The game interaction is regulated as follows. The Leader evaluates the possible payoffs for her actions by predicting the Follower's optimal reaction in assumption that the Follower is economically rational and malevolent. Then the Leader realizes the method of impulsion by determining a mechanism of reward and punishment in the form $p \in P^{U(q)}$ where $P^{U(q)}$ is a set of maps in the form $p : U(q) \rightarrow [0,1]$. Thus, the Leader makes the most advantageous for her Follower's strategies as well advantageous for the Follower herself without restricting her domain of admissible strategies. On the next stage the Leader realizes the method of compulsion by determining the most acceptable for her range of quotas

$$Q_v = \{q : \forall s \in [1-a,1], \forall p \in P^{U(q)} \ J_L(p,s) \leq J_L(p,q)\}$$

that narrows the domain of admissible strategies of the Follower to the subset advantageous for the Leader. At last, the Leader makes a move by choosing her strategy and informing the Follower about it. The Follower reacts by choosing the values of bribes and the part of resource used from the set of optimal reaction

$$R(p,q) = \{(\beta_p, \beta_q, u) \in [0,+\infty) \times [0,+\infty) \times [0,a] : \forall \mu \in [0,+\infty), \forall \eta \in [0,+\infty), \forall s \in [0,a]$$

$J_F(\beta_p,\beta_q,u,p,q) \geq J_F(\mu,\eta,s,p,q)\}$. Two kinds of corruption interaction are presented in the model: p-corruption as a diminution of the tax rate for resource use for a bribe and q-corruption as an augmentation of the quotas for resource use for a bribe. The Leader's optimization problem has the form

$$J_L = c_1(p_\beta u^{k_1} - M\rho(U,u)) \to \max_{q \in Q_v} \max_{p \in P^U(q)} \min_{u \in R(p,q)} ; \qquad (6.2.1)$$

with restrictions

$$p_\beta = p - \gamma\beta_p + d_p; \qquad (6.2.2)$$

$$u \in [0, 1 - q_\beta]; \qquad (6.2.3)$$

$$q_\beta = q - \sigma\beta_q + d_q; \qquad (6.2.4)$$

$$p, q, p_\beta, q_\beta \in [0,1]; \qquad (6.2.5)$$

$$U = [0, a]; \qquad (6.2.6)$$

$$a \in [0,1]; \qquad (6.2.7)$$

$$d_p \in [0, \gamma]; \qquad (6.2.8)$$

$$d_q \in [0, \sigma]; \qquad (6.2.9)$$

$$k_1, k_2, \gamma, \sigma > 0; \qquad (6.2.10)$$

$$\beta_p, \beta_q \geq 0; \qquad (6.2.11)$$

$$M \to +\infty; \qquad (6.2.12)$$

$$\rho(u,U) = \begin{cases} 1, & u \in U \\ 0, & u \notin U \end{cases}; \qquad (6.2.13)$$

The model parameters can be described as follows: U is the domain of homeostasis, i.e. the set of values of environmentally admissible resource extraction parts; a — the maximal allowable value of resource extraction; u — a part of the resource extraction (the Follower's control variable); p – a tax rate for the resource extraction (the Leader's control variable); p_β – the tax rate with consideration of bribing; q – a part of the resource which represents a necessary reserve for its reproduction. In this case the quota is defined as $1-q$ (the Leader's control variable); q_β – a part of the resource with consideration of bribing; M – an infinitely big penalty constant using in the case of violation of the homeostatic condition; $\rho(\cdot)$ – an indicator function for the violation of the homeostatic condition ($u \notin U$); γ – an efficiency of the p-corruption defined as a quantity on which the Leader diminishes the tax rate if the bribe is equal to the total expected income of the Follower; σ – an efficiency of the q-corruption defined as a quantity on which the Leader increases the quota if the bribe is equal to the total expected income of the Follower; d_p – a roughness of the p-corruption, i.e. an estimate of the Leader's benevolence to the Follower as applied to the diminution of the tax rate; d_q – a roughness of the q-corruption, i.e. an estimate of the Leader's benevolence to the Follower as applied to the extension of the homeostatic domain; β_p – a part of the Follower's income assigned for a bribe aimed to the diminution of the tax rate (the Follower's control variable); β_q – a part of the Follower's income assigned for a bribe aimed to the augmentation of the quota (the Follower's control variable); c_1 – a profitableness of the transaction for the Leader per unit of the resource used by the Follower; k_1 – a technological coefficient of the resource usage for the Leader.

The Follower's problem consists in the resource extraction in the limits of quotas determining by the Leader and in the tax payments. But the Follower could try to increase her income by bribing. So, the Follower's problem has the form

$$J_F = c_2(1-p_\beta)u^{k_2}(1-\beta_p-\beta_q) \to \max_{u,\beta_p,\beta_q} . \tag{6.2.14}$$

The expressions (6.2.2)-(6.2.11) are common for the problems of the Leader and the Follower. The parameters u, p, p_β, q, q_β, γ, σ, d_p, d_q, β_p, β_q and the restrictions (6.2.2)-(6.2.11) in both problems have the same meaning. Besides, two additional parameters are introduced: c_2 – a profitableness of the transaction for the Follower per unit of the resource with consideration of her costs; k_2 – a technological coefficient of the resource usage for the Follower.

On the first stage of the model investigation the analytical solution of the non-linear optimization problem (6.2.2)-(6.2.11), (6.2.14) was found for the identification of the Follower's reaction domains and the determination of the Leader's optimal control parameters for each class of the domains. Then a parameter which permits to describe the roughness of corruption in the model including more than one type of bribes was found. The parameter was named an indicator of the summary relative roughness (ISRR). In the case of two types of bribes it has the form

$$I_{pq} = 1 - \frac{d_p}{\gamma} - \frac{d_q}{\sigma} \in [-1,1]. \tag{6.2.15}$$

Basing on this parameter in the model (6.2.11)-(6.2.14) the roughness of corruption was ranged in accordance with the following scale the grades of which generalize the notions of connivance and extortion: «soft» $<=> I_{pq} = 1$; «half-soft» $<=> I_{pq} \in (0,1)$; «moderate» $<=> I_{pq} = 0$; «half-rough» $<=> I_{pq} \in (-1,0)$; «rough» $<=> I_{pq} = -1$.

The scale permits to evaluate the efforts of the Follower required for providing her activity in different cases of the barriers established by the Leader. In the following study of the model a criterial function named reaction charasteristic function (RCF) was found. The function permits to select and characterize the Follower's domains of reaction to the Leader's strategies. It has the form

$$RCF(p,q) = I_{pq} + \frac{1-p}{\gamma} + \frac{1-q}{\sigma}.$$

The values of the RCF with consideration of the sign of an additional expression

$$I_{RCF} = \gamma a - \sigma k_2$$

uniqely determine the Follower's reaction.

In the process of solution of the optimization problem (6.2.2)-(6.2.11),(6.2.14) five domains of the essentially different reactions of the Follower were differentiated. The domains represent an intersection of the rectangle $(p,q) \in [0,1] \times [1-a,1]$ in the axes p and (1– q) and the set of half-planes formed by the parallel straight lines which are described by the following systems of inequalities:

$$\mathbf{I} = RCF(p,q) < 0; \tag{6.2.16}$$

$$\mathbf{II} = \begin{cases} 0 \le RCF(p,q) \le \dfrac{k_2+2}{\gamma} \\[2mm] RCF(p,q) > \dfrac{(k_2+2)a}{\sigma k_2} \end{cases} ; \tag{6.2.17}$$

$$\mathbf{III} = \begin{cases} 0 \le RCF(p,q) \le \dfrac{(k_2+2)a}{\sigma k_2} \\[2mm] RCF(p,q) > \dfrac{k_2+2}{\gamma} \end{cases} ; \tag{6.2.18}$$

$$IV = \begin{cases} RCF(p,q) \geq 0 \\ RCF(p,q) \leq \dfrac{(k_2+2)a}{\sigma k_2} \\ RCF(p,q) \leq \dfrac{k_2+2}{\gamma} \end{cases} ; \qquad (6.2.19)$$

$$V = \begin{cases} RCF(p,q) > \dfrac{k_2+2}{\gamma} \\ RCF(p,q) > \dfrac{(k_2+2)a}{\sigma k_2} \end{cases} ; \qquad (6.2.20)$$

For any given collection of exogenous parameters the domains do not intersect and their union covers the rectangle $(p,q) \in [0,1] \times [1-a,1]$. An additional criterion of the non-emptiness of the domains of the types II and III is the sign of the expression (6.2.13) but the two domains can not exist simultaneously. It is proved that for any fixed collection of the exogenous parameters the domains of not less than one and not more than four types can exist simultaneously.

The optimal strategies of the agent are determined for all types of the domains (6.2.16)–(6.2.20). The bribe strategies for the respective domains have the form

$$\begin{pmatrix} \beta_{pI}^* \\ \beta_{qI}^* \end{pmatrix} = \begin{pmatrix} \dfrac{d_p + p - 1}{\gamma} \\ \dfrac{d_q + q - 1}{\sigma} \end{pmatrix}$$

when $(p,q) \in \mathbf{I}$;

$$\begin{pmatrix} \beta_{pII}^* \\ \beta_{qII}^* \end{pmatrix} = \begin{pmatrix} \dfrac{\left(1 + \dfrac{C}{\sigma} - \dfrac{(k_2+1)A}{\gamma}\right)}{k_2+2} \\ \dfrac{q - (1-a) + d_q}{\sigma} \end{pmatrix}$$

when $(p,q) \in \mathbf{II}$;

$$\begin{pmatrix} \beta_{pIII}^* \\ \beta_{qIII}^* \end{pmatrix} = \begin{pmatrix} \dfrac{p+d_p}{\gamma} \\ \dfrac{\left(k_2 - 2*\dfrac{C}{\sigma} + k_2\dfrac{A}{\gamma}\right)}{k_2 + 2} \end{pmatrix}$$

when $(p,q) \in \mathbf{III}$;

$$\begin{pmatrix} \beta_{pIV}^* \\ \beta_{qIV}^* \end{pmatrix} = \begin{pmatrix} \dfrac{\left(1 + \dfrac{C}{\sigma} - \dfrac{(k_2+1)A}{\gamma}\right)}{k_2 + 2} \\ \dfrac{\left(k_2 - \dfrac{2C}{\sigma} + \dfrac{k_2 A}{\gamma}\right)}{k_2 + 2} \end{pmatrix}$$

when $(p,q) \in \mathbf{IV}$;

$$\begin{pmatrix} \beta_{pV}^* \\ \beta_{qV}^* \end{pmatrix} = \begin{pmatrix} \dfrac{p+d_p}{\gamma} \\ \dfrac{q - (1-a) + d_q}{\sigma} \end{pmatrix}$$

when $(p,q) \in \mathbf{V}$,

where $A = 1 - p - d_p$; $C = 1 - q - d_q$.

The optimal values of the payoff functions for the Follower's strategies from the domains I-V are equal respectively:

1. $J_L^* = 0$; $J_F^* = 0$

when $(p,q) \in \mathbf{I}$.

If the Leader chooses a control belonging to the domain of the type I then both agents receive no income because it becomes not profitable for the Follower to use the resource. The malevolence of the Leader is maximal and the Follower is obliged to give a bribe only for the right of the resource extraction because initially the quota is negative or the tax rate exceeds 100%. This extreme variant is absolutely disadvantageous for both players.

2. $J_L^* = c_1 \left[1 - \dfrac{\gamma}{k_2 + 2} RCF(p,q) \right] a^{k_1}$ when $(p,q) \in \mathbf{II}$;

$$J_F^* = c_2 \left[\dfrac{\gamma}{k_2 + 2} RCF(p,q) \right] \left(\dfrac{k_1 + 1}{k_1 + 2} RCF(p,q) - \dfrac{a}{\sigma} \right) a^{k_2} \text{ when } (p,q) \in \mathbf{II}.$$

In this case it is more profitable for the Follower to maximize her income by an augmentation of the quota than by a diminution of the tax rate. This effect results from the fact that the Leader's benevolence in the quotas fixation is much greater than in the tax rating. This variant is relatively advantageous for the Leader who receives a guaranteed positive income. The Follower's income is also positive.

3. $J_L^* = 0$

when $(p,q) \in \mathbf{III}$;

$$J_F^* = c_2 \left[1 - q - d_q \right]^{k_2} \left(1 - \dfrac{p + d_p}{\gamma} \right)$$

when $(p,q) \in \mathbf{III}$.

In this case it is more advantageous for the Follower to give a bribe for the deliverance from taxes than for the extension of quotas because the Leader's benevolence is high in relation to the taxes but not the quotas. This strategy is not advantageous for the Leader because the deliverance of the Follower from the taxes gives to the Leader no income.

4. $J_L^* = c_1 \left(\dfrac{\sigma k_1 k_2}{(k_1 + 1)\gamma} \right)^{k_1} \left(\dfrac{1}{k_1 + 1} \right)$

when $(p,q) \in \mathbf{IV}$;

$$J_F^* = c_2 (\sigma k_2)^{k_2} \gamma \left(\dfrac{k_1}{(k_1 + 1)\gamma} \right)^{k_2 + 2}$$

when $(p,q) \in \mathbf{IV}$.

It is proved that the choice of a strategy from this set gives to the Leader the global maximum of her payoff function with satisfaction of the restrictions (6.2.13)-(6.2.14). Along with this the conditions of existence of the domain of this type described by the formula

(6.2.7) are essential. It is simple to find a collection of exogenous parameters when the domain of the type IV is empty.

5. $J_L^* = 0$ when $(p,q) \in \mathbf{V}$; $J_F^* = c_2 I_{pq} a^{k_2}$

when $(p,q) \in \mathbf{V}$.

If the Leader chooses a strategy from the domain of the type V then the Follower acquires the complete deliverance from the taxes and the maximal value a of the quota. This strategy is the most advantageous for the Follower but the Leader will choose it only if the domains of the types II and IV are empty because the strategy of the type V gives to the Leader no income.

Thus, the enumerated domains can be ordered by decrease from the point of view of the Leader's preference as follows:

1. the domain of the type IV (if it is not empty);
2. the domain of the type II (if it is not empty and the domain IV is empty);
3. the domains of the types I, III, V if the domains II and IV are empty.

Consider as an example the model (6.2.1)-(6.2.14) for the collection of parameters: $\gamma=1.63$; $\sigma=0.171$; $d_p=0.488$; $d_q=0.145$; $a=0.3$; $c_1=1$; $c_2=1$; $k_1=1$; $k_2=1$. In this case the value of ISRR is equal to $I_{pq} = 1 - \dfrac{0.488}{1.63} - \dfrac{0.145}{0.171} = -0.15$ that permits to classify the corruption as "half-rough". This class is characterized by a moderate malevolence of the Leader. For the determination of existence of the domains of different classes the value of RCF should be calculated:

$$RCF(p,q) = -0.15 + \frac{1-p}{1.63} + \frac{1-q}{0.171};$$

$$\frac{k_2 + 2}{\gamma} \approx 1.84; \quad \frac{(k_2 + 2)*a}{\sigma k_2} \approx 2.63;$$

$$I_{RCF} = 0.318.$$

In the strength of (6.2.3) the domain of the type II for this collection of parameters is empty. Besides, the domain of the type V is also empty because the maximal value of RCF is equal to $RCF(0, 0.7) \approx 2.217 < 2.63$. The minimal value of RCF is equal to $RCF(1, 1) = -0.15$. Therefore, non-empty domains of the three types exist: I,III,IV. The optimal strategy should be searched in the domain IV. In fact, the maximizing strategy is the pair $(1, 0.757)$ which gives to the Leader the payoff $J_L^* = 0.304$. The quantities of roughness for taxes and quota are equal to $\dfrac{d_p}{\gamma}=0.3$; $\dfrac{d_q}{\sigma}=0.85$ respectively that impels the Follower to buy the decrease of taxes rather than the increase of quota. Therefore the Leader fixes the initial tax rate as 100% and extorts a bribe for the diminution. As a result the Follower gives out 72.4% from her expected payoff and decreases the tax rate down to 31%. In the same time the Leader who is malevolent to the quota distribution increases the part of reserved resource from 0.757 to 0.902 that leaves to the Follower the maximal allowable quota for the resource extraction equal to $1-0.902=0.098$. It is not advantageous to the Follower to buy more quotas because the q-corruption has a low efficiency and a high partial roughness. Therefore the Follower chooses the strategy $(\beta_p^*, \beta_q^*, u^*) = (0.724\,, 0\,, 0.098)$ which permits to use the maximal allowable quantity of resource without a bribe and provides the payoff $J_F^* = 0.0186$.

An evaluation of the applicability of the methods of hierarchical management was also made in the model. An essential structural restriction resulting from an interdependence of the bribing strategies and the model criterial parameters for the method of impulsion was found. In the model the mechanism of impulsion is not applicable because when the Follower realizes the optimal strategies of reaction (6.2.9)-(6.2.13) the following chain of dependences appears: $u^*=u^*(\beta_q^*)=u^*(\beta_q^*(p))=u^*(p)$ that generates a vicious circle. Namely, the Leader is unable to establish a system of reward and punishment for the taxes because she can not determine the set of optimal for the Follower parts of resource extraction which in turn depends on the tax rate which should also be fixed by the Leader, and all the enumerated actions are to be fulfilled in the same move. The similar situation arises in application of the impulsion method for the quotas distribution, therefore impulsion was substituted by compulsion in the process of model investigation. This restriction can not be eliminated for the definition of impulsion made in the model. A potential solution could be an introduction to the model a mechanism of the Leader's manipulation or using of the Germeyer games of the class Γ_3 as a basic model of the hierarchical interaction.

6.3. CONSIDERATION OF PRIVATE INTERESTS IN RESOURCE ALLOCATION

Let's consider the following example (Kurbatov and Ougolnitsky 1998). Assume that an economic system consists of the control unit (Leader) and several subordinated enterprises (Followers). The Leader has a financial resource at a rate of R and allocates it among the Followers each of which receives a quantity x_i of the resource. The i-th Follower realizes a product at a rate $\varphi_i(x_i)$ where φ_i is a production function. Then a natural objective of the Leader is a maximization of the total product output

$$J_0 = \sum_{i=1}^{n} \varphi_i(x_i) \to \max \tag{6.3.1}$$

with obvious restrictions

$$\sum_{i=1}^{n} x_i = R \qquad (6.3.2)$$

$$x_i \geq 0 , i=1,...,n. \qquad (6.3.3)$$

The problem (6.3.1)-(6.3.3) is a non-linear problem of conditional optimization which could be solved by the method of Lagrange multipliers. For the illustration the production function is chosen in the form

$$\varphi_i(x_i) = r_i\sqrt{x_i} , i=1,...n \qquad (6.3.4)$$

where $r_i \geq 0$ is a parameter characterizing the productive capacity of i-th enterprise. A Lagrange function has the form

$$L(x,\lambda) = \sum_{i=1}^{n} r_i\sqrt{x_i} + \lambda(R - \sum_{i=1}^{n} x_i). \qquad (6.3.5)$$

According to the Lagrange method the system of algebraic equations

$$\partial L/\partial x_i = 0 \ (i=1,...,n), \ \partial L/\partial\lambda = 0$$

should be solved from where we get the value of a potential extremum point:

$$x_i^* = Rr_i^2/(\sum_{i=1}^{n} r_i^2) , i=1,...,n. \qquad (6.3.6)$$

It is easy to check that the value (6.3.6) is the maximum point of the function (6.3.5) and therefore the maximum point of the initial objective function (6.3.1). This solution has a clear economic interpretation: the Leader should allocate the resource proportionally to the production capacity of i-th Follower characterizing by the parameter r_i. It seems that the problem of resource allocation aimed to the maximal total product output is solved. However, a more precise analysis permits to find some nuances.

First of all it should be noticed that any production function characterizes the marginal productive capacities being only an upper limit of the whole set of production abilities. An investment of x_i^0 resource units could result in the product output at any rate in the segment $[0,\varphi_i^0]$ and not at all necessary the maximal quantity φ_i^0 that is ignored by the notion of production function.

To impel a Follower to use the production abilities to the maximal extent her interests should be taken into consideration, for example, an economically rational striving for the maximization of profit

$$J_i = \varphi_i(x_i) - c_i x_i \rightarrow \max \tag{6.3.7}$$

where c_i is a price of the resource unit for i-th Follower.

The following reasoning is even more essential. To calculate an optimal solution by the formula (6.3.6) in the numerical form the Leader should know the values r_i of the Followers' productive capacities. But in fact the Leader does not know them!

Certainly, the Leader can officially request the values of parameters $r_1, ..., r_n$ from the Followers; however, she receives in answer a collection of values $s_1, ..., s_n$ which are not at all obliged to coincide with the true values. To illustrate the fact that it could be advantageous for the Followers to deliberate the information about the values of r_i consider the following numerical example.

Assume that the system includes only three elements (one Leader and two Followers) and $R = 100$, $r_1 = 100$, $r_2 = 10$. Then the problem (6.3.1)-(6.3.3) takes the form

$$J_0 = 100\sqrt{x_1} + 10\sqrt{x_2} \rightarrow \max$$

with restrictions

$$x_1 + x_2 = 100 \,,\, x_1 \geq 0 \,,\, x_2 \geq 0.$$

Consider different variants of the information about the Followers' productive capacities available to the Leader.

1. The Leader has no information about the Followers' productive capacities. In this case it seems the most natural to divide the resource equally: $x_1 = x_2 = 50$ whence $\varphi_1(50) = 707.11$; $\varphi_2(50) = 70.71$ and the total product output is equal to $J_0^1 = 777.82$.
2. The Leader knows that the first Follower has essentially greater capacities than the second one: suppose $x_1 = 90$, $x_2 = 10$ and receive $\varphi_1(90) = 948.68$; $\varphi_2(10) = 31.62$; $J_0^2 = 980.30$.
3. At last suppose that the Leader knows the values r_1 and r_2 exactly; then by the formula (6.3.6) $x_1{}^* = 99.01$; $x_2{}^* = 0.99$ and finally $\varphi_1(99.01) = 995.04$; $\varphi_2(0.99) = 9.95$; $J_0^3 = 1004.99$.

Thus, the exact information about the Followers' production capacities in comparison with its complete absence permits to the Leader to get an important rise

$$\Delta = (J_0^3 - J_0^1)/J_0^3 * 100\% \approx 22.6\%. \tag{6.3.8}$$

Comparing the values of allocated resource in the variants 1 and 3 it is easy to understand that the Leader hardly receives from the second Follower the true information about the production capacities of the former.

So, a detailed analysis of the situation impels to pass from an optimization problem formulation to the game theoretic one taking into consideration not only the Leader's interests but also the interests of other agents. Namely, a game in the normal form of n+1 person could be constructed as follows:

$$G = <\{B_0, B_1, ..., B_n\}, \{x_i\}_{i=1}^{n}, \{c_i\}_{i=1}^{n}, \{s_i\}_{i=1}^{n}, \{J_i\}_{i=0}^{n} >. \qquad (6.3.9)$$

Here

$\{B_0, B_1, ..., B_n\}$ is the set of players (Leader B_0 and Followers $B_1, ..., B_n$);
$\{x_i\}, \{c_i\}, i=1, ..., n$ – the sets of Leader's strategies;
$\{s_i\}, i=1, ..., n$ - the sets of Followers' strategies;
$\{J_i\}, i=0, 1, ..., n$ – the payoff functions.

The payoff functions in the game (6.3.9) are defined by the formulas (6.3.1), (6.3.7) and formalize the interests of players: the Leader tends to maximize the total product output and each Follower to maximize her profit. In the example the Leader's set of strategies includes the quantities of allocated resource x_i and the price for the resource unit c_i , and each Follower's set of strategies include admissible values s_i of the real parameters r_i informed to the Leader by the Followers. Thus, the information passed to the Leader by the Followers is their strategy that naturally generates a possibility of their opportunistic behavior and a necessity of the hierarchical management.

A problem of concordance of the private and public interests is known for a long time. In his book "The Economics of Welfare" (1920) a British economist Arthur Pigoux has given a big number of examples of "externalities", i.e. not planned consequences of a deal between the first and the second parts which have an effect to the third (probably fourth, fifth and so on) part. The examples are a deterioration of the environment by the construction works, an increase of the customer expenses as a result of the competitive advertisement, an environmental damage by the rabbits breed in hunting reserves and so on. Environmental externalities (first of all pollution) are the object of a serious attention in the modern economic science. The free-rider problem is also well known; for example, an individual could refuse to pay taxes because she thinks that her personal refusal has no essential consequences for the whole society.

One of the most interesting examples of the mathematical formalization of an interaction of the private and public interests is so-called Germeyer-Vatel model (1974). It represents n-person game in normal form in which the payoff functions have the form

$$u_i(x_1, ..., x_n) = f_i(x_i) + f(a_1 - x_1, ..., a_n - x_n), i = 1, ..., n, \qquad (6.3.10)$$

and the sets of admissible strategies are $0 \le x_i \le a_i$, $i=1, ..., n$. Thus, each player shares her resource a_i between private and public needs where the private interests are described by the first summand of the payoff function and the public ones by the second summand (the same for all players). Germeyer and Vatel have proved that if the functions f and f_i , $i=1, ..., n$, monotonically increase than a Pareto optimal Nash equilibrium exists in the game. Besides, they have proposed an efficient way of finding the game solutions. Order the players by the principle

$$\lambda_1 f_1(a_1) \ge \lambda_2 f_2(a_2) \ge ... \ge \lambda_n f_n(a_n).$$

Then such p≤n exists that for i≥p it should be taken $x_i=a_i$, i.e. the players for which the quantities $\lambda_i f_i(a_i)$ are small can spend all the resource for the private interests. Another x_i should be determined from the system of equations $\lambda_i f_i(a_i-x_i)=f(a_1-x_1 ,..., a_p-x_p)$, i=1,...,p. Therefore some players are "free-riders": they miss the resource (a_i is small) or have a poor technology ($f_i(a_i)$ is small) or have a small interest in the results of a collective decision (λ_i is small).

The Germeyer-Vatel model serves a natural formalization of situation of the type "travelers in the same boat" in which all agents besides their personal interests have also the common interest ("to get the shore"). First of all this class of situations contains environmental problems which require joint cooperative decisions (environmental pollution, global warming, biodiversity and so on). A number of generalizations and applications of the Germeyer-Vatel model was proposed in the last years.

We think it expedient to consider as one of the generalizations of the Germeyer-Vatel model (6.3.10) a game with partly coincident interests in which the payoff functions have the form

$$u_i(x_1,...,x_n) = f_i(x_1,...,x_n) + f(x_1,...,x_n), i = 1,...,n, \qquad (6.3.11)$$

where the first summand describes a private interest of i-th player and the second one the common interests. This model reflects a number of typical situations of the organizational management. For example, a non-objective use of the unit resource could be described by the model of a hierarchical game in the form

$$u_1(x_1,x_2) = f(x_1,x_2) + f_1(1-x_1), 0 \le x_1 \le 1,$$
$$u_2(x_1,x_2) = f(x_1,x_2) + f_2(x_1 - x_2), 0 \le x_2 \le 1, \qquad (6.3.12)$$

where f is a function of the common interest, f_1, f_2 are functions of the private interests of the Leader and the Follower respectively, x_1 is a part of the resource allocated by the Leader to the Follower (a part $1-x_1$ of the resource is used by the Leader for her private needs), x_2 is a part of the resource used by the Follower for the needs of the whole organization (a part $1-x_2$ of the resource is used by the Follower for her private needs).

A more general model of the resource allocation in a hierarchical system considering corruption was proposed by Gorbaneva and Ougolnitsky (2009). A two-level tree-like game theoretic model consists of the Leader and n subordinated Followers. The Leader has a resource at a rate of R which is to be allocated between the Followers. Both the Leader and the Followers could use a part of the resource for their private purposes. The Followers can try to increase the allocated quantity of the resource by corruption. Both the Leader and the Followers are striving for the maximization of their payoff functions J_0 and J_i, i=1,...,n, respectively. Without lack of generality assume that $R=1$.

The Leader's payoff function includes: 1) an income from the usage of the resource by the Followers for the needs of the whole organization; 2) an income from the usage of a part of the resource in her personal interests and 3) an income from bribing.

The Follower's payoff consists of 1) an income from the activity aimed to the needs of the whole organization and 2) an income from the activity aimed to the private needs. The

Leader can give a lower bound of the part aimed to the needs of the whole organization. So, the model has the following form.

The problem of the Leader:

$$J_0 = H\left(1 - \sum_{i=1}^{n} r_i(b_i)\right) + \sum_{i=1}^{n} g_i(u_i r_i) + \sum_{i=1}^{n} b_i r_i(b_i) \to \max$$

$$0 \le q_i(b_i) \le 1 ; 0 \le r_i(b_i) \le 1 ; \sum_{i=1}^{n} r_i(b_i) \le 1 .$$

The problem of the Follower:

$$J_i = h_i\left((1 - b_i - u_i)r_i\right) + g_i\left(u_i r_i\right) \to \max$$

$$q_i(b_i) \le u_i \le 1 ; b_i + u_i \le 1 ; 0 \le b_i \le 1, \ i = 1,...,n,$$

where b_i is a part of the allocated resource returned to the Leader by i-th Follower as a bribe (from r_i); $r_i(b_i)$ – a part of the resource allocated to i-th Follower by the Leader (from R); u_i – a part of the allocated resource used by i-th Follower for the needs of the whole organization; $q_i(b_i)$ – a lower bound of the values of u_i controlled by the Leader (from r_i); $g_i(u_i r_i)$ – a payoff of the organization from the activity of i-th Follower; $h_i((1-u_i-b_i)r_i)$ – a private payoff of i-th agent; $H\left(1 - \sum_{i=1}^{n} r_i(b_i)\right)$ – a private payoff of the Leader.

In totality the problems form a hierarchical two-person game in normal form. The Leader's strategies are the resource allocation r_i and the control of resource use q_i. The Follower's strategies are the part of the allocated resource used for the needs of the whole organization u_i and the part of the resource used as a bribe b_i. The Leader moves first. A Stackelberg equilibrium is found as the solution.

The following corruption mechanisms are considered:

1. $r_i = r_i(b_i)$ – a corruption concerned with the resource allocation;
2. $q_i = q_i(b_i)$ – a corruption concerned with control of the resource use. In both cases connivance and extortion are considered.

The following parameterizations are used:

1. the resource use control function depending on a bribe $q_i(b_i)$:

- $q_i(b_i) \equiv q_{i0}$ (the corruption is absent);

- $q_i(b_i) = q_{i0}(1 - b_i)$ (the case of connivance, q_{i0} is an initial level of control of the resource use in the absence of bribe which diminishes to zero while the bribe part increases from zero to one);

- $q_i(b_i) = 1 - (1 - q_{i0})b_i$ (the case of extortion, q_{i0} is a final level of control);

2. the resource allocation function depending on a bribe ri(bi);

- $r_i(b_i) \equiv r_{i0}$ (the corruption is absent);

- $r_i(b_i) = r_{i0} + \dfrac{(k-1)b_i}{n}$ (the case of connivance, r_{i0} is an initial part of the allocated resource which increases while the bribe part increases from zero to one);

- $r_i(b_i) = \dfrac{b_i}{n}$ (the case of extortion, the initial part of the allocated resource is equal to zero and increases while the bribe part increases).

If the corruption is absent then the Stackelberg equilibrium has the form:
$u_i = 1$, $b_i = 0$, $q_i = 1$,

$$r_i^* = \frac{\sqrt[1-\beta]{g_i(x)}}{\sum_{i=1}^{n} \sqrt[1-\beta]{g_i(x)} + \sqrt[1-\beta]{H(x)}}, \quad r_0^* = \frac{\sqrt[1-\beta]{H(x)}}{\sum_{i=1}^{n} \sqrt[1-\beta]{g_i(x)} + \sqrt[1-\beta]{H(x)}},$$

$$J_i(r_i^*) = \frac{g_i^{\frac{1}{1-\beta}}(1)}{\left(\sum_{i=1}^{n} g_i^{\frac{1}{1-\beta}}(1) + H^{\frac{1}{1-\beta}}(1)\right)^{\beta}}, \quad J_0(r^*) = \left(\sum_{i=1}^{n} g_i^{\frac{1}{1-\beta}}(1) + H^{\frac{1}{1-\beta}}(1)\right)^{1-\beta}.$$

In the case of extortion in resource allocation the Follower's optimal strategy has the form

$$u_i = \frac{\sqrt[1-\beta]{g_i(x)}}{2\left(\sqrt[1-\beta]{g_i(x)} + \sqrt[1-\beta]{h_i(x)}\right)}, \quad b_i = 1/2,$$

and the Leader's optimal strategy is $q_{i0} = 1$, $r_i = \dfrac{1}{2n}$.

Here the Leader does not let the Followers to use the resource for their private purposes because she takes away all free resource as a bribe.

In the case of connivance only the optimal strategy of the Followers could be found analytically:

$$b_i = \frac{1}{2} - \frac{nr_{i0}}{2(k-1)}, \quad u_i = \frac{\sqrt[1-\beta]{g_i(x)}}{\sqrt[1-\beta]{g_i(x)} + \sqrt[1-\beta]{h_i(x)}}\left(\frac{1}{2} + \frac{nr_{i0}}{2(k-1)}\right)$$

where x is an arbitrary point from the interval $(0; 1]$ whence $b_i \le \dfrac{1}{2}$.

In this case the Leader's optimal strategy q_i could be found by means of the method of successive approximations, and the set of optimal strategies r_i by means of the method of linearization.

Both in presence and in absence of the private interest of the Follower a quantity of the resource returned to the Leader as a bribe is the same. As for the left part of the resource, it is allocated among the Followers in dependence on their private interests and productive capacities.

Denote $N=\{0, 1, 2, \ldots, n\}$ the finite set of elements of the considered economic system, $\{0\}$ is the Leader. Assume now that coalitions $K \subseteq N$ are admissible. In two-level hierarchical control system the following types of coalitions are possible: 1) a vertical coalition as the coalition of the Leader and a Follower; 2) a horizontal coalition of two or more Followers; 3) a complex coalition of the Leader with several Followers. The payoffs of each coalition in the Shapley value and in the vector of proportional distribution are found for the problem of resource allocation as a cooperative game. For each coalition the quantity of excess $\Delta_K = v(K) - \sum_{i \in K} v(i)$ is calculated. The payoff of the grand coalition is equal to

$$v(N) = \left(\sum_{i=1}^{n} \left((2g_i(1))^{\frac{1}{1-\beta}} + h_i(1)^{\frac{1}{1-\beta}} \right) + H(1)^{\frac{1}{1-\beta}} \right)^{1-\beta}.$$

The Shapley value has the form

$$\Phi_0 = \frac{1}{n+1}\left(\sqrt[1-\beta]{H(1)} + \sum_{i=1}^{n}\left(\sqrt[1-\beta]{2g_i(1)} + \sqrt[1-\beta]{h_i(1)} \right) \right)^{1-\beta} - \frac{n-1}{2(n+1)}\left(\sqrt[1-\beta]{H(1)} + \sum_{i=1}^{n}\sqrt[1-\beta]{h_i(1)} \right)^{1-\beta} +$$

$$+ \sum_{s=2}^{n}\gamma(s) \sum_{\substack{\forall K \\ |K|=s-1}} \left(\sqrt[1-\beta]{H(1)} + \sum_{i \notin K}\sqrt[1-\beta]{g_i(1)} + \sum_{i \in K}\left(\sqrt[1-\beta]{2g_i(1)} + \sqrt[1-\beta]{h_i(1)} \right) \right)^{1-\beta}$$

$$\Phi_i = \frac{1}{2} \cdot \frac{\sqrt[1-\beta]{g_i(1)}}{\left(\sqrt[1-\beta]{H(1)} + \sum_{i=1}^{n}\sqrt[1-\beta]{g_i(1)} \right)^{\beta}} + \sum_{s=2}^{n}\gamma(s) \sum_{\substack{\forall K \\ |K|=s-1 \\ l \in K}} \left[\left(\sqrt[1-\beta]{H(1)} + \sum_{i \notin K}\sqrt[1-\beta]{g_i(1)} + \sum_{i \in K}\left(\sqrt[1-\beta]{2g_i(1)} + \sqrt[1-\beta]{h_i(1)} \right) \right)^{1-\beta} - \right.$$

$$\left. - \left(\sqrt[1-\beta]{H(1)} + \sum_{i \notin K \setminus \{l\}}\sqrt[1-\beta]{g_i(1)} + \sum_{i \in K \setminus \{l\}}\left(\sqrt[1-\beta]{2g_i(1)} + \sqrt[1-\beta]{h_i(1)} \right) \right)^{1-\beta} \right],$$

The vector of proportional distribution has the form:

$$x_0 = \left(\sum_{i=1}^{n}\sqrt[1-\beta]{H(1)} + \left(\sqrt[1-\beta]{2g_i(1)} + \sqrt[1-\beta]{h_i(1)} \right) \right)^{1-\beta} \frac{\sum_{i=1}^{n}\sqrt[1-\beta]{g_i(1)} + \sqrt[1-\beta]{H(1)}}{2\sum_{i=1}^{n}\sqrt[1-\beta]{g_i(1)} + \sqrt[1-\beta]{H(1)}}$$

$$x_i = \frac{\sqrt[1-\beta]{g_i(1)}}{2\sum_{i=1}^{n}\sqrt[1-\beta]{g_i(1)} + \sqrt[1-\beta]{H(1)}} \left(\sqrt[1-\beta]{H(1)} + \sum_{i=1}^{n}\left(\sqrt[1-\beta]{2g_i(1)} + \sqrt[1-\beta]{h_i(1)} \right) \right)^{1-\beta}.$$

Organizational Management and Opportunistic Behavior

A more general dynamic model of hierarchical control by resource allocation in a tree-like environmental-economic system may be represented as follows:

$$f_0(x(t),u_1(\bullet),...,u_n(\bullet)) = \sum_{i\in M}\int_{t_0}^T g_i(x(t),u_i(t))dt \to \max;$$

$$0 \le q_i(t) \le 1;\ r_i(t) \ge 0, i \in M; \sum_{i\in M} r_i(t) = 1, t \in [t_0,T];$$

$$f_i(x(t),u_i(t)) = g_i(x(t),u_i(t)) + h_i(x(t),u_i(t)), i \in M, t \in [t_0,T];$$

$$q_i(t) \le u_i(t) \le r_i(t), i \in M, t \in [t_0,T];$$

$$\frac{dx}{dt} = F(x(t),u_1(t),...,u_n(t)), x(0) = x_0.$$

The tree-like hierarchical structure consists of n+1 element: one element of the higher level (Leader) designated by index 0 and n elements of the lower level (Followers). Let's denote the whole set of elements by N={0,1,...,n}, and the set of elements on lower level by M={1,...,n}. The Leader controls the Followers separately by control variables of compulsion q_i (administrative impacts) and control variables r_i of impulsion (resources). Without lack of generality we may consider the total resource equal to one. After receiving the values of q_i and r_i each Follower $i\in M$ chooses the control value u_i (environmental protection efforts). The objective of Leader is to maximize the payoff function f_0, and the objective of each Follower is to maximize f_i . We suppose that g_i represents the ecological interests for the whole system, and h_i represents private economic interests of i-th Follower; functions g_i are non-negative, continuous, differentiable, monotonically increase on u_i, $g_i(x(t),0)=0$; functions h_i are non-negative, continuous, differentiable, monotonically decrease on u_i , $h_i(x(t),r_i(t))=0$ for each $t\in[t_0,T]$.

To define a cooperative differential game with initial state x_0 and time horizon $[t_0,T]$ on the base of compulsion it is sufficient to build a characteristic function v: $2^N \to R$ using the definition of compulsion (3.1.5). In this case the values of r_i are fixed, and the Leader chooses q_i, $i\in M$, as open-loop strategies $q_i(\cdot)=\{q_i(t)\}$, $t\in[t_0,T]$. We have

$$v(\{0\};x_0,T-t_0) = \max_{0\le q_i(\bullet)\le r_i(\bullet)\delta i\in M}\ \min_{u(t)\in R_i(q_i(\bullet),r_i(\bullet)),i\in M} \sum_{i\in M}\int_{t_0}^T g_i(x(t),u_i(t))dt = \sum_{i\in M}\int_{t_0}^T g_i(x(t),r_i(t))dt;$$

$$R_i(q_i(t),r_i(t)) = Arg\ \max_{q_i(\bullet)\le u_i(\bullet)\le r_i(\bullet)} f_i(x(t),u_i(t)), i \in M, t \in [t_0,T];$$

the compulsion mechanism has the form $q_i(t)=r_i(t)=>u_i^*(t)=r_i(t)$, $i\in M$, where $u_i^*(t)$ is an optimal reaction of i-th Follower on $q_i(t)$, $t\in[t_0,T]$. Respectively,

$$v(\{i\}; x_0, T - t_0) = \int_{t_0}^{T} g_i(x(t), r_i(t)) dt + \int_{t_0}^{T} h_i(x(t), r_i(t)) dt = \int_{t_0}^{T} g_i(x(t), r_i(t)) dt, j \in M;$$

$$v(K; x_0, T - t_0) = \sum_{i \in K} \int_{t_0}^{T} f_i(x(t), r_i(t)) dt = \sum_{i \in K} \int_{t_0}^{T} g_i(x(t), r_i(t)) dt, K \subseteq M.$$

So, if Leader has full possibilities of compulsion, he can compel all Followers to follow the ecological interests only. Farther we get

$$v(\{0\} \cup K; x_0, T - t_0) = \max_{0 \le q_i(\bullet) \le r_i(\bullet), i \in M} \max_{q_i(\bullet) \le u_i(\bullet) \le r_i(\bullet), i \in K} \min_{q_i(\bullet) \le u_i(\bullet) \le r_i(\bullet), i \in M \setminus K} [\sum_{i \in M} \int_{t_0}^{T} g_i(x(t), u_i(t)) dt +$$

$$+ \sum_{i \in K} \int_{t_0}^{T} g_i(x(t), u_i(t)) dt + \sum_{i \in K} \int_{t_0}^{T} h_i(x(t), u_i(t)) dt] =$$

$$= \max_{0 \le q_i(\bullet) \le r_i(\bullet) i \in M} \max_{q_i(\bullet) \le u_i(\bullet) \le r_i(\bullet), i \in K} \min_{q_i(\bullet) \le u_i(\bullet) \le r_i(\bullet), i \in M \setminus K} [\sum_{i \in K} (2 \int_{t_0}^{T} g_i(x(t), u_i(t)) dt +$$

$$+ \int_{t_0}^{T} h_i(x(t), u_i(t)) dt) + \sum_{i \in M \setminus K} \int_{t_0}^{T} g_i(x(t), u_i(t)) dt] = \sum_{i \in K} \int_{t_0}^{T} (2 g_i(x(t), u_i * (t)) + h_i(x(t), u_i * (t))) dt +$$

$$+ \sum_{i \in M \setminus K} \int_{t_0}^{T} g_i(x(t), r_i(t)) dt,$$

where

$$\sum_{i \in K} \int_{t_0}^{T} (2 g_i(u_i * (t)) + h_i(u_i * (t))) dt =$$

$$= \max_{0 \le q_i(\bullet) \le r_i(\bullet), i \in K} \max_{q_i(\bullet) \le u_i(\bullet) \le r_i(\bullet), i \in K} \sum_{i \in K} \int_{t_0}^{T} (2 g_i(x(t), u_i(t)) + h_i(x(t), u_i(t))) dt,$$

the mechanism of compulsion is $q_i * (\bullet) = \begin{cases} u_i * (\bullet), i \in K, \\ r_i(\bullet), i \in M \setminus K. \end{cases}$ At last,

$$v(N; x_0, T - t_0) = \max_{0 \le q_i(\bullet) \le r_i(\bullet), i \in M} \max_{q_i(\bullet) \le u_i(\bullet) \le r_i(\bullet), i \in M} \sum_{i \in M} \int_{t_0}^{T} [2 g_i(x(t), u_i(t)) + h_i(x(t), u_i(t))] dt =$$

$$= \sum_{i \in M} \int_{t_0}^{T} [2 g_i(x(t), u_i * (t)) + h_i(x(t), u_i * (t))] dt.$$

So, if the Leader forms a coalition with Followers, he begins to consider their private interests, and the point of maximum shifts.

Lemma. Function v is superadditive.

Proof. It is sufficient to consider three cases:

1) $\forall K, L \subseteq M (K \cap L = \varnothing)$

$$v(K; x_0, T - t_0) + v(L; x_0, T - t_0) = \sum_{i \in K} \int_{t_0}^{T} g_i(x(t), r_i(t)) dt + \sum_{i \in L} \int_{t_0}^{T} g_i(x(t), r_i(t)) dt =$$

$$= \sum_{i \in K \cup L} \int_{t_0}^{T} g_i(x(t), r_i(t)) dt = v(K \cup L; x_0, T - t_0);$$

2) $\forall K \subseteq M$

$$v(\{0\} \cup K; x_0, T - t_0) - v(\{0\}; x_0, T - t_0) - v(K; x_0, T - t_0) =$$

$$= \sum_{i \in K} \int_{t_0}^{T} [2g_i(x(t), u_i *(t)) + h_i(x(t), u_i *(t))] dt + \sum_{i \in M \setminus K} \int_{t_0}^{T} g_i(x(t), r_i(t)) dt - \sum_{i \in M} \int_{t_0}^{T} g_i(x(t), r_i(t)) dt -$$

$$- \sum_{i \in K} \int_{t_0}^{T} g_i(x(t), r_i(t)) dt = \sum_{i \in K} \int_{t_0}^{T} [2g_i(x(t), u_i *(t)) + h_i(x(t), u_i *(t)) - 2g_i(x(t), r_i(t))] dt \geq 0;$$

3) for $\forall K, L \subseteq M (K \cap L = \varnothing)$ as far $M \setminus K = M \setminus (K \cup L) \cup L$ we get

$$v(\{0\} \cup K \cup L; x_0, T - t_0) - v(\{0\} \cup K; x_0, T - t_0) - v(L; x_0, T - t_0) =$$

$$= \sum_{i \in K \cup L} \int_{t}^{T} [2g_i(x(t), u_i *(t)) + h_i(x(t), u_i *(t))] dt + \sum_{i \in M \setminus (K \cup L)} \int_{t_0}^{T} g_i(x(t), r_i(t)) dt -$$

$$- \sum_{i \in K} \int_{t_0}^{T} [2g_i(x(t), u_i *(t)) + h_i(x(t), u_i *(t))] dt - \sum_{i \in M \setminus K} \int_{t_0}^{T} g_i(x(t), r_i(t)) dt - \sum_{i \in L} \int_{t_0}^{T} g_i(x(t), r_i(t)) dt =$$

$$= \sum_{i \in L} \int_{t_0}^{T} [2g_i(x(t), u_i *(t)) + h_i(x(t), u_i *(t)) - 2g_i(x(t), r_i(t))] dt \geq 0.$$

Thus, the function v is superadditive and generates a cooperative differential game on the base of compulsion $\Gamma_v = \langle N; v; x_0, T - t_0 \rangle = \Gamma_v(x_0, T - t_0)$. Let's remind that the set of non-dominated imputations in the game $\Gamma_v(x_0, T - t_0)$ is called C-core and denoted as $C_v(x_0, T - t_0)$, and the Shapley value $\Phi^v(x_0, T - t_0)$ is determined by formulas

$$\Phi_i^v(x_0, T - t_0) = \sum_{K \subset N(i \in K)} \gamma(k)[v(K; x_0, T - t_0) - v(K \setminus \{i\}; x_0, T - t_0)], i = 1, ..., n,$$

$$\gamma(k) = \frac{(n-k)!(k-1)!}{n!}, k = |K|, n = |N|.$$

(6.3.13)

Theorem. In the game $\Gamma_v(x_0, T-t_0)$ it is true that $\Phi^v(x_0, T-t_0) \in C_v(x_0, T-t_0)$.

Proof. Let's calculate the components of Shapley value subject to (6.3.13):

$$\Phi_0^{\ v}(x_0, T-t_0) = \gamma(1)v(\{0\}; x_0, T-t_0) + \gamma(2) \sum_{\{0\}\in K, |K|=2}[v(K; x_0, T-t_0) - v(K \setminus \{0\}; x_0, T-t_0)] + \ldots +$$

$$+ \gamma(n) \sum_{\{0\}\in K, |K|=n}[v(K; x_0, T-t_0) - v(K \setminus \{0\}; x_0, T-t_0)] + \gamma(n+1)[v(N; x_0, T-t_0) - v(M; x_0, T-t_0)] =$$

$$= \gamma(1)\sum_{i\in M}\int_{t_0}^{T}g_i(x(t), r_i(t))dt + \gamma(2) \sum_{\{0\}\in K, |K|=2}\int_{t_0}^{T}[\sum_{i\in K}(2g_i(x(t), u_i*(t)) + h_i(x(t), u_i*(t))) +$$

$$+ \sum_{i\in M\setminus K}g_i(x(t), r_i(t)) - \sum_{i\in K}g_i(x(t), r_i(t))]dt + \ldots + \gamma(n) \sum_{\{0\}\in K, |K|=n}\int_{t_0}^{T}[\sum_{i\in K}(2g_i(x(t), u_i*(t)) + h_i(x(t), u_i*(t))) +$$

$$+ \sum_{i\in M\setminus K}g_i(x(t), r_i(t)) - \sum_{i\in K}g_i(x(t), r_i(t))]dt + \gamma(n+1)[\sum_{i\in M}\int_{t_0}^{T}(2g_i(x(t), u_i*(t)) + h_i(x(t), u_i*(t)))dt +$$

$$+ \sum_{i\in M}\int_{t_0}^{T}g_i(x(t), r_i(t))dt] = \gamma(2) \sum_{\{0\}\in K, |K|=2}\sum_{i\in K}\int_{t_0}^{T}(2g_i(x(t), u_i*(t)) + h_i(x(t), u_i*(t)))dt +$$

$$+ \gamma(3) \sum_{\{0\}\in K, |K|=3}\sum_{i\in K}\int_{t_0}^{T}(2g_i(x(t), u_i*(t)) + h_i(x(t), u_i*(t)))dt + \ldots +$$

$$+ \gamma(n) \sum_{\{0\}\in K, |K|=n}\sum_{i\in K}\int_{t_0}^{T}(2g_i(x(t), u_i*(t)) + h_i(x(t), u_i*(t)))dt + \gamma(n+1)\sum_{i\in N}\int_{t_0}^{T}(2g_i(x(t), u_i*(t)) +$$

$$+ h_i(x(t), u_i*(t)))dt = \sum_{s=2}^{n+1}\gamma(s) \sum_{\{0\}\in K, |K|=s}\sum_{i\in K}\int_{t_0}^{T}A_i(t)dt, A_i(t) = 2g_i(x(t), u_i*(t)) + h_i(x(t), u_i*(t)).$$

As each of n players of lower level takes part $C_{n-1}^{\ s-1}$ times in the set of coalitions of s players than

$$\Phi_0^{\ v}(x_0, T-t_0) = \sum_{s=2}^{n+1}\gamma(s)C_{n-1}^{\ s-2}\sum_{i\in M}\int_{t_0}^{T}A_i(t)dt = 0.5\sum_{i\in M}\int_{t_0}^{T}A_i(t)dt. \text{ Thus,}$$

$$\Phi_0^{\ v}(x_0, T-t_0) = \sum_{i\in M}\int_{t_0}^{T}(g_i(x(t), u_i*(t)) + 0.5h_i(x(t), u_i*(t)))dt = 0.5v(N; x_0, T-t_0).$$

As far Shapley value is Pareto-optimal we get

$$\sum_{i\in M}\Phi_i^{\ v}(x_0, T-t_0) = 0.5v(N; x_0, T-t_0) = \Phi_0^{\ v}(x_0, T-t_0),$$

and as far all Followers are completely symmetrical we get

$$\Phi_i^{\ v}(x_0, T-t_0) = \int_{t_0}^{T}(g_i(x(t), u_i*(t)) + 0.5h_i(x(t), u_i*(t)))dt, i \in M.$$

To complete the proof it is sufficient to verify directly the inequalities of three types:

1) $\displaystyle\sum_{i\in K}\Phi_0^v(x_0,T-t_0)+\sum_{j\in L}\Phi_j^v(x_0,T-t_0)\geq v(K\cup L;x_0,T-t_0);$

2) $\displaystyle\Phi_0^v(x_0,T-t_0)+\sum_{i\in K}\Phi_i^v(x_0,T-t_0)\geq v(\{0\}\cup K;x_0,T-t_0);$

3) $\displaystyle\Phi_0^v(x_0,T-t_0)+\sum_{i\in K}\Phi_i^v(x_0,T-t_0)+\sum_{j\in L}\Phi_j^v(x_0,T-t_0)\geq v(\{0\}\cup(K\cup L)),$

$$K\cap L=\varnothing, K,L\subseteq M.$$

A cooperative game on the base of impulsion is built similarly. Unfortunately, the optimality principle $\Phi^v(x_0,T-t_0)\in C_v(x_0,T-t_0)$ is not dynamically stable (time consistent). To ensure the dynamic stability a regularization procedure (payoff distribution procedure) has to be used (Petrosyan and Zenkevich 2007). Define

$$\Phi_i^v(x_0,T-t_0)=\int_{t_0}^{T}B_i(s)ds, B_i(t)\geq 0, \sum_{i\in N}B_i(t)=1, t\in[t_0,T].$$

The quantity $B_i(t)=\dfrac{d\Phi_i^v(x_0,T-t_0)}{dt}$ is the instantaneous payoff to the player i at the moment t. The vector $B(t)=(B_0(t),B_1(t),\ldots,B_n(t))$ determines a distribution of the total gain among all players. By properly choosing $B(t)$ it is possible to ensure that at each instant $t\in[t_0,T]$ there will be no objections against realization of the original agreement $\Phi^v(x_0,T-t_0)$, i.e. the imputation $\Phi^v(x_0,T-t_0)$ is time consistent. It is proved under general conditions that the regularization procedure $B(t)$, $t\in[t_0,T]$, leading to the time consistent cooperative solution, exists and is realizable (Petrosyan and Zenkevich 1996).

Chapter 7

CORPORATIVE INFORMATION-MODELING SYSTEMS

Creating of the sustainable management systems in organizations requires structuring of the data which describe the state of controlled objects, external and internal impacts, norms and regulations. The structuring is made on the base of information modeling which permits to describe the data and concerned operations and create databases and corporation information systems as well as to identify simulation models and other mathematical models.

A general theory of information modeling and database design is being developed for a long time that has resulted in generally adopted notions of data models and their elements such as objects, relations, operations, attributes and so on. There is a mathematical formalism convenient for description of not only a current state of the organization but also of its change in time such as Markov processes, finite automates, Petri nets and other models. The modeling to an extent takes into consideration a structure of the modeled system. In this monograph the author's concept of dynamical multidigraphs is considered as an example. There are also specific methods of the information modeling of business processes among which the IDEF0 notation plays a leading role. This notation is well compatible with the requirements of quality management and is recommended for the formalization of the product realization processes.

A practical realization of the sustainable management technologies requires the usage of computer information systems (CIS). The CIS ensures an automation of the control in organization on the base of modern information technologies. The notion of CIS is a product of a rather long evolution from the second half of the last century. In this process of evolution the requirements to the CIS were determined, a number of standards such as MRP, MRP II, ERP, CRP and others was developed, an experience of using was accumulated. The modern notion of CIS includes not only a software of complex automation of the control processes and document flows but also a program implementation of data analysis, monitoring and predicting on the base of mathematical modeling. Here a number of concepts are used such as data mining, data warehouses, OLAP technologies, simulation and expert systems. In the second paragraph of the chapter an overview of the concepts is given, a simulation system of business processes modeling as a queuing system is driven as an example.

In the third paragraph the author's concept of the corporative information-modeling system (CIMS) of decision support in organizations and territories is presented, a description of the technology of sustainable management of an organization based on the CIMS is given.

7.1. Information Modeling of Organizations

Information modeling is a part of system analysis that identifies the data and relationships between them as well as operations with the data. By the figure of speech used by Matt Flavin (1981:1), "information modeling is a marriage of the art of system analysis with the science of data representation". The principal destination of information models is a development of the databases which ensure computer storage and processing of the necessary information about a modeled system.

The databases represent the state of a modeled system in any moment of time by describing the system elements (objects, entities), the relationships between them and the operations with them. The description of operations contains explicit or implicit transfer to the dynamics of modeled system, i.e. the representation of its subsequent states with consideration of the internal and external factors. For determination of the essential objects, relationships and operations an analysis of the system and its laws of functioning are required. In the case of organizations one could speak about its policy research. In accordance with the general principles of mathematical modeling the logical database design is completely determined by the objectives and resources of the information system project which establish a set of the objects, relationships and operations and the level of their specification.

Information modeling permits to increase essentially the accuracy of description of the problem domain that creates a reliable base for the further database design. In the same time it is necessary to underline that it is impossible to formalize the problem of building an information model completely (in other words, to pass its solution to the computer).

The five logical components of an information model are selected (Flavin 1981):

1) object types, or entities which play a specific role in the system being modeled. Examples are persons, things, documents, organizations, agreements, policies and so on;
2) relationships, or named associations between two or more object types. They are the result of interactions between the participating object types or logical associations between them and contain the names of the participating object types as attributes;
3) operations that change the state of the system being modeled and therefore provide a transfer to the description of its dynamics. There are two classes of operations: standard (add/delete, modify/rewrite) and user defined (sign contract, confirm purchase);
4) data elements, or unit facts (order number, department name) that characterize object types or relationships;
5) regulations, or rules that govern the content, structure, integrity, and operational activity of the model. They apply to the model as a whole and express, in general, high-level policy constraints.

Each logical component is described by six subcomponents which are defined below.

1. Name – a unique identifier of the logical component within the information model. The name may consist of multiple words (compound name).

2. Definition in terms of the role that the element plays in the model. In organizations business policy is generally the source of valid component definitions.
3. Content – a set of data elements associated with the object type or relationship.
4. Structure – data elements associated with some component can be classified as single-valued or multi-valued for this component. Single-valued data elements (name, number) are grouped in a so-called "base segment" and multi-valued data elements (names of subordinates, customers) are grouped into one or more "dependent segments". The collection of all segments makes up the data structure associated with the given component.
5. Allowable operations are all operations that can be performed on a given component. Since operations change the state of the model, each allowable operation is described by a set of pre- and post-conditions. Pre-conditions must be true before the operation and post-conditions must be true immediately after the operation has been performed. Therefore an information model combines the elements of "entity-relationship" analysis and the elements of "state-transaction" analysis.
6. Data dependencies – rules that determine logical connections between the components. They are the chief tool for logical integration of an information model.

Database is a systematic and logically organized collection of facts the logical structure of which is derived from an information model. All occurrences of object types, relationships, and data elements are stored in the database. Finally, an information model is composed of graphic and analytic specifications of the components and a database (Flavin 1981).

The information modeling process can be subdivided into two major phases: analysis and representation. The analysis phase is composed of procedures for the analysis of the problem domain and permits to identify the data components, to produce augmented entity-relationship diagrams, to complete partially the analytic specifications, and to create policy definitions.

The representation phase is concerned with creating data structures for the data components, and completing and logical integration of the model. Data dependencies, pre- and post-conditions, and regulations are also specified in this phase.

Levels of specifications include:

- name of domain of information;
- entity-relationship diagram of domain;
- entity-relationship diagram and complete set of required data elements for the domain;
- fully defined and completed information model of the domain of information.

In order to complete the information model, it is necessary to define each component unambiguously and consistently in the context of their meaning in the real-world system being modeled. Definitions of the model components will depend on discovering the rules, laws, and conventions that are the policy that govern the system. Most often, the policy is not written down neatly in a manual and must be extracted piece by piece from the combine knowledge of managers and experts. By the way, one of the main tasks of the quality management system is to document this vague knowledge. A number of special methods are used for the solution of this problem such as functional analysis, scenario analysis, transaction analysis, abstraction analysis and anchor-point analysis (Flavin 1981).

A traditional approach to database design selects three levels of representation: conceptual (from the point of view of an administrator), logical (from the point of view of an applied programmer and user) and physical (from the point of view of a system analyst and system programmer). On the conceptual level entities, relationships between them and their attributes are differentiated as it was described above; on the logical level one of the known data models (relational, hierarchical or network one) is used; on the physical level physical blocks, stored records, pointers and overflow data are defined (Teorey and Fry 1982).

There are a number of mathematical models which permit to describe the state of complex system including explicit or implicit consideration of their dynamics. Some examples are Markov processes, finite automates, Petri nets, queuing systems.

The description of the state of a complex system in the moment of time t taking into consideration its structure by means of dynamic multidigraphs (Ougolnitsky 1996) includes the following elements.

1. A set of vertices $Y(t)=(y_1(t),...,y_n(t))$ where $n(t)$ is a number of vertices in the moment t. Decompose the set $Y(t)$ onto two non-intersecting subsets: $\forall t \ Y(t) = Y_1(t) \cup Y_2(t), Y_1(t) \cap Y_2(t)=\varnothing$ (it is possible that $Y_2(t)= \varnothing$). Let's name the vertices from the subset $Y_1(t)$ compartments and denote them by squares and the vertices from the subset $Y_2(t)$ transformers and denote by circles.

2. A set of arcs $Z(t)=\{z_{ij}^{k}(t)\}$, $1 \le i,j \le n(t)$, $1 \le k \le N$, where $z_{ij}^{k}(t)$ is the arc from the vertex y_i to the vertex y_j (in particular the loop if $i=j$) on which a resource k can move in the moment n; N – a total number of resources within the system.

3. A set of state variables of the compartments $X(t) = \{x_i^{k}(t)\}$, $1 \le i \le n(t)$, $1 \le k \le N$, where $x_i^{k}(t)$ is a number of the resource k in the compartment $y_i \in Y_1$ in the moment t. Then $x_i(t)$ is a state vector of the compartment y_i in the moment t (the collection of all its resources).

4. A set of state variables of the arcs $F(t) = \{f_{ij}^{k}(t)\}$, $1 \le i,j \le n(t)$, $1 \le k \le N$, where $f_{ij}^{k}(t)$ is a weight of the arc $z_{ij}^{k}(t)$, i.e. a number of the resource k moved during the time $[t,t+1]$ from the vertex y_i to the vertex y_j, $i \ne j$, or a quantity of increase (decrease) of the resource k in the compartment y_i during the same time, $i=j$ ($\Delta t=1$). In each considered situation (problem) the set $F(t)$ can be split into two non-intersecting subsets: $\forall t \ F(t)=F_1(t) \cup F_2(t)$, $F_1(t) \cap F_2(t)= \varnothing$ (in particular it is possible that $F_2(t)= \varnothing$). Variables from the set $F_1(t)$ are called regulated (they change in the strength of given rules) and variables from the subset $F_2(t)$ are called regulators (they can change arbitrarily in the admissible set).

5. A set of limitations on the compartments capacity $\underline{X} = \{\underline{x}_i^{k}\}$, $1 \le i \le n(t)$, $1 \le k \le N$, where $\underline{x}_i^{k}$ is a maximal number of the resource k which can be stored in the compartment y_i.

6. A set of limitations on the carrying capacity of the arcs $\underline{F} = \{\underline{f}_{ij}^{k}\}$, $1 \le i,j \le n(t)$, $1 \le k \le N$, where $\underline{f}_{ij}^{k}$ is a maximal number of the resource k which can be moved from the vertex y_i to the vertex y_j, $i \ne j$, or produced (destructed) in the compartment y_i, $i=j$, during the time unit. Thus, the extended state of a complex system is a set $S(t) = \ <Y(t), Z(t), X(t), F(t), \underline{X}, \underline{F}>$.

To avoid a consideration of digraphs with multiple arcs let's map to each vertex $y_i \in Y$ the only weight $x_i(t)$ and to each arc $z_{ij} \in Z$ the only weight $a_{ij}(t)$. Then a dynamic structure of the system consists of the separate "scalar" structures each of which represent a certain aspect of matter and energy interactions within the system. The partition of a set of vertices of the dynamic digraph onto two parts permits to describe the principal matter-energetic processes in the real-world systems such as 1) movement (transfer, exchange) of resource between the compartments; 2) production/destruction of the resource in the compartments; 3) transformation of the resource. Describe the processes by the dynamic digraphs.

1. A movement of the resource k between two compartments y_i and y_j in the moment t can be performed if the arc $z_{ij}^k(t)$ exists (Figure 7.1.1).

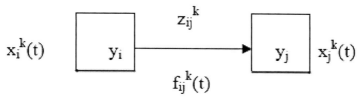

Figure 7.1.1. A movement of the resource k between compartments y_i and y_j.

Assume that in the moment t the stocks of the resource k in the compartments y_i and y_j are equal to $x_i^k(t)$ and $x_j^k(t)$ respectively and the state variable of the arc $z_{ij}^k(t)$ is $f_{ij}^k(t)$. Then

$$x_i^k(t+1) = x_i^k(t) - f_{ij}^k(t), \quad x_j^k(t+1) = x_j^k(t) + f_{ij}^k(t). \tag{7.1.1}$$

2. Production/destruction of the resource k in the compartment y_i in the moment t is possible if the loop $z_{ii}^k(t)$ exists (Figure 7.1.2).

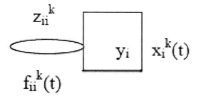

Figure 7.1.2. Production/destruction of the resource k in the compartment y_i.

The case $f_{ii}^k(t) > 0$ corresponds to the production and the case $f_{ii}^k(t) < 0$ to the destruction of the resource k. The result is

$$x_i^k(t+1) = x_i^k(t) + f_{ii}^k(t). \tag{7.1.2}$$

3. A transformation of some resource into other one is possible if a vertex-transformer from the set Y_2 exists. It is the most complicated class of processes which contains a number of subclasses. The subclasses can be classified by different criterions such as

a) a simple transformation (resource k into resource l);
b) a composite transformation (one resource into several ones, many resources into one or many to many); or

A. a unit transformation (within one compartment);
B. a binary transformation (between two compartments);
C. a multiple transformation (between several compartments).

Consider the case bB as an example. Assume that initial stocks of the resource are $x_i^k(t)$, $x_i^l(t)$, $x_j^l(t)$. The transformation satisfies the equations

$$x_i^k(t+1) = x_i^k(t) - f_{ip}^k(t),$$
$$x_i^l(t+1) = x_i^l(t) - f_{ip}^l(t), x_j^l(t+1) = x_j^l(t) + f_{pj}^l(t),$$
(7.1.3)

where y_i, y_j are compartments, y_p is a transformer.

Now consider as a more detailed example a known predator-prey model

$$\frac{dx_1}{dt} = \varepsilon_1 x_1 - \gamma_1 x_1 x_2, \frac{dx_2}{dt} = -\varepsilon_2 x_2 + \gamma_2 x_1 x_2,$$
(7.1.4)

where $x_1(t)$, $x_2(t)$ are biomasses of the prey and predator respectively in the moment t; ε_1, ε_2 are coefficients of the natural increase of the populations; γ_1, γ_2 are coefficients of the predator-prey interaction. A representation of the model (7.1.4) by means of the dynamical digraph is shown in Figure 7.1.3.

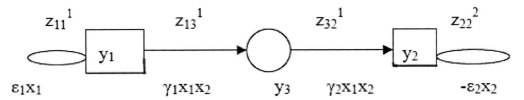

Figure 7.1.3. A representation of the predator-prey model by means of the dynamical hierarchical digraph.

The loops z_{11}^1 and z_{22}^2 describe an increase of the prey biomass (resource 1) and a decrease of the predator biomass (resource 2) in the compartments y_1 and y_2 respectively, and the transformation y_3 describes a simple binary transformation of the prey biomass into the predator biomass. In the general case a natural dynamics of the system resources is represented by a balance equation for each compartment and each resource:

$$x_j^k(t+1) = x_j^k(t) + \sum_{y_j \in S_j^+(t)} f_{ij}^k(t) - \sum_{y_l \in S_j^-(t)} f_{jl}^k(t),$$
(7.1.5)

$$1 \leq i, j, l \leq n(t), 1 \leq k \leq N,$$

The relation (7.1.5) added by initial data represents in fact a simulation model describing the system dynamics with consideration of its structure. The equation (7.1.5) considers both a passive regulation of the system (for the sake of change of f_{jl}^k, $f_{mj}^k \in F_1$ in the strength of given relations) and an active one (for the sake of choice of f_{jp}^k, $f_{qj}^k \in F_2$). The active regulation could additionally change the sets Y and Z. It is natural to name the changes of the sets X and F resource ones and the changes of the sets Y and Z structural ones. The totality of resource and structural changes determines the dynamics of the system S.

An extended state of the system S(t) is also changed by external impacts. The system environment can be represented by a vertex y_0 with the state vector $x_0(t) = (x_0^1(t), \ldots, x_0^N(t))$. Respectively the set of arcs Z(t) is added by elements of the type $z_{0i}^k(t)$, $z_{i0}^k(t)$ and the set of state variables of the arcs F(t) by elements $f_{0i}^k(t)$, $f_{i0}^k(t)$, $1 \leq i \leq n(t)$, $1 \leq k \leq N$. An influence of the environment is considered in (7.1.5) without loss of generality with the condition that y_0 can belong to the sets S_j^+, S_j^-. Besides, an external impact can change the sets Y(t), Z(t). If there are several sources of impact then it is necessary to introduce several external vertices $y_{01}, \ldots, y_{0M}$, respective arcs and state variables.

Consider as an example the predator-prey model with man-made impact

$$\frac{dx_1}{dt} = \varepsilon_1 x_1 - \gamma_1 x_1 x_2 - \alpha \lambda x_1, \frac{dx_2}{dt} = -\varepsilon_2 x_2 + \gamma_2 x_1 x_2 - \beta \lambda x_2, \qquad (7.1.6)$$

where in comparison with the model (7.1.4) the characteristics of man-made exploitation of the community are added, namely an intensity of use λ and methods of use α, β. A representation of the model (7.1.6) by means of the dynamical hierarchical digraph is given in Figure 7.1.4. In comparison with the Figure 7.1.3 to the compartments y_1 ("preys") and y_2 ("predators") the compartment y_0 reflecting the community environment (a source of exploitation) and arcs z_{10}^1, z_{20}^2 with state variables $\alpha \lambda x_1$, $\beta \lambda x_2$ are added.

Besides the relation (7.1.5) other rules of change of the values of vertices are also possible (Roberts 1976).

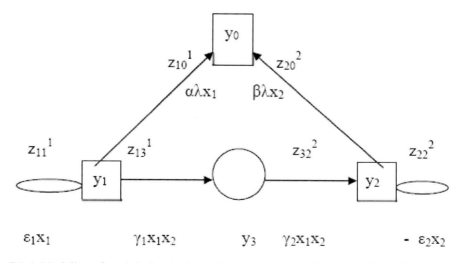

Figure 7.1.4. Modeling of exploitation in the predator-prey system by means of the dynamical digraph.

Return to the model of an organization as a controlled dynamical system

$$\frac{dx}{dt} = f(t, x(t), u(t), \xi(t))$$

where x(t) is the vector of state (phase vector), u(t) is the vector of control impacts, $\xi(t)$ is the vector of external impacts in the moment of time t, the control objective is a transfer of the system from the initial state $x(0)=x_0$ to the final state $x(T)=x_T$. Information modeling permits to determine, store and process the values of vectors x, u, ξ as well as the parameters of a transformation function f for t=0,1,...,T. The described models of system dynamics propose a tool for the description and analysis of changes in the organizational state for different transformation functions f.

The most widespread problem domain of information modeling is business processes. Consider the principal methods and models of information modeling of the business processes (Tikhonov 2009).

Different definitions of a business process are known. Havey (2005) proposes a simple definition of a business process as "a collection of stepwise rules of the business problem solution". In the majority of literary sources two main definitions are cited. One of them belongs to Hammer and Champy (1993) who have defined a business process as "a collection of actions having one or more inputs and creating an output having a customer value". The second definition is proposed by Davenport (1993) who states that a business process is a given sequence of actions the final objective of which is the production of an output for the specific client or market. The process orders the actions and works in time and space, and it has a beginning and an end as well as precisely given inputs and outputs.

Ferrie (1995) treats a process as a definite collection of actions beginning in the known initial point. According to Omrani (1992) a process is a cycle of actions the totality of which permits to achieve a certain objective. Pall (1987) defines a process as a logical organization of people, materials, energy, equipment and procedures to the works and actions aimed to the creation of a final result (product). Earl (1994) interprets a process as a horizontal form which encapsulates the interactions of problems, roles, human resources and functions so that to provide a product or service to the customer. Saxena (1996) underlines that a process creates an added value and Talwar (1993) defines a process as a sequence of predetermined actions performed for the achievement of a predetermined range of output products.

Thus, a business process is characterized by the following elements: a collection of inputs; a transformation of the inputs into the outputs determined by the process objective; a mechanism of the process realization; control impacts.

Modeling of business processes plays an important role in their perception and understanding. There are a number of methods of the modeling directed to different aspects of business processes, and each of the methods has its own advantages and shortages. A conceptual base of the representation and classification of the methods of business processes modeling is given by Kettinger et al. (2004) and Melao and Pidd (2000).

According to Agilar-Saven (2004) the modeling of business processes can be performed for the following purposes:

1) description of the processes for their study. A model of the processes should represent the structure and business processes of an organization in a unified form. This representation can be aimed to the learning and instructing of the employees, preparing reports for the top management and audits, analysis of the business processes within a reengineering activity and so on;

2) decision making support in process development and design. A model of the business processes is the main source of information for their analysis, validation and verification. It is also a means of fixing of the introduced changes before they will be reflected in the system of normative documentation. It should be noticed that the processes model is both the main means of an evaluation of different variants of the system structure and the tool for development of the variants;

3) decision making support in process realization: the model support to develop and analyze management decisions, to propose different scenarios of the resource use and evaluate their optimality, to control quality and take corrective and preventive actions aimed to the providing of the target state of the system;

4) information technologies introduction support. A development of the systems of automation of different aspects of the production activity, of the structure of software integration, of the database models and means of collection and analytical processing of the information is based on the business processes model.

There are many points of view to the nature and essence of business processes determined at first by the objectives of their modeling and analysis. The diversity of objectives results in the respective diversity of the models being developed by different researchers independently and by means of different tools. Vergidis et al. (2008) have differentiated three types of the methods of business process modeling: chart models, mathematical models and business process modeling languages. The first type includes the models illustrating processes by graphic charts. Models of the second type have a mathematical or other formal ground. The third type contains artificial languages which support modeling of business processes and as a rule their realization. Table 7.1.1 illustrates the classification and gives a list of literary sources on every key modeling technology.

The first methods of business process modeling were simple graphic representations (flow diagrams) initially developed for the software specification. These simple diagrams in the majority of cases represent a business process without use of some standard denotations (Havey 2005). These technologies are useful for a quick informal description of the process but they lack a semantics which is necessary for the determination of more complicated and standardized constructs. The standards based on chart models are simple enough and therefore widespread. However, they are criticized by a number of authors. The main critical argument is that the models are based on a graphical representation only and they lack a formal ground. They also miss both quantitative information that impedes the consequent analysis and formal instruments of the logical validation (Valiris and Gykas 1999). Phalp and Shepperd (2000) have noticed that any analysis of the models consists completely in the charts study and the conclusions depend to a great extent on the analyst qualification.

The necessity of a formal semantics in business process models has leaded to the appearance of their second generation. A model is formal if the process is defined strictly and accurately and therefore mathematical methods can be used for the analysis, knowledge elucidation and causal relations determination.

Table 7.1.1. A classification of the methods of business processes modeling (Tikhonov 2009)

Methods of modeling	Model type	Main works
Charts	Chart models	Knuth (1963), Chapin (1971)
IDEF	Chart models	Mayer et al. (1994), Menzel and Mayer (1998), Peters and Peters(1997), Zakarian (2001), Badica et al. (2003), Shimizu and Sahara (2000), Chou and Chen (2002)
Role Activity Diagrams (RAD)	Chart models	Ould (1995), Phalp and Shepperd (2000), Badica et al. (2003)
Unified Modeling Language (UML)	Chart models Business process modeling languages	Quatrani (2001), Wohed et al. (2004)
Petri Nets	Chart models Mathematical and other formal models	Aalst (1998), Li et al. (2004), Donatelli et al. (1995), Raposo (2000), Peters and Peters (1997)
Business process models based on mathematical and algorithmic models	Mathematical and other formal models	Hofacker and Vetschera (2001), Powell et al. (2001), Valiris and Gykas (1999)
BPEL BPMN	Business process modeling languages	Havey (2005), Grigori et al. (2004)
jPDL (jBPM)	Chart models Business process modeling languages	Koenig (2004)

An advantage of the formal models is the possibility of the mathematical validation of their consistency and other properties (Koubarakis and Plexousakis 2002). But the shortage is that business processes have a qualitative nature that troubles their formalization in the form applicable for the analytical methods. This explains the complexity of development of the business process models and the fact that only several practical examples of the development are presented in the literature.

Petri net is an example of the method of business process modeling which combines a visual representation using a standard notation and a mathematical formalism. Shortages of Petri nets are conditioned by the process of their programming implementation. Petri nets have no strict notion of a process which could be implemented on a given processor. There is no also a fixed consequence of the Petri net realization because the basic theory gives a language for the description of parallel processes. Besides, in the case of complex systems the model has a huge volume and is hardly observable. Therefore, its graphic notation is not available for business analysts and other users what impedes the practical use.

The methods based on mathematical models only are still not widespread and are criticized by a number of authors. Building a formal business process model is much more complicated and expensive than traditional technologies where a chart model is quite sufficient (Hofacker and Vetschera 2001). Koubarakis and Plexousakis (2002) have noticed that complex mathematical notation can trouble the model use to business analysts because a lot of work is required for the creation, support and keeping of the formal business process logic. However, charts can lead to ambiguity in the process description meanwhile a formal model proves that the process is described accurately, and analytical instruments permit to receive quantitative information about the process being modeled. This is the principal advantage of the formal methods of business process modeling.

Modeling languages form the third and the newest generation of the methods of business process modeling which try to consider the complexity and in the same time to keep the logic and a possibility of the subsequent analysis. As the first generation this group of the methods is inherited from the domain of software development. Context dependent executed languages are the last trend in business process modeling including such semantic packages as BPEL4WS (Business Process Execution Language for Web Services) and BPML (Business Process Modeling Language). It is noticed in (Aalst 1998) that process languages with their precise semantics are useful in the description of business process models and analysis of their structural properties. Other examples of languages from this group are BPMN (White 2004), UML and UML2, XPDL, YAWL (Aalst and Hofstede 2003).

The business process modeling languages have proved their reliability as a tool of the formal modeling and visualization of business processes in terms of the standardized models valid for the multiple use.

The survey demonstrates a wide diversity of the methods and tools of business process modeling. Some of them are developed long ago but keep their actuality due to the simplicity and flexibility and are widespread in spite of some shortages. In contrary, other methods are rather new and powerful but in the same time are characterized by the high complexity and expensiveness that can trouble their practical introduction. Thus, new and new methods are being developed. Some examples of the methods and their practical use are given below.

In the work by Chinese authors Gou et al. (2000) a method of business process modeling based on Petri nets is proposed. This method is a typical representative of the group of mathematical models based on the Petri nets theory with all respective advantages and shortages.

Another bright example of the mathematical modeling of business process is described in Yan and Yu-quiang (2006). The authors have proposed a new method of process mining based on the construction of a matrix of transient probabilities using so-called process logs. The proposed algorithm to a great extent eliminates the constraints of the known methods of process mining and increases the quality of models. A theoretical description of the method without its computer implementation and practical recommendations is proposed yet.

Vick and Harrell (1998) have described the systems of discrete-event modeling Process Model and Process Model 9000. The system Process Model 9000 is a modification of the Process Model which permits to quality managers to document, analyze and improve the quality management processes within certification according to the standards ISO 9000 and QS-9000.

Another direction of research in the domain of business process management is development of the technologies of integration and improvement of the existing methods of modeling aimed at the increase of efficiency of models, convenience of their use and creation of the new instrumental means. An example is given by Badica et al. (2005). The authors have presented an approach for the integration of two notations of business process modeling: Role Activity Diagrams (RAD) and Hybrid IDEF (Integrated Definition). Besides, they have proposed a prototype of the instrumental system based on the Eclipse platform.

One of the most widespread is the methodology of functional business process modeling IDEF0 which belongs to the group of graphical methods (see above). The methods of IDEF family have been created within a US Air Force program of computerization ICAM (Integrated Computer Aided Manufacturing) in the end of 1970-s. After its publication the standard was successfully used in the very different domains of business as an efficient tool of the analysis, design and description of business processes as well as investigation of their structure, parameters and different characteristics. An appearance of the main ideas of BPR (Business Process Reengineering) is also connected with IDEF technologies.

The objects of functional modeling and structural analysis in IDEF0 are organizational-economic and industrial-technical systems. The main conceptual principle of the IDEF0 methodology is a representation of any modeled system as a collection of interacting and interconnected blocks which reflect the processes, operations and actions in the system. Each function is mapped to its own block which is represented by a rectangle on the IDEF0 diagram. The interfaces of interaction of the block with other blocks or system environment are represented by input or output arrows. The input arrows show which conditions must be satisfied simultaneously so that the function described by the block can be performed. The main notions of IDEF0 are the following:

- Block – a rectangle which contains the name and the number and is used for description of the function.
- Arrow – a directed line which consists of one or more segments and models an open channel or a channel of transmission of data or material objects from the source (initial point of the arrow) to the customer (final point of the arrow). There are four classes of arrows: input, output, control, mechanism (including the call arrow).
- Input arrow – a class of arrows reflecting the input of IDEF0 block, i.e. data or material objects which are transformed to the output by the function. The input arrows are connected to the left side of the IDEF0 block.
- Output arrow – a class of arrows reflecting the output of IDEF0 block, i.e. data or material objects which are produced by the function. The output arrows are connected with the right side of the IDEF0 block.
- Decomposition – a subdivision of the function being modeled into the component functions.
- Diagram – a part of the model which describes the block decomposition.
- Context diagram – a diagram having the node number $A-n$, $n \geq 0$, which represents the model context, i.e. the model environment.
- Binding/unbinding – a unification of the arrows values to a compound value (binding to the "bunch") or division of the arrow values (unbinding of the "bunch").
- Mechanism arrow – a class of arrows which reflect the IDEF0 mechanisms, i.e. the means used for a function realization. The mechanism arrows are connected with the bottom part of the IDEF0 block.
- Call arrow – a kind of the mechanism arrow which denotes a call from the model block (or a part of the model) to the block of other model (or another part of the same model) and provides a connections between models or different parts of the same model.

- Control arrow – a class of arrows which denotes controls, i.e. the conditions which are to be satisfied so that the block output will be correct. The control arrows are connected with the top part of the IDEF0 block. The standard disposition of the arrows is shown in Figure 7.1.5.

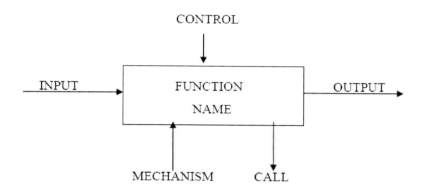

Figure 7.1.5. The standard disposition of arrows on the IDEF0 diagram.

The main advantages of the IDEF0 methodology are the following:

- low cost of models development;
- possibility of the quick and efficient correction of the system being modeled according to new conditions and requirements;
- precise reflection of the logic of interaction of the organizational processes, clearness of the visual representation;
- availability of the complete information (control, informational and material flows, feed back) about each work, procedure, operation due to the strictly regulated structure;
- possibility of aggregation and specification of the data and information flows;
- improvement of the quality of documents describing the structure and functioning of the organizational departments, a possibility of optimization of the organizational structure based on the model;
- compatibility of the approach to processes description to the requirements of ISO 9000:2008.

By virtue of the enumerated factors IDEF0 is still one of the most acceptable methods of business process modeling. But it has also a number of shortages such as:

- IDEF0 is a method of functional modeling and therefore does not fit well to process modeling;
- on its base it is impossible to reflect the process dynamics or parallel works;
- insufficient level of formalism and impossibility of the application of mathematical methods of analysis;

- complexity of perception in the case of a big system being modeled, and the necessity of analysis of a great number of diagrams corresponding to many decomposition levels;
- presence of logical and linguistic contradictions which determines the necessity of different additional interpretations and specifications for the analyzed problem domain.

Thus, IDEF0 is a quite attractive modeling tool, especially at the initial phases of business process reengineering by virtue of such properties as simplicity, clearness and relative low cost. It permits to develop rather quickly an optimal organizational structure with consideration to the changing environment and requirements.

However, in the same time the methodology has a number of shortages the main of which are an insufficient level of formalism and impossibility to model the process dynamics and therefore is hardly applicable for the deep process analysis. That's why it is necessary to use more complicated and in the same time more powerful tools which permit to consider the process interaction and dynamics, resource allocation and joint use, temporal and financial characteristics of the system functioning (Tikhonov 2009).

An important branch of information modeling is the construction of so-called ontological models. Ontology is a philosophic theory which studies entity and its being, types, structure and laws of the being. In the end of the last century by the efforts of Barry Smith, Nicola Guarino and other researchers the ontological ideas were applied to the information modeling and information system development (Smith 1998). Specifically, the enterprise ontology is treated as a collection of terms and definitions relevant to the enterprise (The Enterprise Ontology 1995).

Boris Shvedin (2006) formulates the following theses which form a base of the intellectual technology based on the experience approach to ontological modeling:

- each enterprise is treated as a business entity having its own individual destiny (an anthropomorphic approach);
- the base of enterprise existence is its unique individual experience which should be saved, structured and stored by information systems. A system of the experience inheritance of the enterprise is an analogue of the human memory;
- it is a specific activity of the enterprise on a certain period of time that forms its unique individual experience;
- in the present time the enterprise experience is not saved specially but exists only in the heads of the managers that results in the inevitable loss of the experience when the managers leave the organization;
- the system of experience inheritance should be the organizational "brain" and an instrument of its adaptation in the continuously changing environment;
- the majority of management information systems have no feedback. The systems can provide only a reactive behavior of the business entities and does not permit to achieve the proactive reactions to the environmental change;
- by contrast to a human being, an enterprise as a social organism has no subconsciousness therefore its "brain" is able to use only discursive models of decision making;

- the proposed system QuaSy is a tool that permits to provide the corporative information systems its own "brain" and to include them into the process of organization, accumulation and structuring of the individual experience of social entities.

Basing on this methodology Boris Shvedin proposes an ontological Business Entity Ontological Model (BEOM) as the holistic model of the business entity ensuring its self-control, surviving and adaptive behavior during the complete life cycle. The BEOM structure contains such components as subjects, objects, tasks and relationships of the business activity as well as description of the time and space, ontological classifier and technologies of object naming. The BEOM provides an ontologically connected description of the organizational architecture, the solved problems and concerned norms, regulations, relations and situations.

The subjects of business activity are subdivided into the subjects of internal and external activity. The subjects of external activity are partners of the organization, and the subjects of internal activity are its departments and employees. Another criterion of the business activity subject classification is its differentiation on principal and supporting ones. The objects of the business activity are subdivided to material and non-material ones. As well as the subjects they should be named and attributed. The tasks of business activity arise in principal and supporting processes of product realization. A construction of the task tree is a complex problem that is solved on the base of a grounded decomposition and subsequent integration of the tasks. The relationships of internal and external business activity are differentiated onto norms, regulations, contracts and organizational structures.

The proposed QuaSy technology promotes information systems to acquire an ontological status which makes its distinction from the simple systems of operative control (Shvedin 2006).

7.2. CORPORATIVE INFORMATION SYSTEMS AND ITS MODELING COMPONENTS

Corporative information system (CIS) is a computer system aimed at the complex automation of business activity of big and middle enterprises, first of all corporations and holdings. It is considered as a rule that CIS is a system which automates more than 80% of the departments of an enterprise. The obligatory requirements for a CIS are the following: client-server architecture which allows to use industrial database systems; safety providing by the methods of access control; distributed data processing support; modular principle of construction from the operationally independent functional blocks with extension using open standards (API, COM and others); Internet/Intranet technological support; exploitation characteristics such as simplicity of administration, ergonomics, presence of the localized interface.

The most natural and efficient way of the CIS development ensuring the enumerated above functions and technological requirements is usage of the business process automation system as a core of the whole information system. This approach is explained by that the activity of any enterprise is in fact a totality of the developed in every day practice business processes involving financial, material, personal, information and other resource. It is business processes that determine an order of interaction of the employees and departments as well as principles of the information systems development.

During several decades a number of CIS standards were elaborated such as MRP, MRP II, CRP, ERP, CSRP and others. Up to the present time the main CIS standard is ERP (Enterprise Resource Planning). The key concept of ERP is a repository which contains all the information accumulated by an organization in its business activity. The repository delivers from the necessity to allocate the data between different applications. Besides, all the information existing in the organization is available for all employees having the respective authority.

The main purpose of ERP-systems is an automation of the planning, accounting and control processes therefore the systems can be considered as an integrated totality of such main subsystems as finance control, material flow control, production control, project management, service management, quality management, human resource management. Each of the enumerated subsystems can contain its own functional blocks which can be realized as separate subsystems. For example, the subsystem of material flow control includes as a rule the functional block "Transportation control". In the same time the subsystems of material flow control, production control, project management, and service management form in their totality the logistic information system of the enterprise. ERP-systems consist of many program modules which could be bought separately and support control in many kinds of business activity. They are modules of sales and distribution, financial accounting and controlling (including MRP and CRP), human resource, project and quality management, plant maintenance, workflow control, industry solutions.

The application of ERP methodology becomes a standard thing. The producers who want to compete successfully should actively use ERP just to correspond the production efficiency of their competitors. The ERP methods promote integration, elimination of mistakes, decrease of useless operations, amelioration of planning and forecasting, complex automation of organizational control that can ensure cost reduction and product realization improvement. Due to ERP system the top management of an organization receives a tool of the real business activity control. ERP systems are compatible with CAD/CAM systems that permit to get an integrated solution joining development, production and purchases. ERP systems are oriented at the work with financial information for the solution of management problems in big corporations with spatially distributed resources.

From the point of view of modern approaches, the CIS is treated in a wide sense and it is required that CIS include software of at least three classes:

- complex enterprise management systems (automated information decision support systems),
- electronic document flow systems,
- products which permit to create functional models, to analyze and optimize the organizational activity. Automated systems of technological process control, CAD systems, and intellectual data analysis programs belong to the former class.

Each enterprise has its own specifics which depends on the kind of its activity and determines to a great extent the choice of specialized information systems. For example, for oil companies it is important to have geographic information systems which support spatially distributed data processing. An industrial enterprise should have CAD/CAM/CAE/PDM systems which support design and other technological works. The economic departments need information systems of financial analysis, planning and programming, the commercial departments – customer control systems and so on. In many cases an integration of existing and additionally developed subsystems could be required.

A modern CIS in a wide sense may contain:

- a system of enterprise resource control (ERP-system);

- a system of distributed logistic control (SCM-system);

- a system of purchases, sales and post-sales service control;

- a system of industrial articles data control (PDM-system);

- CAD/CAM/CAE-systems;

- a system of electronic documents control (DocFlow system);

- a system of working space organization (Workflow system);

- Internet / Intranet environment;

- a system of electronic commerce (e-commerce);

- a system of information resource control;

- Data Warehouse system;

- a system of on-line analytical data processing (OLAP);

- Data Mining systems;

- a system of management support (MIS);

- specialized working places of autonomous users;

- systems of business process modeling and representation;

- systems of analytical and simulation process modeling;

- systems of mathematical (including statistical) data analysis;

- specialized products or systems for the solution of specific problems.

Each of the enumerated components is quite complicated and consists of several software products. A number of the components have been just developed or even are being developed. Therefore, no one product can pretend for a separate solution of the whole totality of the problems.

An electronic document flow control system is the system of automation of the work with information documents during all its life cycle (creation, change, storage, search, classification and so on) as well as interaction processes between the employees. First of all the documents are treated as non-structured electronic ones (Word, Excel files and others). As a rule, such systems include an electronic data archive and a system of business process automation. Examples of application of the document flow automation include: correspondence registration (incoming and outgoing documents), electronic documents archive, automation of contracting process, library of management regulations, business trips registration, internal organizational portals, and so on.

In the ground of Data Warehouse concept is the idea of differentiation of the data for operative processing and for analytical problems. The first detailed description of the concept was made by William Inmon (2002) who had defined the Data Warehouse as an integrated, subject-oriented, non-changeable, supporting chronology data set organized for decision support purposes. According to this definition, the principal distinctions of the Data Warehouse (DW) from the operative databases (DB) are the following.

1. Subject orientation. Different DB contain data characterizing an organization from the different points of view (human resource management, accounting, logistics and so on) meanwhile DW realize a unified approach to all organizational data. Besides, the subject orientation permits to store in the DW only those data attributes which are required for their subsequent analysis that reduces costs and increases the safety of data access.
2. Integration. Heterogeneous data from different DB are transformed in the DW to the unified format that facilitates their subsequent analysis.
3. Chronology support. Data in DB are used for current needs and are not obliged to be connected with some moments in time. In DW historical data are stored having a necessary time attribute.
4. Non-changeability. The data in DB are continuously actualized and removed as soon as possible for the purposes of space economy. In contrary, the data in DW are read only that provides the archive storage of chronologically ordered data.

The DW development is concerned with the following problems:

-   necessity of the integration of data from different sources in the distributed environment;
-   need in the efficient methods of storage and processing of the very big information arrays;
-   necessity of the multilevel meta-data glossaries (stored data catalogues);
-   high requirements to the safety of data providing a holistic historical picture of the organizational functioning.

DW include detailed, aggregated, archive data and metadata. The detailed data are subdivided into measurements (data sets necessary for an event description) and facts (data reflecting the essence of the event). The aggregated data are formed from the detailed ones by summation of the measurements. For augmentation of the access speed the aggregated data are stored in the DW instead of being generated in each request. The metadata provide to the user some information about the stored data. According to John Zachman principles, the metadata should describe the modeled objects from a problem domain, places of the data storage, the operations with data, processing time and causes of the data modification.

A very important task of the data transfer from DB to DW is their refinement which includes the following phases: revealing data problems, determination of the refinement rules and their testing, the refinement itself. The refined data are stored in the DW and are used for analysis and decision making.

In the process of data analysis and search of solutions a necessity of the construction of dependencies between the variables often arises, and the number of variables can be big enough. The most widespread relational data model badly fits to the solution of this problem. Therefore in 1993 the founder of the relational approach Ed Codd has recognized some shortages of his model and has proposed the concept of OLAP (On-Line Analytical Processing), a technology of operative analytical data processing for their multidimensional analysis (Codd et al. 1993). Codd has formulated twelve rules that determine the essence of OLAP–technology: 1) multidimensionality; 2) transparency; 3) availability; 4) constant performance in report development; 5) client-server architecture; 6) equality of measurements; 7) dynamic control of sparse matrices; 8) multi-user mode support; 9) non-restricted cross operations; 10) intuitive data manipulation; 11) flexible abilities of report generation; 12) unlimited dimensionality and number of aggregation levels.

In 1995 six more rules with consideration of the accumulated experience were added: 13) package elucidation versus interpretation; 14) all OLAP-analysis models support; 15) non-normalized data processing; 16) separate storage of the OLAP results and original data; 17) elimination of the absent data; 18) processing of the absent data.

An OLAP-system includes two main components: OLAP-server and OLAP-client. The OLAP-server ensures data storage, required operations performance and formation of the multidimensional data model on the conceptual level. Now the OLAP-server is joined with a DW as a rule. OLAP-servers hide from the user details of the physical implementation of the multidimensional data model. They form a "hypercube" providing all necessary data processing operations for the user. Nevertheless a method of implementation is important because it determines the performance and required resource. Three main methods of implementation are differentiated: MOLAP based on multidimensional databases. The advantages of this approach are high performance and simplicity of the embedded functions usage; ROLAP based on relational databases. The advantages are the possibility of work with existing relational databases, more economic resource use and flexibility in the case of addition of new dimensions; HOLAP which synthesized both approaches. OLAP-client provides to the user a friendly interface for the work with a multidimensional data model.

Methods of intellectual data analysis permit to receive some new, still unknown information using a computer. This direction was called Data Mining. Its main tasks are classification, regression, search of associative rules and clustering. The classification problem consists in the attribution of an object to one of the known classes. In the problem of regression it is required to find the value of a parameter of the object by its known characteristics. These problems are predictive and can be joined to the problem of evaluation of the dependent variable of the object by its independent variables. It the dependent variable takes numerical values then it is possible to say about regression else about classification.

In the search of associative rules the objective is to find stable dependences (associations) between objects or events. At last, the clustering problem consists in the search of independent groups (clusters) in which the analyzed data set may be subdivided. The problems of clustering and search of associative rules are descriptive.

By way of solution the Data Mining problems are selected on the learning problems with a teacher and without a teacher. In the first case at the beginning a model of the analyzed data (classifier) is built by the learning sample then its quality of work is examined by the control sample and if the quality is bad then a modification of the model (learning) is performed. The learning without a teacher relates to descriptive models where the laws are known and any learning is required. The methods of Data Mining include sorting algorithms, fuzzy logic, genetic algorithms, and neural networks.

An application of simulation models requires its combination with an expert knowledge in the dialogue with a computer system. This idea finds its expression in the notion of simulation system which may be used both independently and as a CIS subsystem.

One of the authors of the term Robert Shannon defines a simulation system as the system which permits to reproduce the behavior of an object of the environment (Shannon 1975). The behavior is considered here as a set of reactions of the object to the external impacts. Yuri Pavlovsky (2000) defines a simulation system as a form of usage of the mathematical models which is a part of a wider class of the problem oriented interactive systems including expert, optimization and simulation systems. The systems are a result of the combination of the traditional technology of mathematical modeling and the information technology based on computers. The simulation system is also interpreted as an interactive system which is able to reproduce and simulate different scenarios of development of the system being modeled, first of all in the education purposes in the form of a game.

So, there are three points of view to the simulation system: 1) a program realization of the simulation model; 2) an external superstructure which ensures a convenient and efficient use of the simulation model; 3) an interactive training system which reproduces different situations and respective reactions of the system being modeled in dependence on the user's actions (Tikhonov 2009). In spite of the external distinction all three approaches have a common feature, namely they based on a model which is able to simulate the system behavior as a response on different external impacts therefore the three types are in fact the different ways of usage of the simulation model. Really, a computer realization of the simulation model permits to make the calculations for different scenarios and primary processing of the received results. It is not very convenient to use the model for a deep analysis of the system being modeled because the researcher is obliged to do a lot of work by hands or by using additional instruments. That's why the second approach proposes an integration of the simulation model and the analytical tools in the unified system which provides simulation experiments by different scenarios, collection and ordering of the experimental results, and the analysis and optimization of the system being modeled using the received information. As for the third approach, the systems of this type are constructed on the base of the well approbated and adequate simulation model which describes a real world system known in details. In this case the main objective is not an investigation but the understanding of the known functioning laws by the trained person. So, the enumerated types of the simulation systems realize different phases of the simulation model application cycle. In this book the second approach is considered as the principal one.

Let's consider the composition of a simulation system and the interaction of its elements. As it is shown in Figure 7.2.1 for the initial determination of the model structure the input subsystem which includes as a rule a text or graphical editor is used. This module is also used for the specification of the parts of the system being modeled which are considered in the given simulation experiment and on the level of modeling which is comprehensive for each block belonging to the system. For the accurate calculation of the functional characteristics and statistical parameters of the system being modeled a special subsystem is used which permits to determine a specific type of the functions used in simulation and the values characterizing the structural elements of the system such as performance, capacity, speed and others. This information is kept in the data base and can be used by other blocks of the simulation system.

The modeling subsystem reads the information about the model structure from the data base and creates its own data structures which are used in the numerical algorithms. The calculation results are saved in special files containing the information about the system trajectories on the whole modeling period or in the data base for the present step of modeling. Besides, the system creates checkpoints which contain the complete set of the data in a current moment of time. The checkpoints are used for the continuation of the calculations from the exact required moment of time.

Graphical editors and compilers are used for the creation, updating and displaying of the graphical representation of the data saved in the files of calculation results.

As a rule the simulation subsystems read data as text lists describing the connections between the model blocks. The lists are created on the base of data kept in the data base in the moment when a command for the beginning of simulation is given. Then the lists are analyzed by the simulation subsystem for creation or updating the data structures used in the calculation process. The outgoing results are also presented in a text format which is to be analyzed and transformed for the use by the graphical editor.

Let's consider as an example the simulation system of business processes of an organization as a queuing system (Tikhonov 2009).

The system is realized by the client-server technology with a "thin" client. This architecture permits to locate all numerical operations on the separate server and to avoid a necessity to provide the user's working place by the powerful and expensive equipment.

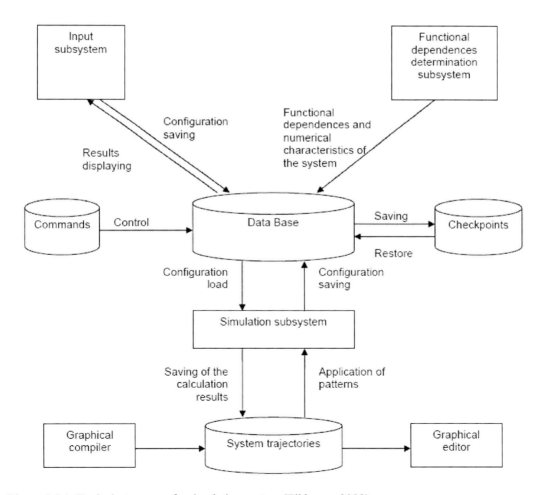

Figure 7.2.1. Typical structure of a simulation system (Tikhonov 2009).

The proposed system can be logically subdivided onto three main nodes: client terminal, server module and database management system with the data base (Figure 7.2.2).

The client terminal is installed on any workstation and is in fact an implementation of the user graphical interface. Via the client interface the user inputs data, builds a model and controls the organization of simulation experiments. The output of calculation results is made also by the client terminal.

All calculations and data transforming operations are realized inside the server module which can be physically situated on other, more powerful one.

The system structure is shown in Figure 7.2.3. The client terminal consists of the input-output subsystem and the data transfer subsystem. The first subsystem provides the data input by the user, its displaying, transformation and saving including the user graphical interface. The total user interaction with the simulation system is realized only via the client terminal. The subsystem of data transfer is a streak between the client terminal and the server module which is responsible for the data transfer by a local network or via Internet.

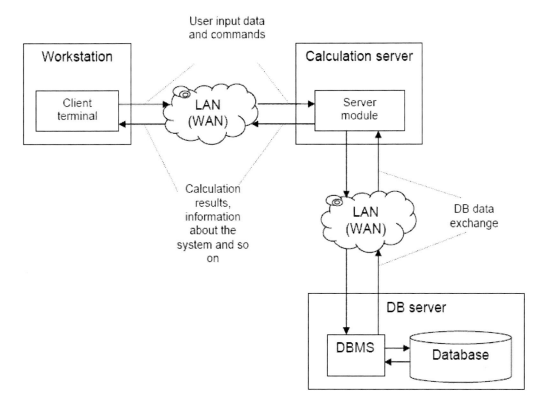

Figure 7.2.2. Logical organization of the simulation system according to client-server technology (Tikhonov 2009).

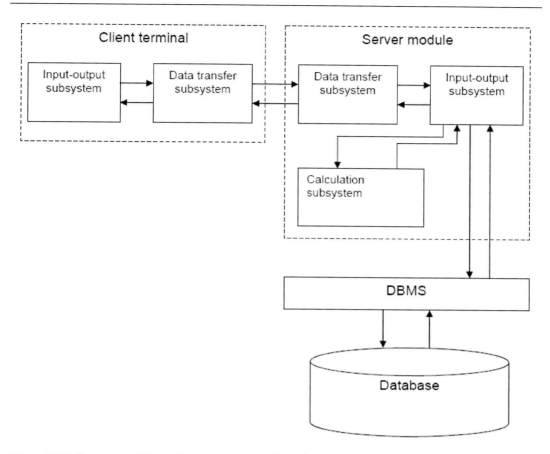

Figure 7.2.3. Structure of the business process modeling simulation system (Tikhonov 2009).

The server module has the central place in the simulation system. It is this module that ensures the information transfer from the client terminal to the database and back, the realization of simulation experiments, the operations of results processing and their storage. The module includes the data transfer system which ensures a connection with the client terminal, the input-output subsystem and the calculation subsystem. The input-output subsystem of the server module differs by its functions from the analogous system of the client terminal and includes the means of interaction with the DBMS.

The main components of the client terminal and their interaction are shown in Figure 7.2.4. The principal element of the client terminal is the input-output system which includes the user graphical interface and the means of data transformation and displaying.

In initial phases of the work with the system the user should determine the structure of the system being modeled by IDEF0 diagrams. Their input can be performed by the import of a diagram from Microsoft Visio, by an embedded text editor in the XML format or by loading from a XML file.

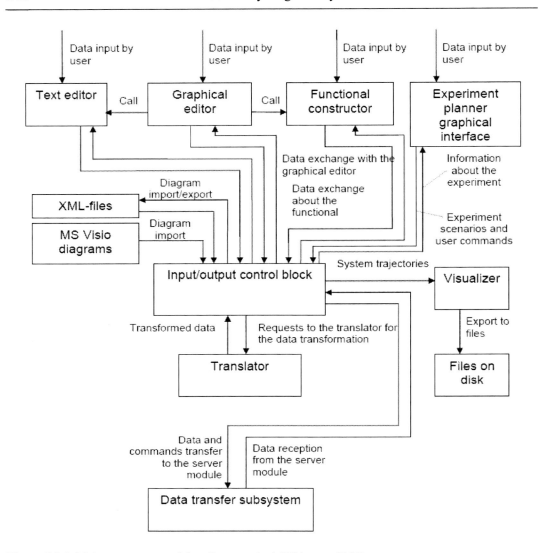

Figure 7.2.4. Main components of the client terminal (Tikhonov 2009).

The embedded graphical editor is the main tool of diagram input. When a diagram is input the information is saved in the operative memory in the form of special data structures and can be exported to an external XML file or imported from it to the editor according to the user request. An opportunity of the diagram input from Microsoft Visio also exists. For the input of information in text form the embedded text editor exists which allows the synchronization in the real time mode. It is called from the graphical editor. The input diagrams are accumulated in the database from which they can be read by other modules.

Saving, loading and export-import of the information are made by a special translator which transforms the data into a corresponding format in dependence on the performed operation. The translator is called by the control block which processes the requests of other modules and performs its transfer using the respective subsystem.

Structural and numerical identification of the model is fulfilled by a special functional constructor which permits to give the form of the model functions and their numerical parameters using interface elements and choosing the required functions and variables from the lists. The input information is also saved in the database. Though the functional constructor is an independent module it is called only from the graphical editor to ensure the user convenience and to avoid the mistakes connected with an underdefinition or logical contradiction in the data. In the same time the data exchange with the database passes over the graphical editor because the data synchronization with it is ensured by the input-output control block.

Data output and displaying are performed by an embedded visualizer which displays the system trajectories on a monitor and ensures basic functions of image editing such as coloring, scaling, printing, as well as exporting of both graphical image and initial data to an external file. The created graph is interactive, i.e. the user can change its parameters by moving some points or adding new ones. All the changes can be saved in the database for the subsequent use.

The main functions of the client terminal are:

1. Data input: IDEF0 diagrams input in the graphical mode; IDEF0 diagrams input in the text mode; diagram import from XML-files; diagram import from Microsoft Visio; determination of the functional dependences between model components by the functional constructor; determination of the numerical values of the model parameters by the functional constructor; computer experiments planning by the graphical interface of the experiment planner; system trajectories editing by the visualizer interface.
2. Data output: displaying of the information about the model structure and the functional dependences between its components in graphical and text modes; animation of the computer experiments by means of the planner graphical interface; results displaying and experiments animation by the trajectories visualizer; export of the information about the model structure to an XML-file; export of the experimental results to external files.
3. Data and calculations control: control commands and data exchange with the server module; control of the simulation and optimization experiments by different scenarios; data saving and restoring control; data transformation.

The server module of the simulation system is shown in Figure 7.2.5.

The input-output subsystem of the server module is much simpler than the same subsystem of the client terminal because it does not contain elements of graphical interface and is intended to the coordination of the interaction between the calculation modules and the client terminal and database. The subsystem includes: the data transfer subsystem ensuring the connection with the client terminal; the DBMS client part performing data and requests transfer; the translator transforming the data by requests from the control block; at last, the control input-output block coordinating the work of the enumerated modules and their interaction with the calculation subsystem.

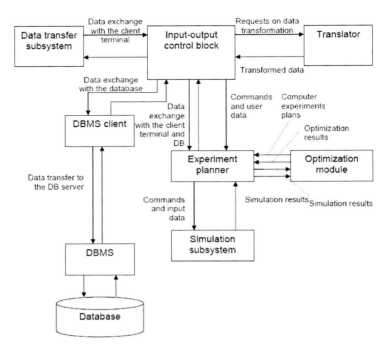

Figure 7.2.5. Structure of the server module of the simulation system (Tikhonov 2009).

The central place in the calculation subsystem belongs to the experiment planner which organizes computer simulation experiments by scenarios. The scenarios and simulation control commands are received from the user via the planner graphical interface (see Figure 7.2.4) or from the optimization subsystem which generates experiment scenarios and plans automatically basing on criteria determined by the user.

In the simulation mode of work the experiment planner basing on the scenarios received from the user creates the calculation plan and generates the sets of variables and parameters for the simulation. The calculations themselves are performed in the simulation subsystem. The user can control the calculation process by means of the planner graphical interface. The received system trajectories are passed back to the experiment planner and after that to the input-output subsystem for their saving in the database and/or for the transfer to the client terminal for their displaying and editing.

In the optimization mode of work the computer experiments are controlled by the optimization module. Basing on the user data and commands the optimization module develops computer simulation scenarios and passes them to the planner. The planner organizes simulation experiments the results of which are returned by the simulation subsystem to the planner and passed by it to the optimization module for their analysis. After the optimization procedure the results are passed to the input-output system for their saving or transfer to the client terminal if the visualization is required.

The simulation subsystem also collects statistical data and calculates a number of statistical parameters such as waiting time of the claims in the queue; number of claims in the queue in a moment of time; general number of claims in the system in a moment of time; average delay value; response time for a claim (in the queue and in general); virtual response time; occupation period of the system and so on.

So, the principal functions of the server module are the following.

1. Realization of the computer simulation experiments:
- Organization of calculations by the experiments planner:
- Realization of the computer simulation by the simulation subsystem;
- Calculation results processing by the planner;
- Organization of optimization calculations by the optimization module including automatic scenario generation for the planner.

2. Data collection, processing and storage:
- Data transformation by the translator;
- Data exchange with the database by interaction with the DBMS client part;
- Data transfer to the client terminal;
- Data collection and statistical parameters calculation in the queuing system model;
- Primary processing of the simulation experiments results.

The proposed simulation system of business process modeling as a queuing system is rather universal and can be used for the investigation of business process in almost any organization. The high degree of integration permits to do without additional expensive analytical tools which are not obligatory for the majority of arising problems. The client-server architecture permits to distribute the calculation load between several computers and delivers from the necessity of installation of the whole software complex on each workstation as well as diminishes the requirements to the equipment on a user working place. The distant interaction with DB allows usage of an existing DBMS or even its integration to the corporative DB (Tikhonov 2009).

Another important kind of information systems which could be used independently or as a block of CIS is expert systems (Giarratano and Riley 2004). An expert system (ES) accumulates the practical experience of the experts-specialists in a specific problem domain and provides recommendations on decision making based on the experience. The main component of the ES is a knowledge base. As a rule, the ES knowledge base contains facts (static information about the problem domain) and rules (a set of instructions which permit to receive new facts basing on the known ones). Within a logical model the knowledge base is recorded by a predicate language (for example, Prolog) for the description of facts, rules of logical deduction, generalized and specific information as well as specific and general requests to the databases and knowledge bases. As a rule, the facts in a knowledge base describe the phenomena which are constant for the problem domain. The characteristics which values depend on conditions of a specific problem are received by the ES from the user and are saved in the working memory. For example, in a medical ES the fact "A healthy person has two legs" is kept in the knowledge base and the fact "The patient has one leg" is kept in the working memory. The ES knowledge base is developed by three groups of people: experts in the analyzed problem domain; knowledge engineers who are specialists in information systems; programmers who implement the ES. An important part of the ES is an inference engine which realizes the logical transformations. At last, a component of explanation is obligatory to demonstrate the user the logical chain of deduction and to increase the degree of confidence to the ES. The following phases of the ES development are selected: problem identification – the problems that are to be solved are formulated, the objectives of development are determined, the experts and users are identified; knowledge elucidation – a comprehensive analysis of the problem domain is made, the notions used and their interactions are revealed, the methods of problem solving are determined; knowledge structuring – the ways of representation of all types of knowledge are determined, the principal notions are formalized, the ways of knowledge interpretation are determined, the work of the system is modeled, the adequacy of the determined notions, methods and procedures to the system objectives is evaluated; formalization – the filling of the knowledge base by an expert.

7.3. CORPORATIVE INFORMATION-MODELING SYSTEMS IN ENSURING SUSTAINABLE MANAGEMENT OF ORGANIZATION

The quality management which principal requirements are determined by the ISO 9000 standards (see Paragraph 4.1) represents a technology of organizational management ensuring the sustainable management of the organization. The main line of the technology basing on the interpretation of an organization as a hierarchically controlled dynamic system proposes the following set of actions aimed to the creation and support of the management system.

1. Selection and description of the business processes structuring the organizational activity. Different information modeling tools are used here (see Paragraph 7.1) including the special tools of business process information modeling. One of the main means of business process description is IDEF0 notation.
2. Determination of the parameters of functioning for each process which form in their totality the vector of state of the organization $x^t = (x_1^t, ..., x_n^t)$ where x_i^t is the value of i-th parameter in the moment t; n is the total number of selected parameters (Paragraph 4.2).
3. Determination of the plan (target) values of the parameters which describe the organizational homeostasis (Paragraph 4.2). The conditions of homeostasis can be formulated in two forms: the strong one and the weak one. The weak form of homeostasis is treated as the condition

$$\forall t \in [0, T]: x(t) \in X * \tag{7.3.1}$$

where x(t) is the vector of state of an organizational system, X* - the domain of homeostasis, T – the period of functioning of the system. Assume that for each state parameter x_i its target value x_i* is defined and the domain of homeostasis X* represents a parallelepiped

$$\prod_{i=1}^{n} [x_i * - \varepsilon, x_i * + \varepsilon]. \tag{7.3.2}$$

Corporative Information-Modeling Systems

Then the segments $[x_i^* - \varepsilon, x_i^* + \varepsilon]$ are admittances for the parameter x_i and the requirement (7.3.1) for $t \to \infty$ is the condition of neutral stability of the stationary point x* for the controlled dynamical system

$$\frac{dx}{dt} = f(x(t), u(t)) \tag{7.3.3}$$

which describes the trajectory of an organizational system with the state vector x(t) for the specific set of control impacts u(t).

The strong form of homeostasis (W.E.Deming requirement of continuous improvement) is described by the additional condition

$$\lim_{t \to \infty} x(t) = x^* \tag{7.3.4}$$

which together with the condition (7.3.1) and consideration of (7.3.2) means the Lyapunov asymptotic stability of the stationary point x*.

Thus, if the development of an organizational system is being modeled by the equation (7.3.3) and the totality of target values of its state parameters by the stationary point x* then the traditional approach is formalized as the requirement of neutral stability of the equilibrium and the Deming approach of continuous improvement as the requirement of its Lyapunov asymptotic stability. The requirement of neutral stability is considered as the weak form of organizational homeostasis and the requirement of asymptotic stability as the strong form. The asymptotic stability (strong condition of homeostasis) includes the neutral one (weak condition). Therefore the Deming approach reinforces the admittance approach.

4. Regular measurement of the values of process parameters and key parameters of the environment. The measurement is necessary for checking whether the formulated above requirements of homeostasis are satisfied. Collection of information about the organizational state is a very important task of the organizational monitoring system (Paragraph 4.3).

5. Analysis of the measurement results and the evaluation of the organizational state. These are monitoring problems inseparably linked with the previous problem from the step 4 which give together an answer to the question whether the organizational development is homeostatic.

6. Development and realization of corrective action if necessary (Paragraph 5.2). As far as an organization is continuously impacted by external and internal disturbing factors then current deviations from the homeostatic conditions are inevitable. Therefore it is necessary to develop and realize adaptation mechanisms ensuring the return of the organizational system to the desirable trajectory (Paragraph 5.1). A natural way of ensuring adaptation is the development of incentive mechanisms which impel the employees to satisfy the requirements of homeostasis (Paragraph 5.2).

7. Development and realization of preventive action (Paragraph 5.3). According to the requirements of the standard ISO 9001-2008 the organization shall determine action to eliminate the causes of potential nonconformities in order to prevent their occurrence. Here it is necessary to use simulation modeling which permits to predict the state of internal and external milieu.

8. Overcoming of the opportunistic behavior. There is a hope that an ideal management based on cooperation and conviction would permit to avoid an organizational opportunism. However, a thorny path leads to the ideal and in the present real conditions it is necessary to consider personal interests and individualistic strategies of the employees that do not fit the requirements of sustainable development of the whole organization. Therefore models of the opportunistic behavior are actual and useful (Paragraph 6.2). For description of the compromise interaction of the stakeholders associated with the organization it is necessary to use game theoretic models which solution should satisfy the requirements of strategic and dynamical stability (Paragraph 2.2). In their totality the conditions of homeostasis (neutral and asymptotic stability) and compromise (which is strategically and dynamically stable) represent the necessary and sufficient conditions of the organizational sustainable management.

9. Automation of document flow and decision support based on the corporative information-analytical system. Practical tools of realization of the described management technology are given by corporative information systems (Paragraph 7.2) providing the computer automation of collection, storage and analysis of the required information. In this paragraph the author's concept of the corporative information-modeling system (CIMS) as a tool of the organizational sustainable management is described. The structure of CIMS is shown in Figure 7.3.1.

The CIMS is realized according to the client-server pattern. The client part includes data and model interfaces, other system blocks relate to the server part (a case of several servers is also possible).

Operative databases contain information about separate directions of the organizational activity. The well known examples are accounting database, human resource database, operative production control database, archive of contracts and so on. All those databases in fact exist in all organizations: if the organization has a CIS then on the unified platform else on different platforms up to the complete absence of the computer representation. The problem is an integration of the uncoordinated data for the support of the described technology of sustainable management.

The problem is solved based on the concept of data warehouse (Paragraph 7.2). The data warehouse supports the following functions:

- data import from the operative databases (the problems of data refining, aggregation, safety and integration are solved in this process);
- processing of big arrays describing all aspects of activity of the large organizations and necessary information about their environment;
- creation of the multilevel metadata glossaries (user catalogues);
- user request processing and report generation. In this case not only standard reports but also intellectual ones based on OLAP and Data Mining are formed.

The users can interact with both operative databases and data warehouse in the dialogue mode. An interaction between the operative bases and the data warehouse is supported by the programs of internal interface and is one-way (data import from the databases to the data warehouse).

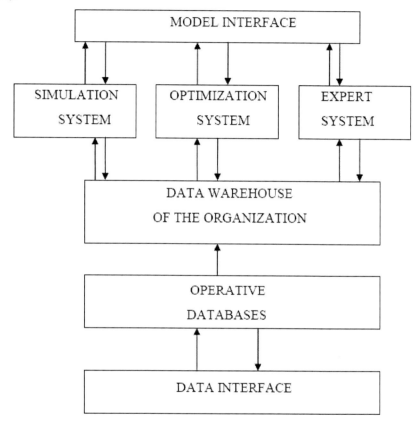

Figure 7.3.1. Structure of the CIMS of sustainable management support.

Simulation, optimization and expert systems (subsystems) are selected within the CIMS on the logic level. The differentiation of the simulation and optimization systems is quite conventional, and they can be joined as a model subsystem which is characterized in Table 7.3.1.

Table 7.3.1. Model subsystem of CIMS

Methods Modes	Numerical methods	Simulation
Optimization	Approximate search of the optimal solution	Checking of suboptimal solutions to the correspondence to additional constraints
Prediction	Approximate calculation of the trajectories	Evaluation of consequences of the control impacts

This approach in general corresponds to the concept of simulation system proposed in the early 1970-s in the Computing Center of the Russian Academy of Sciences (Pavlovsky 2000). A generalized pattern of the simulation system is shown in Figure 7.3.2.

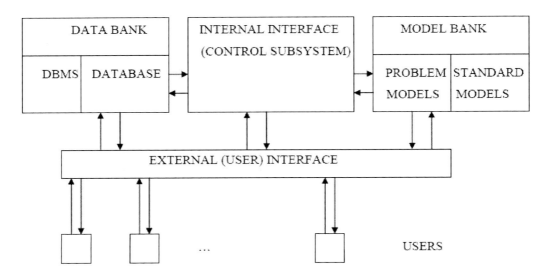

Figure 7.3.2. Pattern of simulation system.

The experience has shown that simulation computer experiments with a model of the type (5.3.1)-(5.3.2) alone do not permit to answer all questions of the system research. It is necessary to combine formal analytical methods and computer simulation with expert knowledge that permit to take into consideration badly formalized specific reasoning. It is convenient to realize the combination in the form of the specially organized simulation system. The main idea of the simulation system is an organization of its dialogue with a user so that the user could interactively correct models and calculation schemes with consideration to the informal knowledge and the results received up to the present moment.

The model bank (more accurately, the bank of program realizations of the models) has the central place in the simulation system. The used models are differentiated into two groups: problem ones and standard ones. Problem models describe how the model variables change in the considered processes. For example, Verhulst-Pearl-Reed model of dynamics of population number or von Neumann model of economics are problem ones. Standard models realize well investigated classes of mathematical models for which the methods of solution are known. For example, a linear programming problem with a modification of the simplex method can be realized as a standard model.

The same situation can be formalized by means of different standard models. Thus, a problem of allocation of industrial enterprises can be described by the linear programming model or by a more complicated model which takes into consideration the non-linearity of some relations. The same dynamic system can be described by a system of ordinary or partial differential equations, and so on. From the other side, the same standard model can be used for the formalization of different objects. For example, the linear programming model can be applied to the problem of optimal allocation of industrial or agricultural resource or to the

Corporative Information-Modeling Systems

problem of optimal rationing. A system of ordinary differential equations can describe processes of the different nature in mechanical, biological, economic systems, and so on.

The problem of information support is solved by the data warehouse described above. The internal interface ensures an interaction of the data warehouse and the model bank by the user defined scheme. Initial values of the variables and parameter values are transferred from the data warehouse to the model bank and the calculation results (values of the state variables in the end of prediction period) are returned. The internal interface programs solve also a number of technical problems: value range control, data format transformation and so on.

The external interface provides to the user a possibility of the dialogue with the simulation system. As far the user is not obliged to be an expert in modeling and programming it is very important to make the external interface as a user friendly one. The characteristics of convenience are:

- speed of the system response to the user request;
- simplicity of the input language in which the user should communicate with the system;
- ability of correction of the modeling process in the interactive real-time mode, and so on.

The described property is one of the most important features of the simulation system as an essential factor of its practical applicability. A totality of nice models, accurate data and control programs deprived of a user-friendly interface remains a thing in itself suitable for internal needs of the developers only. Real managers will not deal with the system. In this connection the form of representation of the modeling results acquires an important role. The most obvious and illustrative ways of data displaying which facilitate their understanding and interpretation should be encouraged. These ways are maps, graphs, diagrams, tables, figures and so on. For the realization of convenient data output both program-technical (plotters, graphical editors) and analytical (methods of aggregation) tools could be required.

It is evident that the most complete and comprehensive representation of the organization as a complex system could be received by using several models which are different by their mathematical nature and degree of complexity. Simulation models can be differentiated into three types: detailed, aggregated and macro-models. To the first type the simulation models having more than ten state variables, to the second one the models with 5-10 variables and to the third type the models describing 2-4 main characteristics of the system being modeled are related. The need in different types of complexity of the simulation models is explained by the following reasons.

First, for the solution of each separate problem which forms a part of the total problem its own level of detail of the real system description and therefore its own level of the simulation model detailing is required. For example, it is hardly reasonable to consider in details a process of building separate houses for the general evaluation of the efficiency of a real estate development project. But the details can be useful for the specification of building schedules. In other words, the choice of modeling method is determined by the requirements to the accuracy of the modeling results.

Second, a unified system of organizational monitoring is not developed yet, and therefore an absence of some data can impede the determination of the quantitative dependences with a sufficient accuracy. In this case one has to use macro-models aimed not to the quantitative description of the system functioning but to the revealing of its qualitative properties and development trends. If a volume of the available information increases then detailed and aggregated models become the most adequate.

Third, having organizational models of all three types it is convenient to control the quality of their work by comparison of the results of solution of the same problem by means of different models. In the majority of cases the complexity of a detailed simulation model is comparable to the complexity of the real organization. Therefore the results received by means of a detailed model are far from trivial, their analysis, interpretation and validation are troubled. It is possible to consider aggregated models and macro-models as consequent simplifications of a detailed simulation model up to the degree which permits to understand the essence of the model behavior. For example, the structure of stationary states of a complex system has an essential influence to its dynamical behavior. It is easy to find the stationary states by means of a simplified model and then to underline a possible domain of stationary states of a more complicated model. In practice this approach leads to the transfer of ideas developed on one level of modeling to another level for the evaluation of their applicability from the point of view of validity of the received results. This leads to the concept of simplified models illustrated in Figure 7.3.3.

A combined use of simulation and optimization models is of big interest. The solution of an optimization problem answers the question "How to act the best way?" and this selection of the optimal variant from the set of allowable ones is the most attractive for practical workers. However, it is not always possible to solve an optimization problem; it is even more important that often it is difficult to formulate it, or to select the only criterion which describes the agent's interests.

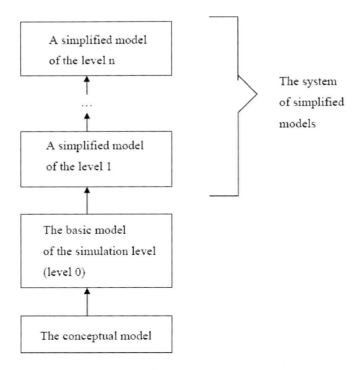

Figure 7.3.3. The scheme of concept of simplified models.

A simulation model answers a less ambitious question "What will be with the system if it is impacted so and so?" and therefore is always realizable but the own problems arise here. First, an identification problem is to be solved, i.e. the form of functional dependences and the numerical values of parameters are to be found (as a rule, there is much more dependences and parameters than in the optimization problem). Second, a set of scenarios for the computer simulation experiments is to be determined. Third, it is not always clear how to use the simulation results in practice, and so on.

So, the simulation and optimization techniques are complementary and their combination can reinforce the advantages of both approaches. Different schemes of coordination of simulation and optimization models are possible. Consider as an example a managerial modification of the scheme oriented for the investigation of environmental-economic systems (Ougolnitsky 1999). The procedure includes the following phases.

1. The system analysis of the organization is performed which results in the main organizational processes and their interaction determination.
2. An optimization problem (or a set of the problems) is formulated so that its objective function and constraints reflect the economic requirements.
3. The problem is solved by mathematical programming methods and the optimal solution

$$u^* = \text{Arg max } g(u)$$
$$u \in U$$

is determined where $g(u)$ is the objective function; U is the set of constraints.

4. A simulation model of the type (5.3.1)-(5.3.2) describing the organizational functioning is built. The vector u should belong to the set of control variables of the model.
5. A computer simulation experiment with the built model for $u=u^*$ is performed and the respective organizational phase trajectory $x(u^*,t)$ is determined for the period of prediction.
6. If the organizational trajectory $x(u^*,t)$ for the period of prediction belongs to the domain of homeostasis Ω then u^* is economically optimal and homeostatically admissible solution which can be recommended as the control impact.
7. Otherwise the constraints of the optimization problem should be weakened, i.e. a set $U' \supset U$ is to be considered as the new set of constraints. For the finding of U' different methods could be used, especially heuristic ones based on the content of the problem domain. After that the optimization problem is solved again on the set U', the received optimal solution $u^{**} \in U'$ is checked for its satisfaction of the homeostatic conditions, and so on.

The flow chart of the proposed procedure is shown in Figure 7.3.4.

Nevertheless the subdivision of the CIMS into simulation and optimization subsystems on the logic level seems reasonable because simulation and optimization models have a different nature.

For example, a balance simulation model of a real estate development company describes its financial flows for different scenarios of the production activity, credit policy and customer demand. The income part of the balance model includes own and credit means, means of the strategic and private investors, rental payments.

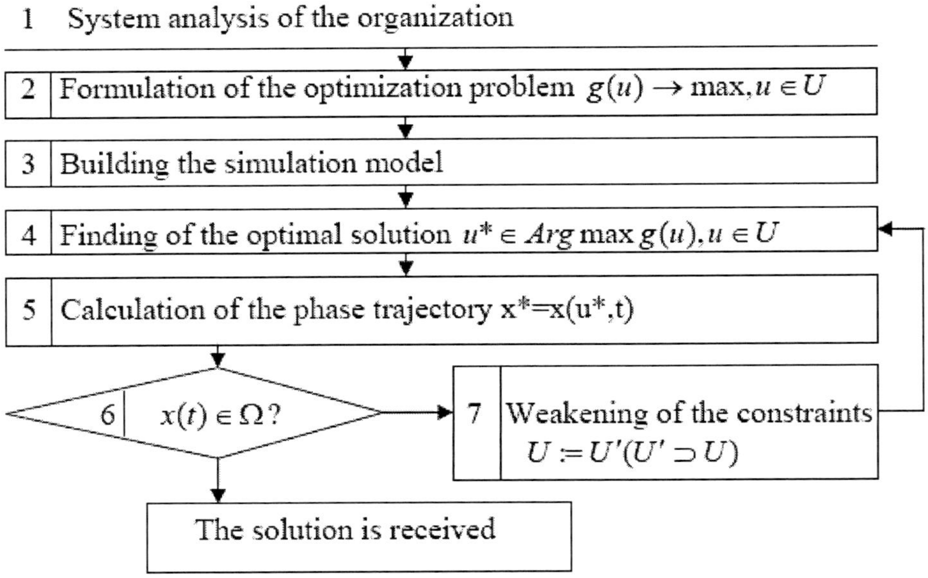

1 System analysis of the organization

2 Formulation of the optimization problem $g(u) \to \max, u \in U$

3 Building the simulation model

4 Finding of the optimal solution $u^* \in Arg \max g(u), u \in U$

5 Calculation of the phase trajectory $x^*=x(u^*,t)$

6 $x(t) \in \Omega$? → 7 Weakening of the constraints $U := U'(U' \supset U)$

The solution is received

Figure 7.3.4. Flow chart of the procedure of coordination of simulation and optimization in organizational sustainable management.

The expenditure part of the balance considers the return of credits with percents, expenditures for design and building of new real estate objects, maintenance of the leased lodgings, marketing, advertisement and customer service, internal organizational expenses.

The control variables are the cost rate for 1 m^2, the rental rate for 1 m^2 per month, the expenditures for marketing, advertisement and customer service, the ratio between volumes of sales and rental for commercial real estate. The scenario part includes schedules of design, building, sales and rentals, credit return, obligatory payments and so on. It is evident that the model contains a big number of parameters such as threshold dates, different rates, norms and others. Optimization and game theoretic models in real estate development are considered in (Ougolnitsky 2010).

Expert subsystem is described in the previous paragraph. Let's note that the simulation and optimization models also can be considered as specific inference engines.

Graphical editors and compilers are used for the creation, updating and displaying of the graphical representation of the data saved in the files of calculation results.

As a rule the simulation subsystems read data as text lists describing the connections between the model blocks. The lists are created on the base of data kept in the data base in the moment when a command for the beginning of simulation is given. Then the lists are analyzed by the simulation subsystem for creation or updating the data structures used in the calculation process. The outgoing results are also presented in a text format which is to be analyzed and transformed for the use by the graphical editor.

CONCLUSION

Let's return to the principal theses of the book and discuss the concerned achievements, unsolved problems and prospective research.

1. A correspondence between different rationality concepts and mathematical models formalizing them is established.

The correspondence is shown in more details in the following table.

Rationality concept	Mathematical model
Economic rationality	(Scalar) optimization problem
Sociological rationality	Vector optimization problem
Competition of economic agents	Games in normal form
Cooperation of economic agents	Games in the form of characteristic function (cooperative games)
Competition of sociological agents	Games in normal form with vector payoff functions
Cooperation of sociological agents	Games in the form of vector characteristic function
Competition and cooperation of the hierarchically organized agents	Hierarchical games in normal form and in the form of characteristic function in scalar and vector case
Sustainable management	Game theoretic models of sustainable management

The main author's hypothesis consists here in the identification of the economic rationality with the decision making problem with one criterion of optimality and the sociological rationality with the problem with several criterions. A development of the theory of games in normal form and in the form of characteristic function for the case of vector payoff functions (vector characteristic functions) and its specification for the hierarchically organized players (coalitions) is of great interest.

2. Possibility and appropriateness of generalization of the concept of sustainable development to the case of arbitrary dynamic systems including human beings are

justified, and the conditions of sustainable management of a dynamic system (homeostasis, compromise, dynamic consistency) are formulated.

The term "sustainable development" acquires a great popularity during the last decades and is often used in conformity with very different objects (natural systems, organizations, territories and so on) in a very broad sense. We think that it is natural and correct to spread the term beyond the limits of the environmental-economic systems and disseminate it to the economics, sociology, organizations theory, and arbitrary dynamic systems including the human beings. However, it is important to give a strict definition of the term preferably on the level of mathematical formalization. It is this approach that is realized in the book: the requirements of homeostasis, compromise and dynamic consistency are differentiated as the conditions of sustainable development, their formalization in the game theoretic model is proposed.

3. A scantiness of the classic model of controlled dynamic system is shown, a necessity of transition to the model of the hierarchically controlled dynamic system is proved. Here the main idea is that personal objectives of separate agents impacting a system often contradict to the conditions of sustainable development of the whole system. Therefore it is required to introduce the higher level of management the elements of which together with their personal interests first of all pursue the objectives of the whole organization identified with the requirements of sustainable development.

4. A subject of the hierarchical sustainable management (subject of hierarchical rationality) is described. The subject is defined as a structured control system with a number of internal connections and relations which only conditionally could be considered as a whole unit.

    This thesis is a direct development of the previous idea. In the real world the agent having an influence to the dynamic system contains at least two levels, and the elements of the lower one pursue only their private interests meanwhile the elements of the higher one are also responsible for the satisfaction of requirements of the sustainable development using for this the different methods of hierarchical management. In a sense a new type of the rationality of behavior could be spoken about here.

5. A static game theoretic model of the sustainable management is built. The methods of the hierarchical management (compulsion, impulsion, conviction) are formalized as solutions of a hierarchical game, the necessary and sufficient conditions of their existence are found.

    All the diversity of methods of the hierarchical management can be differentiated into three groups: compulsion, impulsion, conviction. Almost all known classes of the models of contract theory and other mathematical theories of hierarchical management from the point of view of this terminology relate to only one of the three methods, namely impulsion. The leading player (Leader, Principal) impacts to the payoff function of the leaded player (Follower, Agent). This method has a pure economic nature. However, in the real world there are also other methods such as compulsion when the set of admissible strategies of the Follower is impacted, i.e. and administrative impact, and conviction when hierarchical relations are transformed into cooperative ones, i.e. social-psychological impact. In this work a unified

Conclusion 261

approach to the description of all three methods in a game theoretic model is realized.

6. Dynamic models of sustainable management in complete and reduced forms are built, their interpretation for the case of hierarchically controlled environmental-economic systems is proposed.

A static model of sustainable management is inevitably conventional and illustrative because the concept of sustainable development by definition relates to the long (in the limit infinite) period of time. Only the dynamic model permits to define and study the notion of time (dynamic) consistency which should be done for the different classes of models. The dynamic model of sustainable management seems a typical object that requires usage of the "experimental mathematics" – modern technologies of building problem-oriented programming systems and realizing computer simulation experiments. In the books (Gorstko and Ougolnitsky 1996; Ougolnitsky 1999) the methodology of applied system analysis which combines mathematical methods, expert estimates and computers for the solution of complicated practical problems is described. It seems natural to use this methodology for the investigation of the dynamic models of sustainable management.

7. Specific models of sustainable management of the water resources, forest resources, recreational systems, construction projects are built and investigated.

It is important to note that though the environmental-economic problem domain has historically served a natural base for the development of the concept of sustainable management it is not at all the only domain of application of the concept. The universal character of the concept is illustrated by the examples from different problem domains, and the process of extension of the applications should be prolonged. Specifically, the models of state regulation of economic processes are of great interest.

8. An approach to the consideration of corruption in the models of organizational sustainable management is realized, some models of description of private interests in resource allocation are developed.

Corruption is one of the brightest and most social important examples of the opportunistic behavior. The main author's ideas of the corruption modeling in the context of sustainable management consist in the differentiation of two types of corruption, namely connivance and extortion, and three kinds of corruption, namely p-corruption, q-corruption and a-corruption. In the case of connivance a basic level of service is guaranteed meanwhile the additional services and preferences are given for a bribe. In the case of extortion the bribe is required already on the basic level of service. In the case of p-corruption the bribe ensures economic preferences, i.e. the conditions of payoff getting are ameliorated. In the case of q-corruption the bribe ensures administrative preferences, i.e. the set of admissible strategies of the bribe-giver is extended. In the case of a-corruption the conditions of homeostasis are for sale. Some preliminary results of the application of this methodology to the modeling of sustainable management are received.

9. A general approach to the modeling and optimization of monitoring as an integral part of the sustainable management is proposed, a technology of organizational monitoring based on mathematical models and information-modeling systems is characterized.

Monitoring is treated as an integral part of the sustainable management which provides the higher control level by the information about the state of controlled system and therefore by the feedback. The possibility of a unified approach to the monitoring of dynamic systems of the arbitrary nature is proved, and its specification for the case of organizational systems is given. Some approaches to the optimization of the monitoring structure are presented. It seems rational to consider the opportunistic behavior in the monitoring process when it is profitable for the agents to deliberate the information about the state of the controlled system in their personal interests.

10. A consistency of the quality management principles and the conditions of sustainable management is shown. An interpretation of corrective and preventive action in quality management as the adaptive behavior of organization is substantiated. The quality management based on the ISO 9000 standards is a generally accepted technology of the management improvement. In the book the complete consistency of the quality management principles and the requirements of sustainable management is shown, and the methodology of ensuring the adaptive sustainable management compatible with the ISO 9000 standards is proposed.

11. Dynamic multidigraphs as a means of information modeling are proposed. Information modeling forms a base for the improvement of the management in organizations based on computerization. A number of mathematical tools of information modeling in static and dynamic form exist (finite automates, Petri nets, queuing systems and others). A one more mathematical instrument facilitating the building of information model and the transition to the simulation modeling is proposed in the book.

12. A necessity of development of the corporative information-modeling systems as a tool of providing sustainable management is proved.
    Corporative information systems represent the material base of sustainable management in organizations. A necessary condition of their efficient use is the addition of modeling components which provide the possibilities of analysis, prediction, optimization and expert recommendations. The author's concept of the corporative information-modeling systems as a tool of sustainable management in organizations is presented in the book.

Thus, the concept of sustainable management is stated in the book. Three sources of the concept can be selected.

First, it is the theory of sustainable development of the relations between the mankind and its natural environment. In the process of investigation and public discussion of this direction generated by the aggravation of environmental problems in the end of the last century an understanding of the sustainable development as an economic development compatible with the requirements of ecological equilibrium has been achieved. In other aspect, the interests of consumption of the present generation should not violate the rights and interests of the next generations. Thus, the essential conditions of sustainable development are the following: satisfaction of the requirements of both economic development and ecological equilibrium; observance of the requirements on very long or even infinite interval of time; need in coordination of non-coincident interests with an obligatory maintenance of the key requirements.

Second, it is the theory of control of the dynamic systems. Within the theory models of the controlled dynamic systems in different modifications are built and studied, such notions as state vector, control vector, control and controlled subsystem, control objective, criterion of optimality of control, stability, feedback and others are introduced and formalized.

Third, it is the methods of hierarchical control (management) and their mathematical formalization. Three groups of control methods in the hierarchical systems are selected: administrative-legislative (compulsion), economic (impulsion), social-psychological (conviction). The main directions of the mathematical formalization of control mechanisms in the hierarchical systems are information theory of hierarchical systems, theory of active systems, and theory of contracts. The main mathematical formalism is here the hierarchical game theory.

In turn, on the next stage of research the general concept of sustainable development becomes one of the three sources of analysis of the sustainable management in organizations. The second source is the quality management and the strategic management. Within this problem domain the theory of strategic reference points of corporation is developed, the interests and influence potential of the key stakeholders are revealed and analyzed, the principles of quality management are formulated, and the standards of quality management determining a number of requirements to the management in organizations are approved. The third source is information technologies of modeling of the big systems. It is conditioned by the fact that the problems of sustainable management in organizations are obviously practical and need for their realization a material base the role of which is played by information systems. Within this direction the structure, functions and methods of implementation of the corporative information systems are studied, the understanding of the need of their addition by the analytical and modeling components is achieved, and certain results on the way of development of the corresponding instrumental means are received.

Three components of the theory of sustainable management can be selected, namely system analysis, mathematical modeling and information technologies.

In the process of author's research and development was shown: the compatibility of the quality management principles and the conditions of sustainable development in organizations; the possibility of representation of the condition of organizational homeostasis as the stability of its stationary point given by the totality of target values of the processes of its activity; the necessity of the organizational monitoring and the possibility of its optimization on the base of dual problems of the type "accuracy-cost"; the expediency of development of the incentive system which encourages the observance of the target values of the process parameters and fines for the deviation from them as a mechanism of the automation of corrective action in the quality management; the prospects of usage of simulation modeling based on the scenario method for the realization of preventive action in the quality management; the need in consideration and overcoming of the opportunistic behavior on the base of game theoretic models describing the conditions of compromise and dynamic consistency; the necessity of development and maintenance of the corporative information-modeling system as a practical tool of ensuring of the sustainable management in organizations.

The whole logical construct can be schematically depicted as two tetrahedrons with the common vertex (see Figure C1).

Let's note again that the proposed monograph has a principally synthetic character. In the process of the writing the author was using the concepts, methods and models from the very different domains of knowledge such as environmental science and sustainable development, economic sociology, theory of social space and stratification, management theory, theory of optimization and optimal control, game theory, theory of contracts and others. It is absolutely evident that in this case the ratio between the width and the depth of research is solved in favor of the first one. This approach badly combines with the trend of specialization dominating in the modern science. Though declarations of the benefit of a multidisciplinary approach and the prospects of research made on the junction of sciences appear quite often, in fact the publications with a clear specialization which can be characterized by the only code of any classification are encouraged. The attempts of the interdisciplinary approach result in the obvious difficulties of perception, such works are hard to read and easy to criticize using (grounded by definition) the accusations in superficiality and dilettantism. Nevertheless we want to hope that the book will found its readers and will serve a source for the irreproachable specialized research.

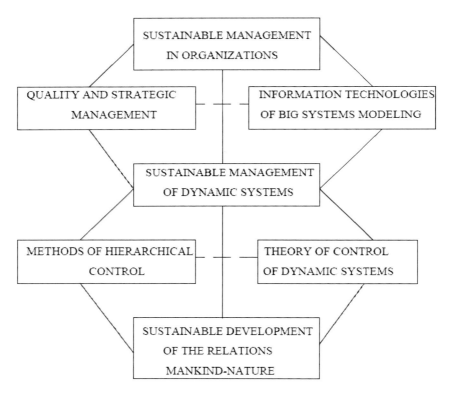

Figure C1. Logical construct of the presented research.

REFERENCES

Aall C. Sustainability Concept as Viewed by the Local Authorities // Regions. 2000. P.39-44.

Aalst W.M.P. van der. The application of Petri nets to workflow management // *J. Circuits, Syst. Comp.* – 1998. – Vol. 8. – No. 1. – P. 21-66.

Aalst W.M.P. van der and Hofstede A.H.M. ter. YAWL: Yet another workflow language (revised version) // Queensland Univ. Technol., Brisbane, Australia: *QUT Tech. Rep.* - FIT-TR-2003-04. – 2003.

Adizes I. Managing Corporate Lifecycles. – Adizes Institute Publications, 2004.

Agilar-Saven R.S. Business process modeling: Review and framework // *Int. J. Prod. Econ.* - 2004. - Vol. 90. - P. 129-149.

Avtonomov V.S. A Model of Man in Economics. – Saint Petersbourg, 1998 (in Russian).

Bac M. Corruption and Supervision Costs in Hierarchies // *Journal of Comparative Economics*. 1996. N22.

Badica C. et al. A new formal IDEF-based modeling of business processes // *In Proc. 1st Balkan Conf. Inf., Y. Manolopopulos and P.Spirakis, Eds.* – Thessalonica, Greece, 2003. – P. 535-549.

Badica K., Teodorescu M., Spahiu C., Badica A. Integrating Role Activity Diagrams and Hybrid IDEF for Business Process Modeling using MDA // Proc. 17th International Symposium on Symbolic and Numeric Algorithms for Scientific Computing (SYNASC'05). – 2005.

Bardhan P. Corruption and Development: a Review of Issues // *Journal of Political Economy*. - 1996. - N 31.

Basar T., Olsder G. *Dynamic Non-Cooperative Game Theory*. – L., 1995.

Beer St. *Cybernetics and Management.* – The English Universities Press, 1959.

Bell D. *The Coming of Post-Industrial Society*. – N.Y., 1976.

Bellman R.E. *Dynamic Programming.* – Princeton University Press, 1957.

Bolton P., Dewatripont M. *Contract Theory.* – MIT Press, 2004.

Boulding K. Ethics of the Critique of Preferences // *The Morality of Scarcity*. Eds.W.Finnin, G.Smith. – Louisiana, 1979.

Boyett J.H., Cohn H.P. Workplace 2000: *The Revolution Reshaping American Business*. – N.Y.: Dutton, 1991.

Burkov V.N. *Mathematical Theory of Active Systems*. – Moscow, 1977 (in Russian).

Burkov V.N., Novikov D.A. *Theory of Active Systems: State and Prospects.* – Moscow, 1999 (in Russian).

Burkov V.N., Novikov D.A., Shchepkin A.V. *Mechanisms of Control in the Environmental-Economic Systems.* – Moscow, 2008 (in Russian).

Cannon W. *The Wisdom of the Body.* - L., 1932.

Canter L.W. Environmental Impact Assessment. – McGraw-Hill Book Company, 1977.

Carley M., Christie I. Managing Sustainable Development. - Minneapolis, 1993.

Case J. Competition: *The Birth of a New Science.* – Hill and Wang, 2007.

Castels M. *The Information Age. Economy, Society and Culture.* –Vol. 1-3. – Oxford: Blackwell Publishers, 1996-1998.

Chang Ni-Bin, Tseng C.C. Optimal Design of a Multi-Pollutant Air Quality Monitoring Network in a Metropolitan Region Using Kaohsiung, Taiwan as an Example // *Env.Monitoring and Assessment*, 1999, v.57, iss.2, p.121-148.

Chapin N. Flowcharts. – Princeton, NJ: Auerbach, 1971.

Chou Y. and Chen Y. The methodology for business process optimized design // *In Proc. Ind. Electron. Conf. (IECON).* – 2003. – Vol. 2. – P. 1819-1824.

Codd E.F., Codd S.B., Salley C.T. Providing OLAP (On-Line Analytical Processing) to user-analysts: An IT mandate. *Technical report,* 1993.

Coenen F., Eckerberg K., Lafferty W.M. Implementation of Local Agenda 21 in twelve European countries. *A comparative analysis* // Regions. 2000. P.99-108.

Competitive Challenges and Business Opportunities. - Washington, 1995.

Dahrendorf R. Homo sociologicus: Ein Verzuch zur Geschichte, Bedeutung und Kritik der Kategorie der sozialen Rolle. – 12 Aufl.Opladen, 1973.

Danilov-Danilyan V.I., Losev K.S. *Environmental Challenge and Sustainable Development.* - Moscow, 2000 (in Russian).

Dantzig G. Linear Programming and Extentions. – Princeton University Press, 1963.

Davis K. Conceptual Analysis of Stratification // *Amer. Sociol. Review.* June 1942. Vol.7. N3.

De Crespigny A. Power and Its Forms // *Political Studies.* 1968. Vol.16. N2. P.192-205.

Deming W.E. *Out of the Crisis.* – The MIT Press, 1986.

Denin K.I., Ougolnitsky G.A. Game-Theoretic Model of Corruption in the Hierarchical Management Systems // Izvestia RAS. *Control Theory and Systems.* - 2010. - Vol. 1 (in Russian).

Di Zio S., Fontanella L., Ippoliti L. Optimal spatial sampling schemes for environmental surveys // *Environmental and Ecological Statistics,* 2004, v.11, iss.4, p.397-414.

Donatelli S., Ribaudo M. and Hillston J. A comparison of performance evaluation process algebra and generalized stochastic Petri nets // Proc. 6th Int. Workshop Petri Nets Perform. Models (PNPM 1995). – 1995. – P. 158.

Drucker P.F. *The New Realities.* – Oxford, 1996.

Drucker on Asia. A Dialogue between Peter Drucker and Isao Nakauchi. – Oxford, 1997.

Dubrov D.V., Ougolnitsky G.A. Two-Level Model of Control of the Forest Resource Use // *Problems of Environment and Natural Resource.* 2001. N6. P.83-98 (in Russian).

Earl M.J. The new and the old business process redesign // *Journal of Strategic Information Systems.* – 1994. – 3(1). – pp. 5-22.

Easton D. *The Perception of Authority and Political Change* // Authority. Nomos 1. Ed. by C. J. Friedrich. Cambridge, 1958. P.170-196.

Eliferov V.G. *Quality Management.* – M., 2006 (in Russian).

Elster J. Sour Grapes: *Studies in the Subversion of Rationality.* – Paris, 1983.

Elster J. Explaining Social Behavior: *More Nuts and Bolts for the Social Sciences.* – Cambridge University Press, 2007.

Environmental Assessment of Socioeconomic Systems / Ed. by D. F. Burkhardt and W. H. Ittelson. – Plenum Press, 1978.

Environmental Finance Program. *A Guidebook on Financial Tools.* - Washington, 1995.

Environmental Impact Assessment: Principles and Procedures. Ed. by R. E .Munn. – *J. Wiley and Sons,* 1979.

Ferrie J. Business processes: a natural approach / ESRC Business Processes Resource Centre, University of Warwick. – 1995.

Forrester J.W. *World Dynamics.* – Wright-Allen Press, 1971.

French J. R. P. Jr., Raven B. The Bases of Social Power // *Studies in Social Power.* Ed. D. Cartwright. Ann Arbor, 1959. P.150-167.

Fudenberg D., *Tirole J. Game Theory.* – Mass.: MIT Press, 1991.

Fundamentals of Geographic Information Systems: A Compendium / *Ed. W. J. Ripple.* Bethesda, MD, 1989.

Garkavy L. Kh., Kvakina E.B., Ukolova M.A. Adaptation Reactions and Resistance of Organism. – Rostov State University Publishers, 1979 (in Russian).

Germeyer Yu.B. Games with Non-Antagonistic Interests. – M., 1976 (in Russian).

Germeyer Yu.B., Vatel I.A. Games with hierarchical vector of interests // Izvestia AN SSSR. *Technical cybernetics.* 1974. Vol. 3 (in Russian).

Giarratano J., Riley G. Expert Systems: *Principles and Programming.* – 2004.

Gorbaneva O.I., Ougolnitsky G.A. Models of Resource Allocation in the Hierarchical Systems of River Water Quality Control // *Control in big systems.* – Vol. 26. – M., 2009. – P.64-80 (in Russian).

Gore A. Earth in the Balance. *Ecology and the Human Spirit.* - N.Y., 1993.

Gorelik V.A., Kononenko A.F. *Game Theoretic Models of Decision Making in Environmental-Economic Systems.* – M., 1982 (in Russian).

Gorstko A.B., Ougolnitsky G.A. *An Introduction to Modeling of the Environmental-Economic Systems.* – Rostov State University Publishers, 1990 (in Russian).

Gorstko A.B., Ougolnitsky G.A. *An Introduction to the Applied Systems Analysis.* – Rostov-on-Don, 1996 (in Russian).

Gorstko A.B., Sukhodolsky Ya.S. Some Questions of the Theory of Optimal Monitoring of Water Ecosystems // *Problems of Environmental Monitoring and Ecosystems Modeling.* – SPb., 1981. - Vol.4. - P.67-85 (in Russian).

Gossen H.H. Entwicklung der Gezetze des menschlichen Verkehrs und der daraus fliessenden Regeln fur menschliches Handeln. – Berlin, 1927.

Gou H., Huang B., Liu W., Ren S., Li Y. Petri-net-based business process modeling for virtual enterprises // 2000 IEEE International Conference on Systems, Man, and Cybernetics. – 2000. – Vol. 5. – P. 3183-3188.

Grigori D., Casati F., Castellanos M., Dayal U., Sayal M., Shan M.-C. Business Process Intelligence // Computers in Industry Journal. – 2004. – April. - *Special issue on workflow mining.* – Vol. 53/3. – P. 321-343.

Gurman V. I., Kulbaka N. E., Ryumina E. V. An experience of the social – environmental – economic modeling of a region // *Economics and Mathematical Methods.* 1999. Vol.35. №3. P.69-79. (in Russian)

Haken H. Synergetics: An Introduction. – *Springer,* 1983.

Hammer M. Beyond Reengineering. How the Process-Centered Organization is Changing Our Work and Our Lives. – N.Y., 1996.

Hammer M. and Champy J. Reengineering the Corporation: *A Manifesto for Business Revolution.* - London, U.K.: Brealey, 1993.

Handbook of Operations Research / Ed. by J. J. Moder, S. E. Elmaghraby. – Van Nostrand Reinhold Company, 1978.

Hargreaves Heap S. *Rationality in Economics.* – Oxford, 1989.

Hartfiel G. Wirtschaftliche und soziale Rationalitat: Untersuchungen zum Menschenbild in *Okonomie und Sozialogie.* - Stuttgart, 1968.

Havey M. Essential business process modeling. - Sebastopol, CA: O'Reilly, 2005.

Heiner R. The Origin of Predictable Behavior // *Amer. Econ. Rev.* 1983. – Vol.73. – N4.

Hicks J.R. Value and Capital. An Inquiry into *Some Fundamental Principles of Economic Theory.* – Oxford, 1939.

Hlupic V. and Robinson S. Business Process Modeling and Analysis Using Discrete-Event Simulation // Proc. of 1998 *Winter Simulation Conference.* – 1998. - P. 1363-1369.

Hofacker I. and Vetschera R. Algorithmical approaches to business process design // *Comp. Oper. Res.* – 2001. – Vol. 28. – P. 1253-1275.

Hudak P.F. A method for monitoring ground water quality near waste storage facilities // *Env.Monitoring and Assessment,* 1994, v.30, iss.2, p.197-210.

IDEF3 Process Description Capture: Method Report // Armstrong Laboratory, Human Resources Directorate, Logistics Research Division. - Wright-Patterson AFB, 1995.

Inmon W.H. *Building the Data Warehouse.* – J. Wiley and Sons, 2002.

Inosemzev V.I. Creative Bases of a Modern Corporation // *World Economy and International Relations.* – 1997. – Vol.11. – P.18-30 (in Russian).

Iooss G., Joseph D.D. *Elementary Stability and Bifurcation Theory.* – Springer-Verlag: N.Y. et al., 1980.

Isaaks R. Differential Games. *A Mathematical Theory with Applications to Warfare and Pursuit, Control and Optimization.* - J.Wiley and Sons, 1965.

Jeremy Bentham's Economic Writings. Vol.1. – L., 1952.

Jevons W.S. *The Theory of Political Economy.* – L., 1924.

Kettinger W. J., Teng J.T.C. and Guha S. Business process change: A study of methodologies, techniques and tools // *MIS Q.* – 1997. - Vol. 21. - No. 1. - P. 55-80.

Kidland F.E., Prescott E.C. Rules rather than decisions: the inconsistency of optimal plans // *Journal of Political Economy,* 1977. Vol.85. P.473-490.

Knies K. Die politische Okonomie vom geschichtlichen Standpunkte. – Braunschweig, 1880.

Knight F.H. Risc, Uncertainty, and Profit. – Chicago, 1971.

Knuth D.E. Computer-drawn flowcharts // *ACM Comm.* – 1963. – Vol. 6. – No. 9. – P. 555-563.

Koenig J. JBoss jBPM: White Paper. – 2006. – Version 2004.

Koubarakis M. and Plexousakis D. A formal framework for business process modeling and design // *Inf. Syst.* – 2002. – Vol. 27. – P. 299-319.

Kuhn H.W. Extensive games and the problem of information // *Annals of Math. Studies,* 1953, 28, 193-216.

Kurbatov V.I., Ougolnitsky G.A. *Mathematical Methods of Social Technologies.* – Moscow, 1998 (in Russian).

Kuznetsov O. L., Bolshakov B. E. Sustainable Development. Scientific Bases of Design in the System Nature-Society-Man. - SPb. – M. – Dubna, 2002 (in Russian).

Laffont J.-J., Martimort D. The Theory of Incentives: *The Principal-Agent Model.* – Princeton, 2002.

Law, Averill M. and David W. Kelton, *Simulation Modeling and Analysis*, McGraw-Hill, 1991.

Ledyaev V. Power: *A Conceptual Analysis.* – N.Y.: Nova Science Publishers, 1998.

Leibenstein H. Beyond the Economic Man: A New Foundation for Microeconomics. – Cambridge, Mass., 1976.

Leitmann G. Cooperative and Non-Cooperative Many Players Differential Games. – N.Y.: Springer-Verlag, 1974.

Lewin K. Dynamic Theory of Personality. – N.Y., 1935.

Li H., Yang Y., Chen T.Y. Resource constraints analysis of workflow specifications // Syst. Software. – 2004. – Vol. 73. – P. 271-285.

Loucks D.P., Stedinger J.R., Haith D.A. *Water Resource Systems Planning and Analysis.* – Englewood Cliffs, 1981.

Luce R.D., Raiffa H. Games and Decisions. *Introduction and critical survey.* – J.Wiley and Sons, 1957.

Malik F. Fuhren, Leisten, Leben. Wirksames Management fur eine neue Zeit. – Campus Ferlag, 2006.

May R. M. *Stability and Complexity in Model Ecosystems. –* N.Y., 1973.

Mayer R.J., DeWitte P.S., Blinn T.M. Framework of Frameworks. Knowledge Based Systems, Inc.: Internal Report / College Station, TX. – 1994.

McConnell J., Servaes H. Additional Evidence on Equity Ownership and Corporate Value // *Journal of Financial Economics.* 1990. V.17.

Meadows D.H., Meadows D.L., Randers J., Behrens W.W.III. *The Limits to Growth.* - N.Y., 1972.

Melao N., Pidd M. A conceptual framework for understanding business process modeling // *Inf. Syst.* – 2000. – Vol. 10. - P. 105-129.

Menzel C., Mayer R. Modeling Process Structure // *Proceedings Joint Standards Workshop* on Data that Defines Business Processes, published at www.NIST.gov. – September 1998.

Mescon M.H., Albert M., Khedouri F. Management. Harper and Row, 1988.

Methods of Structural Adjustment of the Control Mechanisms / Syroegin I.M. et al. – Moscow, 1976 (in Russian).

Milgrom P., Roberts J. *Economics, Organization and Management.* – Prentice Hall, 1992.

Mill J.S. On the Definition of Political Economy and on Method of Investigation Proper to it // Collected Works. – Toronto, 1970. – Vol.4.

Mintzberg H. Structure in Fives. *Designing Effective Organizations.* – Prentice/Hall International, 1983.

Mises L.von. *Human Action. A Treatise on Economics.* – Contemporary Books, 1996.

Modak P.M., Lohani B.N. Optimization of ambient air quality monitoring networks // *Environmental Monitoring and Assessment,* 1985, v.5, iss.1, p.1-19.

Moiseev N.N. Mathematical Problems of Systems Analysis. – Moscow, 1981 (in Russian).

Moiseev N.N. *A Farewell to Simplicity.* – Moscow, 1998 (in Russian).

Moulin H. *Game Theory for the Social Sciences.* – N.Y. University Press, 1986.

Moulin H. *Axioms of cooperative decision making.* – Cambridge University Press, 1988.

Naylor T. H. *Computer Simulation Experiments with Models of Economic Systems.* – J. Wiley and Sons, 1971.

Neave H.R. *The Deming Dimension.* – SPC Press, 1990.

Nelson R., Winter S. Evolutionary *Theory of Economic Change.* – Cambridge, Mass., 1982.

Neumann J.von, Morgenstern O. *Theory of Games and Economic Behavior.* – Princeton University Press, 1953.

New Paradigm of the Development of Russia. Complex Investigations of the Problems of Sustainable Development / Eds. V. A. Koptyug, V. M .Matrosov, V. K. Levashov. – M., 1999 (in Russian).

Ning Shu-Kuang, Chang Ni-Bin. Optimal Expansion of Water Quality Monitoring Network by Fuzzy Optimization Approach // *Env.Monitoring and Assessment,* 2004, v.91, iss.1, p.145-170.

Novikov D.A. Theory of Control of the Organizational Systems. – M., 2007 (in Russian).

Novikov D.A., Chkhartishvily A.G. *Reflexive Games.* – M., 2003 (in Russian).

Nurutdinova I.K., Ougolnitsky G.A. Construction of Incentive Mechanism Based on Reapportionment of Wage Fund // Control of Big Systems. Iss.31. – Moscow, 2010. P.250-264 (in Russian).

Oakeshott M. Rationalism in Politics and Other Essays. – L.: Methuen, 1949.

Olson R.L. Alternative images of a sustainable future // *Futures.* 1994. V.26. P.156-169.

Omrani D. Business process reengineering: a business revolution // *Management Services.* – 1992. – Oct.

Ougolnitsky G.A. Linear Theory of the Hierarchical Systems. – Moscow, 1996 (in Russian).

Ougolnitsky G.A. *Control of the Environmental-Economic Systems.* – Moscow: Vuzovskaya Kniga, 1999 (in Russian).

Ougolnitsky G.A. Game theoretic modeling of the hierarchical control of sustainable development // *Game Theory and Applications.* 2002. Vol.8. P.82-91.

Ougolnitsky G.A. Hierarchical Management of the Sustainable Development of Social Organizations // *Social Sciences and Modernity.* 2002. №3. P.133-140 (in Russian).

Ougolnitsky G.A. Mathematical Modeling of the Hierarchical Control of Sustainable Development // Computer Modeling. *Ecology.* Iss.2 / Ed. by G.A.Ougolnitsky. – Moscow: *Vuzovskaya Kniga*, 2004. P.101-125 (in Russian).

Ougolnitsky G.A. Game Theoretic Principles of Optimality of the Hierarchical Control of Sustainable Development // Izvestiya RAS. *Theory and Systems of Control.* 2005. №4. P.72-78 (in Russian).

Ougolnitsky G.A. Optimization and Game-Theoretic Models of Management of the Construction Projects // *Mathematical Game Theory and Applications.* - 2009. – Iss.2. – P.82-97 (in Russian).

Ougolnitsky G.A. Hierarchical Control of Sustainable Development. – Moscow: Fizmatlit, 2010 (in Russian).

Ougolnitsky G.A., Demyanenko Ya.M., Dubrov D.V. Methods of Hierarchical Optimization in Problems of the Forest Resource Use // Computer Modeling. Ecology. / Ed. by G.A.Ougolnitsky. - Moscow: *Vuzovskaya Kniga*, 2000. - P.79-89. (in Russian)

Ougolnitsky G.A., Cherdyntseva M.I. Computer Simulation of the Sustainable Development of Environmental-Economic Systems // Computer Modeling. Ecology. Iss.2 / Ed. by G.A.Ougolnitsky. – Moscow: *Vuzovskaya Kniga,* 2004. P.126-135 (in Russian).

References

Ougolnitsky G.A., Usov A.B. An Information-Analytical System of Control of the Environmental-Economic Objects // *Izvestia RAS. Control Theory and Systems.* – 2008. Vol.2. P.168-176 (in Russian).

Ougolnitsky G.A., Usov A.B. Managing Big Environmental-Economic Systems // *Remote Control Systems.* – 2009. – Vol. 5. – P.169-179 (in Russian).

Ougolnitsky G.A., Usov A.B. Problems of the sustainable development of ecological-economic systems // Global Climatology and Ecodynamics: Anthropogenic Changes to Planet Earth / Eds.A.P.Cracknell, V.P.Krapivin, C.A.Varotsos. – *Springer-Praxis,* 2009. – P.427-444.

Ould M.A. Business Processes: *Modeling and Analysis for Reengineering and Improvement.* – Chichester, UK: Wiley, 1995.

Our Common Future. *World Commission on Environment and Development* (WCED). - Oxford, 1987.

Our Common Journey. A Transition toward Sustainability. – National Academy Press: Washington, D.C., 1999.

Pall G.A. Quality Press Management. – Englewood Cliffs: Prentice-Hall, 1987.

Passarella G., Vurro M., D'Agostino V., Barcelona M.J. Cokriging Optimization of Monitoring Network Configuration Based on Fuzzy and Non-Fuzzy Variogram Evaluation // *Env.Monitoring and Assessment*, 2003, v.82, iss.1, p.1-21.

Paul R.J., Hlupic V., Giaglis G. Simulation modeling of business processes // UK Academy of Information Systems Conference, Lincoln, UK. – April 1998.

Pavlovsky Yu.N. *Simulation Models and Systems.* – Moscow, 2000 (in Russian).

Peters L. and Peters J. Using IDEF0 for dynamic process analysis // In Proc. 1997 *IEEE Int. Conf. Robot.* Autom., Albuquerque, NM, 1997. – 1997. – P. 3203-3208.

Petrosjan L.A. Stable solutions of differential games with many participants // *Vestnik of Leningrad University*, 1977, 19. P.46-52 (in Russian).

Petrosjan, L.A., Zenkevich, N.A. Game Theory. - World Scientific Publ.Co., Singapore, 1996.

Petrosjan L.A., Zenkevich N.A. Time Consistency of Cooperative Solutions. In: Contributions to game theory and management. Petrosjan, L.A., Zenkevich, N.A. (Eds.). Collected papers presented on the International Conference Game *Theory and Management.* SPb: Graduate School of Management SPbU, 2007, pp.413-440.

Pezzey J. *Economic Analysis of Sustainable Growth and Sustainable Development.* The World Bank, 1989.

Pfeffer J., Sutton R.I. Hard Facts, Dangerous Half-Truths, and Total Nonsense. Profit from Evidence-Based Management. – Harvard Business School Press, 2006.

Phalp K., Shepperd M. Quantitative analysis of static models of processes // *System Software.* – 2000. - Vol. 52. - P. 105-112.

Pinter J. Stochastic modeling and optimization for environmental management // *Annals of Oper.Res.*, 1991, v.31, iss.1, p.527-544.

Pontryagin L.S., Boltyanskii V.G., Gamkrelidze R.V., Mishchenko E.F. *Mathematical Theory of Optimal Processes.* – N.Y.: Interscience Publishers, 1962.

Powell S.G., Schwaninger M., Trimble C. Measurement and control of business processes // *System Dynamics Rev.* – 2001. – Vol. 17. – No. 1. – P. 63-91.

Quatrani T. Visual Modeling with Rational Rose 2000 and UML. - 2nd Edition. – N.Y.: Addison Wesley, 2001.

Raposo A.B., Magalhaes L.P. and Ricarte I. L. M. Petri nets based coordination mechanisms for multi-flow environments // *Int. J. Comp. Syst. Sci. Eng.* – 2000. – Vol. 15. – No. 5. – P. 315-326.

Reklaitis G.V., Ravindran A., Ragsdell K.M. Engineering Optimization. Methods and Applications. – *J. Wiley and Sons*, 1983.

Roberts F.S. Discrete Mathematical Models with application to social, biological and ecological problems. – Prentice-Hall, 1976.

Rose-Ackerman S. The Economics of Corruption // *J. of Political Economy* 1975. V. 4. P. 187-203.

Roseland M. Toward Sustainable Communities. *A Resource Book for Municipal and Local Governments.* - NRTEE, 1992.

Rosenmuller J. Kooperative Spiele und Markte. – *Springer-Verlag,* 1971.

Runciman W.G. Weber: *Selections in Translation.* – Cambridge University Press, 1991.

Rybasov E.A., Ougolnitsky G.A. Mathematical Modeling of the Hierarchical Control of the Environmental-Economic Systems Considering Corruption// *Computer Modeling.* Ecology. Iss.2 / Ed. by G.A.Ougolnitsky. – Moscow: Vuzovskaya Kniga, 2004. P. 46-65 (in Russian).

Salanie B. *The Economics of Contracts.* – MIT Press, 1997.

Samuelson P. *Foundations of Economic Analysis.* – Cambridge, Mass., 1948.

Saxena K.B.C. Reengineering public administration in developing countries // Long Range Planning. – 1996. – 26 (6). – P. 703-711.

Senior N.W. Introductory Lecture on Political Economy. – L., 1827.

Selten R. Models of Strategic Rationality. – Dordrecht-Boston-London, 1988.

Selten R. Bounded Rationality // *J. Institutional and Theoretical Econ.* – 1990. – Vol.146. - P.649-658.

Seron Arbeloa F.J., Perez Caseiras C., Nogue Lahuerta L.J., Latorre Andres P.M. Air quality monitoring for multiple pollutants: Optimization of a network around a hypothetical potash plant and two thermal power stations in open countryside // *Env.Monitoring and Assessment,* 1993, v.27, iss.2, p.107-134.

Shannon R.E. Systems Simulation: the art and science. – Prentice-Hall, 1975.

Shimizu Y. and Sahara Y. A supporting system for evaluation and review of business process through activity-based approach // *Comp. Chem. Eng.* – 2000. – Vol. 24. – P. 997-1003.

Shvedin B. Ontological Model for Human Resource Management and Organizational Development of the Large-Scale Organization // *Science-consuming Technologies.* 2006. N6. Vol.7. P.13-35 (in Russian).

Simon H. *Models of Bounded Rationality,* Vols. 1 and 2. MIT Press, 1982.

Simon H. *Models of Bounded Rationality,* Vol. 3. MIT Press, 1997.

Skitovsky T. The Joyless Economy: *An Inquiry into Human Satisfaction and Consumer Dissatisfaction.* – N.Y., 1976.

Sloan A.P., Jr. My Years with General Motors. – N.Y., 1964.

Smith A. An Inquiry into the Nature and Causes of the Wealth of Nations: A Selected Edition / Ed. Kathryn Sutherland. – Oxford Paperbacks, 2008.

Smith B. The Basic Tools of Formal Ontology / Formal Ontology in Information Systems. Ed. by N.Guarino. – IOS Press, 1998. – P.19-28.

Smith J.M. Optimization theory in evolution // *Ann.Rev.Ecol.Syst.,* 1978, v.9, p.31-56.

Sorokin P. Social and Cultural Dynamics. A Study of Change in Major Systems of Art, Truth, Ethics, Law and Social Relationships. – Porter Sargent Publisher, 1957.

Soros G. The Alchemy of Finance. Reading the Mind of the Market. – J.Wiley and Sons, 1994.

Spellenberg I.F. *Monitoring Ecological Change.* – Cambridge, 2005.

Steuer R.E. Multiple Criteria Optimization: Theory, Computations, and Application. – *J.Wiley and Sons,* 1986.

Stigler G. Smith's Travels on the Ship of State // *Hist.Polit.Econ.,* 1971, vol.3.

Stigler G. The Economist as Preacher: Three Tanner Lectures. - Cambridge, 1980.

Taha H.A. Operations Research: An Introduction. – Macmillan Publ., 1982.

Talwar R. Business reengineering – a strategy-driven approach // Long Range Planning. – 1993. - №26 (6). – P. 22-40.

Teorey T.J., Fry J.P. Design of Database Structures. – Prentice-Hall, 1982.

Thaler R., Shefrin H. An Economic Theory of Self-Control // *Journ. Polit. Econ.* 1981. Vol. 89. P.392-406.

The Enterprise Ontology. Mike Ushold, Martin King, Stuart Moralee and Yannis Zorgios. - http://citeseer.ist.psu.edu/ushold95enterprise.html.

The Essential Drucker. Selections from the Management Works of Peter F. Drucker. – Harper Business, 2001.

The Local Agenda 21 Planning Guide. 1996.

The Portable MBA in Strategy. Ed. L. Fahey and R. M. Randall. – J. Wiley, 2001.

The Sociology of Economic Life / Eds. Granovetter M., Swedberg R. – Boulder: Westview Press, 1992.

The Works and Correspondence of David Ricardo. Vol. 1 / Eds. P. Sraffa and M. H. Dobb. – Indianapolis: Liberty Fund, 2005.

Tikhonov S.V. *Simulation Modeling of Business Processes in the Queuing Systems.* Ph.D. Thesis. – Rostov-on-Don: SFU, 2009 (in Russian).

Toffler A. The Adaptive Corporation. – Aldershot, Gower, 1985.

Transition to the Sustainable Development: Global, Regional and Local Levels. *Foreign Experience and Russian Problems* / Ed. by N. F. Glazovsky. - M., 2002.

Vaisbord E.M., Zhukovskiy V.I. Introduction to Multiplayer Differential Games and Their Applications. – N.Y.: *Gordon and Breach Sci. Publ.,* 1988.

Valiris G. and Gykas M. Critical review for existing BPR methodologies: The need for a holistic approach // *Bus. Process Manage. J.* 1999. – Vol. 5. – N. 1. – P. 65-86.

Vasin A.A., Agapova O. Game Theoretic Model of the Tax Inspection Organization // International Year-Book of Game Theory and Applications. 1993. V. 1. P. 83 - 94.

Veblen T. The Theory of Leisure Class: An Economic Study of Institutions, 1899.

Vergidis K. et al. Business Process Analysis and Optimization: Beyond Reengineering // IEEE Transactions on Systems, Man, and Cybernetics. – 2008. - Part C. – Vol. 38. – No.1.

Vick J.F., Harrell C.R. Introduction to ProcessModel and ProcessModel 9000 // Proc. 1998 Winter Simulation Conference. – 1998.

Weizsaeker E.U.von, Lovins A.B., Lovins L.H. Factor Four. Doubling Wealth – Halving Resource Use. A Report to the Club of Rome. - L., 1997.

Wen A. T., Song L, Fan Y. Zero-Time Enterprise Modeling with Component Assembly and Process Model Optimization Techniques // The Fifth International Conference on

Computer and Information Technology, CIT 2005. - Sept. 2005. – 21-23. – P. 1135 – 1139.

White S. Business Process Modeling Notation (BPMN): specification. – 2004. – Version 1.0. – May 3.

Wicksteed P.H. The Common Sense of Political Economy. – L., 1933. – Vol.1-2.

Williamson O. Corporate Control and Business Behavior: An Inquiry into the Effects of Organization Form on Enterprise Behavior. – Prentice Hall, 1970.

Wohed P., Aalst W.M.P. van der, Dumas M. and Hofstede A.H.M. ter. Pattern-based analysis of BPEL4WS // Queensland Univ. Tech., Brisbane, Australia: *QUT Tech. Rep.* - FIT-TR-2002-04, 2002.

Womack J.P., Jones D.T. Lean Thinking. Banish waste and create wealth in your corporation. – Free Press, 2003.

Wrong D.H. Power: Its Forms, Bases, and Uses. – Oxford, 1988.

Yan L., Yu-quiang F. An Automated Business Process Modeling Method Based on Markov Transition Matrix in BPM // 2006 *International Conference on Management Science and Engineering*, 5-7 Oct. 2006. – 2006. – P. 46–51.

Yilmaz Icaga. Genetic Algorithm Usage in Water Quality Monitoring Networks Optimization in Gediz (Turkey) River Basin // *Env.Monitoring and Assessment*, 2005, v.108, iss.1, p.261-277.

Zakarian A. Analysis of process models: A fuzzy logic approach // *Int. J. Adv. Manuf. Technol.* – 2001. – Vol. 17. – P. 444-452.

Zangwill W.I. Nonlinear Programming: *A Unified Approach*. – Prentice Hall, 1969.

ABOUT THE AUTHOR

Guennady Ougolnitsky was born in 1962. He is Professor and Head, Department of Applied Mathematics and Computer Sciences, Southern Federal University, Rostov-on-Don, Russian Federation. The principal domain of his scientific interests is mathematical modeling of the hierarchical structures and control mechanisms in organizational and environmental-economic systems.

e-mail: ougoln@mail.ru

INDEX

A

abatement, 143
abstraction, 11, 12, 75, 226
abuse, 15
access, 237, 240
accommodation, 155
accounting, 130, 137, 150, 238, 240, 252
acquisitions, 186
actuality, 233
ADA, 179
adaptation, 4, 58, 68, 69, 152, 153, 155, 156, 160, 162, 236, 251, 267
Adaptivity, 155
adjustment, 156
age, 51, 103, 104, 107, 108, 109
agencies, 34, 59, 152, 186
aggregation, 150, 235, 241, 252, 255
agriculture, 45, 59, 65
Air Force, 234
alcohol consumption, 51
algorithm, 72, 76, 112, 113, 117, 119, 124, 167, 168, 171, 174, 179, 233
ambient air, 269
amortization, 35, 45
antagonism, 30
anthropocentrism, 42
applied mathematics, vii, 3
arbitrage, 37
Arrow theorem, 29
Asia, 266
aspiration, 11
assessment, 33, 34, 60, 119
assets, 151
atmosphere, 32, 33, 52, 59, 132
attribution, 241

B

audit, 133, 151
audits, 150, 151, 152, 231
Austrian economic school, 11, 12
authorities, 41, 138, 157
authority, 131, 158, 238
automate, 6, 180
automation, 5, 135, 153, 223, 231, 237, 238, 239, 252, 263

bankruptcy, 75
banks, 35, 186
barriers, 132, 133, 204
base, 2, 3, 4, 5, 6, 9, 10, 11, 12, 14, 15, 16, 17, 18, 19, 24, 29, 30, 32, 34, 40, 41, 43, 46, 52, 59, 81, 114, 116, 121, 122, 123, 128, 129, 132, 134, 136, 142, 143, 145, 149, 150, 151, 153, 157, 159, 160, 217, 219, 221, 223, 224, 225, 230, 235, 236, 237, 242, 243, 244, 249, 258, 261, 262, 263
base year, 121
Bayes theorem, 18
biodiversity, 1, 51, 213
biological systems, 3
biomass, 45, 65, 69, 70, 77, 228
biosphere, 40, 41, 48
birth rate, 45
blood, 12, 49, 57
blood pressure, 49, 57
bonds, 35
bonuses, 9, 32
bounds, 16, 174
brain, 16, 236, 237
bribes, 201, 203
Buddhism, 42
budget deficit, 57
Business Entity Ontological Model (BEOM), 237

business processes, 128, 152, 223, 230, 231, 232, 233, 234, 237, 243, 250, 265, 271

C

C++, 180
CAD, 238, 239
calculus, 14
calibration, 147
CAM, 238, 239
career prospects, 33
catastrophes, 41, 42
centigrade, 49
certification, 33, 127, 132, 151, 233
certification audits, 151
challenges, 160
changing environment, 236
Chicago, 268
children, 159
CIS, 223, 237, 238, 239, 242, 249, 252
civil society, 42
civilization, 15
clarity, 177
classes, 9, 12, 13, 14, 18, 19, 44, 49, 143, 179, 180, 186, 208, 224, 234, 238, 241, 254, 260, 261
classification, 2, 4, 14, 29, 88, 103, 230, 231, 232, 237, 239, 241, 264
clients, 130, 138, 158, 197
climate, 196
closure, 176
clustering, 241
clusters, 241
collusion, 20
commerce, 239
commercial, 149, 152, 186, 188, 239, 258
commodity, 15
common sense, 122, 151, 182
communication, 16, 131
communism, 52
communities, 42, 51
community, 10, 26, 70, 77, 159, 229
comparative analysis, 200, 266
compatibility, 235, 263
compensation, 115
competition, 129, 132, 186, 197
competitive advantage, 35
competitiveness, 132, 155, 156, 158
competitors, 145, 152, 175, 176, 238
complexity, 3, 15, 41, 91, 134, 174, 232, 233, 236, 255, 256
compliance, 30
composite transformation, 228
composition, 67, 176, 180, 242

Compromise, 18, 49, 51, 136, 145
compulsion, 2, 4, 5, 9, 31, 32, 33, 40, 48, 61, 81, 82, 83, 84, 85, 86, 87, 88, 93, 107, 108, 110, 132, 185, 192, 197, 200, 201, 209, 217, 218, 219, 260, 263
computer, 4, 5, 6, 44, 72, 73, 81, 91, 92, 97, 102, 103, 107, 109, 113, 122, 147, 155, 171, 173, 174, 178, 179, 181, 182, 223, 224, 233, 237, 241, 242, 247, 248, 249, 252, 254, 257, 261
computerization, 5, 234, 262
conception, 4
conceptual model, 92, 113, 115, 117, 118, 148, 174, 176, 177, 178, 181
conceptualization, 92
concordance, 212
configuration, 56, 158
conflict, 1, 9, 18, 22, 29, 49, 51, 52, 136, 143, 144, 158
conformity, 33, 39, 127, 134, 138, 146, 147, 151, 260
Confucianism, 42
consciousness, 52
conservation, 48, 51, 52, 58, 97, 114, 175
constant load, 68
construction, 4, 6, 91, 92, 121, 122, 124, 136, 137, 142, 150, 152, 177, 185, 186, 190, 191, 192, 193, 212, 233, 236, 237, 240, 261
consulting, 35, 186
consumers, 1, 15
consumption, 15, 42, 43, 46, 47, 123, 262
contradiction, 16, 247
control, 3, 32, 53, 57, 138, 235, 266, 267, 268, 269, 270, 271, 272, 273, 274
control impact, 3, 53, 57, 62, 67, 90, 94, 112, 113, 141, 143, 148, 161, 174, 230, 251, 253, 257
control objective, 3, 54, 55, 161, 230, 263
controlled systems, 2, 3
conviction, 2, 3, 4, 5, 10, 31, 32, 33, 34, 40, 61, 81, 84, 85, 86, 87, 88, 89, 93, 107, 132, 159, 185, 192, 196, 197, 200, 252, 260, 263
cooperation, 10, 25, 32, 35, 107, 127, 129, 132, 145, 151, 185, 186, 192, 196, 197, 252, 259
coordination, 41, 49, 50, 51, 53, 60, 61, 131, 136, 137, 176, 185, 247, 257, 258, 262, 272
corporate life, 128
Corporative information system (CIS), 237
Corrective action, 4
correlation, 31
corruption, 5, 6, 61, 131, 185, 197, 198, 199, 200, 201, 202, 203, 208, 209, 213, 214, 215, 261
cost, 1, 5, 17, 41, 58, 66, 67, 85, 86, 96, 105, 106, 121, 137, 164, 165, 168, 171, 187, 188, 190, 235, 236, 238, 258, 263

Index 279

cost minimization, 58
counter-game, 33
creative personality, 159
critical value, 69, 77, 106, 142
criticism, 43, 152
CRP, 223, 238
cultural conditions, 47
cultural transformation, 43
cultural values, 10
culture, 42, 51, 52
customer preferences, 149
customer service, 258
customers, 129, 130, 136, 138, 139, 149, 151, 157, 158, 159, 173, 176, 197, 225
cybernetics, 3, 134, 135, 267
cycles, 114, 115, 128

diseases, 132
disposition, 74, 235
distress, 156
distribution, 25, 26, 67, 102, 103, 115, 118, 138, 157, 175, 183, 209, 216, 221, 238
diversity, 97, 106, 114, 134, 231, 233, 260
dominance, 22, 27, 42, 47
dominant strategy, 19, 189
draft, 137
drawing, 41
drugs, 51
dynamic consistency, 51, 136
dynamic control, 111, 241
dynamic multidigraphs, 6, 262
dynamic systems, 4, 5, 48, 81, 91, 156, 179, 259, 260, 262, 263

D

damages, iv
danger, 21
data analysis, 223, 238, 239, 240, 241
data mining, 5, 223, 239, 241, 252
data processing, 180, 237, 238, 239, 241
data set, 240, 241
data structure, 121, 225, 242, 243, 246, 258
data transfer, 240, 244, 245, 247
database, 102, 103, 179, 223, 224, 225, 226, 231, 237, 244, 245, 246, 247, 248, 249, 252
database management, 179, 244
decay, 67
decentralization, 158
decision makers, 47
decomposition, 177, 178, 234, 236, 237
deduction, 249
defects, 145
deforestation, 1
degenerate, 17
degradation, 41, 120
democracy, 32
dependent variable, 241
deposits, 35
depth, 175, 264
destiny, 236
destruction, 227
developed countries, 1
developing countries, 1, 272
deviation, 21, 51, 108, 109, 110, 140, 142, 148, 263
differential equations, 135, 179, 182
dimensionality, 241
direct payment, 34
directors, 131
disaster, 1, 42, 66

E

ecological requirements, 60
ecological systems, 177
ecology, 67
economic activity, 12, 14, 42, 43, 59, 66
economic change, 16
economic damage, 10
economic development, 40, 41, 42, 43, 48, 66, 95, 262
economic efficiency, 118, 120, 121
economic growth, 39, 40, 41, 43, 47
economic power, 129
economic problem, 85, 159, 261
economic rationality, 10, 11, 12, 13, 15, 16, 17, 19, 25, 76, 78, 157, 259
economic relations, 52, 186
economic sociology, 264
economic systems, 4, 5, 36, 47, 48, 59, 60, 102, 103, 113, 201, 255, 257, 260, 261, 271
economic theory, 12, 14, 60, 196
economics, 10, 13, 25, 41, 43, 47, 160, 254, 260
ecosystem, 33, 59, 65, 67, 69, 95, 115, 117, 118, 119, 123
editors, 243, 255, 258
education, 10, 11, 15, 48, 51, 133, 242
egoism, 15
e-learning, 130
elucidation, 231, 241, 250
emigration, 47
emission, 33
employees, 1, 4, 6, 49, 52, 60, 128, 130, 131, 132, 133, 135, 136, 138, 144, 146, 149, 157, 158, 159, 160, 163, 166, 168, 171, 196, 197, 231, 237, 238, 239, 251, 252
employment, 114

280 Index

encouragement, 66
energy, 1, 43, 59, 65, 177, 227, 230
engineering, 59
environment, 1, 34, 40, 41, 46, 52, 53, 59, 65, 123, 148, 150, 152, 158, 160, 175, 176, 197, 212, 229, 234, 239, 240, 242, 251, 252, 262
environmental change, 236
environmental control, 66
environmental degradation, 42
environmental factors, 52
environmental impact, 2, 33, 34, 47, 48, 59, 60, 65, 85, 115, 117, 118, 126
environmental management, 33, 151, 271
environmental organizations, 59
environmental policy, 41
environmental protection, 33, 34, 40, 41, 42, 43, 59, 60, 66, 114, 118, 217
Environmental Protection Act, 34
Environmental Protection Agency, 34
environmental quality, 34, 43, 59, 115, 117, 119, 120, 125, 126
equality, 29, 85, 241
equilibrium, 1, 2, 14, 20, 21, 36, 39, 41, 57, 81, 82, 83, 84, 86, 87, 95, 141, 142, 144, 145, 189, 192, 196, 212, 214, 215, 251, 262
equipment, 35, 49, 118, 146, 147, 175, 230, 243, 249
ergonomics, 237
erosion, 1
ethnic groups, 1
eustress, 156
evidence, 128, 146
evolution, 40, 223, 272
exchange rate, 57
exclusion, 22
expenditures, 13, 16, 34, 35, 43, 97, 106, 121, 166, 187, 192, 193, 258
expert systems, 5, 223, 249, 253
expertise, 34
exploitation, 43, 58, 115, 125, 229, 237
externalities, 1, 34, 212
extinction, 1, 52, 70
extraction, 96, 98, 100, 104, 202, 203, 206, 209

F

families, 30
farmers, 159
fear, 132
fears, 132
feelings, 10, 29
financial, 2, 9, 11, 13, 30, 33, 96, 108, 109, 110, 138, 158, 175, 179, 209, 236, 237, 238, 239, 258
financial crisis, 33

first generation, 233
first side audit, 151
fish, 65, 85
fishing, 51, 65
fixation, 18, 183, 207
flexibility, 233, 241
fluctuations, 45, 57, 161
Follower, 9, 10, 22, 23, 24, 28, 31, 32, 33, 35, 37, 56, 57, 58, 60, 62, 63, 64, 65, 66, 67, 68, 69, 70, 71, 72, 73, 74, 75, 76, 77, 81, 82, 85, 86, 87, 90, 91, 94, 95, 96, 98, 100, 104, 105, 106, 107, 108, 109, 110, 111, 112, 113, 118, 123, 124, 125, 126, 144, 146, 156, 186, 197, 198, 199, 200, 201, 202, 203, 204, 206, 207, 208, 209, 210, 211, 212, 213, 214, 215, 216, 217, 260
food, 45, 51, 59, 118
force, 11, 35, 196
forecasting, 5, 58, 62, 102, 147, 148, 175, 176, 238
forest ecosystem, 103, 104, 106, 107, 108, 109, 110, 111
forest resources, 4, 261
formation, 26, 29, 43, 159, 186, 190, 241
formula, 28, 30, 72, 119, 120, 121, 124, 166, 167, 189, 192, 207, 211
foundations, 4
fraud, 196
freedom, 31, 42, 198
functional analysis, 226
funds, 45, 47, 49

G

game theory, 9, 10, 18, 19, 25, 26, 48, 143, 263, 264, 271
General Motors, 157, 272
geography, 67
Germany, 15
Germeyer-Vatel model, 185, 212, 213
global consequences, 41
global security, 45
global warming, 1, 213
globalization, 43, 129
God, 11
goods and services, 42, 157, 158, 159
grades, 102, 108, 109, 110, 203
grants, 35, 65, 66, 77, 85, 94, 192
graph, 25, 79, 135, 173, 247
gravity, 129
Great Depression, 42
Greece, 265
growth, 1, 43, 46, 126, 127, 129, 157, 158
guidance, 136

Index

H

harmonization, 42
harmony, 40
harvesting, 65, 69, 70, 77
health, 114
Henry Ford, 128
heterogeneity, 102, 115
heterogeneous notions, vii, 3
hiring, 175
histogram, 183
historical data, 240
history, 15, 52
homeostasis, 3, 4, 5, 6, 39, 48, 49, 50, 51, 52, 55, 57, 58, 61, 62, 66, 81, 82, 87, 90, 92, 95, 97, 106, 107, 109, 110, 127, 136, 139, 140, 141, 142, 143, 144, 146, 148, 152, 155, 156, 157, 174, 175, 185, 194, 196, 197, 198, 199, 200, 201, 202, 250, 251, 252, 257, 260, 261, 263
Homeostasis, 48, 51, 136, 137, 141, 145
Homo sociologicus, 266
homogeneity, 103
hostility, 30
hotels, 114, 115, 123, 125, 126
human, 1, 2, 4, 5, 9, 11, 12, 15, 16, 17, 29, 39, 41, 42, 47, 48, 49, 50, 51, 52, 57, 58, 59, 61, 113, 128, 134, 137, 138, 156, 159, 174, 230, 236, 238, 240, 252, 259, 260
human actions, 17
human activity, 12, 42, 59, 113
human behavior, 11, 17
human genome, 42
human nature, 11, 16
Human Resource Management, 272
human resources, 1, 134, 230
hunting, 33, 51, 65, 212
hypercube, 241
hypothesis, 10, 13, 14, 15, 66, 82, 83, 85, 115, 118, 164, 259

I

ICAM, 234
ideal, 31, 57, 72, 120, 133, 138, 140, 142, 145, 163, 185, 197, 252
ideals, 52
identification, 45, 60, 92, 118, 122, 123, 137, 147, 156, 165, 174, 180, 181, 183, 203, 247, 250, 257, 259
identification problem, 92, 118, 174, 180, 181, 257
identity, 47
ideology, 149, 158

image, 52, 137, 247
images, 270
imagination, 16
immigration, 47
impact assessment, 60, 119
Impact Assessment, 266, 267
imperialism, 12
imprisonment, 34
improvements, 142, 150
Impulsion, 35, 88, 107
incentive effect, 165
income, 10, 13, 25, 26, 55, 66, 69, 73, 85, 86, 90, 91, 94, 95, 98, 100, 101, 104, 105, 107, 108, 109, 110, 111, 124, 125, 126, 166, 171, 175, 203, 206, 207, 208, 213, 258
independence, 2, 64
Independence, 64
independent variable, 241
individuality, 159
individualization, 159
individuals, 53, 79
industry, 5, 59, 65, 157, 238
inequality, 20, 26, 85, 191, 193
inflation, 57
information exchange, 36
Information model, 224, 230, 262
information technology, 242
infrastructure, 41, 42, 114, 115, 121
inheritance, 236
initial state, 57, 62, 90, 94, 143, 161, 174, 179, 217, 230
injury, iv
institutions, 30, 34, 42, 186
integration, 182, 225, 231, 233, 237, 238, 239, 240, 242, 249, 252
integrity, 2, 155, 224
interaction process, 239
interdependence, 29, 209
interface, 237, 241, 244, 245, 247, 248, 253, 255
interface programs, 255
International Monetary Fund, 57
intervention, 42, 163
investment, 152, 178, 210
investments, 115, 129, 186
investors, 138, 186, 258
ISO 9000, 4, 127, 128, 129, 130, 133, 151, 233, 235, 250, 262

J

Japan, 128, 131, 132

K

Keynes, 15

L

laconism, 129
Lagrange multipliers, 210
landscapes, 51
languages, 179, 231, 232, 233
laws, 11, 33, 59, 118, 134, 178, 182, 224, 225, 236, 241, 242
lawyers, 30
Le Chatelier principle, 57
lead, 131, 182, 233
leadership, 60, 128, 132
lean production, 128
learning, 32, 132, 133, 180, 231, 241
legislation, 34
legs, 249
leisure, 113
leisure time, 113
life cycle, 237, 239
light, 49
linear dependence, 198
linear function, 62, 188, 191, 194, 198
linear model, 98
linear programming, 13, 14, 77, 254
local authorities, 41
local community, 157
local conditions, 41
logical reasoning, 16
logistics, 240
Louisiana, 265
love, 2, 30
Ludwig von Mises, 12

M

magnitude, 34
majority, 14, 15, 17, 26, 30, 39, 43, 47, 49, 61, 122, 131, 135, 137, 140, 143, 163, 176, 230, 231, 236, 249, 256
man, 1, 10, 12, 40, 41, 42, 60, 65, 67, 229
manipulation, 32, 33, 87, 88, 107, 146, 185, 196, 209, 241
marginal product, 210
market economy, 30
marketing, 127, 129, 130, 149, 152, 159, 178, 258
Markov process, 223, 226
marriage, 224
Marx, 12

Maslow pyramid, 132
mass, 15, 40, 135
materials, 33, 137, 230
mathematical formalization, vii, 3, 4, 13, 49, 113, 118, 185, 196, 212, 260, 263
mathematical knowledge, 3
mathematical methods, 128, 135, 231, 235, 261
mathematical programming, 78, 257
mathematics, 3, 135, 261
matrix, 4, 47, 102, 124, 142, 233
matter, 131, 132, 143, 163, 177, 178, 227
maximal allowable concentration, 33
maximal allowable emission, 33
measurement, 142, 146, 147, 150, 151, 152, 162, 163, 251
measurements, 140, 240, 241
medical, 114, 123, 249
memory, 178, 236, 246, 249
mental activity, 29
mental energy, 16
mental power, 113
mercury, 49
mergers, 186
methodology, 41, 103, 113, 133, 138, 143, 234, 235, 236, 237, 238, 261, 262, 266
microeconomics, 12
Microsoft, 245, 246, 247
middle class, 126
military, 30, 43
Minneapolis, 266
minorities, 157
mission, 131
modern science, 264
modernization, 52
modifications, 36, 43, 180, 182, 197, 263
modules, 238, 246, 247
Monitoring, 4, 6, 144, 151, 262, 266, 267, 268, 269, 270, 271, 272, 273, 274
monopoly, 197
moral hazard, 37
mortality, 45, 51
mortality rate, 45
Moscow, 265, 266, 268, 269, 270, 271, 272
motivation, 4, 6, 9, 32, 33, 55, 128, 132, 136, 137, 152, 155, 159, 160, 163
multidimensional, 147, 241
museums, 114

N

naming, 2, 237
Nash equilibrium, 20, 144, 145, 189, 212
natural resources, 1, 33, 42, 95

neglect, 115
neural network, 241
neural networks, 241
neutral, 66, 131, 141, 142, 143, 145, 251, 252
next generation, 262
nodes, 244
non-linear equations, 67
non-renewable resources, 45
normal development, 65

O

objectivity, 57
oil, 238
operations, 128, 134, 140, 159, 223, 224, 225, 234, 238, 240, 241, 243, 244, 245
opportunism, 5, 132, 185, 196, 197, 252
optimization, 4, 5, 6, 9, 10, 11, 12, 13, 14, 17, 18, 19, 29, 55, 61, 63, 65, 77, 111, 112, 113, 133, 135, 165, 167, 175, 179, 186, 187, 191, 196, 202, 203, 204, 210, 211, 235, 242, 247, 248, 249, 253, 256, 257, 258, 259, 261, 262, 263, 264, 271
optimization method, 113
ordinary differential equations, 255
organ, 248
organism, 48, 49, 57, 58, 128, 139, 155, 156, 158, 159, 236
organizational development, 52, 53, 60, 127, 134, 139, 159, 251
organize, 33, 132
oxygen, 123

P

palliative, 185
parallel, 178, 204, 232, 235
Pareto, 12, 17, 20, 26, 168, 212, 220
Pareto optimal, 17, 20, 26, 212
Pareto optimality, 17, 20, 26
partial differential equations, 254
participants, 27, 30, 50, 127, 159, 178, 185, 197, 271
partition, 78, 227
penalties, 9, 32, 34, 55, 66, 73, 94, 110, 118, 124
permission, 34
permit, 1, 10, 33, 47, 77, 100, 102, 110, 118, 122, 124, 125, 126, 129, 131, 132, 135, 142, 150, 156, 177, 178, 179, 226, 233, 236, 238, 241, 249, 252, 254
personal computers, 130, 179
personal development, 113
personal problems, 1
persuasion, 127, 129

Petri nets, 223, 226, 232, 233, 262, 265, 266, 272
physiology, 139
plants, 45, 59
platform, 149, 233, 252
playing, 182
pleasure, 30
policy, 129, 131, 133, 150, 151, 224, 225, 258
political parties, 51
political problems, 42
politics, 25
pollutants, 33, 51, 65, 85, 95, 97, 117, 118, 120, 122, 123, 124, 272
pollution, 1, 33, 34, 35, 43, 45, 47, 51, 52, 60, 65, 67, 68, 69, 85, 94, 95, 96, 98, 118, 124, 125, 126, 212, 213
Pontryagin principle of maximum, 68
population, 1, 40, 41, 42, 43, 45, 47, 51, 52, 55, 59, 65, 69, 70, 129, 175, 189, 254
post-industrial society, 31, 157, 158, 160
poverty, 51
power plants, 65
practical activity, 16
precedent, 2, 156, 162
predators, 229
predicate, 249
preparation, iv, 131, 137, 150
present value, 134, 152, 162
preservation, 46
president, 131
prestige, 11, 12
prevention, 35
Preventive action, 173
principles, 4, 6, 19, 25, 26, 27, 40, 43, 44, 47, 49, 63, 66, 79, 81, 127, 128, 129, 130, 131, 132, 134, 136, 137, 143, 149, 150, 151, 158, 160, 163, 180, 196, 224, 238, 240, 262, 263
private enterprises, 35
probability, 11, 16, 73, 135, 161
probability theory, 135
problem solving, 42, 175, 250
Process approach, 136
process control, 135, 179, 238
process indicators, 4, 6
producers, 238
production costs, 34, 139, 186
production function, 95, 104, 209, 210
productive capacity, 210
professionalism, 151
profit, 11, 13, 25, 30, 49, 52, 55, 58, 98, 121, 126, 129, 132, 157, 158, 165, 171, 172, 173, 175, 185, 187, 188, 192, 210, 212
programming, 3, 14, 157, 177, 179, 180, 232, 239, 254, 255, 261

programming languages, 179, 180

project, 4, 41, 124, 137, 142, 150, 152, 185, 186, 187, 188, 190, 193, 224, 238, 255

proposition, 14, 98

protection, 33, 34, 40, 41, 43, 59, 66

prototype, 233

psychologist, 32

psychology, 15

public administration, 272

public interest, 185, 212

punishment, 31, 66, 70, 73, 74, 75, 76, 85, 87, 132, 201, 209

Q

quality control, 128, 135

quality improvement, 127, 129, 133, 135, 142

Quality management, 127

quality of life, 45

quantitative estimation, 48

Queensland, 265, 274

queuing systems, 177, 179, 226, 262

queuing theory, 113, 115, 117

quotas, 43, 66, 85, 87, 94, 107, 108, 201, 202, 203, 207, 209

R

radiation, 51

radius, 57, 170

rationality, 4, 5, 9, 10, 11, 12, 13, 15, 16, 17, 18, 19, 25, 26, 28, 29, 39, 49, 55, 61, 76, 78, 143, 157, 259, 260

raw materials, 1, 43, 59, 175

reactions, 3, 4, 23, 58, 155, 156, 160, 204, 236, 242

reactivity, 156

reading, 140, 177

real estate, 137, 150, 152, 185, 186, 194, 195, 196, 255, 258

real time, 135, 177, 246

reality, 13, 15, 30

reasoning, 25, 26, 118, 140, 211, 254

recall, 33, 163, 183

recession, 42

recognition, 132

recommendations, iv, 5, 6, 14, 41, 47, 128, 129, 143, 152, 233, 249, 262

recovery, 113, 114

recreation, 59, 103, 115, 118

recreational, 4, 6, 65, 81, 113, 114, 115, 116, 117, 118, 120, 122, 123, 261

recurrence, 114, 155, 162

reengineering, 128, 231, 236, 270, 273

reflexivity, 25

regeneration, 45

regional problem, 46

regression, 183, 241

regression analysis, 183

regulations, 36, 138, 157, 223, 224, 225, 237, 239

regulatory requirements, 130

relativity, 1, 134, 176

reliability, 16, 233

representativeness, 147

reproduction, 46, 103, 104, 114, 203

reputation, 52, 175

requirements, 4, 5, 6, 14, 33, 39, 41, 42, 47, 49, 50, 51, 52, 53, 55, 58, 60, 61, 63, 66, 86, 95, 128, 130, 131, 133, 134, 139, 140, 141, 142, 143, 145, 146, 147, 148, 149, 151, 152, 158, 162, 173, 174, 179, 182, 183, 193, 200, 223, 235, 236, 237, 240, 249, 250, 251, 252, 255, 257, 260, 262, 263

researchers, 2, 39, 43, 128, 157, 231, 236

reserves, 212

resistance, 35, 131, 156

resolution, 9, 18, 136, 156

resource allocation, 5, 6, 79, 157, 210, 213, 214, 215, 216, 217, 236, 261

resource management, 238, 240

resources, 1, 2, 16, 18, 25, 33, 42, 47, 49, 52, 59, 60, 95, 127, 130, 131, 137, 138, 139, 143, 149, 150, 175, 176, 179, 186, 189, 190, 217, 224, 226, 228, 238

response, 22, 156, 182, 183, 196, 242, 248, 255

response time, 248

restaurants, 114, 115, 118, 123

restrictions, 10, 13, 31, 33, 34, 35, 39, 53, 61, 77, 78, 97, 100, 101, 111, 112, 122, 158, 161, 164, 168, 170, 176, 185, 202, 203, 207, 210, 211

restructuring, 156, 181

retardation, 68

revenue, 164

Ricker model, 98

rights, 262

risk, 15, 191

risks, 191

root, 195

roots, 195

roughness, 178, 199, 201, 203, 209

rules, 16, 17, 33, 36, 60, 85, 103, 177, 178, 190, 224, 225, 226, 229, 230, 240, 241, 249

Russia, 270

S

safety, 52, 97, 107, 129, 237, 240, 252

Index

sanctions, 35, 43

scaling, 102, 142, 177, 247

school, 11, 12, 15, 128

science, 5, 12, 43, 134, 157, 185, 196, 212, 224, 264, 272

scientific method, 127

second generation, 231

security, 130, 137, 150

sedimentation, 120

self-actualization, 157

self-control, 60, 237

semantics, 231, 233

Sen paradox, 29

sensitivity, 182

servers, 241, 252

services, iv, 35, 42, 47, 122, 123, 127, 129, 130, 135, 137, 149, 159, 261

settlements, 59, 65

sewage, 33, 55, 67, 68, 120, 124

Shapley value, 28, 190, 216, 219, 220

shareholders, 52, 60, 130, 158, 159, 160

shortage, 20, 232

simulation, 4, 6, 65, 70, 72, 73, 81, 91, 92, 95, 97, 98, 103, 107, 109, 113, 118, 121, 122, 124, 135, 143, 155, 173, 174, 177, 178, 179, 180, 181, 182, 183, 223, 229, 239, 242, 243, 244, 245, 247, 248, 249, 252, 253, 254, 255, 256, 257, 258, 261, 262, 263

Simulation modeling, 271

Singapore, 271

social class, 185, 186, 192, 193, 194, 195

social environment, 47

social group, 30

social interactions, 30

social norms, 16, 17

social organization, 52, 53

social problems, 158

social relations, 2, 9, 29, 30

social responsibility, 158

social sciences, 4, 12

social status, 15, 31

social structure, 129

socialization, 17, 159

society, 4, 9, 18, 40, 46, 57, 59, 129, 130, 133, 138, 157, 158, 159, 160, 212

sociology, 2, 7, 260

software, 130, 147, 179, 223, 231, 233, 238, 239, 249

solidarity, 30

solution, 4, 14, 17, 19, 27, 39, 41, 42, 43, 44, 45, 46, 47, 49, 50, 51, 52, 55, 58, 60, 63, 64, 74, 75, 76, 78, 88, 91, 92, 103, 110, 112, 113, 143, 144, 145, 146, 148, 150, 156, 157, 158, 159, 164, 165, 166, 167, 168, 169, 170, 171, 172, 176, 177, 178, 179, 180, 182, 183, 188, 189, 190, 193, 203, 204, 209, 210, 211, 214, 221, 224, 226, 230, 238, 239, 241, 252, 253, 254, 255, 256, 257, 261

sovereignty, 1

Soviet Union, 52

specialists, 2, 52, 156, 160, 162, 175, 249

specialization, 114, 115, 264

species, 51, 103, 104

specifications, 225, 236, 269

speech, 224

stability, 16, 21, 28, 40, 48, 57, 127, 129, 135, 139, 141, 142, 143, 144, 145, 156, 165, 182, 221, 251, 252, 263

stakeholders, 6, 127, 129, 130, 143, 145, 197, 252, 263

standardization, 33, 34, 127, 146, 148

stars, 115, 123

state, 1, 4, 6, 33, 34, 35, 39, 41, 42, 44, 45, 47, 49, 51, 53, 54, 55, 57, 58, 62, 63, 64, 65, 67, 77, 90, 94, 95, 102, 103, 107, 108, 109, 110, 112, 113, 127, 134, 135, 140, 141, 142, 143, 144, 146, 147, 148, 149, 150, 151, 152, 156, 157, 161, 162, 174, 175, 177, 180, 182, 192, 223, 224, 225, 226, 227, 229, 230, 231, 250, 251, 252, 255, 261, 262, 263

state control, 34

states, 1, 42, 47, 52, 54, 62, 66, 112, 174, 175, 224, 230, 256

statistics, 147

stochastic model, 15

stock markets, 25

storage, 5, 147, 149, 183, 224, 239, 240, 241, 245, 249, 252, 268

strategic management, 263

stratification, 30, 78, 264

stress, 156

structural changes, 44, 229

structure, 4, 9, 10, 14, 24, 29, 36, 40, 51, 52, 55, 56, 58, 59, 60, 61, 79, 92, 117, 134, 135, 138, 149, 156, 157, 158, 160, 176, 178, 181, 186, 217, 223, 224, 225, 226, 227, 229, 231, 234, 235, 236, 237, 242, 243, 244, 245, 247, 252, 256, 262, 263

structuring, 128, 174, 223, 237, 250

style, 152, 157

subjectivity, 140

substitution, 68

successive approximations, 216

Sun, 41

supplier, 131, 133

suppliers, 128, 130, 131, 132, 133, 136, 138, 149, 150, 175, 176, 186, 197

surplus, 12

sustainability, 41, 46, 47

sustainable development, 1, 3, 4, 5, 6, 39, 40, 41, 42, 43, 45, 46, 47, 48, 49, 50, 51, 52, 61, 66, 74, 76, 81, 86, 97, 104, 111, 127, 143, 185, 186, 192, 193, 196, 198, 252, 259, 260, 261, 262, 263, 264, 270, 271
Sustainable development, iv, 40
Sustainable management, iv, 259
synchronization, 246, 247
syndrome, 14
synergetics, 18
synthesis, 3, 162
system analysis, 81, 92, 115, 153, 174, 224, 257, 261, 263
systems theory, 3

T

Taguchi function of losses, 142
Tail coefficient, 181
Taiwan, 266
target, 4, 6, 52, 90, 94, 127, 134, 136, 139, 140, 141, 142, 143, 148, 152, 187, 231, 250, 251, 263
tax base, 85
tax rates, 98, 107
taxation, 34
taxes, 34, 66, 85, 94, 188, 201, 207, 208, 209, 212
teachers, 16
teams, 159
technical support, 150
techniques, 135, 147, 150, 162, 163, 182, 183, 257, 268
technologies, 1, 5, 44, 104, 128, 135, 148, 160, 223, 231, 232, 233, 237, 261, 263
technology, 6, 96, 98, 104, 106, 137, 152, 153, 160, 179, 180, 213, 223, 231, 236, 237, 241, 242, 243, 244, 250, 252, 261, 262
temperature, 49, 57
tenants, 152
tension, 43, 158
territorial, 2, 51, 60
territory, 1, 51, 59, 102, 117, 176, 186, 189, 190
terrorism, 1
testing, 180, 240
theoretical approaches, 11
thesaurus, 47
threats, 30
throws, 67
total product, 209, 210, 211, 212
trade, 1, 9, 15, 18, 30, 127, 130, 186
trade-off, 1, 9, 15, 18, 30, 130
traditions, 17
training, 156, 242

trajectory, 50, 57, 63, 69, 71, 72, 143, 148, 162, 174, 181, 182, 251, 257
transaction costs, 1
transformation, 1, 32, 43, 95, 117, 127, 134, 137, 149, 157, 158, 197, 227, 228, 230, 244, 245, 247, 249, 255
transformations, 249
transmission, 23, 32, 34, 138, 234
transnational corporations, 129
transparency, 139, 241
transport, 65
transportation, 103, 104, 105
treatment, 114
Turkey, 274

U

UK, 78, 271
UN, 78
unification, 30, 234
Unified Modeling Language (UML), 232
uniform, 158, 177
unions, 25, 26
unit transformation, 228
universalism, 12, 15
UNO World Commission on Environment and Development, 3, 40
updating, 133, 243, 258
urban, 186
USA, 34, 35
user data, 248
USSR, 52, 156

V

validation, 115, 231, 232, 256
valuation, 103
variables, 37, 44, 45, 47, 49, 53, 54, 64, 66, 78, 86, 107, 112, 118, 119, 121, 122, 123, 124, 148, 162, 167, 174, 178, 180, 181, 182, 183, 187, 188, 194, 197, 217, 226, 229, 240, 247, 248, 254, 255, 257, 258
variations, 135, 142, 163, 182
vector, 4, 9, 17, 19, 28, 29, 36, 47, 49, 51, 53, 54, 57, 62, 66, 68, 70, 77, 78, 82, 90, 95, 96, 102, 103, 106, 140, 141, 146, 148, 152, 161, 163, 164, 165, 166, 167, 174, 177, 182, 189, 193, 216, 221, 226, 229, 230, 250, 251, 257, 259, 263, 267
velocity, 100
Verhulst-Pearl model, 98
violence, 2
visualization, 233, 248

voting, 189

W

Washington, 266, 267, 271
waste, 33, 35, 42, 43, 45, 51, 68, 268, 274
waste disposal, 33, 35, 45, 68
water, 1, 4, 6, 33, 55, 59, 67, 117, 119, 120, 126, 261, 268
water quality, 33, 55, 268
water resources, 4, 261
watershed, 129
wealth, 129, 274
well-being, 178
Western countries, 43
Western Europe, 128
witnesses, 64, 103, 139, 152, 182
wood, 103, 104, 105, 106, 108, 109, 110, 111
work environment, 150

workers, 128, 133, 140, 157, 159, 160, 175, 176, 197, 256
workflow, 238, 265, 267, 269
working conditions, 175
working hours, 163
working memory, 249
workstation, 244, 249
World Bank, 271
World War I, 128

X

XML, 245, 246, 247

Z

zero growth, 42, 47